MW01268499

World War II Through Polish Eyes

In the Nazi-Soviet Grip

M. B. Szonert

EAST EUROPEAN MONOGRAPHS, BOULDER
DISTRIBUTED BY COLUMBIA UNIVERSITY PRESS, NEW YORK
2002

EAST EUROPEAN MONOGRAPHS, NO. DCIV

Copyright 2002 by M. B. Szonert
ISBN: 0-88033-502-5
Library of Congress Control Number 2002112278

Printed in the United States of America

Danuta's Legacy

At the twilight of her days, Danuta entrusted me with her dramatic life story. This book evolved over a period of several years—it is the result of countless hours of digging into Danuta's remarkably vivid memory of the most brutal war ever fought. All the events and facts described in this story are true; the characters are real people and their names have not been changed. By the time the last chapter was written, Danuta's health had deteriorated rapidly. She passed away on April 20, 2002, several months before this book appeared in print.

She left us knowing, however, that the lessons of her tragic life would not be forgotten. Let us draw wisdom from her story. Let us strive for a better understanding among the peoples and nations of our world. Let us always remember the price of senseless, cruel war.

Katyń Monument Over the Smoldering Ruins of the World Trade Center; Jersey City, New Jersey, September 2001. Photo: Tony Classe.

Contents

Acknowledgments

I would like to express my deepest gratitude to all those who helped me in various ways to bring this project to fruition. I am indebted to Doctors Kathleen and Jerzy Maciuszko for their priceless advice and support. I am also very grateful to Katharine Reilly who expended much time and effort in editing my drafts, and to Pat Reilly for sacrificing so much of Katharine's companionship time for this project. Mrs. Brigitte Hirst helped me uncover the mystery of important German language documents. Ms. Susan M. Malone and Prof. Robert Pope assisted me with the literary flair of this work. Mrs. Elżbieta Szonert undertook an overwhelming task to search the Polish archives. Mrs. Dana Amerio, Professor Michael J. Carley, Professor M. K. Dziewanowski, Professor Donald E. Pienkos, and Mrs. Wanda Pietrzyk-Małysa read the manuscript and provided me with their valuable comments.

Also, I would like to express my gratitude to the Polish-American Congress–Ohio Division for their bold decision to support this effort. I am especially grateful to my editors, Professor Stephen Fischer-Galati for his fatherly guidance and Nancy Tyson for her superb abilities to finalize this project.

In the end, this book was made possible thanks to the unwavering support of my husband, Wiesław, and our children.

Guide to Polish Names

Polish nicknames are not just the shortened versions of the formal names. Frequently nicknames are longer and almost always contain softer consonants such as "ni" or "ń" and "si" or "ś." Below are listed the Polish names used in this book and their nicknames.

Alek – Aluś

Andrzej – Andrzejek, Jędrek, Jędruś

Bolesław – Bolek

Bronisława – Bronia

Danuta – Danusia, Danuś, Danuśka, Danka, Daneczka

Eugeniusz – Gienio

Janina – Jasia

Józef – Józek, Józio

Julian – Julek

Kazimierz – Kazik

Maria – Marysia, Maya

Regina – Renia

Stanisław – Staszek, Staś

Wincenty – Vince

Zbigniew – Zbyszek, Zbyś, Zbyszko

1

Western public opinion towards the Soviet Union had become increasingly sympathetic since the German attack on the Soviet Union, reaching its peak in early spring of 1943, after the Stalingrad victory.[1] At the time of this pro-Soviet euphoria, the German Army stationed near Smolensk in Russia stumbled over mass graves in the Katyń forest. The graves contained thousands of bodies of Polish officers. The Goebbels propaganda machine rushed to announce the gruesome discovery to the world, naming the Soviets as the perpe-trators of the crime.

The Polish Government in London called upon the International Red Cross to conduct an investigation of the Katyń crime scene. Capitalizing on his favorable public image, Stalin labeled the Polish request for investigation as anti-Soviet and broke off diplomatic relations with the Polish Government in London. The Polish Prime Minister responded: "Force is on Russia's side, justice is on our side. I do not advise the British people to cast their lot with brute force and to stampede justice before the eyes of all nations. For this reason I refuse to withdraw the Polish appeal to the International Red Cross."[2]

In the summer of 1943, the political tension over the Polish matter was at its peak. Poland's Western allies found the Katyń affair most inconvenient. A perception was growing that the Poles were playing into the hands of Germany's strategy. The United States treated the Katyń matter as a German attempt to divert international attention from its losses on the Eastern Front.[3] Goebbels, who kept a close eye on the Allied press, wrote in his diary: "The Poles are given a brush-off by the English and Americans as though there were enemies."[4]

In July of 1943, a plane carrying Polish Prime Minister Sikorski plunged into the sea over Gibraltar, instantly killing the Polish head of state and his only daughter but sparing the pilot. With Sikorski's untimely death, Poland lost its most influential statesman, politician, leader, and patriot at the most critical moment for the country's future.[5]

The Roosevelt Administration was determined to contain the public debate over Katyń. The British and American press consistently ignored the subject of Katyń but the issue represented an open wound for the Polish community. In 1944, President Roosevelt stepped up efforts to "quarantine" explosive debate over the Katyń massacre. Polish–American radio stations received directives from Washington requesting restraint concerning sensitive issues like Katyń.[6]

At the Nuremberg trials the Katyń crime was also effectively "contained." The victorious coalition chose the Soviet Union as the lead prosecuting nation with respect to crimes against humanity. This decision meant that the Katyń crime was to be submitted for prosecution to the Soviet Government, the suspected perpetrator of the crime.[7] During the trial, the counsel for the German General Staff asked: "May I have a question put to the Prosecution? Who is to be made responsible for the Katyń case?" The President of the Court, Lord Justice Lawrence, replied: "I do not propose to answer questions of that sort."[8]

After the demise of the Soviet Union, Boris Yeltsin presented the Polish Government with a top-secret document dated March 5, 1940. Signed by Stalin and the members of his Politburo, the document revealed that on Stalin's order 14,700 Polish officers and 11,000 Polish government officials were executed in April and May of 1940, in three main locations: in the Katyń forest, in the NKVD prisons in Kharkov, and in the NKVD complex in Kalinin.[9]

* * * *

Danuta looks through the window of a suburban house. It's very beautiful here. Neatly cut grass and the strip of wild forest embracing a small creek surround a large deck decorated with baskets of perennials. It is also very quiet here. In fact it's so quiet that it's even lonely. A few years ago, she and her husband came to live with their son in this elegant suburban house in Ohio. It is very comfortable here. In fact it's so comfortable that she has become lazy.

At the turn of the millennium, Danuta spends most of her time in the armchair, waking up only to check the mail and make phone calls. She cannot write anymore but loves to read letters and watch TV

Polonia. Only recently, TV Polonia began to broadcast, directly from Poland via satellite, a regular Polish TV program for worldwide audiences. Danusia watches TV Polonia non-stop. It gives her and hundreds of thousands of other Polish people scattered all over the world some sense of belonging, a distant and abstract community of their own, more of a virtual or semi-imaginary world.

Breathing heavily, she slowly scuffs along towards her armchair, her face twisted from exhaustion. The glare of the television screen brightens the gloomy room. As she slumps into the chair, a sonorous voice abruptly awakens her consciousness.

"On the occasion of the sixtieth anniversary of the Katyń Massacre...." She turns around confused. What occasion? What anniversary? A young reporter from the TV Polonia Evening News yells from the screen. "A special train carrying families of the Katyń victims arrived today at Katyń for the first official memorial ceremony." Danusia holds her breath, staring wide-eyed at the screen. The camera zooms on a newly erected memorial wall covered with thousands of small plaques listing the names of the Poles bestially murdered by the Soviets in 1940. "This is my husband," a woman in her eighties cries, out pointing to one of the plaques. Danusia hastily draws nearer the screen. "You see," the woman continues, "I was a happy wife for two years and a widow with two children for sixty years. This is a priceless moment in my life. I feel as if I am at last reunited with my husband. I brought with me today our two sons.... They are already in their sixties."

Danusia freezes. The Evening News starts reporting on the official speeches given at the memorial ceremony by the Polish Prime Minister and a Russian official. "My God! Finally, we got them back!" She whispers, quivering with emotion. Hastily she turns towards the closet, pulls out a small metal case, and scuffs back to her armchair.

The image of the aged woman pointing to her husband's name on the Memorial Wall haunts Danusia as she opens the compact box. The icy chill of the metal frame penetrates through her fingers. Her hand gropes frantically inside the box. Here it is, on the very top. She takes out a white piece of paper and unfolds it with devotion. In the brightness of the television's screen, a circled portion of the text shines at her: "Sierzant, Julian, born 1912, son of Paweł, Second Lieutenant, N 462/21, T 653."[10] Julian, her first true love, her dream. Only now it occurs to her that his name must be listed on the Katyń Memorial Wall. But she still cannot grasp it or, rather, she doesn't want to. Only a few weeks ago, her son brought home this piece of paper—a copy of one page from the list of thousands of Katyń victims slaughtered by the Soviets in 1940.

All these years, she has wondered what could have happened to Julian. Never ever could she imagine that he met such a cruel martyr's death. The memory of the magnificent officer vividly comes back. Closing her eyes, she tries to recall those happy summer days back in 1939 spent with Julian near Brasław. His tall silhouette in the military uniform flickers in her memory. This fragile image of the handsome officer melts quickly with imagination and soon vanishes in cloudy recollection.

She folds the paper and looks inside the box. "Where should I put you?" she ponders. As her fingers caress different photographs and documents inside, she instantly recognizes each of them just by a slight touch. Each one is distinct. Each one conjures up a unique emotional feeling. The collection starts with photographs from her 1939 vacation, and continues with her first marriage wedding pictures, the Auschwitz letters, the Nazi death certificate, the Soviet death certificate, pictures of her cousins deported to Siberia or lost in action in Great Britain, snapshots of her friends and neighbors killed during the defense of Warsaw, in the Warsaw Uprising, and in numerous concentration camps. The collection ends with the wedding pictures from her second marriage.

Now, sixty years after the crime, she adds to her shrine of martyrs yet another face—a victim of the Katyń Massacre, a name from the list of about fifteen thousand Polish officers barbarically exterminated by the Stalin's henchmen. That shot to the back of the head of the prisoner of war standing over the mass grave in an obscure forest is one of the most hideous crimes of World War II. Yet, it has been effectively kept from the public eye for generations, a cowardly policy not to upset the Russians at any price. This thought makes her shiver.

She pulls out the wedding photograph from her first marriage. "Józef, darling, I am going to place Julian next to you and Dad." She talks to a man looking at her from the wedding photograph. "Julian has just returned from oblivion and needs our extra care. I am sure you will welcome him here, next to you." The dark content of the metal box is Danuta's most treasured possession. In moments of despair, she always reaches for this box, finding comfort within and deriving strength from it. A loud noise of the opening garage doors fills the room signaling the arrival of her son. She puts the photograph back and hurriedly places the white piece of paper next to it. "Yes, that's precisely what you want me to do, good!" she whispers with relief. Doors open and a man in his forties waves to her.

"Daddy, Daddy, look, I've just won the battle," Danusia's grandson yells from another room. "Look at the score!"

Danuta's son slowly moves to the computer room and pats the boy on the shoulders. "Very good, Konrad! But that's enough for now. Did you practice piano today?"

Konrad gets up grumbling something.

"Grandma, did he play?"

Danusia makes a puzzled face. "I guess he has played, a little," she replies with some hesitancy. In fact, she has been overwhelmed by the news that she doesn't really know. "There was this news today about Katyń," she relates quietly. "An official memorial at the Katyń Forest. The camera briefly showed this new memorial wall with all the names listed."

"Really?" Her son glances at her, unpacking his suitcase. An uncomfortable silence sets in.

"Grandma, I need your help!" Konrad's energetic voice breaks the discomfort. "I have a project to do. I must write a biography of a famous person. I thought I would write about Marshal Piłsudski and his victory in the Battle of Warsaw."

"Battle of Warsaw, that's right. The 1920 defeat of the Red Army near Warsaw[11] and the Katyń slaughter twenty years later, a striking coincidence," Danusia observes with bitter sadness. She had been a history teacher for almost forty years. She bravely taught Polish history under the Communist regime and later in the Polish Sunday School in New York. History is her passion. She loves to tell the stories from the distant and not so distant past, and she does it with great eloquence and zeal. But today she doesn't feel like talking.

"You love those battles, don't you, especially the victorious ones. But you know, Konrad, the essence of history is what's really behind those battles. What's most important is *why* people fight those battles. Bring me that big red book from upstairs, I'll show you something."

Konrad already knows the big red book. That's Grandma's teaching manual. He finds it instantly. She opens the book ceremoniously and slowly turns the pages.

"You see Konrad, to me Piłsudski is not the symbol of war but the symbol of peace, the symbol of resurrecting and rebuilding the nation, and most of all, the symbol of my happy childhood...."

The red book on the table is opened to a page entitled "Poland Resurrected." Konrad looks at Grandma totally unimpressed. Peace, who cares about peace? She guesses his thoughts and adds. "Yes, he fought all those battles to assure sovereign peace for his nation." Slowly, she puts her glasses on and starts reading from the red book.

> On November 11, 1918, Poland reemerged from the historic chaos through a complicated plot of events of the World War I and Bolshevik Revolution. The ancient nation was reborn after over one hundred years of partition, degradation, and deprivation of rights and happiness of millions of Poles. Poland was resurrected through a series of local wars conducted by newly formed, mostly voluntary Polish Armed Forces, through distant peace conferences, and despite objections of her powerful neighbors and pre-packaged plebiscites. This was yet another historic time that called on the Polish people for great sacrifice.
>
> At this decisive moment, the country was blessed with the great leader. Józef Piłsudski emerged as a great military and political talent. His job was monumental, though. First, he had to recover and preserve ethnic Polish lands from three partitioners: Austria, Prussia and Russia. Next, he had to unify three different provinces with different official languages, different laws, different administration, different schools, and different political systems.
>
> His greatest military challenge came from the East. The leaders of the Bolshevik revolution decided to spread communist ideology to Western Europe and viewed Poland as the first target in their military advances into the West. In the summer of 1920, the Red Army staged a full strength attack on Warsaw. Many volunteers crowded the Polish Army to defend their homeland. Thanks to a brilliant defense strategy designed by Marshal Piłsudski, the Polish Army defeated the Red Army. The Polish victory effectively put an end to Bolshevik expansion into Western Europe. In the Battle of Warsaw, the very existence of Western civilization was at stake. Lord d'Abernon would later call this battle the 18th most important battle in the history of the world.[12]

Danusia's voice dies out. "That's fantastic!" Konrad yells proudly. She looks at him with calm resignation. Two decades later, Great Britain withheld a helping hand in Poland's moment of need and later closely cooperated with Stalin in burying forever the memory of his sweet revenge...the Katyń Massacre. But perhaps Konrad is too young to grasp this complexity.

"Do you know, Konrad, that Karol Wojtyła, the future Pope John Paul II, was born at the time of the Battle of Warsaw? Half a century later, he would become the driving force behind the Solidarity Movement that put an end to the era of Soviet Communism.... The next savior.... One may wonder...." She sights with a hint of sadness in her smile.

> The military activities ended in 1920, and an era of vigorous rebuilding of the nation followed. A new Constitution was adopted and popular elections were held. The elections revealed deep political divisions between the conservative right and liberal left. In December 1922, Professor Gabriel Narutowicz was elected as the First President of resurrected Poland against the objections of the radical right. A few days later, a fanatic rightist killed President Narutowicz.[13] The country was boiling.

Konrad fidgets on his chair. "Grandma, I don't need that much information. I just need to know about Piłsudski," he complains. Danusia closes the book and tenderly touches his golden hair. "Well it's enough for now. Let's take a break." He gives Grandma a hug and rushes to his room.

Danusia follows him with her eyes. He is such a happy boy, full of warmth and creative energy. At his age, she was also a very happy kid. She remembers her mother often telling her about all these dark and tragic years of Poland's partition, the failed uprisings, resurrections, and tragic oppressions. It wasn't fun at all. In fact back then, when she was Konrad's age, all these stories seemed so remote and unreal. They didn't apply to her anyway because she was born in independent Poland, in true liberty and freedom, with plenty of opportunities smiling on her.

A bell rings and Danusia shuffles noisily to the door. A mail woman hands her a long box and a pile of today's mail. "Greeting cards from Poland!" Danusia whispers with excitement.

Her fiftieth wedding anniversary approaches. Suffering from severe Alzheimer's, her second husband has been in a wheelchair for several years but he will most certainly attend the festivities. To celebrate their golden anniversary, their son will drive them to a Polish church in Cleveland for a special Polish mass. An elegant new outfit already hangs in the closet for this occasion. But Danuta is somber. She has always dreamt of celebrating their golden wedding anniversary in the Old Town in Warsaw with all her family and friends, the church full of guests. In reality though only one guest is coming for their anniversary celebration in Cleveland. There will be just six of them, that's all....

Konrad takes a curious peek at the fancy box. "What's that?"

"I don't know. Could you open it, please?" she asks, opening the letters in great rush. A dozen purple-red roses in a crystal vase emerge from the elegant box. Danusia's eyes grow round. Konrad finds a small pink envelope hidden between the leaves.

"This is from my Elunia, my dearest baby," Danusia exclaims with tears. The floral scent spreads through the house. Fancy greeting cards are piled on the table. Danusia reads them one by one with great diligence.

"Wishing you many more happy years in good health," her friends write. "We hope you will come to Poland soon," her oldest son writes from Poland. Another card says: "Wishing you not only material wealth but more importantly spiritual wealth." Danusia looks at the handwritten note on the small card. "Spiritual wealth.... That's right...." After all, there was plenty of spiritual wealth in her life back then, before or even during the war. Her eyes wander around the big house. "This special feeling of spiritual wealth, one's soul, where is it now...?"

* * * *

Danusia is a Warsawian. Born in Warsaw at the time of the first presidential elections in resurrected Poland, she is the first child born to a middleclass couple. Her mother, Janina, nicknamed Jasia, works as a hairstylist and wigmaker. Jasia comes from a noble family named Żmigrodzka. Unfortunately, through a complicated plot of family events her noble roots are of no use to her whatsoever. But Jasia is a self-made and entrepreneurial young lady who relies only on herself.

Danusia's father, Alek, has recently settled in Warsaw after years of adventures. His family lives near Brasław, northeast from Vilnius, at the farthest northeast corner of the Second Polish Republic. His family has been living on those lands for centuries. In 1918, Poland recovered those lands from the Soviet Union. Subsequently, Stalin would invade this territory in World War II, and after the demise of Communism Lithuania, Latvia, and Belarus will share this land.

Young Alek speaks broken Polish with a heavy Russian accent. He knows he needs to improve his Polish quickly in order to get a decent job. While he attends language classes, Jasia runs her own beauty salon in the center of Warsaw. Business is good and Jasia is very busy. Before long, Alek gets a job as an electrician in a publishing company.

Unfortunately, inflation runs high and the economy is worsening. In the fall of 1923, a wave of strikes sweeps through Poland. Economic stability becomes the goal of all political parties and a strong unifying force. The non-partisan Economic Council is formed under the leadership of a prominent economist, Grabski. Within one year, Grabski curbs inflation, restores the national currency, improves the collection of taxes, balances the budget, and initiates a period of relative economic stability.[14]

During Grabski's tenure, the publishing company in which Alek works becomes the official State Mint for the country, a hallowed place where the national currency, the *zloty*, is made. Overnight, Alek's job becomes more lucrative and more secure. The times are stable and Danusia's parents decide to have a second child.

In 1925 Danusia gets a present—a little brother. The boy receives a very special name, Zbigniew, nicknamed Zbyszek. By naming their children Danuta and Zbigniew, the parents make a statement of national pride and patriotism. Danusia and Zbyszko are the heroes of the great Polish novel *Teutonic Knights* written by the Nobel Price winner, Henryk Sienkiewicz. The book is known by heart by all the Poles. It's a national bible. In this tragic story set in fifteenth century Poland, Danusia is kidnapped and tortured by Teutonic Knights. Zbyszek makes heroic efforts to save her. In their worst nightmare, the parents of little Danusia and Zbyszek do not anticipate that the horror of the story in its modern version may actually repeat itself.

Jasia works hard looking after two young children and the business. The family needs a bigger apartment but apartments are very hard to come by these days in Warsaw. In the meantime, little Zbyszek becomes very sick and requires extra care. Jasia quits working and sells her business. The family moves to the suburbs of Warsaw to get a cheaper apartment. Alek commutes to work.

Over their heads and beyond their horizons, the world is slowly moving towards disaster. The international situation of Poland worsens. The unification process left the country isolated from its neighbors—most of them former partitioners. The tide of western politics moves invariably against the vital national interests of the young Polish Republic. In England, John Maynard Keynes, a prominent economist, argues that the policy of war reparations reduces Germany to servitude for a generation, degrades the lives of millions of human beings, thereby depriving the whole nation of happiness. Accordingly, the reparation policy is "abhorrent and detestable." By 1924, England decides to support the war-weakened Germany, thereby preventing France from growing in influence. The United States, through the Charles Dawes Plan, supports Germany by forgiving war reparations and offering new loans.[15] The German economy grows rapidly and looks into Poland for new markets that can absorb German goods. As a result, Polish markets suffocate and a tariff war is triggered.

The 1925 European Peace Conference in Locarno brings a big blow to the security of Poland.[16] The resulting pact confirms the permanency of Germany's northwestern borders with France and Belgium but remains silent on Germany's southeastern borders with Poland and Czechoslovakia, thereby opening the door to German expansion eastward.[17] The German propaganda effectively promotes the idea of unjust separation of Eastern Prussia from German lands and calls the Polish Corridor connecting Warsaw with the Baltic Sea "a strip of flesh torn from German blood."

The fact that Germany itself reduced the Polish nation to servitude for more than a century, degraded the lives of millions of Poles for several generations, and that the so called "Polish Corridor" is near the "Birthplace of the Polish Nation" with Gniezno—the homeland of the first King of Poland—is of no relevance. The Polish voice is not heard on the international scene. The international community remains silent with respect to German demands towards Poland and silence in politics is a gesture of approval. Germany knows it and takes advantage of it. While growing in strength, Germany raises more territorial claims to Polish territories and develops new alliances. The dark clouds gather over Poland.

Danusia's family doesn't look at those clouds though. Preoccupied with their daily chores, the parents raise Danusia and Zbyszek with great care and love. After moving from one apartment to another, the family finally settles in an elegant apartment at the State Mint. An excellent electrician, Alek becomes indispensable at work and is awarded a luxurious apartment on the premises of the State Mint. Their new apartment is located in Powisle, the prominent neighborhood of Warsaw near the Vistula River.

Danusia and Zbyszek attend a nearby school at Rybaki. Under the watchful eyes of great teachers such as the historian known as Aunt Fluff, the children study Polish literature and history, read the poetry of Mickiewicz, and participate in unforgettable school plays and Christmas programs. In one of those programs Danusia plays a man of straw in a patriotic play "Wedding" by Stanisław Wyspiański. In this highly symbolic and tragic play written during the partition years, the Poles rise against their oppressors—the three partitioners: Prussia, Austria and Russia. However when the long-awaited call to arms finally comes to a village, people dance, drink, and celebrate but are not ready to fight. Consequently, the opportunity to regain independence is lost. The memory of the partition years is very vivid in the consciousness of Danuta's parents. However for Danusia, the partition time is only a distant past, mere history....

Like most girls her age, Danusia loves to dance, sing, and act. She grows fast and develops into an attractive young lady, full of poise and personal charm. Cultural life in Warsaw is booming. The National Opera and operettas fill up every day. Jan Kiepura, the Polish tenor, reigns in the opera world. Vaudeville is Danusia's favorite. The first Polish records and movies are made. Every day, big crowds rush to see the movies. Movie theaters mushroom and movie stars become heroes and role models for the young generation.

Danusia absorbs the spirit of the time and draws inspiration from it. She keeps asking her parents to send her to the exclusive Art and Movie School.

"You know..., I went today to the movie school and met some teachers there. They were so nice and friendly. They told me that I could qualify and that...."

Her father looks at her skeptically. "I already told you," he interrupts. "This school is too expensive. And besides, you need to get better grades in the first place before thinking about any movie school."

"But Dad," Danusia groans, "you know, I will get a 3+ in math for this grading period, and a 4 for all other courses this semester. I saw my grades today. And the movie school is only 40 zloty per month. I promise I will work hard."

"If 40 zloty is not much for you then go and earn it," Mama scolds her.

"Okay, I know, it is expensive but this is such an excellent school. Everybody says I have talent. Please give me a chance. I promise I will work hard. You'll see."

The father sighs heavily. "Well, how about if we give it a try? What do you think, Jasia?" The mother slowly nods with approval. "But remember, on one condition—that your grades in the gymnasium[18] will not suffer!"

Danusia jumps like a rocket, gives Dad a big hug, kisses Mama, and yells with excitement: "I promise I will study hard and will even get some 5's. You'll see!" The mother embraces her gently with a smile.

Every day after regular school, Danusia flies to the movie school. She loves every minute of it. She sings and dances, learns phonetics and diction, studies history of art, poetry and acting. She is very good at it. In fact, she is a born actress with a natural talent for acting and public speaking. When she performs, she shines. Her sharp eyes and assertive voice immediately capture the audience. She quickly and effortlessly makes new friends and frequently takes charge in the group. Although she is among the youngest students, she catches the attention of the most influential teachers.

Her adventure with acting doesn't last long, though. The first grading period in the gymnasium is a disaster. It turns out that Danusia got an F in mathematics and in French. Dad is merciless. He turns a deaf ear on Danusia's entreaties and orders that she withdraw from the movie school at once. The school principal, Hanna Osoria, desperately wants to keep Danusia in school. She even offers to waive the tuition. But Alek is determined and rejects her offer.

"Danusia must get a high school diploma first," he declares. "It is not a matter of money. It's a matter of principle."

There was nothing Danusia or anyone else could do to keep her in the movie school. Her dream of becoming an actress would forever remain just a dream. But with such a painful experience, she becomes more mindful of her school responsibilities.

Like many Poles of his time, Alek is a man of principle, loving but rigorous. Most of the time he keeps a distance from daily affairs but when it comes to important matters, he becomes involved. Like many of the time, Alek sympathizes with the Communists, and even though he was raised as a Catholic, he never goes to church. The couple has an unspoken agreement that Jasia is responsible for the religious upbringing of the children.

Jasia is a devout Catholic and scrupulous practitioner. The kids must go to church every Sunday. Sometimes Jasia goes with them. But often she is busy with styling hair and the kids must go by themselves. One of Danusia's childhood dreams has always been to go to Sunday mass with both Mom and Dad. But it never happened. Her Dad never went to mass. She only remembers that one day he slipped into an empty church and spent some time inside. Although Alek approved of his children's religious upbringing, he remained deeply distrustful of the church institution.

As Danusia is coming to terms with the movie school disaster, the country is coming out of the 1933 recession. Danusia didn't really experience the pain of the great recession because the families of State Mint employees were among the privileged and protected ones. But hundreds of thousands of workers across the country suffered great hardship.

In the southwestern region of Silesia, the catastrophic unemployment among the coal miners became the fertile ground for the promotion of fascist ideologies. The German minorities along the Polish–German borders were galvanized. The ranks of the fascist German minority organizations swelled. By 1934 the German Socio-Cultural Association (*Schlesische Volksbund*) had thirty-three thousand members, conservative-right *Deutsche Partei* accounted for five thousand, and the aggressive pro-Hitler *Jungdeutsche Partei* exceeded forty thousand members. The German NSDAP was busy providing these groups with subsidies, training the leaders, and developing networks of spies and paramilitary groups. Thanks to NSDAP financial support, the German minority organizations in Poland were able to offer unemployment compensation and thereby attract thousands of laid-off coal miners to their ranks.[19]

In 1932 Poland signed a ten-year Non-Aggression Pact with the Soviet Union. The Pact included a historically critical clause providing that in the event of military conflict with a third country the signatories of the Pact shall not directly or indirectly assist that third country. Two years later, Poland also signed a ten-year Non-Aggression Pact with Germany. This pact was supplemented by the Moral Disarmament Agreement renouncing propaganda wars. Marshal Piłsudski, the center of the country's political power and the author of Poland's foreign policy, aimed at preserving a balance between the two neighbors. His goal was to maintain relations with both powers but to ally with neither of them.[20]

The role of Marshal Piłsudski in the Polish Government was one of a kind. Although in 1926 the National Assembly elected him as President, he declined the nomination and chose the position of Minister of Defense. Formally the Minister of Defense and for all practical purposes the center of power, he remained in this position until his death.[21]

In the spring of 1934, a new quasi-fascist organization called the Radical National Group (ONR) entered the political scene. Soon thereafter, Minister of Internal Affairs Pieracki was assassinated. Radical National Group was blamed for the assassination and immediately outlawed. As a result of this violent assassination, President Mościcki issued a special presidential decree on proper measures to assure the safety, security, and public order. Although it would be revealed later that the Ukrainian Military Organization was behind the assassination of Minister Pieracki, the 1934 Decree gave the administration the right to detain indefinitely and without any cause any political opponent. Once introduced, this convenient tool quickly became the primary method of eradicating any opposition. Pursuant to the Decree, a detention camp was created in Bereza Kartuska and several hundred political opponents from far right and far left alike were preventively detained there.[22]

In the spring of 1935, news had broken that Marshal Piłsudski was seriously ill. By then, Piłsudski had a mixed record of accomplishments. Faced with a highly polarized and divided society, the Great Marshal had moved over the years away from the democratic style of governance towards more of an autocratic style. His record included a 1926 military coup, the 1930 Brest detention and trial of opposition leaders, the 1934 imprisonment of Communists in Bereza Kartuska, and the 1935 Constitution that curbed democratic privileges.

And yet, the Great Marshal was perceived as the father of the country, the greatest moral, political, and patriotic authority. The loyalty of his soldiers represented the cornerstone of his power. Piłsudski's soldiers from the time of the Battle of Warsaw have moved into civil service and government posts. For the young people, military service has been offering opportunities for professional and social advancement. Piłsudski's heroic struggle for resurrection of Poland made him a true national hero, and for most Poles he would remain that national hero forever. During his final days, the whole nation prayed for his recovery. Everybody, from youngsters to the elderly, was deeply saddened by the news of his illness and wished him well.

On a sunny day in May 1935, the word comes. Marshal Piłsudski is dead. Danusia gets the news from her mother and bursts into tears. Inexplicable fear settles in her heart, and the same fear settles in the hearts of millions of others. Piłsudski was the symbol of independent Poland, the statesman that, as some historians would later say, could save the world from World War II. Does that mean that Poland may be lost again without him? Who would protect us now? What does the future hold? Grieving people are asking these terrifying questions everywhere. Even Piłsudski's direct political opponents pay last respect to the man of unquestionable and unparalleled patriotism. Only Piłsudski's moral authority could solidify the many different interest groups and orientations. Only Piłsudski could find middle ground between right and left, West and East, democracy and autocracy. Above all, Piłsudski was the most powerful symbol of resurrected Poland.

The funeral of the Great Marshal is a weeklong event. First, his body is displayed for viewing in the National Cathedral in Warsaw, then the casket will be transported to Kraków, and the Great Marshal will be laid to rest at Wawel, the burial place for all the Polish kings for over one thousand years. Warsaw is so crowded that people can hardly approach the Cathedral. Countless crowds gather in the center of the city, blocking all the streets. No one can freely move around.

Danusia and her mother join the crowd with a secret plan to get to the Great Marshal. One of their neighbors, Mr. Bojewski, works as a security guard at the King's Palace near the Cathedral. Apparently, the Cathedral is connected with the Palace by a secret underground passage. The plan is that Danusia and her mother would come to the Palace and Mr. Bojewski would take them through the secret passageway to the Cathedral. Danusia is anxious. Her imagination boils.

The first challenge is to reach the gate of the Palace. For several hours, Danusia and Mama revolve round the Palace in smaller and smaller circles until they push to the gate where, as planned, Mr. Bojewski lets them in. He takes them through humid, labyrinthine halls, stairs and passages to the basement of the Cathedral and from there up a concealed, chilly staircase to the nave balcony. Here, Danusia finds herself right above the glowing nave of the Cathedral. The breathtaking view spreads in front of her curious eyes. The majestic walls of the gothic Cathedral nave are filled with sadness and candle warmth. She looks down and here he is. The Great Marshal, with this familiar stringent face, his dark, bushy eyebrows and big mustache, he is lying beneath in the open casket, his numerous military insignia gleaming from the distance. Tears veil Danusia's eyes for a moment, but the scene is so spectacular she has to absorb every moment of it.

The casket of the Great Marshal, buried in the flowers, rests high on the pedestal. Military and honor guards with representatives of the government, political organizations, and scouts surround the casket. The never-ending procession of sobbing people slowly moves by the casket. The monumental ascetic Cathedral is silent, but from time to time, loud weeping and sobbing break the silence.

Danusia's farewell with the Great Marshal doesn't last long. After a few minutes, Mr. Bojewski hastily waves to them. "We have to go. I must be back at the Palace."

Danusia finishes her prayer, takes a last glimpse at the spectacular scene below, and pulls Mama away from the balustrade. In a few minutes, they are back at the Palace and on their way home. Danusia is exhausted and bewildered. The view from the nave balcony deeply touched her heart and would remain engraved upon her memory for the rest of her life.

After the funeral, life seems to go back to normal. As summer comes, people head to the countryside. But a certain anxiety remains. Who would succeed the Great Marshal? What will happen to various political groups unified under his leadership? Who would take on the lead in foreign policy? The Piłsudski coalition doesn't waste time and selects Edward Rydz-Śmigły as Commander-in-Chief of the Armed Forces. In early fall, the coalition forms a new cabinet with Edward Kwiatkowski as the Treasury Minister. Energetic and skilled Kwiatkowski develops an ambitious four-year industrialization plan for a carefully selected Central Industrial Region. Although financial support from England and the United States is beyond Poland's reach, Kwiatkowski arranges credits from France, Poland's closet ally. In an atmosphere of increasing tension with Germany, he focuses the limited resources of the country on the development of the military industry: military plants, steel mills, power plants, airplane plants, tire and machine tool plants. His policy stimulates growth and brings down unemployment. By 1937, the economy has improved and the country has reached relative political stability.[23]

The first years without the Great Marshal seem good for ordinary Poles. Danusia and her family are happy and prosperous. One day, Alek comes home carrying a big package in both hands. "Hello everybody, guess what I have for you!"

"Wow, this must be an airplane," Zbyszek exclaims, goggling at the box.

"No, no, this is some kind of a scooter, I guess," Danusia declares.

The mother checks the box. "Well, since Christmas is not here yet, you have to wait a little longer for your wishes to come true. I think this present is for the house, in other words, for all of us. Right, Alek?"

"Exactly!" he thunders.

The kids are not discouraged. They rush to the neatly packed box. Danusia grabs the scissors while Zbyszek peels off heavy paper and spots a shiny piece of light wood.

"Hurrah! Hurrah!"

The kids tear off the paper with the speed of light. A big wooden box with a fabric covered frame and black plastic panel in the center emerges from the rubbish.

"Radio! Radio!" Zbyszek screams.

Indeed, a beautiful brand new radio stands on the dining table. Alek looks at it with admiration while Jasia shakes her head in disbelief. "Alek, this must cost a fortune. How much did you pay for it?"

"Don't worry, Jasia, I got a special deal." Alek always talks about a special deal when he wants to calm down Jasia. "You know that store in Żelazna Street? They set this unit aside for me. It's the latest model. I buy so many things from them that they gave me a great discount."

"Yes, but how about your old radio, Dad?" Danusia asks with concern. "Do you want to throw it out?"

Alek looks at the ugly gray box standing on the windowsill. This is his first radio, his baby, and the source of great pride. Before anybody else could even dream of having a radio, he put it together himself with great diligence. The whole family treats this simple gray box as their darling. The memories of the best times of togetherness came back. They would gather around the little radio in the evening and listen to the Warsaw station broadcasts, music and poetry programs, and the Lwów Wave Station with the all time favorite talk show of Toncio and Szczepcio. Thanks to this little radio, they listened to the very first radio broadcasts in Poland. Now, they look at each other with consternation. At last Zbyszek breaks the silence.

"Can I have it, Dad? I will be very careful with it, I promise."

"Sure," Alek replies with relief.

The new radio is placed prominently on the commode in the living room. Alek frequently invites friends for an evening of radio listening. With this new top of the line equipment, he catches many stations, including some Russian music stations. He loves to listen to the Russian songs that remind him of his youth times far away near Brasław.

His job at the State Mint is getting better and better every day. The company takes good care of the most valuable employees. With his electronics expertise, Alek is one of them. Together with other innovators, he arranges for the installation of a telephone line in the reception area of their apartment building. The phone, paid for and maintained by the company, immediately becomes indispensable to all the residents.

Another important benefit of working at the State Mint is the sports club. For Danusia and Zbyszek, it is their summer paradise. Located on the opposite side of the Vistula River, the club stretches before the eyes of all the children from the Powisle neighborhood like a magic kingdom. Equipped with rowboats and kayaks, the club is the envy of all the neighbors. A fancy clubhouse with a golden sand beach protected by handsome lifeguards is surrounded with adjacent volleyball fields. Although across the river, the club is within a walking distance from the State Mint either through Kierbedzia Bridge or through the pedestrian walkway of the Railroad Bridge.

Almost every morning during the summer, Danusia and Zbyszek rush to the club and spend all day playing there. The only problem is to be back home on time for dinner. And they cannot be late one minute because it makes their mother furious and spells trouble. If everything goes well and Mama is not upset, Danusia can even go back to the club in the evening for dancing. This is the only place where she is allowed to go dancing, but only if she takes along her little brother. Zbyszek likes to play billiards, chess and checkers with his friends there.

One hot and sluggish day in the summer of 1938, Danusia is tanning on the boat deck of the club and her young body, coated with a thick layer of Nivea cream, is scorching in the sun. Small waves of the lethargic river stream bang on the side of the boat. As in a cradle, Danusia rocks while daydreaming. From time to time, the rumble of a train passing over the railroad bridge invades her privacy while a blurred monotonous noise coming from the public beach soothes her like a lullaby.

"Excuse me, what time is it?" All of a sudden, an energetic male voice interrupts her daydreaming.

She looks around and spots a good-looking young man swimming toward her. "A quarter to one," she replies and falls back into her dreaming position. But the young man doesn't give up. "I am sorry for interrupting but I come from the other club over there." He points to the crowded public beach next door. "One of my friends, Staszek, is working here. He invited me to come over here but I can't find him now. Do you know Staszek?"

"Oh yes, Staszek, sure I know him. I think he must be inside," Danusia points to the main building.

"He is lucky to be around such beautiful girls around here." The young man reaches the boat. "May I join you?"

"Yes, of course." Danusia already understands his intentions and leans upward with curiosity.

"I notice you come here frequently," the trespasser continues.

"How do you know?"

"Well, everybody notices a beautiful girl like you. I like to come to the beach to relax a little before my exams. I am a law student at the University of Warsaw, just across the river, there. I have seen you several times already."

Danusia carefully studies the man. He wears his ash blond hair straight back. His sharp blue eyes give him an intelligent look. His easy talk and polite manner please her. A law student, that sounds interesting, but he must be much older. "Thank you for your compliment," she replies without embarrassment. She knows she is attractive and is used to compliments. "If you want, I can take you to Staszek," she offers her help.

"Oh, that would be great!"

They jump to the footbridge and walk down towards the club. At the end of the footbridge, the young man stops abruptly and draws himself up. "Since we are on solid ground, let me introduce myself. My name is Józef Fijałkowski. It is a pleasure to meet you." He extends his hand.

Danusia looks at him slightly bewildered. Such a formal introduction from a man in a swimsuit, how funny. "And I am Danusia." She quickly shakes his hand and moves on. As they approach the club, Zbyszek runs to them yelling, "I won, I won, Danusia, I won two games."

"That's great, Zbyszek. But listen, this is Mr. Fijałkowski. He is looking for Staszek. Did you see him?"

"Oh, sure, Staszek was cheering for me. They are inside."

"This is my little brother, Zbyszek." Danusia turns to Józek.

"Nice to meet you, Zbyszek. You can call me Joseph or Józek, not Mr. Fijałkowski, okay?"

"That's great, Joseph. Are you good at playing chess, because I want to play chess with someone very good!"

"I can certainly play with you and then we'll see," Józek replies as they enter the building.

"Józek, you made it here!" Staszek spots them immediately. "How are you, buddy? Where are your clothes?" They hug each other warmly.

"I left my clothes and my books in the club next door," Józek replies.

"So, let's go and bring them here. I see you already made some friends here. That's great!" Staszek sends him a suspicious smile.

Exhausted by the sun, Danusia throws herself on the couch. The room is dark and pleasantly chilly. In the opposite corner, a group of children plays billiards. Zbyszek keeps jumping all over her, talking about his glorious victories. Before long, Staszek and Józek are back. Józek is neatly dressed in a white shirt and pastel pants. With heavy books under his arm, he looks like a real student. Danusia rushes to put her white dress on. She, too, wants to look her best. They chat and joke for a while. In the early afternoon, the whole group moves to the dance club. Józek dances well and stays with Danusia all the time until Zbyszek grabs her hand and pulls her away.

"Danusia, we have to go home! We are late, very late! Mama must be furious!"

Danusia, like Cinderella, wakes up from her dream, waves good-bye to Józek, and with horror in her eyes rushes home. Too late! Mama is already on her way to the club. But they miss each other. The children rush home through Kierbedzia Bridge while Mama takes the Railroad Bridge. They reach home out of breath and Dad opens the door. "Did you see Mama? She just left to get you!"

"Oh, no!" Danusia groans. "Dad, I am sorry, it's my fault. You know, we met a new friend, a very nice boy. He's a law student. We went dancing and it was so great I forgot to check the time. I am sorry, but please tell Mama not to holler. Please, please, save us, Dad!"

"All right, but you shouldn't do this to Mama. She always waits for you with dinner. This is the last time I am going to risk my life for you, remember that!"

Danusia is Daddy's girl. Not only do they love each other but they also understand each other in a split second. When it comes to daily problems, Daddy is more forbearing and often protects Danusia from Mama's rage. As in the past, he does his best when Mama comes home looking like a thundercloud.

"Jasia, don't holler, they came home right after you left. They apologized already and promised not to do it again."

Mama grumbles for a while but soon life goes back to normal.

A few days later, a gatekeeper named Gara knocks at the door. "Danusia, phone for you, a lover, I guess." Danusia runs down the steps.

"Hallo?"

"Hi, Danusia. This is Józek. You see I've found you."

"Józek! How are you?"

"Good. I had my last exam yesterday. So, I thought maybe you would have time to go out tomorrow."

"Oh, that's great. I think I could," Danusia replies eagerly.

"How about if we meet tomorrow in front of the Fate Movie Theater at about six? Do you know that movie theater?"

"Yes, of course I know. At six, right?" Danusia hangs up the phone and starts dancing. Finally he found her. She has been looking for him at the club for several days. Exams, exams, he should have called her earlier.

The next day, she wakes up excited. To assure that the evening goes well, she decides to stay home and do some good deeds. Ironing is the thing she hates the most, but she needs to get her favorite dress ready. So she takes a big pile of things waiting to be ironed and starts working. As the day goes by, she decides to mention to Mama that she wants to go out in the evening. After several more good deeds and some more negotiations, she finally gets permission and by 5:30 is ready to go.

At the Fate Movie Theater, Józek is waiting. Danusia approaches him from behind and surprises him. He greets her with a smile. "I am so glad to see you again. You look very pretty today."

"Thank you. And how are your exams?"

"Oh, I am finally done with all of my exams for this semester."

They stare at each other in silence then Józek slowly starts: "You know, I checked the movie schedule and there was nothing interesting tonight. So, how about if we go to the park. It's such a nice evening."

"That's a good idea," Danusia agrees. "Let's go to the Vistula Park, that's my favorite place." They walk down the street, leaving behind the Fate Movie Theater.

"I was wondering whether we would meet again. I didn't give you my address, and I didn't know yours."

"You just flew away like a butterfly. But I knew you were from the State Mint. That's how I found you."

They enter the park. The aroma of lush grass and dense shrubs pleasantly greets them. Here and there lovers sneak past or sit on the benches. Some elderly people feed pigeons. Józek discreetly reaches for Danusia's hand.

She looks at him slightly embarrassed. "Tell me a little more about yourself. I know you are a law student, but where are you from?"

"Oh, you want to know my story." Józek is pleasantly surprised. "Well, I am from Koło, West of Warsaw, towards Poznań. Have you been to Poznań?"

"No, I've never been in Poznań, but I was in Gniezno and Biskupin. That's northwest from Warsaw, I think. We went on a school trip to see the Cathedral in Gniezno and this oldest Polish settlement in Biskupin. But Koło, I don't remember going through Koło."

"That is because you went northwest and Koło is more west, about three hundred kilometers from Warsaw in that direction." He points towards the park entrance. "But how about if we go this way." He points in the opposite side and gently turns her towards the quiet path leading deeper into the park. "I was supposed to become a priest," he says. "I spent three years in the seminary, here on Krakowskie Przedmiescie Street."

"Oh, really?" Danusia stops for a moment. How exciting to have a date with a would-be priest! "So, why did you quit?" She eagerly anticipates hearing some romantic story.

"It's difficult to say. I didn't really feel the call from God. I didn't like it there."

"So why did you go there in the first place?"

"My father wanted me to. And when I decided to leave, everybody was upset, my father and my teachers. Without even my asking, Father Fiatoski gave me one-year leave of absence. He was hoping I would be back. But for the past two years, I haven't even been in the vicinity of the seminary. But I still keep in touch with all my friends there."

"So you must be happy with law school?"

"Yes, pretty much so. But my father was quite upset for a while. He suspected that I fell in love with some girl and that's why I left the seminary. I tried to convince him that I simply didn't want to be a priest and that the girls had nothing to do with it. To convince him, I even told him that I would never get married."

Until this moment, Danusia has been listening attentively. However, the last statement hit her hard. Her father's admonition flashed through her mind loud and clear: "Stay away from the boys who just want to play around with you and don't want to get married. They will take advantage of you. They may destroy your life. Remember that!"

"Aha!" Danusia thinks. "He is just one of those fellows who merely wants to take advantage of me." She tunes out the rest of Józek's story. He's good-looking and nice but she can survive without him. For all practical purposes, she loses all interest in Józek. Eventually, he senses her change of heart and they head towards the gate. Without saying much, Danusia catches the bus. She has a bad feeling about the entire evening and doesn't want to see Józek again.

"*Panie* Gara, if this fellow, Józek, calls and asks for me, tell him I am not home, okay?"

"Okay, Danusia." Gatekeeper Gara shakes his head. He has five daughters and worries about those boys all the time, sometimes because there are too many of them, sometimes because there are not enough of them.

* * * *

As the summer of 1938 passes by, the European scene is boiling. After annexation of Rhineland in 1936 and Austria in 1937–1938, Hitler turns his fury against Czechoslovakia. As expected, England and France continue the policy of appeasement. To make matters worse, Czechoslovakia's relations with Poland move from bad to worse. Back in 1919, Czechoslovakia invaded the Duchy of Cieszyn inhabited by the majority of ethnic Poles and strained relations with Poland. Subsequently, the government of Czechoslovakia took the position that Poland would be the first target of Hitler's aggression and decided not to seek any alliances with Poland. At the same time, Poland raised territorial claims to Czechoslovakia with respect to the Zaolzie region, heavily populated by ethnic Poles.[24] Consequently, in the summer of 1938, Czechoslovakia found itself in political isolation.

Towards the end of the summer, Hitler concentrates his military forces on the border with Czechoslovakia. In response, France and England undertake intense diplomatic negotiations. British Prime Minister Chamberlain pressures the government of Czechoslovakia to accept Hitler's territorial claims to Sudety. He also persuades France to disregard its commitments to Czechoslovakia and lessen its criticism of Germany.[25]

At the end of September, the leaders of England and France meet with those of Germany and Italy in Munich and accept the German annexation of Czechoslovakia's Sudety region. The Munich meeting becomes the symbol of the policy of appeasement towards German imperialism and marks the end of an era of Franco–British influence in Europe.[26] The Western Powers attempt to buy peace for themselves by selling Czechoslovakia. Poland will be next.

During the Munich crisis, the Polish Army takes over Zaolzie (Teschen) from Czechoslovakia. Colonel Beck, the Polish Minister for Foreign Affairs responsible for this decision, is often blamed for being petty-minded and opportunistic with respect to Zaolzie. However, Colonel Beck holds a very impressive record of standing up in a very non-opportunistic manner to enormous German political and military pressure. His defenders argue that his annexation of Zaolzie was aimed at the Munich policy and Germany's increasing power rather than at Czechoslovakia as such. If not Poland, then Germany would take over Zaolzie with its sizable Polish population and strategic industrial base with the largest steel mill in Europe.[27] Colonel Beck makes this bold move to prevent the German penetration of Poland's southern borders vital to Polish defense.[28]

In October of 1938, Germany reveals to Colonel Beck its intention to annex the free city of Gdańsk (Danzig) and the so-called "Polish Corridor" linking Germany with East Prussia. The German policy of revision promoting German exclusive rights to Danzig and Corridor was put in place back in 1926. Government subsidized propaganda programs at an expenditure of million of marks were intended to stimulate interest in the Germany's eastern borders at home and abroad, in particular in Britain, France, and the United States. Public sympathy for the German cause was necessary to supplement the diplomatic pressure on Western Powers for the revision of German borders. The results of this intricate propaganda war were excellent. In secret talks conducted in July of 1939 between Dirksen, German Ambassador to London, and Wilson, Chamberlain's advisor, Wilson stated that the British side was ready to make a commitment not to interfere into affairs of Great Germany. This commitment would also apply to Danzig.[29]

To the Polish Government, the true German intent behind the "corridor" rhetoric was straightforward and the same for centuries. First, Germany cuts off Poland's access to the Baltic Sea. Next, it turns already weakened Poland into a territory exploitable by the Germans.[30]

Colonel Beck understands this strategy all too well. Counting on some solution in further talks, he decides to keep secret Hitler's October communication demanding Gdańsk and the "Corridor." However, three months later, Hitler renews his territorial demands. Considering that Poland has the largest Jewish population in Europe and strong anticommunist forces, Hitler pressures Poland to join the Axis Powers. In his plans, Poland has to be turned into an obedient puppet like other recently overtaken countries. In January of 1939, he sends Ribbentrop to Warsaw with the final offer. At this moment, Hitler still plans the attack first on France and England, and next on the Soviet Union. Poland is not on his agenda. In the ultimatum, Hitler does not request Poland's support on the Western front but makes it clear that he expects Poland's support in the subsequent invasion of the Soviet Union.[31]

Accustomed to success with his policy of coercion and assault, Hitler does not anticipate any trouble with Poland and turns his attention to Czechoslovakia. There, he forces President Hach to accept the German ultimatum. On March 15, 1939, German troops enter Prague without firing a single shot, turn Bohemia and Moravia into Nazi Protectorates, Slovakia into a puppet republic, and cede Ruthenia to Hungary. Czechoslovakia is dead. A few days later, Hitler takes over Kłajpeda [Memel] from Lithuania. The world stands still and watches the rising of the vicious beast.

After his abhorrent successes, Hitler wakes up to the realization that Poland has not accepted his ultimatum. Even worse! In the meantime, Poland initiated discussions with the Soviet Union. It appears that he miscalculated Warsaw. Indeed, he disregarded the fact that Warsaw has been led by the heirs of the Great Marshal. His legacy —to die but not to surrender—is vivid and powerful in the nation. Colonel Beck could buy some time by bowing to Hitler's ultimatum. Instead, he chooses to fight. His decision is the reflection of the will of the entire nation.[32]

Furious at Poland's defiance, Hitler changes his strategy overnight. He decides to finish with Poland first and then turn to France and Britain. By this time, however, France and Great Britain finally understand their imminent danger and the role that Poland plays in this equation. In March of 1939, the British government rushes with territorial guarantees and a week later with military guarantees to Poland. France follows with its own military guarantees to Poland. Hitler embraces this opportunity to renounce the 1934 Non-Aggression Pact with Poland and unleashes an aggressive propaganda campaign against his next target.[33]

In response Colonel Beck, in his memorable parliamentary speech of May 5, 1939, declares: "Peace is precious and desirable.... However peace, like almost everything in this world, has its price, high but defined. We in Poland do not know the term 'peace at any price.' There is one thing priceless in the life of the people, nations, and states. That one thing is honor."[34]

1. Danusia with Parents, Warsaw, 1926

2. Danusia in the Movie School

2

The summer of 1939 looks marvelous. In May Danusia turns seventeen. Her vacation plans are fantastic. For the first time she will travel to Dad's birthplace in the far northeastern corner of Poland. For the first time, she will meet her relatives living near Brasław: uncles, aunts, and cousins of her age. It is a historic trip for all of them but by far the most significant trip for Dad. He left his home twenty-five years ago and only now he is returning. Just a few years ago, he managed to renew correspondence with his family. Although his parents are no longer alive, his beloved brother is still there and his sisters live nearby.

Every year, for as long as Danusia can remember, Dad talked about going to Brasław. But always something interrupted his plans. Either the kids were too little to endure the trip, or there was not enough money, or there was some emergency at work. This year Dad is determined to go. To everybody's disappointment, Mama decides to stay home. She argues that by staying home she will save money and the children can enjoy a longer vacation. But everybody knows that Mama is not an adventurer and would have a lot of problems coping with country life for more than a week. Hence, they don't press.

The trip to Brasław is going to be very long and exhaustive. The whole journey from home to Uncle Vince takes two days if everything goes well. First they will take a regular train to Vilnius; next they will switch to the light rail to Dukszty. Mysterious Uncle Vince will meet them at the Dukszty station and take them by buggy another 30 kilometers or so to his farm near the Dryświaty Lake.

By the middle of June, everything is ready for the trip. School is finished, shopping is done, presents are packed, and tickets are in hand. Mama walks them to the train station. Danusia is visibly upset.

"Mama, it would be so much better if you could go with us. We can't really enjoy this vacation knowing that you are lonely and so far away."

"Don't worry," Mama smiles. "At last, I will have time for myself. This will be my best vacation. There will be no washing, cooking, and cleaning for a while, and I will even get more sleep."

"She won't be lonely," Dad adds. "I asked Mrs. Sowińska to come over more often. She has some interesting plans for Mama."

As they enter the station, a majestic train slowly puffs in. A white board with big black letters "WILNO" appears on the side of each passenger car. A nervous energy overtakes the crowd. Danusia feels queasy. After all, this is the first time she will take such a long trip.

"Alek!" Mama yells from behind. "Are you in the front or in the back of the train?"

"In the middle, I guess," Dad yells back.

The big crowd flows in different directions. People begin to run, wave, scream, and blindly push into one another.

"Follow me!" Dad orders, trying to push his way through the chaos.

The train puffs and blusters. The brakes screech as the colossus comes to a halt. Immediately, the voyagers are all over the train like ants invading a piece of candy. Some jump through the windows, some run on the roof. The doors are taken by storm.

"Thank God you have the seats reserved," Mama groans at this scene.

"But we have to get on the train somehow," Danusia replies, bemused.

"Zbyszek! Where is Zbyszek? Do you see him?" Mama panics.

Indeed! Zbyszek is nowhere near. The waves of anxious passengers could carry him off in any direction.

"There he is! Waving for us!" Danusia's sharp eyes spot him towards the rear of the train.

Zbyszek has somehow wiggled his way to the steps of the train and is clinging there waving and screaming. "Here, here, this is our wagon!" he yells.

They push through the crowd with Mama forcefully leading the way. She reaches him first, hugs him quickly, and passes a bag full of delicious goodies. Danusia and Dad clamber up the steps behind Zbyszek. Whew, they made it! Now the compartment. But Zbyszek has already found it. They move in quickly, place the luggage overhead, and rush to the window to say good-bye to Mama. A few more instructions, a few more expressions of love, and the train is slowly leaving the station. For a moment, they all have tears in their eyes. But this brief moment of sadness quickly fades away and their thoughts run to the great adventure ahead.

The journey to Vilnius is uneventful. A young couple with three children shares their compartment. They are also headed for vacation. After chatting a little and eating some strawberries from Mama's bag, everybody quickly succumbs to sleep. The warm summer night descends upon them.

Early in the morning, the train arrives in Vilnius. No need to rush this time. The morning is chilly and muggy. Dressed in sweaters and blazers, the children pick up valises and slowly move with the crowd. Dad anxiously looks around trying to recall the place and find the train to Dukszty. It is supposed to depart from the same station. He checks the schedule. The train leaves in an hour from another platform. Soon, a small, light, toy-like train leisurely draws up. No reserved seats this time, but very few people are waiting. A few more passengers show up and off they go.

The weather improves as the train enters the countryside. The sun comes out. Everything around looks and smells vacation. Zbyszek opens the window. The refreshing aroma of meadows and woods blows at them. The train slowly passes through dense forests and open rolling hills with shiny wild lakes surrounded by colorful, sweet-smelling meadows. They are in the first car and several more joyfully wind behind them. From the slow moving train, they can almost touch the branches of the trees. Occasionally, they see small farms and countryside homes far away on the horizon.

"It's so beautiful here!" Danusia whispers.

Zbyszek catches a breath of fresh air and starts singing a scout song. Danusia joins him.

Where creeks flow idly
And May scatters herbs,
Field daisies sprout
And woods above sigh.

"Yes, this countryside is very beautiful," Dad whispers melancholically. As a boy, he didn't really appreciate the beauty of nature around here. The countryside only meant the daily hard work in the fields. Back then, he felt as if it was the forgotten corner of the world, far from anything interesting, far from the cities full of life, far from the sea full of adventure, far from the politics and power, and far from theaters, movies, and schools. But later, as the years passed, he often ventured back in his memory to those vast fields, forests, rolling hills, and shiny lakes where his life was so peaceful and simple.

As the journey continues, Dad grows visibly nervous. He no longer jokes or smiles. Instead, he sits quietly, playing tensely with his fingers. Danusia glances at him and hugs him gently.

"Dad, what's wrong? Why don't you sing with us? Are you upset?"

"No, I am not upset," he replies. "I am just tired."

"What time are we supposed to be in Dukszty?" Zbyszek asks.

"In less than two hours," Dad replies.

They look at each other and the silence sets in.

"Do you think they will be waiting for us?" Danusia breaks the silence with hesitancy.

"I hope so," Dad replies. "I wrote to them several times and they wrote back that they would be picking us up. You remember that last letter, right?"

"But who do you think will pick us up?" Zbyszek wonders.

"Probably Vince and maybe his son, Bolek. I am not sure."

"Do you think you will recognize them? They didn't send us any pictures," Danusia worries.

"I should." Dad tries to sound reassuring. "We grew up together. He is my big brother. We were playing together all the time, we were swimming, and fishing, and hiking. We worked together in the fields in the summer and hunted together in the winter. He was closer to me than my father."

As the train approaches Dukszty, Danusia and Zbyszek also grow increasingly nervous. Soon they will meet the legendary uncle and will discover their "new" family. Who are they? Do they look like Dad? Will they welcome them? Life here seems so different. They stare at the countryside without saying much until the conductor loudly announces: "Next station—Dukszty!"

All three spring to their feet at once, grab the valises, and move to the door. The train slows down. No one else is getting off here. Dad opens the door, steps down onto the platform and quickly reaches for the luggage. In a great rush, the kids pass all the valises to him. This is a very short stop; there is no time to waste. Once Danusia gets off, the train starts moving again and Zbyszek has to jump. The train chugs away whistling.

* * * *

They find themselves alone at the empty station. A small building with a big sign "Dukszty" stands like an abandoned ship on the lonesome sea. Only at the other end of the platform, a small silhouette moves towards them. Alek grabs the valises in both hands and without saying a word moves in that direction. Before Danusia and Zbyszek make a move, he is already way ahead and keeps quickening his pace. Danusia and Zbyszek follow him. Now they can see better. An elderly man is coming from the other side of the platform.

"That can't be Uncle Vince," Danusia thinks. "That can't be him." The man is short and heavy, with a mixture of blond and gray bushy hair, while Dad is tall and slim with dark, almost black, sleek hair. The children look hypnotized as the two men approach each other. The old man's face is tense, his eyes riveted on Dad. He is already running. Dad drops the valises and also runs with his arms wide open.

"Alek! Alek!" the old man cries.

They fling themselves into each other's arms and remain motionless. As Danusia comes closer, she notices the two men quietly sobbing. Dad is crying? But Dad never cries! She has never seen Dad crying! She realizes that something extraordinary is happening in front of her eyes. And this strange expression on Dad's face, evincing both pain and happiness. Just by watching this scene, Danusia and Zbyszek develop a special feeling for the old man. If he is so important to Dad then he must be someone special to them, too. After a few more moments to themselves, the two men slowly turn to them.

"Vince, these are my children: Danusia and Zbyszek."

Vince looks at them shaking his head.

"Oh, my dear, my dear...," he tries to reach to both of them at once but Danusia is faster.

"Uncle Vince, how nice to meet you at last," she hears her voice filled with emotion. They warmly hug each other. By the time Uncle

Vince reaches for Zbyszek, a young man quietly joins them from behind. Dad carefully looks at him.

"Bolek!"

"Yes" the young man replies and they reach for each other. Danusia greets Bolek with some reservation but Zbyszek gives him a big hug and immediately strikes up a conversation. Laughing and talking vigorously, the group moves to the street. Bolek is very warm and direct. He immediately assumes the role of a host. Within minutes, they feel as if they knew each other for years. A buggy with two horses awaits them outside the station. Danusia hesitates for a moment but Zbyszek jumps eagerly on the buggy. "Danusia, look, this is great, come on!" She climbs up, valises are flying behind her, and soon they all are on their way. Dad sits with Uncle Vince at the front and the youth together behind them. Bolek is eighteen, the oldest of the three of them. Like Uncle Vince, he is rather short for his age and slightly overweight. But he also has good-natured blue eyes like Uncle Vince that smile most of the time. The buggy moves slowly through narrow streets of Dukszty. Soon they are traveling again through the woods. Only this time they can reach out and really touch the branches of the old majestic oaks, lindens, poplars, and a multitude of shrubs. The boys talk non-stop while Danusia quietly looks around with some apprehension. She is not used to the buggy or the proximity of the virgin forest. This is the entirely new experience for her. After several kilometers, Dad points to Mama's goodie bag. "There are still some sandwiches left."

Uncle Vince gives them a bag with fresh cookies and a bottle of milk. After the feast, Danusia falls asleep just to wake up when the buggy is passing along a huge lake and Uncle Vince thunders: "There, there, you see those contours of the houses on the other side of the lake? That's Brasław. Our sister, Bronia, lives there with her daughter, Gienia. You will visit them later, after you get some rest."

"But it's very far," Danusia points out.

"Oh, don't worry, we will go by boat. It takes about two hours through the lake."

Night is fast approaching as they turn away from the lake into the open fields. Ten more minutes and the buggy pulls into a sparsely inhabited village. Several small houses and huts stand in the middle of wide-open green fields. Uncle Vince's house is just nearby, closest to the lake.

As the buggy turns into the yard, a meager woman appears in the doorway with a big loaf of bread and a saucer with salt in her hands. It is the centuries old Polish custom to welcome the honored guests with bread and salt. It's the symbol of old Polish hospitality. Flushed with joy, Aunt Regina walks to them, hands the gifts to Alek, and cautiously hugs him. It is an uneasy moment for them. They never met before and don't really know each other. They only know about each other through letters. Visibly excited, Aunt Regina turns to Danusia and Zbyszek, warmly embraces them and invites everybody inside.

"I am sorry, our house is so small. I hope you won't mind," she says with abashment. "Please sit down and rest a little. You must be very tired."

Exhausted and overwhelmed, they sink into the chairs. For the next few hours, they eat, drink, talk, joke, and laugh. Near midnight, Aunt Regina, or Renia as they call her here, takes them to the small bedroom prepared just for them. It's not the most comfortable place in the world; stuffy air and hordes of mosquitoes would normally scare them away but not this time. Within minutes, they fall into soundless sleep.

A commotion in the backyard awakes them. The sun's morning rays already drop in through the window. Cows moo, dogs bark, cocks crow, and doors creak. Danusia checks her watch. It's 6:30 in the morning.

"Oh, noooo!" she protests. "This is awful, I need a couple more hours of sleep!" she cries.

But Dad is already up. "Danusia, Zbyszek, you have to get up, now! They are already preparing breakfast for us. That's how it is around here. Later on you can have a nap. But now you have to get up. Up, up, one, two, three...."

They argue for a while until Dad pulls them out of bed putting them upright one by one.

"Now, go outside and wash up, faster, faster!"

This drastic, merciless treatment awakes them completely. They slowly move outside. The sunny, refreshing morning greets them as they drowsily look around. A big draw well stands in the middle of the yard. White linen is drying in the sun on the clothesline against the wooded, neatly painted white fence. A big barn stands on the opposite side of the yard, its doors wide open. The buggy stands next to it. All sorts of domesticated animals are enjoying breakfast all over the place. Zbyszek goes straight to the well and inspects it. "What should I do with it?" he looks at Dad skeptically.

"Watch, this is how you do it."

Taking hold of the empty bucket that stands on the stony well, Dad lowers it slowly. The bucket is tied to a long chain reeled on the wooded shaft. He carefully cranks the shaft until the bucket reaches deep crystal cold water. A few seconds later, he cranks up the bucket, grabs the chain as the bucket reaches the top, then pulls and puts it on the wooded flap that partially covers the well opening. The whole procedure horrifies Danusia but Zbyszek is intrigued and wants to try it. He experiments with the bucket until he is completely wet. Eventually everybody gets wet. This early morning "shower" raises their spirits.

Another challenging experience awaits them at the breakfast table. The smell of freshly baked bread permeates the house. At the center of the big kitchen table is this huge round loaf of crispy, golden-brown bread.

Uncle Vince sharpens the blade of the slicing knife. "This bread is the specialty of the house. Renia just made it. I hope you will like it." He solemnly takes the big loaf in his hands. While holding the knife in one hand, he draws the sign of a cross on the bottom of the bread, then presses the loaf against his chest and starts cutting huge thick hunks. Danusia looks at the hunks with mixed feelings.

"How am I supposed to eat these monsters?" she wonders. As they all sit down, Aunt Renia places before them a big can of milk, an earthenware bowl with cottage cheese, a plate of butter, a crock of honey, and a jar of aromatic strawberry jam. Everybody grabs the thick chunks of crunchy bread that Uncle Vince piles up on the table in front of their noses. Zbyszek grabs the biggest one. To him, this hunk with crispy delicate crust enveloping a warm and fleshy inside is a heavenly delight. As he stuffs himself with it, Danusia cautiously takes one hunk and puts some butter, cheese, and jam on it. Before long, she also stuffs herself with another hunk. Uncle Vince pours milk into the cups and affectionately pats Dad on the back.

"It's great to have you back, Alek, after all these years. Bolek, why don't you show Danusia and Zbyszek around after the breakfast."

"Aren't we going to Brasław today?" Bolek asks confused.

"Not today, later. They need to rest and get used to the countryside, and I have many things to talk about with Alek. You all have time for yourself. Just be careful, though."

The children eagerly rush outside. There are so many things to see and so many things to do around here. Danusia and Zbyszek can hardly catch up with Bolek. Occasionally, they show up hungry as lions, hastily grab something to eat, and disappear in a jiffy. At sunset they return home all dirty and exhausted. Bolek is especially excited.

"Dad, I took them to our covert and showed them deer. We saw at least six deer, that close," he extends his hands. "We were only two meters away from them, that close!"

"We also saw some rabbits and storks," Danusia adds.

"Yes, of course Danusia prefers rabbits and storks," Zbyszek teases her. "You know, she was afraid of this big hart with its huge antlers that was so close to us," Zbyszek adds, pretending he wasn't afraid at all.

Danusia looks at him ominously. She is ready to strike back but Uncle Vince is faster.

"Tomorrow, you all will go to visit Aunt Tosia."

Alek turns to Danusia and Zbyszek to explain. "Aunt Tosia is my oldest sister. She is the one who prepared me for First Communion. Remember? I told you about her. She lives about twenty kilometers from here. We need to visit her first, and later we will visit my other sister who lives in Brasław, across the lake. We may even be able to stay a couple of days in Brasław before I leave."

"Where do you want to go?" Bolek asks.

Danusia and Zbyszek put their heads down as if they don't want to hear the answer.

"I have to go back to work," Alek replies. "I have only three weeks of vacation. But Danusia and Zbyszek will stay here longer," he adds apologetically.

The prospect of Dad's leaving is daunting. The conversation dies out and soon they disappear into the beds. They have to get up early, almost with the sunrise, right after the hen and cows.

In the morning, Alek tries to speed up things as Danusia and Zbyszek chaotically move around. Bolek puts horses to the cart and readies the buggy for the trip. He is the tour guide today because Uncle

Vince has to work. They dress more formally than normal. Dad brings a fancy bonbonnière of chocolate candies purchased in Warsaw. With the blessing of the hosts, they leave. The dirt road meanders like a river in multi-shaded greens. The buggy passes through small hills and valleys. The morning is serene. Expansive fields of rye, wheat, and potatoes alternate with colorful meadows and picturesque groves. The overwhelming calmness surrounding them creates the illusion of paradise.

Alek goes back in time to his childhood. Aunt Tosia was like a mother to him, always watching after him, always helping and caring for him. But over the years, they completely lost contact with each other. "I wonder whether she will recognize me after all this time. Bolek, does she know when I am supposed to come?"

"She knows that you may be coming this year but nothing more specific than that, I think."

"So, she doesn't really know that I am here," Alek speculates.

The buggy reaches the crossroad and turns abruptly left. Soon some houses emerge on the horizon. The horses quicken the pace.

"I know what I'll do!" Alek exclaims. "I will go first by myself to see whether she will recognize me."

"A good idea. So just call us. We'll be waiting outside," Danusia replies.

"Bolek, don't drive too close. Just stop here. I will walk in as a stranger."

Bolek stops the buggy one block before the house and Alek slowly gets off. The children remain silent as Alek passes along a wooden fence, opens the gate, and walks towards the door of a modest house. The knock at the door and a woman's voice answers: "Come in!"

In the twilight of the room, an elderly woman sitting on a bench bends over a bucket, peeling potatoes.

"God bless you!" Alek says. "I am on my way to Vilnius and I am thirsty. Can you give me something to drink, good woman?"

The elderly woman raises her head and stares at him. A moment of silence. They look at each other. She measures the stranger intensely and springs to her feet. "Jesus Christ! Aluś, Aluś! You came back!" She bursts into tears extending her hands towards him. "Thanks be to God, you came back!" They hug and kiss and cry.

"How did you recognize me?"

"Oh, I have been waiting and praying for you all this time. I will always recognize my little baby brother! But how did you come here?"

"I am with my children. We are staying at Vince's house."

"Where are they?"

"They're waiting outside."

"Oh, God! I am not prepared for such important guests. Let's go! Let's go and bring them here!" They leave the house and wave to Bolek. He sets spur to the horses and with tumult arrives at the gate. There is no end to greetings and heartfelt hugs.

"Can you believe she recognized me immediately! After all those years, she recognized me in the blink of an eye! Unbelievable! Just unbelievable!" Alek marvels, tenderly embracing his sister.

Aunt Tosia is a widow. Since her husband passed away many years ago, she has lived by herself in this run-down hovel. Her two sons are already grown. One of them, Mark, lives nearby with his young wife.

The village quickly learns that Alek, the lost son as they call him here, has come back. Many people stop by to say hello. Mark and his wife are working in the fields when they learn about the unusual guests. They manage to come over later in the afternoon.

Mark was a baby when Uncle Alek left the village. He doesn't really remember his adventurous uncle. He has heard a lot about the handsome uncle who left home at a young age to become a sailor and to travel around the world. Uncle Alek was a hero and a legend to Mark during his childhood years. Later on, Mark learned that his legendary Uncle Alek had settled in Warsaw. His image of Uncle Alek as the adventurer was not compatible with the image of Uncle Alek as a frequenter of the Warsaw saloons. Still the image was sufficiently intriguing. Several more years passed and word came that Uncle Alek was married and had two children. The legendary Uncle became more like an ordinary man. By that time, though, Mark was no longer a boy. He became a man and was in love himself. The transformation of his adventurous hero into a suitable husband and father facilitated Mark's decision to get married. Now, the hero had returned. It is a very special moment for Mark. His childhood fantasies also come back and he is curious, very curious. He surveys the visitor from a distance. Aunt Tosia points to Mark with pride. "This is my older son!"

The two men fondly greet each other. Mark is a tall, handsome young man with dark hair and blue eyes. There is this striking resemblance between the two men. Danusia looks at her newly discovered cousin with great interest. His resemblance to Dad intrigues her. "Quite a good looking man," she observes. "But already married.... It would be nice to meet his younger brother, too."

She won't meet the younger brother, though. After a few more hours of talking and meeting the neighbors, Bolek reminds them that it's time to go back. This is a one-day trip only and it's already getting dark. "We don't want to travel in the night. It's not that safe," he explains.

Aunt Tosia is disappointed. Eventually she capitulates and after much hugging, waving, and a few tears, the buggy leaves the village. Alek and the children leave behind very memorable moments.

* * * *

Over the next few days, they rest and make plans for the trip to Brasław. Again, they will go only with Bolek. This time Uncle Vince worries. "You know, Alek, the lake has become very treacherous lately. These strong sudden gusts that come from nowhere are very dangerous. We rarely go through the lake these days. I am not strong enough any more. Even though Bolek is catching up in strength, the lake seems more and more hazardous."

"It's not the lake. It's the boat that's the problem," Bolek argues. "The boat is very old and is falling apart. We simply need a better boat."

"Don't worry," Alek replies firmly. "I have been sailing on the Atlantic Ocean and through the Pacific. I know how to handle water."

"I know, I know," Vince continues. "But with the adverse wind it can be damn hard to make it to the other side. Especially for someone who doesn't practice rowing every day."

"But there will be three men going. Together we can easily do it, right, boys?"

"Right!" The boys reply eagerly.

"But Daaad, remember, I don't know how to swim!" Danusia worries.

"So, go and learn. The boys can show you. You have two days to learn, that should be enough, right, Bolek?"

"I guess...but only if she wants." Bolek replies with a dose of skepticism.

In fact, Danusia knows how to swim but she is afraid of the huge lake. It's like the sea to her.

Two days later, they are ready to go. The day is calm, the horizon is clear, and the boat is ready. Alek takes the center bench. Bolek will row behind him. Danusia and Zbyszek will be sitting inside the boat. Vince gives them the final push and the boat smoothly flows away.

Alek is delighted. He loves to travel by boat. Cruising and sailing gives him a wonderful feeling of freedom, it brings back the best memories from his early years in Brasław and from his youthful travels around the world. As the boat glides through the lake, his face radiates with joy, and he starts singing an emotional song in the rhythm of a march:

Sea, our sea!
We will faithfully
Guard you!
We are ordered
To protect you
Or to die!

His strong voice echoes through the lake. This is a very powerful song these days. Although Alek hasn't been listening to the radio lately, everybody knows that Hitler put Gdańsk on the long list of his territorial claims, and Gdańsk became the next prey in his mad race for world domination. Throughout history, Gdańsk has played a critical role for Poland. This strategic city located on the Baltic Sea in the delta of Vistula River provides Poland with access to the sea. Gdańsk is an integral part of Poland's blood stream and the country's most important window to the world. Without this vital trade channel, Poland's economy would suffocate. The concern over Gdańsk has been so great that a few years ago the Polish Government decided to build from scratch a brand new city ten kilometers from Gdańsk to preserve Poland's access to the sea in the event the Germans would take over Gdańsk. Within a few years, a completely new city, Gdynia, with its elegant residential neighborhood and impressive industrial district, with the state of the art port and modern shipyard, becomes the second busiest Baltic port only after Copenhagen.[1]

The song, *Sea, our sea!* usually generates enthusiastic and positive thoughts. Today however it brings some mixed feelings. Before long, Alek will leave the children here and will go back to Warsaw. Danusia and Zbyszek will stay with Uncle Vince for at least another month. Who knows what may happen during that time? He can't really name or define his anxiety but in his subconscious he worries.

Western military guarantees given to Poland in the spring of 1939, although important from a moral standpoint, did not have any real teeth attached. To give more credibility to their action, Western Allies sent a military mission to Warsaw in order to assist the Poles in the development of the defense campaign plans. General Gamelin left no doubt as to how the defense strategy should work. In the event of the German aggression on Poland, the objective of the Polish army was to hold the German forces engaged for up to two weeks in order to enable the Western Allies to prepare the counter-attack in the West.[2]

While the defense plans are being drawn up in Warsaw, the prospect for a collective security agreement between the West and the Soviet Union quickly fades away. In May, Stalin appoints a new foreign minister, Molotov. The new appointee quickly reaches out to Berlin. The timing can't be better. In July, Ribbentrop visits Moscow indicating that Germany is willing to work closely with Russia and Molotov is eager for the deal. At the beginning of August, the Western powers send a military mission to Moscow to continue their easygoing talks on collective security. The sudden revival of the Russian–German relations doesn't alarm them. However, the political landscape is already dramatically changed. The British mission accomplishes nothing. Stalin and Hitler waste no time. Upon the departure of the British mission, Ribbentrop and Molotov move full speed into closer cooperation, but the world remains oblivious to the impending catastrophe.[3]

* * * *

"We are sinking! Dad! We are sinking! Water is breaking in!" Danusia's hysterical voice jolts Alek awake. Indeed, the boat is taking water. Their feet are already wet.

"Oh, shit! The old hole is leaking again," Bolek announces. "We have to plug it somehow. We must do something quickly."

"But where is it, where is this hole?" Zbyszek screams.

"Here on the side," Bolek points to the side near the bottom. "I need a handkerchief!" he yells inspecting the leak.

"Here it is." Alek pulls out from his infinite pocket a white handkerchief, nearly the size of a tablecloth.

"Oh, great!" Bolek pants grabbing the kerchief and sticking it into the chink in the side of the boat. "All right! The leak is almost plugged."

"What do you mean 'almost'?" Danusia cries.

"Well, some water gets in no matter what. I know this hole, I keep repairing it but it's getting to the point where no mater what, it will leak. The wood is rotten."

"So, what's going to happen, Dad? We may be drowning here!" Danusia looks helplessly around.

By now the boat is in the middle of the lake or maybe even slightly closer to the other shore. Light clouds cover the sky. To the left of Brasław the clouds look much darker and it seems as if the weather is changing. Alek evaluates the situation and starts shouting commands.

"Zbyszek, try to get the water out just with your hands for now! Or try your shoes if you want! Danusia, look in the blue bag and get something to get the water out. Perhaps Renia put some jar in there. Bolek, let's go full speed. One, two, one, two…." The boat speeds up.

"Dad, there is nothing like that here," Danusia yells hysterically.

"So, how about some towel or shirt?"

"Yes, there are some shirts inhere," she pulls out Dad's Sunday shirt.

"No, not that," Alek groans. "We need something that takes water like a sponge, a towel or maybe some flannel shirt," he tries to explain.

"Like this?" she stretches Zbyszek's favorite checkered shirt.

"Oh, no, not this one!" Zbyszek protests.

"Okay, Danusia, forget it and do it like Zbyszek, with hands and shoes, but quickly please!"

By now Alek is fairly nervous. The wind is picking up and the horizon looks dismal. The lake is no longer smooth. Despite their efforts, the boat is not advancing much. They are going against the wind. The shore is closer, though. They can already recognize the houses. Alek is pushing the water full force. His face is tense turning red from the effort; he starts dripping wet with sweat. Bolek, seating behind him, pushes the water grinding his teeth. From time to time, he bends to adjust the kerchief protruding from the hole.

Suddenly, they hear loud "crraash!" A terrifying sound of snapping wood instantly turns their blood into ice. The boat? No, it's not the boat! Uff.... It's the oar—Dad's oar. Gee, it's a little better but still...they are desperate.

"Bolek, give me your oar!" Alek shouts, throwing out the broken piece. He grabs Bolek's oar and hardly catching his breath pushes the water. Danusia and Zbyszek work hard with their hands, shoes, and other clothes. Despite their efforts, the water in the boat stays much the same. Bolek joins them. The wind is getting stronger with every minute and the waves are already splashing into the boat. They work in silence. All of a sudden, Alek stops paddling, puts the oar upright and pushes it straight down to the bottom of the lake. The oar hits the ground. "Okay, everybody! We've hit rock bottom," he announces.

They pause for a moment. It seems as if the catastrophe is conjured away. Nevertheless, the shore still remains their distant object of desire.

"Hey, don't put your guard down! The wind will blow us back to the lake in a second," Alek yells going back to his routine.

For the next fifteen minutes, they continue battling the waves but make minimal progress.

"That's it. I am going to jump here," Bolek announces. He takes off his clothes and jumps into the water. As he hits the ground, water reaches his lips. "Okay, let's go!" he grabs the front of the boat and slowly moves towards the shore.

"I am going to join him," Zbyszek yells.

"Wait for more shallow water," Danusia begs.

"It's already shallow enough." He jumps in.

Alek still paddles full speed. Another twenty minutes and they reach the shore. It starts raining. Alek gets off and lies down near the water. Drenched, he can hardly catch his breath; his muscular shoulders heave up and down. He is so tired he can't say a word. The rest of them pulls the boat onto the shore and follows suit.

An old man looking like a fisherman comes by. "You are lucky, men, that this storm is so slow moving. I was watching you struggling there and it was looking pretty bad, especially when you were left with this one oar only. Why did you throw out the other one?"

Alek looks at the man with some embarrassment. "It broke in the middle of the lake."

The fisherman shakes his head. "That was a very risky ride."

"You're right! I am afraid, I miscalculated it," Alek confesses. "I should have inspected the boat before leaving. You see we were taking in a lot of water because of the leak."

"So, you are really lucky, man. I have seen many tragedies on this lake over the years. Don't play with nature. Respect it! This lake in its fury already swallowed many lives."

They glance at the lake. The waves are churning, the sky is darkening, and the horizon has already disappeared.

"I am not going back through the lake," Danusia declares.

"Okay, we'll worry about that later. Now let's go," Bolek says. "We have quite a long walk because the wind blew us off course. Let's leave the boat here. Tomorrow we will come back and take it to the port."

"Don't worry about the boat," the fisherman says. "I will keep an eye on your boat."

"Thank you," Bolek shakes the fisherman's hand with gratitude.

With their wet bags and dirty clothes, they enter the small town. Tiny houses are crowded at the steps of a bigger hill that dominates the landscape.

"Do you remember this town?" Bolek looks at his uncle.

"Not much. I remember though that this hill is called the Castle Mountain,"

"Right. But do you remember where Bronia and Gienia live?"

"Not really. Just take us there the shortest possible way!"

"Well, it's quite a distance and it's up the hill," Bolek warns.

"Oh, no! That's too much for today," Danusia groans.

"There used to be a delicious bakery here in town," Alek recalls. "I am wondering whether it's still here?"

"I don't know whether that's the one but there is a bakery near the church. It's almost on our way," Bolek replies.

"Great, then let's go and see. I am buying cookies and drink for everybody," Alek declares.

Normally, such news would result in an outburst of joyful approval but this time the kids are so exhausted they just glance at him. Luckily, the bakery is not that far and the aroma of freshly baked bread guides them. One store in a row of small houses is more crowded than the other places.

"This is it! This is my favorite bakery!" Alek exclaims enthusiastically. "And there are even two small tables inside." For a moment, he feels like a schoolboy over a quarter century ago. Inside the store, a few people wait in line along the glass cases full of cakes and cookies. Yummy *pączki* and charlottes and puffs and bayaderes and éclairs and cheesecakes—square, round, long, short, brown, white and yellow, meticulously decorated, and lined up in neat rows are smiling to them.

"This is fantastic! Oh my, I don't know what to choose." Danusia frets.

"*Pączki* are the best," Bolek suggests.

"Select something for now and I will order a package of twenty to take out. This way you can try something else later," Alek says.

They buy almost half of the bakery produce together with several bottles of sparkling orangeade and grab enough chairs for all of them. This heavenly feast makes their day.

Alek's younger sister, Bronia, and her daughter, Gienia, live at the foot of the Castle Mountain. They aren't expecting guests today. Bronia has just come back from work at the local hospital. Twenty-four-year-old Gienia recently completed her tailor's training and passed all the exams required by the guild. Her diploma entitles her to open her own shop and now she is busy setting up her business. She is trying out her new sewing machine when a knock at the door interrupts her. Bronia, puzzled by an unexpected knocking, comes to the door and opens it slightly. Bolek's smiling face emerges from the dimness of the hall. "Hey, everybody! I have a surprise for you! Look who is with me!" He proudly points to his companions standing behind.

Bronia utters a cry while Gienia dashes for the door. There is no end to the greetings and euphoria.

"We brought you some goodies from the bakery." Alek puts a big bakery package on the table.

"Oh, thank you! That's great. I'll make tea then. Please sit down."

While Alek talks with his sister, Danusia and Zbyszek immediately make friends with Gienia. The age difference doesn't really matter. Gienia is an openhearted and intense young lady with a variety of uncommon interests. There is this striking resemblance between her and Zbyszek: similar deep blue eyes, similar long slim noses, and similar light brown hair. At fourteen, Zbyszek is almost the same height as Gienia. Alek immediately notices this uncanny likeness of the two distant cousins. Looking at each other carefully, Gienia and Zbyszek are also surprised with this sameness.

"But there is also some resemblance between me and Gienia." Danusia moves closer to Gienia and sticks out her face. Alek looks at her rather bemused. "Not at all my dear, not at all. You are just like my copy." Laughing and joking, everybody agrees.

The rest of the day, Danusia spends mostly with Gienia. Soon the girls disappear into the other room talking about clothing and fashion. After examining all dresses in the room, Danusia opens her luggage. Gienia professionally examines each item, curiously checks the fabric, and compliments Danusia's taste.

"My clothes are very modest," Danusia complains. "Dad doesn't allow me to buy anything expensive. He thinks I should have no more than two dresses, one for everyday and one for Sunday."

"Actually, these are very good quality clothes," Gienia concludes professionally. "Let me show you what I am working on." She opens a big armoire and shows her several garments half completed. There is one modest wedding dress, several Sunday dresses, and several regular dresses. "You see I am always looking for some interesting fabrics and new ideas. We have a good store here in town. I might take you there."

The collection of fancy dresses in the process of being made with big tacks, and pins, and the measuring tape hanging over them mesmerizes Danusia. One thing she always dreams of and never has enough of is clothes. Her craving for dresses is proportional to her Dad's desire not to waste money on useless things such as clothes. To make matters worse, Danusia has not been successful in experimenting with needles or sewing machines either in school or at home. She is too impatient. The painstaking precision required for making a dress scares and discourages her. In fact, she can hardly sew a button.

"How long are you going to stay with us?" Gienia asks.

"It depends on how long you can endure us, maybe a couple of days," Alek replies standing in the door. "I see you have a real business here," he says with approval.

"Yes, but for now I focus on women dresses only. I don't make suits."

Alek feigns disappointment, thus Gienia says apologetically, "But let me show you something else that may interest you." She takes him to the small space next to the kitchen.

"Look here!" she says with great pride. "I develop film and make pictures here. See some of my work on the wall?"

Indeed, the space around is covered with big black and white photographs glued to the dark wall. Some chemicals and papers are scattered around big dishes. A dark curtain hangs near two rectangular dishes. She calls them *kuvetas*.

"Photography?" Alek says truly surprised. His thundering voice electrifies the boys.

"Really?" Zbyszek yells. "You mean you have a camera?"

"Yes, a very simple one," Gienia replies modestly. "But it works."

"Show us the camera, please," Zbyszek begs.

She brings a shiny leather case and takes out a small, half-plastic and half-metal, black box. "My boyfriend who is in the Army gave it to me before leaving." She explains. "This is his most prized possession. Before he left, we were developing films together. These are some of the photos that he took." Gienia opens a corpulent blue album with photos neatly pasted to the black thick paper pages. The photos show mostly Gienia in various dresses, poses, and places.

"Show it to me, show it to me!" Danusia grabs the album and disappears with it. Zbyszek is fascinated with the chemicals. He has never seen such a lab before. "Will you be developing some photographs now?"

"Not now. I'll finish the film tomorrow and you can help me develop it then. Okay?"

"Great!" Zbyszek exclaims. "So let's go tomorrow to this famous Castle Mountain."

"But you know there's no castle at the top?" Bolek warns him.

"How can that be? Castle Mountain without the castle?" Zbyszek cries.

"Well that's the mystery of this mountain," Alek pokes while Bronia announces that it's time to go to sleep. She takes Zbyszek and Bolek to her neighbors next door. The boys can sleep comfortably there. Danusia sleeps with Gienia and Alek stays up talking through the night with his sister.

Over the next few days, they all enjoy their time together. Bronia takes a few days off. Gienia concludes that she deserves some good vacation anyway and manages to get a time extension from most of her clients. She must finish a few dresses on time, though. Danusia tries hard to help her, but with minimal success. Nevertheless, Gienia decides to reward her for the effort.

"Danusia, I would like to take you to our fabrics store. It's the best store in town. Even people from Dukszty come here to shop. You could select several fabrics and I will make dresses for you later."

"Are you serious?" Danusia can't believe it. "Gienia, I love you!" she gives her a big hug.

In the fabric store, the girls are lost for hours. The middle-aged, well-built Jew who runs the store follows them around talking about the fabrics, pointing to some better buys, and telling exciting stories about the ones that grab the girls' attention. He knows Gienia very well and promises them a good deal. There is too much here to choose from and Danusia must make some painful decisions. She has always dreamed of the soft, exquisite lengths of silk individually hand painted. Several of those silky lengths of paintings prominently hang along the wall like in the art gallery. But they are way too expensive. After much talking and debating, she settles for several less expensive pieces of chiffon, cretonne, and linen. There is enough material for three or even four dresses. Gienia, like Santa Claus, pays for everything. At home, the girls proudly show the fruits of the shopping but the boys are totally unimpressed.

"Tomorrow we all are going to conquer the Castle Mountain," Alek announces. "You, Bronia, also! Enough of this cooking and spoiling us with your delicious *naleśniki* and other pancakes. You have to go out with us and have some fun."

In the morning, everybody dresses and packs for the trip. They plan to hike for most of the day. Gienia packs her camera and an extra pack of film. Each of them prepares one goodie bag with sandwiches and fruits. Soon, they are on their way passing through the town and heading towards the hill. When they first saw the hill on the arrival day, it appeared gigantic. Today, the challenge to conquer the Castle Mountain seems much more manageable.

On the way up, it looks like a leisurely excursion. Gienia teaches everybody how to take pictures. She explains how to use the camera, especially how to pay attention to light and distance. Everybody has a chance to take two pictures. They will develop them at home and chose the best picture. The photo competition generates a lot of emotions. Most of the pictures are taken from the top of the hill towards the town and the lake because the view from the hill is spectacular. The little town stands like an oasis in a sea of lush greens and flood blues. From the top of the hill, they can fully appreciate the majesty of the Dryświaty Lake stretching with its picturesque bays and lagoons way out and far to the right and far to the left.

"Okay everybody! Lunch time!" Alek orders.

They all sit down near the top of the hill and eagerly take out their lunch bags. On the way down, they choose another path that turns out to be much longer and much more difficult. No further pictures are taken. They reach home exhausted.

* * * *

"Let's develop the film, let's do it now," Zbyszek whines. "We have to find out who won the contest."

"Wait!" Gienia slows him down. "It's not that easy and not that fast. You can easily destroy the film. There is no way we can have any pictures today. It takes longer than that, remember! Today we may try to develop the film but we won't get any pictures! If you want, I can start developing the film now and you can help me."

Gienia looks at Bolek and Alek, already eagerly venturing through the photo equipment. "But I don't need any more help," she says, looking at them categorically. "For now, I only need Zbyszek. If everything goes well, tomorrow we may be actually getting some pictures and then I will need your help, okay?"

They don't protest and Zbyszek looks triumphant. For the rest of the evening the experts work quietly in the darkness behind the curtain while the rest play cards.

The next day, they all gather in the kitchen to assist Gienia in the second stage of the photo development. She carefully takes the negative and places it in the wooden frame on top of the photographic paper. She then exposes the frame to the bright light of the kitchen table for several seconds. Zbyszek assists her with diligence. Next, they go to the darkest corner of the room to remove the paper from the frame and put it quickly into the *kuveta* with developer. Only now some mysterious dark shapes are emerging on the white photographic paper and the picture comes to life through the transparency of the sheet of liquid in the *kuveta*.

"It's like fortune telling with paraffin wax," Danusia comments.

The emerging pictures fascinate Bolek. "I think it is more than fortune telling. This is the real thing!"

Gienia takes out the paper and inspects it carefully. "I think this looks sharp enough, don't you? Okay, let's put it to the other *kuveta* for about 30 minutes to make it permanent."

They are ready to repeat the same procedure with another negative.

"But wait," Gienia stops them. "We still have to rinse and dry the photographs. Mom, I need another bowl of water, please. Danusia, could you quickly dust the window? Here is the cloth. That's going to be our dryer." After a good bath in fresh water, all wet pictures land on the big clean window for several hours.

The moment of truth finally comes. The tension grows as the dry and shiny pictures come down from the window dryer and are lined up on the floor. Everybody gathers around and they look at the pictures over and over again. But to their disappointment, most of the pictures look alike, showing the view from the hill towards the town and lake. The pictures are so similar that they can hardly figure out who made what picture.

One picture stands out, though, in this crowd of uniformity. Aunt Bronia took this one at the beginning of the trip near the bottom of the hill. All the rest of them stand together and smile in good spirit. Everyone likes this picture. Thus, Aunt Bronia wins the contest. The photo is made in five copies and everybody gets one copy as a souvenir.

It's time to go back to Uncle Vince. The boat has been repaired and should withstand the expedition but is not reliable and may start leaking at any time. Alek decides that Danusia and Zbyszek will go by buggy along the lake while he and Bolek will take the boat across the lake. Zbyszek is all upset. He too wants to go by boat.

"I am sorry, Son. But the boat can't take too much load. We won't take any luggage. To have an extra person would make this journey much more dangerous. You have to go by buggy." At the very last moment, Gienia decides to go with them. She will be the tour guide for the buggy since she knows the road.

At the port, the boat already awaits its crew. The morning is warm and quiet. Alek takes Bronia into his arms and embraces her. Who knows whether they will see each other again.... In a minute, the boat smoothly leaves the port and moves full speed onto the lake. Soon Brasław's profile blends with the contour of the horizon.

3. Brasław, Summer 1939

4. Bolek, Danusia, Alek, Gienia, and Zbyszek at the Castle Mountain, Summer 1939

5. Poland Before World War II

3

When the buggy arrives at Uncle Vince's house, Bolek and Alek are already waiting. With a strong tailwind they made it quickly across the lake. But some strangers stand in the yard as well. A group of soldiers is talking with Uncle Vince. Danusia spots them immediately and walks up to the group. The most senior in rank, a tall and handsome lieutenant, greets her with elegant courtesy. "Miss, allow me to introduce myself: Lieutenant Julian Sierżant." Clicking his heels, he salutes chivalrously. "We are from the Border Guard. Our Corps, under the command of General Młot-Fijałkowski and the Unregimented Task Force Narew, is stationed in the nearby Racki Bór."

Danusia knits her brows. Fijałkowski, Fijałkowski, this name sounds familiar. That's right. That law student in Warsaw was Fijałkowski. "I am sorry, what is your first name?" She asks feeling the color rising to her cheeks.

The lieutenant slowly repeats: "Julian, Julian Sierżant."

"My name is Danusia, and this is my cousin, Gienia." She points toward Gienia who timidly glances at the group from a distance. "And...what are you doing here?" she questions.

"We came to the village to say hello. Our horses are getting some rest at the fire station."

Dad gently embraces Danusia. "Lieutenant Sierżant was kind enough to promise that he would watch after both of you once I leave."

"Of course, with pleasure. I didn't even expect that my protégéé would be so charming," the lieutenant replies, eyeing Danusia with great interest.

Usually in this situation, Danusia would expect Dad to react and keep her admirer at a healthy distance. This time, however, maybe because of his anxiety or because of respect for the uniform, Dad remains friendly.

"So how is the spirit in the army these days?" he asks.

"As you see, pretty good so far." The lieutenant talks fast, his face becoming tense. "We don't have the latest news but Great Britain sent a military mission to Warsaw. I understand the French and the British are finally going to give us some line of credit to strengthen our defense forces."

Moving closer to the lieutenant, Dad bows slightly. "I heard that we were negotiating the purchase of some airplanes for the army."

"We hope so. We have a very well trained cadre and our Air Force has been struggling for years to get more of these modern planes. Apparently, the planes that we are making today are state of the art but the engines hold us back. And these days no one wants to sell us the latest engine models. But maybe now the French and British can finally help us with it. I sincerely hope so."

"Excuse me, if I may?" Danusia moves forward. "I would like to know where the lieutenant is from." Her eyes penetrate the lieutenant's swarthy face.

"Oh, I am not from Warsaw, Miss. I am from Zbaraż. Do you know Zbaraż?"

"I'm not sure...."

"Danusia, you don't know?" Zbyszek exclaims, putting down a heavy valise. "Remember the book *With Fire and Swords* by Sienkiewicz? That's where the famous Battle of Zbaraż took place in 1648. There is this old fortress there. Remember?"

The lieutenant smiles. "You are correct, young man. Zbaraż was originally built as a fortress. Historically, this has always been a very important town from a strategic point of view because it's near Tarnopol in the southeast corner of Poland."

Aunt Renia waves to them from the door. "Please come inside. Dinner is ready. You can continue your discussion while eating."

"Thank you, but we will be leaving," the lieutenant replies.

Aunt Renia throws up her hands. "Oh no! You are not leaving without first trying the specialties of the house." Wasting no time, she calls to the soldiers and invites them in. "I am sure you boys will enjoy some homemade food. I made more food today, just in case...."

Uncle Vince puts another table outside for these who can't squeeze inside. The soldiers don't wait for another invitation but greet the hosts warmly and eagerly move to the table.

"We have dumplings today," Aunt Renia announces, putting on the table big bowls with dumplings and smaller bowls with sour cream and fried bacon. "You just dip the dumpling in bacon or sour cream like that." She demonstrates, stuffing her mouth with a dumpling.

"That's my favorite dish. It makes my mouth water," Bolek mumbles.

Once all the guests are seated, more food arrives at the table: *pierogi*, noodles with poppy seed, yogurt, milk, and bread. The lieutenant and his men tell jokes and soldier stories. After the main course, the apple cake appears. Towards the end of the feast, the lieutenant gets up officially. "May I have your attention, please? I would like to thank our hosts for their unsurpassed ancient-Polish hospitality. The dinner has been delicious and will remain in our best memories for a long time. I also would like to take this opportunity to invite our hosts and all our friends gathered here to join us for the Sunday Mass in our field chapel near the military compound. We are stationed in Racki Bór, not that far from here, about ten kilometers west. Please come and be our guests on Sunday."

"Racki Bór?" Bolek repeats out loud. "I think we know where that is, right, Dad?"

"The name sounds familiar," Vince looks slightly puzzled.

"Don't worry. It's very easy to get there. I will show you." The lieutenant draws a map, explaining it diligently to Bolek, then gets up and salutes chivalrously again. "Thank you for your hospitality. I hope to see you on Sunday." The soldiers slowly get up too.

Alek shakes the lieutenant's hand cordially. "Unfortunately, I will not be able to join you on Sunday because I am leaving for Warsaw the day before. But please watch after my family here. We live in such precarious times...." He stops, bites his lips, and adds, "I would like to consign them to your care."

"I am sorry to hear that you can't join us on Sunday, but rest assured that I will watch after your family," the lieutenant replies, holding Alek's hand in both hands. "We should be stationed in Racki Bór for some time and I promise I will take good care of your children and your family here."

* * * *

The next morning, Alek gets up early while the children are still asleep. He and Vince are going to visit their parents' grave. The journey will be long and not very safe. Their parents are buried near Dyneburg, just on the Polish–Latvian border. Dyneburg, in Latvian Daugavpils, lies on the Dvina River. Between 1582 and 1772, the town was part of Poland. After the partition of Poland, Russia took over these lands and renamed the town Dvinsk. Following World War I, the town became part of Latvia. The Warsaw–Vilnius–St. Petersburg railroad built around 1860 passes through the town. The railroad has become instrumental in the growth of the entire Daugavpils region.

For both Alek and Vince, Dyneburg is their birthplace. But they cannot visit Dyneburg because it is in Latvia now. They hope, however, to get to the cemetery at least. Vince doesn't visit his parents' grave very often. With the increasing international tension, the Polish, Latvian, Russian and Lithuanian military patrols are constantly on alert in the region and ethnic relations become tense from time to time. At the end of World War I, many younger Polish families moved from the Dyneburg area to the Brasław area in order to be on the Polish side of the border, and many elderly people, their parents among them, decided to stay. They passed away soon thereafter. Their father's side of the family had been living near the Dvina River for centuries, dating back to the golden pre-partition times. With her maiden name Kimbert, the mother's roots, the family legend goes, are from Scandinavia.

The departure of both men to this hazardous destination creates some anxiety at home. Towards evening, Aunt Renia keeps glancing at the big clock ticking louder and louder high above the door. The men should be headed back by now. They needed no more than an hour at the cemetery—just enough to clean the grave, plant flowers, and say prayers. Danusia also worries. They have only one day left with Dad. Tomorrow he will be leaving.

As darkness falls, familiar hoofbeats clatter through the musical shrill and chirp of field cicadas. Everybody rushes out to the yard while the buggy smoothly rides into the yard. Bolek immediately takes care of the horses while Danusia embraces Dad. Managing to get back and forth without any trouble, Alek and Vince smile despite their fatigue while Zbyszek can't stop asking about the trip. On the way out, near the border, a Polish patrol stopped them, but the soldiers were friendly and even offered some advice on how to go farther. On the way back, only peasants crossed their path. Aunt Renia puts supper on the table.

Alek spends his last hours before the departure mostly with Vince, recalling the past and going back in time to their childhood. As young boys, they used to visit the Big Uncle, their father's brother. The Big Uncle was very rich, owning about half a county with several villages, vast fields and meadows, and rich forests. His house was the center of cultural life for the entire region. At the back of his elegant house, an exquisite garden stretched across the hill. The arboretum with exotic trees, neatly cut shrubs, and rare flowers was the pride of the entire family.

The Big Uncle's son, Józef, was younger than Vince but older than Alek. Occasionally the boys went horseback riding together. They would go after deer and rabbits into dense forests and had to run away from wolves and wild boars. With the Big Uncle no longer alive, Józef took over the estate. Every year the entire family gathers at Uncle Józef house for Easter. As Vince and Alek many years ago, now Gienia and Bolek anxiously await the Easter family gathering at Uncle Józef's house.

Unfortunately, Alek doesn't have time to visit Józef this year. Maybe next year.... But Danusia and Zbyszek will go. Uncle Józef has three children: the oldest, Lodzia, is already married. Wila and Felek are still at home. Wila is Danusia's age and Felek is slightly younger than Zbyszek. They already know about the guests from Warsaw and can't wait to meet their new cousins. It's a very hospitable house. Danusia, Zbyszek, and the rest of the family already have an invitation to stay at Uncle Józef's house for as long as they wish.

On Saturday morning Alek wakes up with a headache. At breakfast, he turns to Vince and lowers his voice. "I don't even remember when was the last time I had such a good time. It was great here with you, Brother. It's very hard for me to leave. There are still so many things I would like to see and so many people I would like to visit...."

"Don't worry, Aluś," Vince gently pats him on the back. "You must come back next year. Next time, we will plan better to make sure you can visit everybody."

"But I would like you and Renia to come over to Warsaw to visit us, and Bolek, and Gienia, too," Alek insists.

"That's a great idea!" Danusia jumps up. "And you, Gienia, could come at any time, right?"

Gienia's eyes search the floor. "Not really. I am starting my own business now. It will be difficult for me to leave for more than a week...." She looks at Danusia's sorrowful face and quickly adds, "But maybe after the New Year, when business is slower."

"We can't leave the farm, you see, but Bolek may want to go in the fall or in the spring, for example," Uncle Vince adds.

Flushed with joy, Bolek fidgets on the chair, ready to go. The time has come to leave for Alek's train. Both Bolek and Vince will take Alek by buggy for the long drive. Tearfully Danusia hugs and kisses Dad. With his head down, Zbyszek hems and haws, trying to hide his emotions. It's not that long, only a month and they will see each other again. But this distance separating them for all this time is scary, very scary. They are not used to it.

As the buggy disappears into the woods, a solitary silence falls on the farmstead. Danusia takes a blanket and decides to do some day-dreaming in the fields while Zbyszek carves a piece of wood with his pocketknife. Before long, hoofbeats break the silence and a group of soldiers led by Lieutenant Sierżant rides in.

"How are you?" The lieutenant waves to Zbyszek.

"Our Dad has just left for Warsaw," he replies quietly.

Attracted by the commotion, Danusia gets up.

"Danusia, how are you?" The lieutenant smiles at her, then turns around to his soldiers. "Free time for everybody. We'll meet at the Fire Station at 1 PM." With joyous understanding, his soldiers ride away.

Inching toward the lieutenant, Danusia erratically smoothens her curly hair and carefully scrutinizes the visitor. In his mid- to late twenties, Julian is tall and slim. His broad shoulders in the elegant military uniform appear powerful. His gestures are decisive and confident, his voice pleasant, sometimes clear and firm, sometimes soft and intimate. His sharp but considerate blue eyes underneath the peak of the elegant officer's hat communicate without words. He gently reaches out to her, slowly leans forward, and solemnly kisses her hand. This wonderful hand-kiss sinks deeply into Danusia's heart. In her girlish imagination, this hand-kiss is a confession of love in a very special, secret way. She blushes slightly. The lieutenant asks about her father, tries to assure her that the journey to Warsaw is safe, and asks about her plans for the next couple of weeks.

They sit at the steps of the house. Zbyszek disappears into the barn. Danusia listens as the lieutenant talks about his home in Zbaraż, about his family he hasn't seen for months, and about life in uniform. As he talks, Danusia realizes she enjoys his company very much. It seems as if they have known each other for years.

"Welcome back, Lieutenant." Aunt's Renia loud voice interrupts them. With Alek's departure, Renia keeps a watchful eye on Danusia and Zbyszek. Apparently the lieutenant's long talk with Danusia has intrigued her.

The lieutenant gets up and bows politely. "Good afternoon, Madam. I stopped by to make sure that you didn't change your plans and that you are coming tomorrow to our Sunday Mass."

"I think we are planning on coming, right, Danusia?" Aunt Renia says. "I would like to see your field chapel. We don't really have a church nearby."

"I hope you will like our Mass. It's a little different than in the regular church. Maybe not that elegant but our choir is excellent and we have an excellent band, although it's a military band.... But I hope you will like it. Well, it's time for me to go. I'll see you tomorrow then." The lieutenant salutes vigorously and turns around. Danusia follows him eagerly with her gaze.

"It looks as if you found a boyfriend." Zbyszek's angry voice startles her. "How about if you play cards with me now?" With cards in his hand, Zbyszek stands in front of her like a warrior ready for battle.

"Oh, Zbyś!" She realizes her little brother is in desperate need of immediate attention. "Okay, let's play." This is the first time they are left without their parents and a certain anxiety settles in their hearts.

* * * *

Sunday morning, Danusia rises before everybody else and takes over the strategic chair in front of the mirror to style her hair. Aunt Renia, with Gienia's help, prepares a light breakfast. The men clean up the buggy and ready the horses. After a quick breakfast consisting of *chałka* with cottage cheese, *powidła*, and delicious cocoa with meringue on top, all of them squeeze into the buggy. Danusia impatiently pushes Zbyszek away. "Hey, watch my dress! Don't sit on it!"

Her snow-white dress might get dirty and wrinkled. The wind might muss her hair.

"Don't worry," Zbyszek shrugs. "It will get dirty anyway. After all, we are going to the forest!"

Uncle Vince drives the buggy while Bolek strives to make sense of the lieutenant's sketchy map. "It's not really that far," he finally concludes. In less than an hour, the buggy arrives at the gate of the military compound. Other buggies with local people also crowd behind and in front of them. The friendly guard in military uniform raises a bar painted in red and white, and shows them the path. As they ride through the bright evergreen forest, many big military tents come into view. In a kilometer or so, a large square opening appears between the trees in front of them. The simple wooden altar dominates over the multitude of young faces dressed in gray-green uniforms. A soldier with a red and while armband directs them to the visitors' section near the altar.

As they park the buggy, Lieutenant Sierżant greets them with an official salute. His probing eyes shine with admiration at Danusia. "I am very glad to welcome you to the camp. I hope you will enjoy the visit. After the Mass, we will have lunch for everybody, so please be our guests."

"You are very well organized here!" Uncle Vince replies. "I am impressed, I must say."

"Thank you. We are trying. We have about two thousand soldiers and several hundreds scouts scattered throughout this forest. That's a nice size to manage. I will have to join my unit for the Mass but I will be back afterward." As soon as the official greetings are over, the lieutenant turns to Danusia. "How are you? I must confess you look very beautiful today." He takes her hand and they walk away chatting.

The Mass starts with the majestic procession of yellow and blue church flags and white and red national flags. Some of the flags are ornamented with the national emblem, some read: "Honor and Country," some have the majestic eagle in the crown painted on the white background. Hundreds of military units standing at attention fill the entire square. The scout formations of boys and girls dressed in khaki uniforms with short pants or skirts and colorful scarves around their necks stand near the altar. The Mass is ceremonial but brief. The sermon is short, dynamic, and full of patriotic references. Throughout the Mass, hymns with a heavy patriotic bent thunder through the woods of Racki Bór. The inspiring flush of emotions spreads around. Many eyes shine with tears of love for the most precious thing in life—their homeland.

After Mass, some units disappear into the forest while others start setting up the kitchen and tables for lunch. Uncle Vince shakes his head in pleasant disbelief. "To see all these good-looking young men and women here is very moving...and very inspiring, I must say."

"I told you, Dad, I must go to the army!" Bolek cries, clenching his fists.

"You know, Bolek, that we need your help at the farm," Aunt Renia shakes her head hastily. "Dad can't take care of the land without your help."

"Don't worry, young man. You may soon have to join the army anyway," a senior officer standing behind them says.

Uncle Vince turns to him abruptly. "What do you mean, Sir?"

"You see, the times are very turbulent these days. We may be heading for war. Please sit down." The senior officer invites them to the table.

His words send chills through Danusia's heart. Although Hitler's venomous acts of violent aggression have been on the front-pages for about two years now, and although people instinctually know that with each new victim Hitler's appetite for more only grows, the word "war" was kept away from people's minds and no one dared to say it so bluntly.

Zbyszek's jaw drops, his eyes bulge. The word "war" hypnotizes him. "Do you think Hitler will invade us?"

"I don't know for sure, young man. But it is possible." The officer tries to soften his tone.

"How are we going to fight?" Zbyszek asks.

"It would be very difficult to resist the Germans if we have to do it alone. But the French and the British will help us." The officer stops and looks at Zbyszek. "Together, we can face up to the Germans!" His fist lands on the table. "Right, young man?"

"Yes, Sir!" Zbyszek replies like a soldier.

Uncle Vince leans towards the officer, piercing him with his glance. "But, Sir, what about if the Soviets decide to attack us from the East?"

"We shouldn't worry about the Soviets. They can hardly keep up with their own internal problems. They are just the colossus with feet of clay."

"With all due respect, Sir," Lieutenant Sierżant joins the discussion cautiously, "the internal opposition in the Soviet Union is pretty much dead by now. The Red Army is growing in strength and gaining ground in the Mongolian conflict with the Japanese. I would not underestimate Stalin."

"Please, don't give us such a depressing scenario!" Danusia gets up, moving an amber bracelet back and forth on her slim hand. The mood at the table turns grim.

"You're right, young lady," the senior officer concludes. "How about if we eat something?" He gets up slowly and directs everyone to one of the kitchen stations set up nearby. Delicious military *bigos* consisting of sauerkraut, *kiełbasa*, mushrooms, and red wine hardly improves their mood, though.

"How much longer do you have to stay in the military service?" Danusia asks the lieutenant.

He looks around and sighs slightly. "I am supposed to conclude my services in a few weeks, if everything goes well," he answers.

"I am sure your mother can't wait to see you," Aunt Renia says.

"That's correct. I haven't been home for over a year. We are always so busy and I like the military service but I miss my family."

"Do you have siblings?" Danusia asks.

"Yes, I have two younger sisters. As a matter of fact, one is your age. Her name is Ania. Sometimes you remind me of her."

"Ania or Anna. One of my best friends is Anna. By the way, her Name Day is July 26. Oh!" Danusia clutches her head. "That's just a few days away. I almost forgot!"

"You're right, it's late. I have to send a Name Day card to my sister tomorrow."

"We can do it together. I have to send my Name Day cards, too," Danusia suggests.

* * * *

Over the few next days, Zbyszek helps with the daily chores around the farm. The harvest is quickly approaching and the farmers are very busy. Danusia spends most of her time with Gienia and Zbyszek and eagerly keeps a lookout for the lieutenant.

By the end of the week, Gienia has to go back to Brasław. The girls have become like real sisters over the past few weeks. Gienia has also spent a lot of time with Zbyszek, playing cards with him, going fishing, and doing many fun things that no one else could or would do. Before long they had become bosom buddies. "Please come to visit us in Warsaw," Zbyszek begs her. "I'll show you our Zoo and our club, and we will take you to the movies."

"And I'll take you for a dance and we could go for some fun shopping," Danusia chimes in.

"I would love to come, believe me. I dream of seeing the Warsaw Photo Exhibition. The best photographers present their works there. But I have to watch my business and I don't know what my boyfriend's plans are. He may be coming home from the army any time now…."

"Those boyfriends! Forget this business, just come over and have fun with us," Zbyszek cries indignantly.

"Don't worry, brother," Bolek gives him a friendly pat. "I will take Gienia with me when I go to Warsaw. Maybe in the spring, okay?"

With Gienia's departure, the evening dates with Julian become even longer. Almost every day, he manages to leave the camp to see Danusia. Sometimes they sit in the yard chatting with everybody around and learning about the challenges of running the farm, sometimes they sneak off alone and walk into the rustling fields around the house. One day Danusia gives Julian a small fancy notebook and asks him to write something for her in memory of this time spent together. He keeps the notebook for a day or so and returns it with a short sentence neatly handwritten on one of the last pages: *"Love is like wine, don't dilute it with water."* Danusia treasures every minute spent with Julian, trying not to think about the inevitable moment when they will have to go their separate ways. Will they ever meet again…?

One evening when Danusia comes back from their walk in the fields, Uncle Vince calls her. "Danusia, we have to plan for a trip to Uncle Józef," he says. "They all are waiting for you there. And your Dad asked me to take you and Zbyszek to Uncle Józef."

"Oh, I see," Danusia replies slowly. "When do you think we should go?"

"We don't need to go tomorrow, but you should plan on going by the end of the week. Bolek will take you to Uncle Józef and will pick you up around August 20th. That way you will still have a couple more days here to pack, okay?"

"Yes, that's okay," she replies quietly. "But maybe we could go to Mass in Racki Bór this Sunday? We would leave for Uncle Józef right after that. It's such a nice trip to Racki Bór. I would love to see it again."

"That's a good idea."

From then on, the evening rendezvous with the lieutenant become even longer. Danusia talks about her life in Warsaw, how much she likes the city, how many interesting things she can do in Warsaw, how she likes to go with her friends to small coffee shops, sit at the tables and watch the busy streets filled with elegant women. Julian listens attentively then talks about the future. His military service is almost over. He can't wait to be back home.

Holding Danusia's hand, he talks of what to do next. Originally he was planning on continuing his education in Lwów. Now it seems as if Warsaw may be a better choice. It's farther away from home, but Warsaw may offer more opportunities. And of course someone very special would be close by. But what about Zbaraż, Tarnopol, and Lwów? That's his real home. Warsaw is big and glamorous but foreign and distant. He has no childhood and high school friends there, no family or relatives, no familiar neighbors who have known one throughout the years, and no sense of belonging to anything anywhere.

This thought steers him back and he starts talking about Zbaraż, his family, the picturesque countryside, the fascinating history of the town, the proximity and cultural ties with Lwów and Kraków. He talks about his house, the street he lives on, his school, then he abruptly stops and with great urgency says, "Korzeniowskiego 25, please remember that! Korzeniowskiego 25. That's my address. Remember this Polish writer, Joseph Conrad Korzeniowski, who became famous by writing in English? That's his last name—Korzeniowski." Contemplating for a moment, he then asks her to repeat the address over and over again. "Please memorize it and never forget it!" He stops, takes her both hands, and squeezes them. "I will always get your letters if you send them there, to my mother in Zbaraż!" His voice is shaking slightly. "I should still be here when you come back from Uncle Józef. But please remember that address. You can always contact me, wherever I am, if you write to my mother. She always knows how to reach me. And anyway, I should be home in September...."

Danusia desperately tries to delay the trip to Uncle Józef. The thought that she will not see Julian for some time causes her heart to drop. She talks with Aunt Renia and Bolek, considers inventing some convenient illness, and even recommends not going at all. But nothing seems to work. The noble Uncle Józef is waiting and Bolek can only drive them on Sunday because the harvest is in full swing and every pair of hands is indispensable in the fields.

Sunday Mass at Racki Bór goes very fast this time. There is no lunch and no time for chatting with the soldiers, just a few short words with Julian and the buggy moves towards the gate.

Once home they don't change their clothes. To be properly dressed for the first visit to the noble Uncle is appropriate. Aunt Renia gives them a bag with sandwiches and fruits, Uncle Vince gives Bolek some last minute advice on how to go and the buggy is on its way, except that this time it is not the heavy, all-purpose buggy but a light passenger carriage called *Linijka* for no more than three persons. *Linijka* is more dangerous than the buggy, though. Faster than the buggy, more elegant, and more agile, *Linijka* is used for shorter trips and for special occasions. The horses like *Linijka*. They know the load will be light, they can run faster, possibly at a trot, and they may even break into a gallop. Danusia curiously checks the soft purple seats and artistic carvings on the side walls. Soon Bolek drives *Linijka* at full speed. Danusia and Zbyszek scream joyfully as the rumble of the speeding wheels grows.

* * * *

The trip to Uncle Józef's usually takes about three hours but today country wagons overloaded with hay and bizarre farming machines and tools, some of which are carried or pulled by horses, plod along the road. Though on Sundays people are supposed to rest, the harvest season allows for the exception, and many people toil in the scorching Sunday sun. Danusia looks around with amazement. She has never seen real haymaking. Bolek greets everybody with the old Polish "*Szczęść*

Boże!" wishing everybody good harvest. Danusia and Zbyszek quickly learn the greeting and wave to the people in the fields.

Bolek looks at the clear blue sky. "It will be raining tonight."

"How do you know?" Zbyszek looks around. "I see no clouds."

"Look at the bugs and birds," Bolek explains. "They fly low, see? And this sultriness in the air…it means a thunderstorm is coming. That's why everybody is rushing to bring the hay in."

Linijka passes through several villages and a small town. At last it turns into a park with ancient, towering oaks, immense linden, and overgrown pines. A few more wide turns through the woods and *Linijka* vigorously stops at the door of a courtly house. The traditional front porch composed of two white columns supporting a small triangle top displays the sign of noble status—the family shield. The house, decorated with roses and perennials, exemplifies the country lifestyle of the Polish gentry.

A school-aged blond boy runs out the door. Bolek gets out and pulls the boy into his arms.

"How are you, young man? Look! I brought you some new cousins, see?" He turns around to Zbyszek and Danusia. "This is Felek, the baby of the family."

A pretty girl of Danusia's age and two elderly ladies appear at the door. They greet the guests with joyful smiles and open arms. "The children couldn't wait to see you," the elegantly dressed woman says. Aunt Michalina, as Bolek calls her, is the lady of the house. Wearing a dark blue frock with a chain of pearls around her neck and her brown-gray hair neatly styled in a chignon, she commands respect. The neatly dressed, plumper woman with a white headband and a white starched apron over her gray dress is the maid of the house. A slim girl with big blue eyes and long blond hair, that's Wila, the younger of the two daughters.

Danusia and Zbyszek are confounded by the luxury of the place. The large rooms of this single-story house have big wide-open windows, elegant furniture, and ornamented tile stoves. Numerous portraits and paintings decorate the walls while colorful plants and snow-white curtains beautify the Venetian windows. The sweet aroma of flowers mixed with the piney smell of the freshly polished wooden floor spreads throughout the house.

After the formal introduction, the guests are invited to the table for a light afternoon meal. Bowls of aromatic raspberries and wild strawberries with homemade sour cream and sugar appear at the table. Aunt Michalina wants to know everything at once. She asks about Dad and Mama in Warsaw, about the stay at Uncle Vince's, about the trips to Brasław, and on and on. Danusia politely tries to answer all the questions but Zbyszek looks around curiously, squirming in his seat.

"Oh, welcome! Welcome! Let me guess...this is Danusia and Zbyszek, right?" A strong baritone interrupts the discussion and a handsome middle-aged man hurries into the room. With tall boots, white shirt, and splendid garments, Uncle Józef looks like a dignitary. He hugs Bolek and keenly embraces the newcomers. The formal introductions are complete. Only the oldest daughter, Lodzia, is missing. She got married this year and moved out of the house but she is expected to stop by later on during the week.

After the initial ice-breaking, Bolek rushes back home as the first drops of rain splash over *Linijka*. Looking fearfully at the sky, Aunt Michalina blesses him for the journey. A thunderstorm is coming and darkness settles in quickly.

Once *Linijka* disappears in the darkness of the park, Danusia and Zbyszek are taken to their rooms to unpack. Later, Wila takes them for a tour of the house showing them their way around. All of a sudden, lightning flashes the room with bright light. Reverberating, violent thunder crashes just outside the window. With every second, heavy rain drums louder and louder on the roof and on the windows. More lightning and booming thunder strike over their heads. Aunt Michalina brings a big consecrated wax candle to the main room and starts praying. Everybody gathers around the table, and real fear settles in the children's hearts. The old trees rustle loudly and thrash fiercely in the wind.

"Last year the lightning destroyed a house in the village," Wila recalls, her voice shaking slightly.

Sitting on the plushy sofa, Uncle Józef stretches his legs. "Yes, but don't worry, we are not in the village. We should only worry about these old trees outside the house. If lightning strikes them, we can be hit by some of the branches."

"But, Dad, remember?" Felek looks through the window. "Last year some people came over and cut these huge dry branches from our linden near the porch."

"That is correct, Son, but there are other trees at the back of the house that may possibly reach the roof, but they are not that tall yet."

Danusia swallows hard and puts her arm around Zbyszek. They have never experienced such a violent thunderstorm in such a strange place, virtually in the middle of a forest. In the stormy night, the elegant house looks gloomy. Long into the night, they stay in the main room, too scared to sleep. Eventually the thunderstorm dies out but they sleep together in one room.

When the warm and cloudy morning finally arrives, the memory of the dreadful thunderstorm still haunts them. The acclimatization in this fancy but scary house takes them longer than expected despite the extra efforts of their hosts. For the first couple of days, they mostly play around the house with Wila and Felek.

One day, Uncle Józef takes them to the stable and shows them the horses. Zbyszek is delighted and keeps returning to the stable over the next days. Danusia, however, is more interested in the neighborhood, the farm, the villages and towns, churches and shops. She explores the farm, gazing with astonishment huge barns and granaries. In one granary, she discovers hundreds of barrels of sour cream and in the other hundreds of barrels of honey. Such wealth!

Every day at 3 PM, the main meal of the day is served. Everyone must be home on time for this daily family ritual. After dinner, the family gathers for a siesta in the garden in front of the dining room. Aunt Michalina always takes her porcelain coffee cup and a book to a small table in the rose garden. Uncle Józef either reads a newspaper next to her or lies down in the hammock in the refreshing shadow of the old oak trees. Danusia and Wila have another hammock nearby. Zbyszek and Felek don't like the siesta and always disappear into the park.

Uncle Józef likes to lounge in the hammock and chat with the girls. Danusia keeps asking him about the farm, about all these barrels, barns, stables, herds of cattle and goat, about his fields, forests, and villages. Uncle Józef talks about his estate with great pride and affection.

"Danusia, you know what? Tomorrow, I will take you and Wila to the Redel store in our village and you can buy whatever you wish there.

I'll pay for everything. How's that?" He watches her closely. Danusia's brown eyes open wide. She takes a deep breath and can't speak for a moment. "Really?" she finally mutters with disbelief. The idea of buying whatever she wishes is mind-boggling. She makes sure that Uncle Józef keeps his promise. She quickly arranges for the trip to the village.

There are several small shops in the village and Uncle's generous offer extends to all of them. But the shopping is not as promising as Danusia would have liked. The village stores have little of interest to her. Eventually, she buys a bag of chocolate candies and, upon the advice of an old Jewish shop-owner, a pair of solid galoshes. Although not very fruitful, the shopping trip leaves a life-long impression of Uncle Józef's boundless wealth and generosity.

One day in the afternoon, a carriage arrives at the porch and a young lady runs into the house. Aunt Michalina and Wila embrace her. The oldest of the three children, Lodzia looks very much like her younger sister, Wila, but is a little taller and has a pleasant, exhilarating voice. Danusia greets her eagerly. Lodzia indicates that she is in a great rush and won't eat anything. The girls sit down on the terrace and talk. Danusia wants to know everything about Lodzia's recent wedding, about her husband, about her new home. Lodzia inquires about life in Warsaw, about Danusia's visit with Uncle Vince, and whether she likes it here at their house. Soon Felek and Zbyszek drop by all dirty and sweaty with sticky hair and scratched legs. They have been riding their bicycles all over the neighborhood.

Lodzia greets them warmly. "Danusia, this gentleman is your little brother Zbyszek, right?"

"Yes, this gentleman who looks like Beelzebub," Danusia smiles. After brief greetings are exchanged, the boys disappear in the park screaming and whistling. Lodzia doesn't stay long. She exchanges addresses with Danusia and runs out.

The next few days Danusia spends mostly with Wila. The girls go to the village and meet Wila's friends. But Danusia seems absent. She doesn't talk much and is not eager to make new friends. Julian is on her mind all the time. Is she going to see him again? Bolek should be coming back soon. Maybe he will bring a letter for her....

That day at the dinner table, Danusia meets a guest who came from Vilnius. The noble dignitary named Witold is an old friend of Uncle Józef's. The two men are deeply immersed in a passionate discussion. Danusia catches some gist of the debate: "provocations," "terrorist attacks," "border guard." Uncle Józef swings a newspaper like a sword. Aunt Michalina paces back and forth, mumbling something like "Unbelievable, unbelievable." She asks the girls to the table without even bothering to introduce anybody. The girls obediently take the seats. Soon Felek and Zbyszek show up at the table.

The two men continue their discourse. "We must somehow stop all this slander and this defamation campaign!" Uncle Józef hollers as he slams the newspaper down on the table. "Savages!" he exclaims, pointing with disgust to a front-page picture: a restaurant window displaying a big banner: "FORBIDDEN TO DOGS AND POLES."[1] "What's that?" Danusia feels a spasm in her stomach.

Enjoying the summer of 1939 in the remote countryside, Danusia doesn't know that Goebbels' propaganda or so-called "war of nerves" is reaching its peak. The mastermind of human madness is unstoppable in pursuing his objective: to promote ethnic hatred and insuppressible aggression, thereby inciting the German people to war and overpowering the Poles. Anything and everything goes. The German paramilitary groups galvanized by Goebbels' propaganda machine are fully preoccupied with sabotage and diversion: they attack trains, bridges, government buildings, industrial plants, restaurants, and spread terror in public places.[2]

In the Free City of Gdańsk (in German, Danzig), the situation is dramatic. The supervision of the city by the High Commissioner from the League of Nations has become pure fiction by now. The Poles are intimidated, offended, and persecuted every day. In northern and southern Poland, German minority groups, organized into the so-called "fifth column," stage numerous terrorists attacks, arranging bombings in German schools and setting fire to German businesses—all that cruelty against their own people in order to blame the Poles for attacking and mistreating the German minority. Detailed reports on how the Poles castrate the German minority appear on a regular basis in the German press. The propaganda about the "pre-arranged" Polish atrocities is also carefully tailored and effectively promoted on the international scene. In August, aggression of the German fascist groups becomes much more blatant. Polish border guards are attacked outright. In Silesia, train stations, factories, and offices are burned.

Only the eastern part of Poland has been relatively stable thus far. Uncle Józef, preoccupied with the harvest, largely missed the political nightmare of the last couple of weeks. His friend from Vilnius brutally brings him up to speed as the rest of the family listens in horror.

"Hitler wants to swallow us like Czechoslovakia!" Witold pounds his fist. "And the West is ready to acquiesce again. They already bought Goebbels' propaganda that Gdańsk should be given to the Germans, just to appease Hitler again. And that's not the end of the story. Next Germany may want to offer us their kind "protectorate" like they did with the others, and the West would not mind that either. It looks to me that once again Marshal Piłsudski was right. We must count only on ourselves."

Uncle Józef looks straight into Witold's eyes. "We must fight for Gdańsk, brother, we must fight, no matter what," he says with determination in his voice. "This discrimination against the Polish people there is unbearable. The Nazis keep increasing their persecutions. They started with taxing the Poles to death, next those who sent their children to Polish schools were losing their jobs; the Nazis were also kidnapping Polish children, sending them to the German schools, and now they openly threaten all the Poles in Gdańsk![3] We must act. We cannot allow this savagery to go on."

"But what if we talk about that later," Aunt Michalina interrupts. "We didn't even have a chance to introduce our cousins from Warsaw. This is Danusia and Zbyszek."

Witold finally notices them. "How do you do?" he says formally.

"Nice to meet you," Danusia replies while Zbyszek murmurs something.

The boys, paying no attention to the adult discussion, swallow their meal in no time and take off. The adults move to the garden for dessert. Danusia follows them and sinks into the wicker chair behind the neatly cut shrubbery thinking about Julian and all the discussions in Racki Bór and here about the German threat.

Watching the boys disappearing into the park, Witold says: "Nice kids, these cousins of yours. But if I were you, I would send them back home as soon as possible. In my opinion, Hitler is setting the stage for war and Warsaw is fully aware of it. We estimate that the German military power is at least twice the size of ours."

Uncle Józef looks at Witold uncertainly. "If this is the case then maybe instead of sending the kids to Warsaw I should ask their parents to come over here. In case of a German invasion, we should be relatively safe here in the east, don't you think so?"

"I don't know. I really don't know what to think. I am sure our defense plans anticipate regrouping in the east. But who knows what the Soviets would do? Colonel Beck, like Marshal Piłsudski, believes that our national interest is to ally with neither the Germans nor the Soviets.[4] In fact, Piłsudski is believed to have said towards the end of his life that the Soviets were the greater danger to Poland than the Germans even though the likelihood of military aggression was greater from the German side. And his reasoning was quite remarkable. In his opinion, Poland could always count on some political or military support from the Western Powers against German aggression but never against Russian aggression. The commonality of interest between France, Great Britain, and Poland against the German zeal for domination and expansion makes the Polish cause viable to the West not only from a moral but also from a practical standpoint. However, it is a totally different story with Russian imperialism. To the West, whether it's Russia or the Soviet Union, it has always been some kind of an exotic and enigmatic terrain totally beyond the realm of their interest."

Uncle Józef rubs his forehead nervously. "But if you look at the Soviets over the past twenty years, they entered into this Non-Aggression Pact with us, they are negotiating with the West on some form of alliance, they don't have any territorial claims to us, and they are not even capable of taking any offensive action right now."

"Apparently that is the thinking in Warsaw," Witold replies. "Colonel Beck doesn't really consider the Soviets in his defense plans. But I am not that certain about it. Ribbentrop recently visited Moscow," he shakes his head with skepticism.

"Are you thinking about some kind of a German–Russian cooperation? That's insane! Hitler adamantly opposes Stalin from an ideological standpoint. He hates communists." Uncle Józef rapidly gets up and paces erratically back and forth.

"Ideological differences quickly fall by the wayside if cooperation can bring territorial gains. We have been getting regular reports from the German press and radio broadcasts. The tone of their propaganda towards Stalin has clearly changed over the last month or so. Goebbels has become suspiciously friendly with Stalin, I must say. And this new face in Kremlin, this Molotov...?"

"That would be a catastrophe for us!" Uncle Józef stops, his wide-open eyes venture to the sky. "Would the West help?" He slowly turns to his friend.

Witold sighs heavily. "If a German–Soviet *rapprochement* is really in the cards, the very existence of our nation is at stake. We don't stand a chance. And the West? They are manipulated and overpowered by Goebbels' propaganda; they don't have the vision and don't understand what's in it for them.... In this situation, I would probably choose cooperation with Germany because, remembering what Piłsudski said, our surrender to them would be less permanent than to Russia. Eventually the West would find us useful. As recently as January, Hitler was very anxious for some sort of a deal with us and was very interested in bringing Poland to the Axis Coalition."[5]

"Let's not be that pessimistic," Aunt Michalina joins the discussion. "After all, we have a good army. I heard that we have over two hundred modern fighter planes, and these so-called German *tanks* are made of cardboard anyway."

"You are right, Madam. We shouldn't be so pessimistic," Witold welcomes the dose of frivolous optimism with a hesitant smile.

* * * *

Danusia nervously awaits Bolek's return. Maybe he will bring a letter from Julian. It's already the middle of August. Assumption Day, the big religious holiday, is approaching. In Poland, this is also a popular Name Day for Maria as well as the time to bless the crops and render thanks to God for a bountiful harvest season.

After the regular church service, a colorful procession passes by the green villages and yellowing fields. Joyful songs resound throughout the countryside. The people are exhausted but satisfied with a job well done. They will rest briefly before starting to prepare for the next farming season.

The next day during lunchtime, *Linijka* wheels rumble outside the house. Everybody springs to the window. Bolek waves to them, running to the house. "Bolek, how are you, boy?" Aunt Michalina exclaims. "We have been worrying about you driving home in that thunderstorm, remember? But we concluded that you must have safely returned home. Otherwise Vince would be already here."

"I am fine. Glad to see you all."

Danusia gives him a big hug. "But how is everything at home? Did you see the soldiers…?"

"The military units that have been stationed in our area are just about to leave, including some of the National Guard units," he scratches his head, eyes searching the floor.

Danusia's face turns pale, her body drops sluggishly into the chair. She may not see Julian again. Different thoughts are running through her mind. "That senior officer in Racki Bór, the newspaper photograph, this guest from Vilnius, war…war, no! It can't be true. No, I am getting unreasonably obsessed with all this."

"Here you go, Julian wrote to you." Bolek hands her a small envelope with her name neatly handwritten in black ink. Everybody eyes the envelope. She grabs the letter and scans the page as she unfolds it. Julian writes that he is trying to delay his departure to see her again but it may not be possible. She skims through the text and catches the ending, "Love you, Julian." Loud steps resound in the hallway as she gently folds the paper.

"Bolek! Good to see you boy!" Uncle Józef thunders. "I hope you will stay for a while this time." He looks at the bewildered faces staring at him in an awkward silence. "What's wrong? Any problems?"

"No, nothing special," replies Bolek greeting Uncle Józef with a hug. "We were talking about the soldiers stationed near us. They are just about to leave and one of Danusia's friends sent her a letter."

"Oh, I see," Uncle Józef sits down, frowning. "Why are they leaving, do you know?"

"I'm not sure, but people think that the Army is moving west to enforce the German borders. They are also taking some of the units to guard against the terrorist provocations of these Jungdeutsche groups."

"That's insane!" Uncle Józef throws up his hands. "What about the Soviet borders? Have you heard about this German–Russian agreement that was just announced?"

"No, not really," Bolek replies with strange tension in his voice.

"You see, the Soviets signed some sort of an agreement with Germany. The thinking is that a military pact between the two is in the works."

"Yes, but the Germans are attacking our border posts in the north, west, and even in the south, and we don't really have any serious border incidents with the Soviets and Lithuanians so far."

"Not yet," Uncle Józef replies shaking his head grimly.

"Well, what about if you get something to eat now? We will talk later." Aunt Michalina takes Bolek to the kitchen.

Danusia goes to the hammock in the rose garden. Closing her eyes, she hears Zbyszek's distant voice. The boys are playing in the park. Two of Felek's friends from the neighborhood are playing with them. The boys draw big circles on the ground and take turns in throwing small sticks at each other.

"Declaration of war!" they shout.

"Declaration of war…," Danusia repeats hopelessly.

"What did you say?" Uncle Józef asks from behind.

"Oh nothing, the boys are playing this game called 'Declaration of War.' Do you know how to play it?"

"No, not really."

"It's getting more popular these days," Danusia observes sarcastically. "Uncle Józef, I think we should be going back soon. It is great here and we both are having a wonderful time. You all are so nice to us! But I feel that we shouldn't stay much longer. With all this talk about war, I would like to go back sooner." Danusia's heart beats fast. This letter from Julian, all the talk of war…. Some unsettling urgency fills her heart. She wants to leave immediately.

"All right, Danusia," Uncle Józef embraces her. "I understand. Don't worry. You will be going soon. But let Bolek rest a little. He just arrived."

Despite her intensive campaign, no one else shares Danusia's urgency to leave. Zbyszek declares outright that he doesn't want to go; Bolek wants to spend time with Uncle Józef; Wila wants Danusia to stay as long as possible. Seeing Danusia's agonized frustration, Aunt Michalina eventually comes to her rescue, and two days later *Linijka* is ready for the trip. Danusia leaves the mansion with sincere sadness. She had a wonderful time in this paradise. Before getting into *Linijka*, she runs to the majestic linden that stretches out near the porch, snaps off a small twig, and declares: "It will always remind me of this wonderful place and my dearest friends here." Tearfully Danusia and Zbyszek wave and yell as *Linijka* takes off in the chill of the early summer morning.

On the way home, Danusia negotiates intensely with Bolek. If the horses go full speed, they could take the longer route and pass by Racki Bór. Then, she could at least find out whether Julian is still around. Bolek is not excited about this idea. It is too far. The horses will be too tired. And besides, the guards may not even let them into the camp. But Danusia is determined. With great persistence she talks him into her idea. The weather is perfect, a pleasant breeze cooperates, and *Linijka* gains speed. Bolek takes a sharp turn and *Linijka* spins into a narrow ditch through the forest. "Remember, I don't know this road very well. We may get lost," he warns.

"I believe in you, Bolek!" she replies. "You are a great guide!"

"I am not afraid to get lost," Zbyszek declares. "That would be fun even."

Bolek indeed turns out to be a great guide. Passing crossroads and changing small paths, he spurs through the forest with confidence and delight. His mood improves. "Last week we had a guest." He becomes conversational. "Our cousin, Giedziun, dropped by. They are in Ryczany, that's the same county—Poraslawsk. It's not that far. He really wanted to meet both of you but unfortunately he won't be able to come back because he is in the military service and his units are moving west as well. So he asked me to say hello. He must be the same age as your Lieutenant Sierżant. A very good fellow this Giedziun." Bolek smiles. Danusia wants to ask more about this unknown cousin of theirs but *Linijka* is already approaching the military compound. A big soldier in the booth measures them with his unfriendly eye.

"What do you want?"

Bolek looks at Danusia.

"Sir," she starts timidly, "we need to see Lieutenant Sierżant. It's urgent."

"We means who?" The giant looks at them suspiciously.

"My name is Danusia and I am here on a private matter."

"Oh, I see," the giant groans, nodding. "Move aside and wait," he orders and turns to some sort of telephone device hanging inside the booth.

Linijka moves toward the fence. "Wait here. I will be back." Danusia jumps out and walks to the booth. Apparently, Julian must be still here. As she approaches the giant, her heart is pounding like a jackhammer but a calculated smile shows on her face. "Did you talk to Lieutenant Sierżant?" she asks at a great peril.

The giant looks at her in an almost friendly way. "Yes, don't worry. He'll be here soon."

Oh, God! He is here! And she will really see him! Her dream comes true. Joy overwhelms her. She wants to shout and cheer, but instead she tries to regain her composure, turns to the boys and raises her hand with two fingers stretched in the "V" sign. With flushed cheeks, she moves closer to the fence, straining her eyes through the forest.

"Miss Danusia!" The familiar voice from behind stuns her. She turns around and falls into open arms. Julian kisses her hands as she presses her head against his muscular shoulder.

"I am so happy to see you, Danusia! You came here, to the camp, at the very last moment. I am so glad!"

"When do you leave?" she asks anxiously.

"Any moment, I am afraid."

She watches him possessively. In his military hat, Julian appears even more handsome than before. His commanding, shining eyes adore her from under the shield. Wearing a brownish-green shirt decorated with Polish Army buttons with its high, tapered collar neatly encasing his slim neck, form-fitting elegantly flared riding pants ,and high black boots made of soft calf leather, he looks like a knight. His alluring eyes smile to her. "The most handsome Polish officer I have ever seen," she thinks, quivering with emotion. This image of Julian smiling to her that day near the gate at Racki Bór is engraved in her deepest memory and becomes a symbol of the ideal for the rest of her life. From that day on, she will always long for that handsome Polish officer. And even many, many years later, she would always advise her cousins, friends, daughters, and even granddaughters to find that "handsome Polish officer." It would become "a must" for all young girls in her family to find that "handsome Polish officer" or someone who could pretend to become that "handsome Polish officer" one day.

"We are on our way home from Uncle Józef's," she explains. "Thank you for your letter."

He smiles. "I am delighted to see you!" He kisses her hand and waves to the boys who are busy cleaning and feeding the horses. "I see your brothers are here." They walk towards *Linijka*. "How are you,"

Julian shakes hands with the boys. “I didn’t expect to see you, Bolek, so soon. After all, you intended to stay about a week at your cousins’ place.”

“Well, Danusia insisted on coming,” Bolek replies.

“I am sorry if my letter caused you any problems,” Julian says apologetically.

“Don’t worry. Uncle Józef suggested that they go back to Warsaw this week because of this war scare.” Bolek stops cleaning the horse and glances at Julian. “And what’s the situation here? Any news?”

“Well, now we are scheduled to leave tomorrow. But there may be another delay, who knows…? We already had several delays.” Julian looks at Danusia with some hesitancy. “But how about if we sit down there in the picnic area?”

“No, no, we don’t have much time. We have to be home before dark,” Bolek protests. “Why don’t you take a walk while the horses rest and let’s say in fifteen minutes we need to be on our way, okay?”

Holding hands, Danusia and Julian walk down the forest path. Not enough time is left to say all they want to say. It feels simply wonderful to be together at last. As they leave the noisy camp behind, Julian reaches into his pocket and takes out a small book.

“Over these days, I have been thinking about you. I even found a poem that described very well how I feel. Do you want to take a look at it?”

“Let’s sit down here,” she moves to a big tree stump away from the path. Julian turns the pages and points to a poem entitled “Separation.” Powerful romantic phrases fly in front of Danusia’s eyes: “remember, white pigeon of sadness… wave of pain… never rejoining… crying nightingale.” These phrases cause pain.

“It’s beautiful, but very sad,” she whispers. “I hope we will meet again. You said you would come to Warsaw to study!” She closes the book. Small golden letters on the white sturdy cover catch her eyes: *Juliusz Słowacki*. “You like Słowacki, don’t you?”

“I like him very much. I think of Juliusz Słowacki as my patron.”

“But he is a very tragic person. His poems are so dramatic. All this patriotic drama of lost independence—it’s his obsession.”

“You are right. He is obsessed with independent Poland. You know which one is my favorite poem? It is ‘My Testament.’ I really feel as if this is my own….”

Danusia mechanically opens the book and a well-worn page meets her fingers. "My Testament," she notices the title and looks at Julian with discontent. She knows the poem very well. Every child in Poland knows this poem by heart. It's a classic piece written during the partition times about those who gave their lives fighting against the Russians for independent Poland. They lost their lives but ultimately triumph through their martyr's death. After glancing at the page, Danusia snaps the book closed.

"I don't want to hear about it!" She bursts into tears. "Why are you so pessimistic?" Her heart is bleeding. Julian embraces her gently and hides his face in her soft curly hair. The precious minutes pass by quickly and it's time to go back. Julian puts his arm around her and they walk back in silence.

"The horses are ready," Bolek announces.

Julian stops. "Your address, Danusia! I don't have your address in Warsaw!" Great urgency sounds in his voice.

"That's right," Danusia quickly puts her hand behind the neckline of her flowery dress and takes out a small piece of paper. That gesture seems so powerful as if she would hand him her heart. "You see, I have it ready." Their hands touch for a last brief moment, their eyes meet closely for the last time, her lips slightly meet his. "I love you," she whispers in despair, jumping onto *Linijka*.

"Thank you for coming," he waves.

Danusia cries, her eyes searching fiercely in the thickening mist as his tall silhouette disappears in the settling dust.

* * * *

A few days later, Danusia and Zbyszek stand on the platform of the Dukszty station. In a great rush, they said good-bye to Aunt Renia and left behind her little friendly house in Dryświaty. Uncle Vince and Bolek drove them to Dukszty. Now Bolek goes back home while Uncle Vince—dear, good-hearted Uncle Vince—will take them as far as Vilnius to make sure they get safely to the Warsaw train. The mood around is grim. Everybody talks about the war. The army has moved west and people are visibly anxious. Mass mobilization is on everyone's mind.

The small Dukszty station is unusually crowded. Many people with large suitcases and school-aged children stand around in small groups. Young men in military uniforms mingle with the crowd. This is quite an unusual scene for Dukszty. They expected crowds in Vilnius but not in Dukszty.

Bolek would like to go to Vilnius but cannot leave the farm when his father is away. He had such a great time with his new cousins. They traveled all over. They hunted together, played together, swam together. Zbyszek helped him in the fields and around the house. Danusia told him so many interesting things about Warsaw. Maybe in the spring, he could go to Warsaw. But who knows what's going to happen by springtime?

A small toy-like train pulls in. They get on with some effort, Uncle Vince right behind them. Soon Bolek and the Dukszty station disappear from the horizon. Uncle Vince worries. If it's so crowded here, they may not be able to get to the Warsaw train in Vilnius at all. They don't have reserved seats this time and people around seem to be panicky.

Indeed, huge crowds welcome them in Vilnius, the biggest crowd of course bound for Warsaw. They squeeze onto the platform and bit by bit are pushed against the wall of a small kiosk. As they watch the nervous crowd in horror, they realize that many people are desperately trying to reach the kiosk. It seems as if everybody is trying to get to the kiosk to buy a newspaper. Why? There must be some big news today.

"No more today's paper!" Upset voices are heard around. It's rather unusual for the newspaper to be sold out at this early hour.

Uncle Vince turns to a man holding a folded newspaper. "What's the special news today?" he asks anxiously.

The man tries to unfold the front-page in the minimal space he has. "I didn't read it yet, but apparently the Germans signed some sort of a deal with the Soviets." He manages to unfold the front-page and displays the headline: "German–Soviet Friendship!" Below, a photo shows the two officials shaking hands. The subheading reads: "Ribbentrop and Molotov Sign Non-Aggression Pact."[6] The men exchange somber looks. Throughout the centuries, there has always been only one reason for this so-called friendship. The two countries come together always for the same purpose—to destroy Poland. Danusia barely comprehends the dimension of this news but Uncle Vince has lived through the horror of this friendship before and his body starts to shake.

The train to Warsaw is already more than full but Danusia and Zbyszek are still on the platform. Uncle Vince with his hands outstretched, his eyes full of despair and determination, cries imploringly. "People! Take pity on these children! They must go home to their parents!"

His desperate voice with the melodic Vilnius accent penetrates the corridor of the train and people react. Some make an effort to move inside, others stick to the side to make room for the children. A large elderly man grabs Danusia's hand and pulls her inside. Someone else pushes Zbyszek from behind. Dear Uncle Vince stands still, his gray hair flyaway, his deep blue eyes slowly swelling with tears.

"Give a big hug to your father. Tell him we are waiting for all of you next year. And don't forget to bring your mother with you! I am going to call your home and let them know that you are on your way." As he yells, a calm comes over him and the hysterical fear of the future slowly eases out. They all will come back next year. Why shouldn't they? He probably overreacted with this newspaper.

"Uncle Vince, don't call! We will find our way home in Warsaw. And it's going to be fun to surprise them like that. They don't expect us until next week. Don't call, please!" Zbyszek and Danusia lean forward but the train is already moving. The big man pulls hard and the heavy door slams shut.

* * * *

Konrad creeps into the house and all of a sudden jumps out at Danusia: "Here I am, Grandma!"

"Oh! You always scare me like that." She smiles.

"Even though I do it every day, you're still scared." He takes off his school book-bag.

"So, how was your presentation today?" Danusia asks.

"Okay, I guess." He shrugs.

"Aren't you satisfied?" She scrutinizes him. "What happened? You have worked so hard on it. Why aren't you satisfied?"

"Well, the kids didn't know anything about Piłsudski, they never heard of him."

"So, now they know, right?"

"Yes, but the teacher didn't know anything about him either. And even worse.... You know, Grandma, what they say?" Konrad looks at her with disbelief and sad exasperation. "They say that World War II started in 1941. I just don't understand that, I just don't, you know? It's as if the invasion of Poland didn't really happen!"

"Oh, don't be so upset." Danusia gently touches his golden hair. "You see America joined the war in 1941. That is why to many the war started in 1941. It's just their perspective here."

"But the schoolbooks also talk about 1941 as the beginning of World War II. And no one knows anything about the invasion of Poland. It's as if no one cares about it; it's not important." He waves his hands in an aggravated gesture. "You know Grandma, I need to know why is it that to us the German invasion of Poland started World War II? Is it because we look only at what happens to us? Or is there another reason why people use this date as the beginning of the World War II?"

"Well, there is a historic reason for it, Konrad. But it is not that easy. It requires certain historical perspective." Danusia moves around the kitchen. "But if you want, I can explain it to you—but on one condition, okay? You must skip your cartoon movie today."

He sighs. "I really have to know...."

"Sit down, then." She puts a bowl of freshly cooked chicken soup sprinkled with aromatic dill in front of him. "What does it mean a 'world war'? It simply means a global conflict, right? From this perspective, two important events took place as a result of the German aggression on Poland on September 1, 1939. In the West, France and Great Britain formally declared war on Germany while in the East the Soviet Union invaded Poland. You must also remember that the countries loyal to Great Britain such as Australia, New Zealand, Canada, and South Africa followed in Great Britain's footsteps and also declared war on Germany.[7] Remember also that the Soviets at that time were engaged in the conflict with Japan in Mongolia. So, the 1939 invasion of Poland in fact linked France, Germany, Poland, the USSR, Japan, and Great Britain with all the British territories in one global military conflict. That is why the historians chose September 1, 1939, as the official beginning of the global conflict known as World War II."

"I think, Grandma, that the Polish determination to fight and not to surrender brought this result, don't you think so?" His blue eyes stare at her intensely.

"Probably indirectly—yes," she replies, weighing words carefully. "But what does that mean, Konrad? Are you proud that because of us a world war started?"

"No," he replies perplexed. "I don't mean that. I mean that... that...," he nervously scratches his head, "I mean that I am proud that we never surrendered to either the Germans or the Russians, and that we never allied ourselves with either of these villains no matter what."

Danuta stares at the bowl of soup in silence. "Well, maybe you're right, you know.... Maybe we should be proud that we stood up for human dignity no matter what. Someone finally had to stand up to Hitler.... But we paid dearly for it." They both sit in silence. "But eat your *rosół*, please. It's getting cold." She moves the bowl closer to him.

"You see," Danusia continues, "when the Germans signed the Friendship Treaty with the Soviets one week before the war, the Western Powers were in state of shock. After meeting with Hitler to clarify the purpose of the pact, the British ambassador to Berlin, Henderson, 'was so wrought up he was speechless,' the *New York Times* declared. But what Henderson and the world didn't know and didn't really want to know was the secret protocol to this 'friendly' non-aggression pact. In the secret protocol, Germany and the Soviet Union blatantly agreed to support each other in dividing Europe between themselves. Paragraph two of the secret protocol from August 23 provided that with respect to the Polish State, the spheres of influence of Germany and the Soviet Union would be established along the Vistula, Narew and San rivers.[8] This line was drawn through the heart of Poland...." Danusia sighs and pauses for a moment.

"The two assailants didn't care about the West any more. Germany was confident it could take care of the French Army. As for Great Britain—no problem there. In Germany's opinion, Great Britain always preferred to use others to fight for their world domination and glory."

"You know, Grandma, I often wonder how it feels to learn that war has broken out and the enemy has invaded your country. How did it feel back then? Were you scared?"

Danusia's eyes venture somewhere far away through the window. "I was young and naïve back then. I didn't worry about myself at all. I worried only about Poland, what's going to happen to my country. That was the most important thing for all of us."

"But how about that one day when you wake up and it's a war?"

"It didn't come like a bolt from the blue. It was more of a gradual process. People were talking about the war for some time already. In fact, Hitler's original date for invading Poland was set one week earlier. That's the date when we were on the train coming back home from vacation. However at the very last moment, Hitler decided to talk with the British about his intentions. He was hoping for another gesture of acquiescence. By that time, though, the British already smelled their imminent danger and decided to demonstrate their support for Poland. On August 25, the British signed an official treaty with us declaring their readiness to help Poland in the event of a threat to our sovereignty and independence.[9] The days that followed were tense but optimistic. People truly believed that France and Great Britain would support Poland in the event of German aggression."

"Does that mean you expected the war?" Konrad fidgets in the chair.

"Yes and no. Belligerent German propaganda and terrorist attacks created a sense of imminent danger. Also, the mass mobilization that began a week before the war gave us a sense of impending peril. But after the new British guarantees, the mobilization was called off because the British insisted on it. They were desperate not to upset the Germans. So, in the last few days before the invasion, the mood was optimistic. Some people speculated that the Germans would not dare to invade. Others thought that even if they attacked, the Polish Army was strong enough to withstand the first impact to give the French and the British enough time to strike Germany from the west. It is human nature not to lose hope." Danuta pauses. The wrinkles on her forehead deepen.

"You know, Grandma, the German army at the time of the invasion of Poland had about 1.7 million soldiers in 57 divisions facing over one million Polish soldiers with about 40 divisions including reserves. Our main problem though was the length of our borders with Germany, about 2800 kilometers in the north, west, and south. They took us in their jaws. Our defense was too stretched out to withstand their concentrated attacks. The Germans had 3000 tanks in six Panzer divisions, about 1000 bombers and 1500 fighter planes. We had a well-trained air force back then, but only 400 fighter planes, mostly Mysliwce PZL[10] and we only had about 600 rather antiquated tanks but we also had state of the art anti-tank "Urugwaj" guns that effectively penetrated 33 mm thick German tanks, and very modern 37 mm Bofor guns.[11] Our real problem was that we didn't have enough reserves behind the lines. And this mobilization that you just told me about!" Konrad bites his lips. "Had we continued with mobilization after August 25, we would have been able to put up a much stronger defense!"

"Would that matter?" Danusia lowers her voice. "Eventually we would be defeated anyway, only with bigger casualties, right? You see, in the first weeks of the war it became obvious that our Western Allies had abandoned us. And then, once the Russians stabbed us in the back, all hopes were shattered, our whole world collapsed."

Konrad fixes his eyes on her. "I don't understand Grandma, why is it that our allies didn't act and that Hitler's big gamble paid off so easily? Do you know that in September of 1939 he left on his western borders only a fraction of his reserves without even a single tank and with ammunition reserves sufficient for only three days while the Allies had 90 French divisions, 3300 mostly modern tanks, and a huge advantage in the sky? While almost all German forces were fighting in Poland, France and Great Britain had a tremendous military advantage over Germany. For 1000 German military planes the Allies had at their disposal 3300 planes including 2200 fighters and bombers. While all German tanks were in Poland, the French kept idle their fleet of 3300 tanks on the German border. The allied superiority in the anti-aircraft defense was also tremendous. The ratio of German to French anti-aircraft artillery was 300:1600."[12]

"Well, as you probably heard, no one in the West wanted to die for Gdańsk, and no one in the West believed that such a noble action of standing up for the other partner would indeed be in their own interest or their best long-term defense." Danusia stops as her shaky hand slowly points at the TV set standing quietly nearby.

"Today again the isolationist attitude is very strong. You see Hitler was able to finish off so many countries one by one because each of these countries fought the battle in isolation. It is even more dramatic to see that today this obvious lesson is widely misinterpreted and conveniently forgotten all together."

"Yes, Grandma. But to me Poland was a very special case in Hitler's collection of captures. We were the first and the only continental country to say 'No' to Hitler."

"You are right, my dear. We put forward the strongest defense in continental Europe. And upon defeat, the resistance movement was immediately put in place. Our historic ability to organize resistance was the reason for the close cooperation of the Nazi–Soviet security forces. But despite the best efforts of these two villains, we did manage to develop by far the strongest resistance movement in the entire occupied Europe,[13] and our government-in-exile was able to organize an excellent Polish Army in the West."

"Yes, Grandma, but do you know what always worries me? I always think about the September campaign and this mobilization that was called off upon request of our allies. Had we continued with full mobilization we would have staged a better defense. We could have evacuated more soldiers through the south and avoid the Soviet gulags and Katyń. People were determined to fight no matter what. We easily exceeded our initial objective to hold the Germans for up to two weeks. Our forces continued fighting long after the Soviet invasion. Warsaw was fighting until October, our last regular unit capitulated at Kock on October 6, and the Hubal Light Cavalry continued fighting on their own for six more months."

"Well, it's hard to speculate, Konrad. Today we know that just before invading Poland Hitler instructed his officers to be very brutal, with no room for pity, that they should aim for the total destruction of Poland. In his system of values the stronger man was always right.[14] And the Germans responded to his call very well. You cannot even imagine how aggressive and brutal the invaders were. Their strategy was to destroy the brain and the heart of the nation, their target was the population at large, not just soldiers but everybody—women, children, elderly, and above all the intelligentsia—in order to annihilate our spiritual and cultural identity.[15] It was the meticulous calculated genocide of the nation." Danusia closes her eyes. The image of a puffed-up SS soldier in tall black boots yelling "*Raus! Raus!*" with a barking attack dog held on leash haunts her nightmares even today.

"Many history books ridicule our defense campaign and portray the Polish horse army as reckless in the fight against the mighty German tanks and their brilliant lightning war," Konrad sighs.

"You are right. The Nazi propaganda was so effective that their cynical interpretation lingers in the West to this day. Let me give you an example how it was done." Danusia ponders, scratching her forehead. "In the first day of the invasion, two Polish Cavalry squadrons under Colonel Mastelarz mounted a saber charge against a German infantry battalion in Tuchola Forest. Just as they wiped out the German infantry, the German armored unit arrived and killed about twenty Poles. The next day the Italian war correspondent was brought to the scene and told that the Polish troopers were killed while charging the German tanks. The German subsequently perpetuated this myth in their propaganda to illustrate to the world Polish backwardness[16] and create the image of the Germans' swift defeat of Poland."

"You know, Grandma, I truly believe that our army did have a chance to resist the Germans. It was only because of the Soviets stabbing us in the back that we were not able to fight back the Germans."

Danusia nods. "One thing that we tend to overlook is the significance of German propaganda power. You know, Konrad, I believe that it was not so much the German military power but the German propaganda power that led to the defeat of Poland. By skillfully masterminding the image of the rapid collapse of the Polish Army, the fifth strongest army in Europe at that time, the Germans manipulated Western opinion into the conclusion that it was too late to help Poland and that the Germans were too strong to fight against. This brilliant propaganda war aimed at Poland's allies was Hitler's greatest victory because it was through this propaganda that he overpowered France and Britain and attracted Stalin to his side."

"Yes, yes," Konrad concurs, "apparently Stalin was sitting on the sidelines, waiting to see whether the West would act. It was only when he realized that the West would not attack Germany that he decided to join Hitler in killing Poland.[17] In ordering the invasion, Stalin took advantage of German propaganda and claimed to the world that Poland collapsed. Therefore, he was compelled to move in to protect the minorities. In reality, however, Poland did not collapse at the time of the Soviet invasion but rather the country was in the process of implementing the second stage of its defense strategy, reorganizing its forces along the shortened defense line in the east. It's true that initially the Germans were able to move fast through the weakest spots of our border defense, destroying roads, bridges, communication centers, energy reserves, and killing thousands in the process. But our defense plans were focused around the second stage of the defense campaign. In that second stage, Poland would have an advantage over the Germans because our army was more maneuverable and could better operate in the familiar terrain, despite destroyed roads and bridges. Also our reserves were mobilized by then. But you know what I realized, Grandma? Our shortened defense line happened to be almost identical to the Ribbentrop–Molotov partition line.

A light smile shows on Danusia's wrinkled face. "You love to analyze these battles, don't you? Luckily, you can just learn about these strategies. I had to live through them." Danusia's thoughts venture back to Warsaw. Not many of her friends live in Warsaw today. Only her oldest son, Jędruś, still lives in the suburbs of Warsaw. The place is called *Radość*, meaning "joy."

6. Danusia and Konrad, Winter 2001, Ohio

7. Polish Tanks

8. Polish Fighter PZL P. 11

9. Army Cooperation Aircraft PZL Karaś

10. 37 mm Bofors Gun

4

Jasia puts the finishing touches on Mrs. Sowińska's fancy coiffure while a loud knocking interrupts her work and old Gara bursts in, hardly able to catch his breath. "What happened, Mr. Gara?"

"They are coming, they are coming!" Mr. Gara stutters, looking at her in quite a state. "I mean Danusia and Zbyszek are coming. Someone has just called from Wilno, the elderly man, probably the uncle. The children are already on the train."

"Thank God! Oh, Lord, You heard my prayer!" Jasia folds her hands the gesture of thanksgiving.

"Oh, I am so glad for you, Jasia." Mrs. Sowińska adjusts her thick curls and gets up. "You see! I told you not to worry. Here they come." She hands Jasia a five zloty bill. "No change, please. Thanks for everything. I'll call you later," she says in her thick German accent and hugs Jasia gently.

"That's too much, wait!"

"Don't worry, my dear." Mrs. Sowińska heads to the door. "Are they on the morning express?"

"I think this is this later Wilno Express," old Gara replies. "They should be here at around 8 PM."

Indeed, the express from Wilno is scheduled to arrive at 8:30 PM Jasia and Alek mix with the anxious crowd at the train station. Many younger and older couples nervously pace back and forth. It looks as if all of them are waiting for their children coming home from vacation. 8:30 passes by and there is no sign of the train. Five, then ten more minutes pass by and nothing happens. Just before 8:45 PM, the loud speaker announces a one-hour delay for the Wilno express. What's happened? Hopefully nothing unusual. The eastern part of the country has been relatively stable. But there are so many rumors lately. And this news about the Germans and the Soviets coming together—anything may happen now.

All these fearful thoughts rush upon Jasia's mind. She squeezes Alek's arm and leans against him. No, no sabotage! They just said only a one-hour delay. That's normal. The weather, probably. Jasia's mind is racing.

"Let's go for a walk outside," Alek suggests. They leave the station and walk along Aleje Jerozolimskie. The evening is warm and pleasant. Bright lights spilling from small elegant shop windows calm them down. But in fifteen minutes they are back at the railway station. Alek checks the information window. The train is expected as announced. A couple more nervous minutes and Alek detects a bright light in the distance. The Wilno express slowly enters the station. Jasia and Alek are ecstatic. A huge wave of people pours out from the train. Where are they? Which direction to go?

It doesn't matter. Danusia had already spotted them as the train passed through the station. She later lost them in the crowd behind. But now they are back together again—for good, for bad, and forever.

"It's so wonderful to be back home," Danusia throws her arms around Mama. Zbyszek can't stop asking questions. Dad also wants to know everything, what happened after he left, about their stay at Uncle Józef's, and about the journey home. Before they know it, Mr. Gara hugs them at the door. His shiny jovial face with bushy hair is very dear to them.

"Thank God, you are back!" he almost jumps with happiness. "We all have been missing you so much! Everybody is asking about you, Wanda, Hania, Janka, Sylwek, and Bruno. They can't wait to see you."

"Yes, yes, but we are first in line," Jasia replies, giving him a friendly pat.

Danusia and Zbyszek look around curiously. It seems as if everything has changed slightly. Bushes around the house are bigger, flowers on the windows are different, and the kitchen has been repainted. Even Mama looks slightly different, a little heavier and a little older. They walk around the house, dizzy with exhaustion and excitement. In the bedroom, two brand new book bags and two piles of notebooks, crayons and school uniforms await them.

"I did some shopping for you," Mama announces proudly. "But leave it for later. First, go and wash your hands. I prepared your favorite supper today."

Indeed, a huge plate of steaming *kopytka* with fried bacon arrives at the table.

"But leave some room for desert. We have something special for you," Dad cautions them.

Danusia looks around. On the kitchen cabinet she finds a small package with the familiar napkin on the top of it.

"Oh, *pączki* from Blikle! Hurrah!" she shouts.

The evening goes by quickly. They drink tea, eat juicy *pączki* and talk long into the night until Mama intervenes and orders everybody to bed. "Tomorrow is another day."

They wake up late. Around noon the radio announces that Great Britain has offered security guarantees to Poland. Overnight the political dynamics have changed and with it the mood in Poland. The Western Allies will stand up for us. With their support we don't need to worry. Dad is particularly delighted. He has been following the news for a while and this is, in his opinion, the critical breakthrough. Now the Germans will not dare risk a global conflict.

"Jasia, you may stop drying bread," he concludes. "We are not going to have any war."

For the past two weeks, Jasia has been stocking up bags of dried bread in preparation for war. After visiting his friends, Zbyszek comes home with the news that the general mobilization has been called off.

The popular euphoria is short-lived, though. Only one day later, the radio reports on another serious German provocation. A small German military detachment broke through the Polish borders in the south, attacked a train station, a bridge, and a tunnel near *Przełęcz Jabłonkowska*. One of the captured Germans contends that Germany has started the war with Poland. The German media are again full of aggressive accusations against Poland for its barbaric mistreatment of German minorities.[1]

"Something is not right," Alek strikes his fist on the table. "We even called off mobilization not to provoke the Germans. And now all this baloney about Polish attacks on poor Germans on the one hand and this lunatic who thinks that Germany is at war with us on the other hand. It doesn't look good."

"Don't worry, Alek. There is a lot of confusion around. Everything will calm down in a couple of days." Mama stands behind Dad, combing his dark thick hair with her slim fingers. "Looks like you're due for haircut, my dear."

"Not yet." He gets up. "Where are the kids, do you know?"

"They will be back soon. They went to the club, I think."

"You know, we should stock up more food and not only bread. Maybe potatoes and kasha, too. And it would be good to buy coal or at least get some wood for emergency supplies for winter." He grabs his suitcase full of specialty tools. "I'll be back later," he bids adieu and is out the door.

"Another false alarm," Mama yells after him.

Lately Dad's mood changes every hour. At one point he was ready to go to Brasław to pick up the kids. Another time he was delighted with the war scare because he could earn extra money as a radio technician. The demand for his expertise has skyrocketed recently. One day, he read about the latest models of the Polish airplane fighters and was ecstatic. The other day, he read how the Germans treated the Poles in Gdańsk and was furious. Mama can't stand his mood swings anymore.

"Mama, listen to this," Danusia bursts into the room like a hurricane. "You know this friend of mine, Basia? She lives down the river, near the park. Can you imagine she is getting married! She is only one year older than I. Oh, my God! Can you imagine?"

"How do you know about that?"

"Oh, I've just seen her. She told me she would be sending wedding invitations soon. The wedding will be in October. I don't know her boy friend. He is from Wola.[2] Oh, that's exciting!"

"What's so exciting? War is around the corner and she is getting married. That doesn't sound like a lot of fun to me," Mama replies with grim face. "And where is Zbyszek? Have you seen him? I sent him to do some shopping three hours ago."

"No, I haven't seen him, but don't worry. He is probably talking with his buddies somewhere here. That's right. He's there." Danusia sticks her head out the window and waves. "Hey, Zbyszek, come home, Mama needs you!"

"Here you are, after all these hours." Irritated, Mama frantically grabs Zbyszek's bags and throws several loaves of deliciously aromatic bread with a shiny crunchy golden crust on the table.

"Now sit down and cut all these loaves into small slices. And you, too, Danusia," she orders flatly. "Dad thinks we need to stockpile more food."

"What for...?" an astonished Zbyszek asks in vain.

"But, Mama," Danusia cries, "I want to write a letter now. I promised this officer I told you about that I would write him right away."

"Oh, that reminds me of something! We have to write to Uncle Vince. We need to thank them for their hospitality and everything they did for you in the summer. Okay, Zbyszek, you start cutting bread, and Danusia, you write to Uncle Vince."

Danusia stays up late that night. Slices of bread on sheets of paper are spread all over the floor, a thick letter to Uncle Vince is ready, and everyone is asleep. Finally, she can write to Julian freely and without interruption.

Julian! She thinks about him all the time. The handsome officer is omnipresent. "My dearest Julian!" she starts writing. In moments of hope, like the recent news about the British guarantees, she envisions Julian arriving in Warsaw to study at the University of Warsaw. In moments of despair, like today's slicing of bread in preparation for war, her mind becomes paralyzed, her ability to think about the future disappears, and some strange scenes from the recent past come vividly to life.

The expression on Uncle Vince's face as he read the newspaper at the train station in Wilno sticks in her memory, giving her butterflies in the stomach. That picture from Witold's newspaper "Forbidden to Dogs and Poles" often reappears in her mind and causes her to flush hotly. She doesn't even want to look at the newspapers anymore but the headlines are all over and all are trumpeting about the war. And all these people around. They only talk about the war. It's disgusting. Her whole soul screams: Stop it now! Just stop it, you fools!

At last, her eyes land on the brand new book bags casually thrown into the corner of the room. School, school.... After all, school starts next week. The new school year always starts on the first day of September but this year that magic date falls on a Friday. So, the first day of school has been moved to Monday, September 4. Why not Friday, September 1, like always? At least we could say hello to each other on Friday. She picks up the book bag from the floor and gently looks it over. Next year she will get her diploma. Then she could even get married, like Basia. But now she needs to make sure that Julian will come to Warsaw this year. The academic year starts in October. Just enough time to arrange for everything. She quietly returns to the table and vigorously starts writing. For an hour or so she moves the pen across the paper without interruption. Late that night, she folds the paper and addresses the envelope from memory: "Korzeniowskiego 25, Zbaraż." That's right!

Over the next few days, the war of nerves is in full swing. Germany makes outright demands for annexation of Gdańsk and the so-called corridor. The Polish newspapers trumpet non-stop that Great Britain and France stand firmly in their commitment to support Poland. The impressive superiority of the British Navy over the German Navy is examined at length in every newspaper. The crushing comparisons of the combined military power of Poland, Britain, and France versus the Germans are on everyone's mind. Together we must succeed, the thinking goes. On August 29, the news breaks that Hitler has accepted the British Government's offer for direct talks with Poland on the peaceful resolution of the conflict.[3] On the streets of Warsaw the mood is mixed. Direct talks? Negotiations? That's a cruel joke. The Allies want to sell us down the river like they sold Czechoslovakia, for their illusory peace. We cannot give up our access to the Baltic Sea. That's our sea, that's always been our sea, that's not only our window to the world, that's our security, that's the main route for receiving critical military supplies from the West, that's our lifeblood.

On August 30, Lipski, the Polish Ambassador in Berlin, calls Ribbentrop and informs him that the Polish Government has accepted the British proposal for direct discussions between Warsaw and Berlin.

"Do you have full powers to treat with us?" Ribbentrop asks.

"No," Lipski replies.

"Then it is completely useless to discuss the matter further," Ribbentrop ends the discussion.

The next day the Polish High Commander, Marshal Rydz-Śmigły, reorders a general mobilization. On the same day, August 31, at 5 PM, General Gerd von Rundstedt in charge of German Army Group South receives the encrypted order: "Y=1.9.0445."[4] Late in the evening, a nervous voice aggressively interrupts the Radio Gliwice program and speaking in broken Polish calls on the people of the border region of Silesia to take up arms against the Nazis. The Gliwice provocation sets the stage for World War II.[5]

* * * *

An old owl readies for sleep. Its neighbors—pelicans, eagles and herons—are slowly waking up. From its favorite branch near the top of a tree, the owl overlooks the Vistula River. The first rays of the sun shine through the morning mist. On the opposite bank of the river, the ancient city is asleep. Daylight slowly unveils the contours of the Old Town, the Cathedral, King's Palace, King Zygmunt's Column, Saint Ann's Church, Kierbedzia Bridge, and Danusia's house. The current in the wide bed of the Vistula River is as serene as the city above. Only in the background of this leisurely silence a deadly sound grows. No one here has ever heard such a mysterious sound.

As the owl is about to close its goggle eyes, something inconceivable happens. A thundering and crashing of unimaginable force cuts through the air and a fountain of water splashes and shoots high into the sky. Another fountain bursts into the air before the first one reaches the water, and another one, and another one. The ferocious noise, hundreds of times louder than any thunderstorm, strikes the resting town.

Danusia jumps out of bed. Mama and Dad and Zbyszek are already up. In the fierce stream of booms, something crashes over their heads. The window glass quivers and trembles.

"To the basement! Run!" Dad shouts. Still half asleep, they rush out the door and down to the basement. "Germans! German bombers! They hit the bridge!" someone shouts behind them. The staircase is jammed. People run, push, scream, and shout in panic, children cry and scream. Danusia is among the first to reach the basement and the incoming crowd pushes her further to the wall. She realizes she is only in pajamas but it doesn't matter. Others are in pajamas, too. In the rumbling background of the warm morning, immense bomb blasts and explosions, single ones as well as several at a time, pierce the air around them. The basement is full. Most of the people freeze and stare speechlessly at the ceiling. Some cry, some can't stop wailing.

"They are going after the bridges," a young voice resounds in the crowd. "And after the airport, I think," someone else comments. "Sons of bitches!" another voice shouts with fury.

"War, war...," Danusia feverishly turns this strange thought over and over in her mind.

Dad embraces her with his muscular arm. "Thank God we are on the first floor. It's closer to the basement and a little safer."

"Shh! Did you hear that distinct series of blasts?" Mr. Tołłoczko yells. "That's our anti-aircraft defense! Our boys are getting at them!" Tołłoczko oversees the security unit at the State Mint. By training, he is a professional soldier, "the Captain," as they call him here. His beautiful daughter, Wanda, is Danusia's age.

"All right! Good job!" the business manager, Falski, enthusiastically welcomes the news. "Our artillery is stationed near us at Cytadela," Falski adds. His son, Bruno, is one of Zbyszek's best friends. Bruno is well-prepared for this emergency, holding his dog under one arm and his precious collection of postage stamps in the other hand.

"Alek, we need to know what's going on," Mr. Owczarek turns to Dad with urgency in his voice. "Is there any way you can get your radio here?" Owczarek is the technical director and Dad's immediate boss at the State Mint.

The blasts slowly ease up. It seems as if the cannonade of bombardments is no longer over their heads. Despite Mama's protests, Dad jumps out of the basement and with lightning speed returns with a small strange object. It's a special emergency radio. As the blare of bombardment fades away, the basement fugitives surround Dad tightly.

"As we speak, the German Luftwaffe is attacking strategic Warsaw locations," the radio reports. "Okęcie Airport and Warsaw bridges have been the primary targets as of this hour. Our anti-aircraft defense forces supported by brilliant air fighters from the Warsaw Pursuit Brigade stage a formidable defense. Already several German airplanes have been brought down. Stefan Starzyński, President of Warsaw, has been appointed the Commissar for Civil Defense of the City of Warsaw. Please stay tuned. In five minutes President Starzyński will be addressing the people of Warsaw." Powerful and deeply treasured piano notes replace the speaker's distant voice. The dramatic chords of Chopin's *Revolutionary Etude* arouse its listeners' burning fury.

"Let's man our posts!" young Sylwek Kotecki yells. "God give us strength!" Mrs. Kotecka cries. "We'll show them!" Bruno supports Sylwek. "Shut up!" Captain Tołłoczko silences them fiercely. "Listen now!" he orders. The powerful music slowly fades away.

Dear Compatriots!

This is the President of Warsaw speaking. This morning German Armed Forces unleashed a vicious attack on our country, invaded our territory from the north, south and west, and dropped bombs on Warsaw. The whole nation is rising to fight! Together we shall stand to defend our country and our capital! Together we shall succeed! I call upon all the citizens of Warsaw to join me in defending our beloved town. Warsaw needs each and every one of us. Today Warsaw needs our courage, our commitment, and our sacrifice! God bless you in this yet another call for sacrifice to defend Warsaw and protect Poland!

The energetic, inspiring voice of President Starzyński sinks deeply into the minds and hearts of the listeners. The radio presenter returns: "On this station, President Starzyński will be addressing Warsawians on a regular basis. Please tune in for updates at the full hour intervals."

As the blasts and rolls of bombardment fade away, the mood in the basement improves. "Our armed forces are well prepared for the attack. With the mass support of the people, we will succeed," a confident male voice proclaims. "And the Western Allies should attack from the West any day," someone else adds. One by one, the residents decide to leave the shelter, looking timidly around.

The warm and sunny morning welcomes them as if nothing tragic has happened. There is no damage in their immediate vicinity. Only the distant roar reminds them of the recent drama. The sense of urgency to organize the defense of the city is everywhere. The State Mint employees are called for the emergency meeting. A big radio is placed on the reception desk and old Gara is charged with the task of following the news around the clock. Children wander around excited and confused. In the afternoon, the radio broadcasts an appeal from the Scouts Commander. All Scouts are called upon to report to their leaders. They will be assigned special tasks in preparation for the defense of the city. Appeals from the Red Cross are broadcast next. They also need volunteers. Danusia and Zbyszek are ready to report. Mama tries to stop them but in vain. All the children go....

The day is hectic and tense. People run around, plan, organize, and pack. Gas masks are distributed. The President orders a total blackout of the city. After dusk, there should be not a chink of light anywhere. Blackout curtains are mandated. Some use heavy fabrics to cover windows, others construct rigid screens and bolt them onto the window frames. Merchants are especially busy. They frantically stock up on extra supplies and try to protect their shop-windows from shattering because of the bomb blasts. They plaster and tape the windows with paper and cover them up with sandbags.

Around noon, the radio reports that the first German airplane was been shot down at 7 AM near Olkusz. Pilot Władysław Gnyś from the Kraków Air Force Squadron is credited with this accomplishment. In the evening, the radio reports that according to Polish estimates, about 100 German fighters attacked Warsaw that day. Against them Poland effectively used 54 fighters from the Air Force Pursuit Brigade and anti-aircraft artillery. Fourteen German planes were brought down during the morning attack on Warsaw.[6]

Danusia comes back home with the first aid kit. Zbyszek stays outside with a group of friends. They talk late into the evening, disregarding repeated calls from the parents. Finally Dad forces Zbyszek to come home. "You must do what I tell you to do, no questions asked! You understand!"

"But Dad, I have some responsibility now. We, the Scouts, are in charge of distributing messages in case there's any communication break down. I have to know all places and all locations by heart."

"Zbyś, I want you to stay home with us!" Mama cries.

"Well, I may as well be hit here at home with you or somewhere on the road. The chances are the same," Zbyszek replies stubbornly, upset.

"But at least we will be together!" Mama replies with despair in her voice.

"You know, Jasia, I am afraid he may be right," Dad appears to be frustrated. "There is no guarantee of safety by staying home. We may be easily killed here while he may be saved out there by moving around."

"You are only partially right," Mama argues. "Knowing Zbyszek, he will be attracted to heavy fighting and the most dangerous places. He just looks for trouble!"

"But you can't lock him up while all his friends are out there with the Scouts."

Mama sends Dad a furious look and turns around. Swallowing her tears, she affectionately hugs Zbyszek and whispers: "Zbysiu, you must be careful, I beg you to be very, very careful now."

The next morning, loud and abrupt pounding at the door wakes them up. It's old Gara. Running from door to door, he knocks, pounds and shouts: "To the shelter, run to the shelter! Take shelter immediately!"

As they all run downstairs, the voice on the radio from the reception desk follows them: ATTENTION! I DECLARE ALERT FOR THE CITY OF WARSAW!

The grim voice repeats the message over and over again: I DECLARE ALERT FOR THE CITY OF WARSAW!

A quick look at the sky. No signs of the planes yet. But the ominous deadly whir already hangs in the air. All the residents jam into the basement. The roll outside intensifies. Soon they can recognize the sinister whistling of falling bombs just before the worst explosions. These are the echoes of the closest hits. The people in the shelter pray together and cheer every indication of Polish anti-aircraft artillery action.

In about an hour, the thunder stops and the radio calls off the raid alert. But during the day, the alerts come back many times. With every passing raid, the people are less confused, though. They already know what to expect and quickly learn how to cope with the alerts. Without even noticing, they gradually adjust to this new way of living.

On the third day of the bombardment, the anxiously awaited news finally comes. Great Britain and France declared war on Germany![7] Now it's a matter of weeks or maybe even days to finish off the aggressors! The mood is vivacious. People on the streets shake hands, kiss and congratulate each other. The mighty Royal Air Force (RAF), the most powerful air force in the world, will come to their rescue any moment now. Dad is ecstatic.

"We only need to hold our ground for another two weeks and this whole war business will be over," he proclaims at the dinner table. "It shouldn't be difficult."

"The city is well fortified," Zbyszek declares proudly.

"The civilian defense is also well staffed," Dad adds. "The delay in general mobilization helps Warsaw now. Many reservists, who were sent home when the mobilization was called off, now eagerly join the Civil Defense forces.

"You see, Dad, you were upset for not being included in the mobilization. It turns out that those who were supposed to report to the army didn't go to the front anyway," Zbyszek points out resolutely. "And now you are in the military anyhow."

"You're right, Son. Now, all the State Mint employees are under the command of Captain Tołłoczko."

"I think," Zbyszek debates with fervor, "that the British Air Force will come first and the French ground offensive will soon follow!"

"I hope so, but why do they wait?" Dad shakes his head with concern. "But, Jasia! If I am not mistaken, tomorrow is the first day of school. Do you know what the radio is saying about that?"

"Not much, unfortunately," Mama replies. "All day the radio only talks about the British declaration of war or the military action on the front. But I think they have recommended that each school make its own decision whether and when to start. And besides, we don't know how heavy the fighting will be tomorrow."

"Is there any shelter, basement or cellar in their schools, do you know?"

"No, but I'll go with them to see what the whole situation looks like," Mama replies. "The children are ready. But I think it would be prudent to postpone school if this horror is to end soon."

That night no one gets any sleep. The air raid alerts are called on and off at regular intervals. On the staircase, throngs move back and forth all night. The attacks are fierce and frequent. In the dense darkness of the night, the roars, blasts, and explosions are much more frightening, too. They are terrifying.

"Apparently, the Germans are infuriated by the action of the Western Allies," Mr. Staniszewski concludes after one of the bigger explosions. "Not only that," Captain Tołłoczko adds, "in the night, our anti-aircraft defense is less effective. I am afraid we may see more of these nightly attacks."

"But it also means the Germans are afraid of our artillery," one of the boys observes.

The following sunny morning brings the first day of school. Danusia is anxious to go and meet all of her friends and teachers. The morning seems quiet and safe enough to make the short trip. Danusia is so excited that she leaves Mama and Zbyszek behind and runs ahead. As they pass through the streets, they are shocked by the extent of damage in the neighborhood. Several houses are ruined. Emergency vehicles and medical personnel maneuver around with difficulty. The streets are damaged as well. But the private gymnasium "Wspólnota" on Miodowa Street is untouched.

Danusia reaches the school first. Not many people hang around outside. She walks into the building. A big group of students and teachers stands close together in the hallway. Some hold hands, some cry, some hug each other in grief. Quietly, she approaches the group. One of the teachers, an older lady, puts her arm around Danusia and embraces her warmly.

"What happened?" Danusia whispers.

"The school principal was killed last night," the woman replies in a shaky voice. "And another teacher was killed on Saturday," she adds.

Danusia freezes. A shiver of fear rushes through her body. This is the first time she learns that someone she knew has been killed. The woman rubs her shoulders. "We won't have any classes today. But let's see what the assistant principal will say." Mama and Zbyszek join the group, looking curiously at Danusia. She reaches out to them in tears.

"Dear students," a strong female voice grabs everyone's attention. "Thank you for coming today in blank defiance of the aggressors' terror! Your commitment to school is your way to stand up for Poland. Always remember that education is yet another way to fight the aggressors!" She stops, takes a deep breath, and continues in a strained voice. "It is my sad duty to report to you that our principal, the greatest leader this school ever had and our best friend," she chokes, "has been killed in the nightly bombardment." Loud sobbing spreads throughout the hallway. She ponders for a moment and continues in a more commanding voice. "It is further my sad duty to inform you that in the Saturday's air raid one of our great teachers has been killed, too…." Her voice breaks down. "But remember! We must be strong and together we shall continue their mission! We must preserve the legacy of those two remarkable women who left us so in such an untimely and tragic manner…. Now, I would like to ask Sister Emily to lead us in prayer for the souls of those two extraordinary members of our community." The students kneel and the passionate prayer mixed with prolonged moments of silence rolls through the old historical building.

"In light of these tragic losses in our school," the assistant principal says after the prayer, "and taking into consideration the latest developments, in particular the French and British declaration of war on Germany, I have therefore decided to postpone the beginning of the school year. Please report to school next Monday. Thank you, God bless you, and God bless Poland!" She rushes to finish the speech, holding back tears.

Danusia mingles with the crowd. She desperately wants to talk more with her friends but Mama pulls her out.

"We must hurry. It's not that safe here." She grabs Danusia's hand, calls on Zbyszek and rushes out. On the way home, Danusia thinks about those teachers, that extraordinary prayer, and those bombs.... They really kill!

"Remember, you must always take shelter in an air raid," Mama shouts out of the blue. The children understand. Their thoughts also wander back to these barbaric killings.

At home, old Gara is engaged in a loud debate with a group of teenaged boys. He tries to prove to the boys that the phone still works. He dials different numbers but each time he dials the phone is completely dead.

"That's not our fault. Our phone is working. It must be the other side that is disconnected," he tries to convince the boys.

"Okay, okay, we need to contact our leader anyway," a boy with a scout scarf around his neck and reddish sticky hair concludes. "Hey, Zbyszek! Are you going with us? We need to report to the Scout Command. The phones are not working."

"No! He can't go now!" Mama snaps back, holding Zbyszek's hand tightly.

During the day several raid alerts are called. People spend more time in the shelters. Anti-aircraft artillery brigades are enforced. A group of sappers delegated to the defense of the railroad bridge takes u[residence in the common room at the State Mint. The Scouts organize a kitchen and provide food to the soldiers. Electricity is down. Old kerosene or carbide lamps are in great demand.

To make matters worse, news from the frontline is devastating. The Polish Army has lost the border battle and is in the process of withdrawing to the shorter defense line in the East behind the Vistula, Narew and San rivers. The Pomorze Army in the North has been encircled and cut off. However, several divisions under the command of General Sosnkowski continue to fight, breaking through the ring as the Germans try to close in on them. In the South, the Kraków Army and Karpaty Army have been split by the Germans' fast-moving motorized and armored divisions enforced by heavy air power.[8] In fact, German air power consisting of two thousand airplanes including 1,640 modern bombers, dive-bombers, and transporters against about four hundred Polish planes including less than 200 fighters, turns out to be the decisive factor in the German success. This "flying artillery" has been used to deliver pointed bomb attacks at the crucial stages of the offensive. Also, it has been used to effectively penetrate strategic targets behind the frontline and deep into Poland, easily reaching Warsaw and other strategic locations. The anxiously awaited Allied help from the powerful British Royal Air Force totaling 3,600 aircraft has not come, as the British debate....

The only good news comes from Gdańsk. The heroic defense of the Polish Post Office in Gdańsk becomes a sacred symbol for the Poles. The Military Repository at Westerplatte on the Baltic Sea with 180 soldiers under the command of Henryk Sucharski has staged a heroic defense. Also Admiral Unruch with his small group still fights at Hell peninsula.[9] The sheer notion that Gdańsk still fights heartens the Polish people.

The first week of the war ends with rumors that the Polish Government is about to evacuate from Warsaw. On September 7, the radio announces that Marshal Rydz-Śmigły and other top officials have left Warsaw and moved east toward Brześć on the Bug River.[10] The Polish Army is in the process of reorganizing in the southeastern part of the country. Hence, all reservists are requested to proceed east to report to the army there. The southeastern part of Poland is covered with forests and marshes that would render German armored divisions and tanks virtually useless and give the advantage to the highly maneuverable Polish forces. The defense of this territory by infantry and cavalry should be very effective. Furthermore, promised weapons from the West, including modern airplanes such as Hurricanes, are expected to arrive through Rumania any day now.[11]

While the Polish Army regroups in the East, all Warsawians are called upon to strengthen fortifications and barricades around the city. President Starzyński announces that civilians who have the means to travel and are not taking part in the fortification works are advised to leave the city.

Warsawians are in a panic. Marshal Rydz-Śmigły has left the city, all men have been summoned to join the army in the East, and the enemy is approaching. The people don't realize yet that their cherished anti-aircraft artillery brigade that has been so bravely and vigorously defending the city, bringing down many enemy planes, will soon be ordered to withdraw east, leaving the city virtually defenseless against the devastating air raids of the Luftwaffe bombers.

Many reservists decide to go east to join the regrouping army; crowds of women with children leave the city in search of shelter in the countryside. Busy roads around Warsaw offer excellent prey for bloodthirsty Luftwaffe dive-bombers and low-flying fighters with machine-guns. Any hopes for resuming school and normal life become more distant with every passing hour.

Danusia's family decides to stay in Warsaw. Dad must defend the State Mint and Mama doesn't want to go anywhere. The State Mint has one of the best bunkers in town. In the worst-case scenario, they can take shelter in the bunker. Zbyszek spends most of his time running around as a messenger. It turns out that his new profession is very profitable. He frequently brings home fresh bread or potatoes.

One day while making his usual trip through the neighborhoods, he notices colorful candies scattered all over on the streets. Several small kids run around picking them up. What's that? The candies wrapped in brightly colored paper look delicious. He picks up several and hastily puts them in his pocket. "It's going to be my surprise treat for supper," he thinks and rushes to his next destination. The message he carries that day from one barricade to another is very disturbing. The German 4th Armored Division advances towards Warsaw and is expected to reach the city at daybreak tomorrow. The fortifications must be ready.

Late into the evening, Zbyszek finally reaches home. Tearfully Mama kisses his blond hair.

Grim-faced, Dad asks in an alarming voice: "Did you eat any candies today?"

"As a matter of fact, not yet…," Zbyszek replies, taken by surprise. "But…." He stops in mid-sentence, stunned by their reaction. The parents lean towards each other in relief, exhaling deeply.

"Thank God, thank God!" Mama raises her hands.

"What's the problem?" Zbyszek looks at them, confused.

"German planes have scattered poisoned candies all over the city. You must have seen some of them. They are all over the place."

Zbyszek is speechless. He tries to reach in his pocket but his hands don't move. They are simply numb from fear and anger.

"I.... I actually have these candies," he stammers out and slowly takes out a handful of the colorful candies from his pocket. "I didn't want to eat them myself, I wanted to share them with you...as a treat for our supper tonight...."

"God must be with you, my son!" Mama kisses him again.

At the supper table that night, they listen to President Starzyński: "Today German planes scatter poisoned candies all over the city. Many children are dying in pain all over Warsaw. We will take vengeance for such cruel barbaric acts! We will remember these cruel deaths of our innocent children! There is justice in the world!"

Danusia swallows hard. The colorful candies are slowly burning in the stove.

"We must fight these mad murderers! We must prevail! Otherwise, they will destroy the human race!" President Starzyński finishes his speech.

"Tomorrow the German artillery will storm Warsaw," Zbyszek says.

"Yes, we heard about it," Dad replies. "I am afraid the bombardment will also intensify. Jasia, you and Danusia will need to take shelter in the bunker."

The German objective is to take Warsaw by storm the first day. But Warsaw stages a heroic defense. The barricades surrounding the city enforced with heavy artillery fire manage to withstand the fierce attacks of the German Armored Division. The German dive-bombers and low-flying fighters ferociously zero in on the barricades, literally tearing them apart. In the powerful blasts, the dead bodies of Polish soldiers fly high into the sky. But the Polish artillery shoots down numerous planes and devastates about eighty German tanks.[12] Losses on both sides are heavy.

Zbyszek moves around hypnotized by the bloody scenes around him. Although machineguns rattle, bullets whistles, and bombs explode all over, he doesn't feel any fear. He gazes at the horrifying scenes as if watching a movie. Everything seems surreal. Ignoring Dad's order, Danusia and Mama do not take shelter. Instead, they report to the Red

Cross to attend the wounded flooding into the hospitals and medical shelters. In the evening, they all return home safely. But the upcoming days will be even tougher.

The German *Blitzkrieg* plan to capture Warsaw in the first week of the invasion fails. A new plan takes its place. The city will be encircled. President Starzyński talks to Warsawians on a regular basis. For all practical purposes, he takes full command of the defense of Warsaw. His passionate energy and iron determination keep Warsawians' spirits high.

It is already mid-September. With despair, the people look to the sky for signs of British airplanes. They must come any moment now. We just need to hold our ground for one more day. But with each passing hour, it is tougher and tougher to withstand the assault. The lack of electricity, water, and medical supplies takes its toll. Soon the time will come when there will be a lack of food and ammunition. On September 17, instead of the British planes, horrifying news strikes the desperate city under siege: the Soviet Army has invaded Poland from the east![13]

"Julian!" Danusia thinks instantly. What will happen to Julian? Until now she hasn't been worrying about him that much. The border troops in the East were the only units not directly engaged in combat against Germans. She is still hoping to get a letter from him soon. For sure, the letter is on its way and once the bombardment stops, she will get this so anxiously awaited letter.

Alek is in a state of shock. "That is impossible! How could they?" The Russian people have always been his friends. He grew up with them, he played with them, and he sailed with them all over the world. In harmony and friendship, they coexisted for centuries near Brasław. And now they simply stabbed us in the back, like that, in blatant disregard of valid bilateral treaties. That's impossible! This must be just a mere rumor.

To invigorate the spirit of the embattled town, the radio broadcasts encouraging reports from the stunning battle near Bzura. Last week, a brave counterattack of the Polish infantry divisions under the command of General Kutrzeba decisively defeated the Germans. The Polish divisions crossed the Bzura River and began advancing towards Warsaw. The Germans called for reinforcements and heavy fighting broke out again. Parts of the Poznań and Pomorze Armies have joined forces and are on their way to give support to Warsaw. Some hope still lingers.

The residents of the State Mint are optimistic. There has been no heavy damage to the building and no one has been lost. The men under the command of Captain Tołłoczo protect the building from looting and plan defensive operations. Each evening, Danusia's family gathers at the supper table. Those moments of awaiting Zbyszek's arrival are excruciating. Mama says prayers and Dad paces fiercely back and forth. When Zbyszek finally shows up, he looks like Lucifer, his clothes dirty and torn, his face and hands full of scratches, his sweaty hair sticking up.

The evening meal becomes more problematic every day. Zbyszek brings less and less food and Mama digs deeper and deeper into her stocks of dried bread. Luckily, thanks to the old but perfectly preserved well on the premises of the State Mint, they have plenty of water. And water becomes more valuable with every passing day. To get water, people from the neighborhood stand day and night in long queues in front of the State Mint.

After supper, Zbyszek and Dad like to chat. Quietly they exchange the latest news. From time to time, they lower their voices to keep bad news away from Mama and Danusia. But this tactic always prompts their fierce objections and instant curiosity.

Today, big news hits the streets of Warsaw. Several thousand soldiers from the battle near the Bzura River near Modlin north of Warsaw broke through the German encirclement and pushed their way through to Warsaw.[14] But there is no news from the East. After the initial announcement about the Soviet invasion, there is no follow-up news. And there is no news about the Allies in the West either. Nothing, no planes, no counterattacks, no news about a delivery of arms, not even supportive statements, simply nothing. Is it a betrayal...?

But Warsaw continues fighting regardless and despite the worsening situation. The Polish airplane fighters from the Pursuit Brigade and the anti-aircraft forces were withdrawn to the East some time ago. German low-flying fighters attack defenseless civilians with impunity.

"Jesus Christ have mercy on us," Mama cries. "The savages killed Basia's son today," she grieves.

"How? What happened?" Zbyszek is stunned. He knew Basia's son very well. His name was Eugene. He was a polite, quiet boy, and a very good student, too.

Sobbing heavily, Mama hides her face in both hands. "They shot him on the street directly from the plane," she chokes out.

"Oh, these low-flying planes with machineguns," Zbyszek wonders. "I know, we have to watch them but you can hear them coming in the distance; you should be able to detect them early and hide."

"But on the crowed street they were shooting defenseless people like ducks," Mama screams in fury. "Oh, God! Such a tragedy! Her only child! She couldn't have a baby for many, many years, and finally this boy was born when she was in her late thirties. He was her whole world. Oh, God! How can You watch all this cruelty!"

Over the next few days, the heroic voice of President Starzyński bolsters Warsawians' spirits, alerts them to the air raids, and informs them of the bravery and numerous successes of the civil defense.

"Warsaw is fighting! Warsaw is fighting!" His charismatic strong voice is heard everywhere. Next, the mass is broadcast from the Church of Saint Cross. Professor Kapusta delivers an inspiring, breathtaking sermon. Warsaw prays with hope.

The Germans become nervous. Their plan to score a fast victory has not been achieved. In their drive for success, the German media rushed to announce the defeat of Warsaw on September 9. That was the latest timetable acceptable to Hitler. But the deadline has not been met. In its fury, the Luftwaffe decides to attack the heart of Warsaw, its most cherished historic and cultural monuments and national treasures. The King's Palace becomes their target. The scenes of the King's Palace in flames and the destruction of the historic library with treasures of the ancient Polish collections bring down the nation's spirit as nothing else does during the entire invasion.

On September 25, Germans under the command of General Blaskowitz storm Warsaw from all directions. Hitler in person oversees the attack. The Luftwaffe starts its greatest assault ever. Warsaw fights to the last bullet. By September 28, there is nothing left to fight with. Flames and fumes of the burning town, a hundred meters high, glow in the heart of Poland day and night. Over a three-day period, the city has endured 1,776 bombing sorties, 500 tons of explosives, and 72 tons of incendiaries. And there is no good news from the West but there is plenty of bad news from the East. Thousands of Polish soldiers are taken prisoners by the Soviets. President Starzyński, as the leader of the courageous free people, talks to the Warsawians for the last time.

> Compatriots!
>
> We have done everything that is humanly possible to defend our Capital. From the bottom of my heart, I thank you for your heroic defense of our beloved Warsaw. Please remember—we didn't lose! We will never lose! We will never yield in this fight for our country and for our freedom. For the time being, we only have to change tactics. Remember that! We don't give up anything! We are only changing tactics, temporarily!

On September 29, the Germans enter Warsaw. General Blaskowitz of the victorious German 8th Army orders that the defenders of Warsaw be treated with respect.[15]

* * * *

The deathly silence of the Cathedral is interrupted from time to time by quiet sobbing or outright crying. It's Thursday. No mass is scheduled during the day, and yet the Cathedral is full. The priests mingle with the crowd of parishioners. On her knees, Danusia hopelessly stares at the altar. "Our Father, Our Father…," she tries to pray, swallowing her tears. In search of God, her eyes venture high up to the sky then stop abruptly. "The balcony," she realizes. "The familiar balcony." Indeed, high up, near the badly damaged ceiling, the small familiar balcony overlooks the dark nave. From this balcony, she watched Marshal Piłsudski in the open casket. It was only four years ago. She was still a child back then. But that feeling, that same awful feeling of unspeakable grief and fear….

Oh, Great Marshal! Help us! Help us in this time of despair! Poland needs you! Now more than ever Poland needs your wisdom and your fatherly shield! Protect us and guide us through this hell on earth! She puts her head down and with closed eyes plunges into a dark abyss, losing any sense of time or place.

"Danusia, my dear," a warm, caring voice rouses her and a heavy hand affectionately touches her hair. Barely opening her eyes, she recognizes the presence of the dearest person.

"Let's go, Danuś, let's go," Dad kisses her brown soft hair.

She gets up. Zbyszek and Mama stand in the doorway. She slowly moves towards them although deep inside she desperately wants to stay in the Cathedral. But Mama and Zbyszek are waiting. She walks into the street and the heavy cathedral door slowly closes behind her. She turns around. In the comforting twilight of the Cathedral, she has left her happiness, her freedom, her sense of belonging and hope. Everything good is left behind this door. Now she steps into the daylight of oppression, cruelty, and despair.

"No! No! I don't want to go anywhere, leave me alone!" she cries hysterically.

"Danusia, darling. Remember what President Starzyński said. We didn't lose! We will never lose because ultimately there is justice in the world. For now, we simply have to change the tactics. We will get our Poland back," Dad tries his best.

"Yes, but when? My life goes on and I will never again be 17," she replies with bottomless despair.

They slowly walk home, Dad holding Danusia and Mama embracing Zbyszek as if she would try to hide him. It is not an easy walk. They have to pass through the barricades, barbed wire entanglements, around bomb craters and the rubble of half-ruined and ghostly burned-out houses. Usually colorful and flowery yards are turned into mini-cemeteries full of wooden crosses. The Church of Our Lady near the State Mint has been heavily hit and rests in ruins.

Haughtily parading through the rubble, viciously victorious German soldiers quickly flood the city. The Polish soldiers must lay down arms. The group of sappers stationed in the State Mint must report to the Athenaeum Theater. Lieutenant Szulc, in charge of the sapper detachment, is devastated but, unlike his soldiers who openly cry, he must keep his composure. Trying to put aside his emotions, he organizes the group and shouts the command. The soldiers in step leave the State Mint as the residents watch in dead silence. The sappers not only have to lay down arms but they immediately become prisoners of war. Their fate is highly uncertain. They will be separated from each other and sent to different camps scattered throughout Germany.

Danusia meets the departing sappers at the gate. In tears, she hugs Lieutenant Szulc.

"Goodbye," he says.

"No," she protests. "See you soon!" she corrects him, stressing the word "soon." Then she looks around for another soldier, a friend of hers. She hasn't seen him for a while but now he should be here. A quick glance through the rows of sappers. But he is not here.

"And where is Marian?" she hastily asks.

Silence. No answer. Only a sad grimace on his face, a gesture "don't ask," and the thump of the measured steps of the departing detachment.

Frozen, she follows them with her eyes, unable to cry, scream or shout.

11. Stefan Starzyński
President of Warsaw

12. Hitler at Victory Parade in Warsaw, October 5, 1939

5

The German invaders immediately take over the administration of the city. First, they order mass registration. They need lists, lists with names; they need to know who is who, what is the role of each and every person in the society, their ethnic background, religion, education, and profession. At the outset, a shocking announcement is made:

> If anyone dares to attack a German, the punishment will be severe. For one German killed one hundred Poles will be killed outright, and for one German wounded fifty Poles will be put to death, no questions asked.

In the meantime, preparations for the victory parade proceed full speed. The streets must be cleared of rubble. The stage for the Führer must be prepared and proper security assured. On October 5, Hitler personally reviews his troops at the victory parade in Warsaw.[1] His speech of a conquering Caesar is full of vicious aggression and hatred. Warsaw holds its breath.

Taking over the Polish territory up to the Ribbentrop–Molotov partition line agreed upon with the Soviet Union, Germans begin to break up its latest kill with more than 22 million Polish people. Half of German occupied Poland is incorporated outright into the Third Reich. The annexed area with more than nine million Poles is to be germanized completely. The Polish language is banned, education for the Poles beyond elementary school is prohibited, and special shopping hours for the Poles are imposed. Even Polish music is forbidden.

The rest of German occupied Poland including Warsaw and Kraków becomes a special German protectorate known as the Government General, the so-called "land of terror." Hans Frank is appointed the Governor General of this experimental hell on earth. Upon taking office, Governor Frank announces that the Poles "shall become the slaves of the German Reich."[2] All the cities are soon plastered with more bizarre announcements:

> In order to prevent impertinent behavior of the Polish population, it is hereby ordered that the Poles give way to representatives of the German nation. The Poles shall step off the sidewalk into the road when passed by the uniformed Germans. In addition, men shall remove their head-gear. The streets belong to the conquerors, not to the conquered!

More appalling and demeaning regulations soon follow. It is against the law for Poles to ride in taxis, carry briefcases, walk in public parks, make calls from public phone booths, etc.

The barbaric cruelty of the German military forces towards the Polish civilian population that were demonstrated in the September campaign were merely the prelude to what was about to happen. General Franz Halder wrote in his diary: "We have no intention of rebuilding Poland. [...] The Polish intelligentsia must be prevented from establishing itself as a governing class. Low standards of living must be conserved. Cheap slaves.... The Reich will give the Governor General the means to carry out this devilish plan."[3] And without a doubt, the Reich did give him the means! Squads of special extermination units *Einsatzgruppen* have followed the German army into Poland to 'clean up' the territory. Reinhard Heydrich, Himmler's right-hand man, announced that these units "undertake a housecleaning of Jews, intelligentsia, clergy, and the nobility!"[4] And without a doubt, they did....

In Warsaw, Commandant Cochenhausen issues an order. All Polish officers, whether regular, reservists or retirees, and all military officials of commissioner rank shall report to the German authorities. Any person from the above categories who does not report will be arrested. Under darkness of the night, brutal arrests are carried out non-stop. People are taken to prisons, shipped to labor camps or to newly formed concentration camps, and shot on the streets.

At the State Mint, new bosses arrive. The Polish managers must report to them. The people are nervous. What to expect? The Germans would need to keep the mint operational and they can't do it themselves. A lot of speculation, a lot of anxiety. But there is no time to waste. The situation is resolved quickly. All the Polish managers are rounded up and taken into custody. Within minutes, they are gone. Only a few are spared. Among the lucky ones is Danuta's Dad, old Gara, and Mr. Sowiński, a graphic artist.

The residents of the mint are in a panic. Danusia Staniszewska, Bruno Falski, Janka Owczerk and Wanda Tołłoczko gather in the yard, scared and confused. Their fathers are being taken away. But why? Where? What for? For how long? To prison or to some kind of a camp? They don't really cry, rather, they are shocked, dismayed, and uncertain. They don't know yet that their fathers will be taken to the concentration camp in Dachau. They don't know yet that none of these men will ever return home....

In Kraków, at the Jagiellonian University, Poland's preeminent educational institution, a general meeting of the faculty is called. "Should we attend?" the professors debate. The most senior and prominent leaders of the Polish academia with their fatherly sense of responsibility for the University and the community obviously attend. And surely, they are rounded up immediately and transported to the concentration camp in Sachsenhausen. Internationally recognized authorities, Professors Stanislaw Estreicher, Ignacy Chrzanowski, Kazimierz Kostanecki, Adam Rożański, Jerzy Smoleński, Michał Siedlecki and 200 others, are rounded up and driven into oblivion. In an act of cold-blooded genocide, the so-called AB-Action, some 15,000 Polish intellectuals, officials, politicians, and clergy were selected for shooting or for consignment to concentration camps.[5] On March 15, 1940, Himmler proclaims that all Poles will disappear from this earth. It is imperative that the great German nation considers the elimination of all Polish people as its chief task.[6]

* * * *

On a golden autumn day in the year 2000, a telephone rings in Ohio.

"Hi, Anetka. How is the Yalie doing?" Konrad yells.

"I want you to come over for the Parents Weekend on October 20th," his big sister says. "There will be a lot of fun here!"

"What did you say, October 20? No way!" Konrad protests. "I have a Halloween Party with my soccer team that weekend."

"But Konrad, we'll have a Yale–Pennsylvania football game here!"

"Is this Anetka?" Danusia asks. "Put her on the speaker phone, please."

"Hi, Grandma, how are you feeling?"

"Okay, darling."

"Grandma, I want you all to come over here to New Haven for the weekend of October 20. All the parents will be coming that weekend."

"I can't go my dear, you know, but your parents may go."

"But Grandma, there will be many interesting events also for you. For example, a lecture by one of the leading American historians on French legacies of collaboration and resistance during World War II. I am sure you would be interested in it."

"Oh darling, I really can't go, but I am sure your parents will go."

"Grandma, please tell them to come. And Konrad, you know what? There'll be a jazz band playing, and do you know who is playing the piano in the band? Konrad Kaczmarek! I'm sure you'd like to hear that."

"Yes, yes, but I must go to my Halloween Party. Bye, Anetka."

Konrad is frowning. "I am not going to give up my Halloween Party. I already have a great costume." He senses another family battle and needs Grandma on his side.

"I think you should go to see your sister," Danusia says. "You don't have that many occasions to be with your big sister since she went to college. Even if you skip this party, you will have other Halloween parties here in the neighborhood the following week."

"But you don't understand, Grandma! I've just found this fantastic mask with a small pump. You put the pump under the costume, squeeze it, and blood oozes and drips down your face. It's fantastic! I can't wait to try it!"

Danusia gently takes his hand. "Konrad, I want you to know something." Lowering her voice, she looks into his burning eyes. "In my life I have seen many faces covered with real blood. I have seen real human corpses and parts of human bodies flying in the air or scattered on the ground. I have met and seen people who were tortured in the most vicious ways. And it was tragic, very tragic. The Polish history is written in blood of our ancestors and for us the memory of the dead is a sacred thing. Do you know what holiday Poland celebrates the day after the Halloween extravaganza?"

Konrad looks at her with impatience. After all, he knows all this stuff....

Danusia reaches for a photo album. "On the first day of November, we celebrate one of the most important national holidays; everybody gets a day off from work. That's All Saints Day, a very beautiful and inspiring holiday." She points to a photo of marble graves buried in chrysanthemums, evergreen twigs, and brightened with warm candlelight. "But very different from Halloween...."

Konrad shrugs. "Oh, I know Grandma, I know."

"You never witnessed that holiday in Poland. One must personally experience the spirit of that day to fully understand its meaning. The spirit of respect, reflection, remembrance of the past, the spirit of solidarity and togetherness is omnipresent. On that single day, all the Polish people visit the cemeteries. We visit family graves, unknown soldiers' graves, national heroes graves, the graves of cousins and friends. And the Polish cemeteries look very different than here. In Poland, the cemeteries play a special role in people's lives, they are treated as the common good, and individual graves are treated as integral parts of the families. When I look at the cemeteries in America, those rows of silent uniform stone tables sticking out from the neatly cut grass...and hardly any human being around, it strikes me how lonely those places are. Maybe it's a cultural thing, but it seems so different here...." Danusia falls silent. Konrad browses TV channels instinctively.

"Anyway," she continues, "All Saints' Day in Poland is the busiest day of the year, with heavy car traffic and crowds of hurrying shoppers. It's the busiest day for the street vendors as well. Everywhere they sell flowers and candles. But those candles are not really the candles. They are *znicze*. Funny when I think about it...the English language doesn't even have a good equivalent for the word *znicze*...."

"But I know what you mean," Konrad interrupts her. "When I go to Poland, Grandma Ela always takes me to the cemetery and she always takes these *znicze* with her. Some *znicze* are as small as an Oreo cookie and some are as big as this bowl." He points to a bowl of tomato soup that Danusia has just put in front of him.

"Why don't you eat," she reminds him. "What's so unprecedented about our All Saints Day tradition is that the cemeteries that day are so crowded you can hardly walk around. And not only that day but during the entire week preceding the holiday, people clean, repair, and decorate the graves, renovate writings, photos or sculptures, rake leaves, plant flowers, etc, etc. People come from great distances, from their busy modern lives in far away cities to their towns, villages, and boroughs to pay respects to their loved ones who passed away, to stop for a moment and take a deep breath of reflection. Old neighbors and childhood friends often meet that day.

"At dusk, thousands of candles brighten the cemeteries and singing processions pass through the alleys. Usually it's a cold and rainy evening. People are warmly dressed for the occasion, in high boots, shawls, hats and gloves. In the flickering light and burning aroma of *znicze,* the processions led by the local catholic priests slowly roll through the glowing cemeteries to the echo of religious and patriotic songs. The graves, some from shiny granite or marble, some from plain concrete, some as high as the table, more prominent family tombs as high as six feet, all buried in flowers, mostly white, violet, and amber chrysanthemum and spruce wreaths, are surrounded by the groups of family members greeting each other, talking, praying, and attentively making last moment improvements to the decorative outlook of the grave. In the spirit of eternity, this is a unifying time for the leaving and the dead, the close and more distant relatives, the neighbors and old friends, respect for our past, for our ancestors, and for our heritage. The cemetery becomes a very warm, pleasant, vibrant, and even cozy place that day. With all the lights, people, processions, resounding songs, flowers, decorated graves, and the aroma of falling colorful leafs mixed with burning candles, All Saints Day is a great attraction and a gentle, civic, and inspiring experience for the children."

Danusia puts down the album, her eyes venture far away. "Only once in my life, All Saints Day was celebrated differently. That was back in 1939, right after the Warsaw defense campaign. That year the country lay in ruins, the cities were covered with fresh graves on the streets and in the backyards. All the cemeteries were badly damaged. In Warsaw alone about ten thousand civilians were killed and about fifty thousand injured.[7] Of course, these losses are nothing in comparison with the losses that Warsaw suffered five years later, during the 1944 Uprising when the city was leveled to the ground and there was virtually no Warsaw left.... For 1944 All Saints Day, there was no living human being left in Warsaw...."

"You know, Grandma," Konrad wakes up from his thoughts. "I was checking the losses on both sides during the September defense campaign and I noticed that different books give different numbers. Most of the time, the losses on the Polish side are estimated at 66 to 70 thousand dead, about 130 thousand wounded, and 620 thousand soldiers taken as prisoners of war. The German losses are often estimated at about 50 thousand dead and wounded, 500 destroyed planes, 1000 destroyed tanks, and about 6,000 trucks."[8]

"These are just mere estimates," Danusia snorts angrily. "And they really don't reflect the real situation because the collusive Soviet invasion from the east makes these estimates less transparent on the Polish side. If you want to be correct, you also need to consider the Soviet losses. True enough, the Soviet losses during the September invasion on Poland were small because Poland was taken by surprise. Orders were even issued not to resist the Soviets. We didn't stand a chance to fight on two fronts. Only several towns like Lwów, Grodno and Wilno organized self-defense against the Soviets. In other parts of Eastern Poland there was a lot of confusion, panic, and chaos. The Soviets did not declare war on Poland. Rather, they entered the country under the banner of saving the Byelorussian, Ukrainian, and Jewish minorities oppressed by the Poles and endangered by the Germans. The Soviets portrayed themselves as the liberators of the masses. Attracted by the populous message, the minorities rose against the Poles and greeted the Soviets with open arms."[9]

Konrad makes a puzzled face. "Most of the books don't talk about the collaboration of Poland's minorities with the Soviets but when I went to Białowieża—it's on the Polish border with Byelorussia now—the forester there told me many stories about it. He told me about the tension between the Poles and the local Jews and Byelorussians in that region."

"The Soviets skillfully turned the local minorities against the Poles. Like the Germans, they too justified their invasion pretending to protect minorities oppressed by the Poles. The Polish Jews, Byelorussians, and Ukrainians were attracted to Soviet propaganda that portrayed the Polish landowners as the oppressors of the masses. The Soviets were promising them liberation and even their own countries." Danusia pauses. "It sounded pretty attractive, especially for the Jews who were already very fearful of the Nazis."

"You know, Grandma, what else the forester told me? He told me some stories how closely the Germans and the Soviets cooperated with each other first in defeating Poland, and later in destroying the Polish resistance. They were the best friends back then, in 1939."

"Well, even today it's very hard to talk about it." Danusia sighs; her eyes become round and fierce. "These things are incomprehensible. Such a blatant crime against humanity committed by two leaders of the twentieth century aiding and abating each other in the most vicious genocide of the Polish nation! It's abhorrent and unprecedented!"

When Grandma's eyes get round it must be a very serious matter. "We took the greatest beating because we dared to say 'no' to the bullies," Konrad takes the matter upon himself. "We were the first to stand up to Hitler and that is why we became his greatest enemy. Also, we defeated the Soviets in 1920, so they were thirsty for revenge."

"I am afraid you are right." Danusia shakes her head. "You see, on the day of Warsaw capitulation, Germany and the Soviet Union formally sealed their agreement to wipe out Poland from the map. On September 28, 1939, Ribbentrop and Molotov signed a new friendship treaty, finalizing the August 23 border deal. The August deal did not anticipate the total annihilation of the Polish State. Some form of a Polish state was still on the table. A number of German and Italian politicians argued against the extreme solution. It was Stalin who opposed that concept and under his pressure a decision was made to kill the Polish State all together.[10] According to the September 28 German–Soviet Friendship Treaty, the Soviet Union took over 51.6% of the Polish territory with 37.3% of the Polish citizenry. The new border deal gave the Soviet Union the same Polish territory as had been annexed by Russia during the third partition of Poland in 1795.[11] Furthermore, Lithuania, initially given to Germany, was transferred to the Soviet sphere of interest in exchange for the Poland's Lublin region and a part of the Warsaw region.[12]"

"Ultimately, the Soviets were able to preserve their prey," Konrad observes.

"But let me finish, please," Danusia silences him with her eyes. "In the secret protocol to the German–Soviet Friendship Treaty, both parties pledged to cooperate closely with each other in order to destroy the Polish underground, Polish resistance, Polish intelligentsia, and all signs of Polish identity. In the winter of 39–40, senior secret police officers of both invaders held regular meetings in such Polish bastions as Kraków and Zakopane, exchanging top-secret information about combating the Polish resistance and developing the best methods to infiltrate the Polish underground and destroy any signs of the Polish identity.[13]

"The German Gestapo highly admired their Soviet counterparts for a wealth of formidable experience developed through decades of oppressing their own people. The NKVD infiltrated every aspect of their people's lives, spread unprecedented mistrust and terror, and bent the nation to the oppressors' every wish. The German police-state apparatus was never so pervasive or effective as the Soviet NKVD. One of the great English writers, Allen Paul, in his book entitled *Katyń* calls this Gestapo–NKVD relation the 'fraternity of miscreants.' His portrayal of the miscreants is a true masterpiece. The Gestapo is bold, impulsive, reckless, and careless, while NKVD is slow, patient, cunning, and thorough. In his words, one played poker, the other played chess."[14]

"Gosh, that's an incredible description, Grandma! But I like to play chess, too, and I don't like poker."

"Well, maybe that's the Slavic nature," Danusia smiles lightly, her fierce eyes getting back to normal. "And maybe that's why we are so good at continuing resistance in defiance of the greatest persecutions ever conceived. Our underground forces under the leadership of the Home Army became by far the largest and the most effective resistance movement in the entire occupied Europe.[15] And our resistance must be put in perspective. The German–Soviet resentment of the Polish underground was so strong that even in the final stages of the war, when the Soviet Army reached the suburbs of Warsaw on its way to Berlin, the fierce enemies at the time once again instinctively came together to kill Warsaw...."

"Yes, but they never destroyed our resistance and couldn't destroy our army abroad," Konrad insists.

"Our army abroad," Danusia whispers melancholically.

"Initially over eighty thousand Polish soldiers managed to escape to the West right after the September campaign,"[16] Konrad's voice vibrates.

"Yes, yes. The escape was relatively easy only for the pilots but not for the others. Most of the men tried to escape to France and Great Britain through Rumania and Hungary. But both countries, even though sympathetic to us, were terrorized by the Nazi and the Soviets to turn in the Polish refugees. They detained many of our men. One of my cousins, Giedziun from Dryświaty near Brasław, escaped through Hungary to France. He later joined the Polish Armored Division under the command of General Maczek, and participated in the Normandy invasion and in the battles at Caen and Falaise. Over the years, many Poles managed to escape the Nazi–Soviet grip and joined the Polish armed forces abroad."

"Is Giedziun still alive?"

"Yes, he lives in Canada, but he must be in his nineties already. We should give him a call. He would be happy to tell you about his feats of arms all over the world in the name of Polish independence."

"And despite all his sacrifices, he couldn't return to Poland after the war," Konrad says with a dose of sarcasm in his voice.

Danusia nods sadly. "Can you imagine? The Polish soldiers who fought the Nazis all over the world couldn't return home upon winning that war! As a result of the Teheran and Yalta agreements, the downfall of the Polish Government in Great Britain, and the emergence of the Soviet-controlled government in Warsaw, the Polish soldiers fighting with British and French forces in the West were viewed as the enemies of the Polish people! The Communists, or rather the Soviet henchmen, were again after the bourgeoisie or rather the few patriotic Poles still left alive. The Polish soldiers who dared to return to Poland from the West were jailed and many of them were simply executed! Only recently, just towards the end of his life, Giedziun was able to visit independent Poland, at last...."

* * * *

Danusia's Lyceum at Miodowa Street hasn't re-opened. The newly installed Nazi regime allows for the re-opening of only a limited number of elementary and vocational schools. High schools and universities are not on their agenda. The Poles should not pursue education beyond elementary and trade schools. A Nazi daily propaganda newspaper written in Polish, *Nowy Kurier Warszawski*, floods the streets. No one buys this trash but no one can escape its screaming venomous headlines calling on people to "cooperate," to sign up for "Volkslists," and trumpeting German glorious victories.

One day Dad comes home with a friend. The man is rather short with a flat face, big lips and friendly soft blue eyes. Eugene Pawłowski, or Gienio as they call him, is a local businessman. In his mid-thirties, Gienio is a decent and polite man.

"Welcome, welcome, please come in," Mama likes Gienio for his restrained drinking habit. "I haven't seen you for a long time."

Dad is a little tense. He shuts the door thoroughly and looks around the house.

"Danusia, cover the windows please," he orders. "Is Zbyszek home?"

"No, but he should be back soon," Mama replies.

"Right, the curfew hour is approaching. We don't have much time, then." Dad observes.

"How do you do, Miss Danusia?" Gienio bows respectfully.

"Hello, nice to see you," Danusia replies politely but indifferently.

Gienio opens his bag and carefully takes out a piece of a thin paper. "*Bulletin*" the big headline reads in Polish. Danusia's eyes are getting round. "Wow! It's a Polish newspaper!" She is scared but curious, very curious; her eyes feverishly scan the tiny pages.

"Alek, it's the death penalty if we are caught with it," Mama says quietly, staring at the paper.

"Don't worry, Jasia. It's everywhere. They would have to kill all of us and that would take them some time. And look what the paper says!"

Dad unfolds the paper and snaps at the headlines with delight: *Poland's Underground Forces Established!* "You see! We already have the solid resistance movement. That's fantastic! We need to celebrate the occasion. Jasia, give us something to warm up, would you please. Maybe this bottle of vodka I brought from Vince. We have a special occasion today."

Mama puts a bottle of homemade vodka on the table.

"To your health, Gienio!" Taking up a glass, Dad taps it at Gienio's glass and drinks the brownish liquid at a draught. Gienio lightly wets his lips and puts the glass down. "Alek, we must be very careful. We must handle the *Bulletin* with great prudence. You should distribute it only to your most trusted people. Otherwise you will put yourself and everybody else at risk. It must circulate because we cannot afford to make many copies. But it must circulate only among the right people."

Mama puts her hands on Alek's shoulders trying to calm him down. "Alek, you must be very careful with the people from the mint. You know this Sowiński, the graphic artist. His wife is from Austria. Just recently they moved to our building."

"Isn't she your client?" Dad sends her a suspicious look.

"Yes, she is. I know her and I like her very much. But you know how the Germans bribe everybody today. This whole Volks- and Reichdeutsche business. The so-called Aryans like Sowiński and their families are classified as the first-class citizens. They become Reichdeutsche, receive German citizenship and all the privileges that go with it. They have special shops, special busses, special restaurants, etc. I am afraid they also have special obligations, for example to report on the others; in other words to spy for the Germans."

Dad shakes his fist. "And all these rascals and scoundrels and traitors who are blond enough to pass for good Aryans fall into the third or fourth category of the semi-privileged Volksdeutsche. It makes them a little better subjects of the Third Reich than we are...." He boils inside and out.

"But Dad," Danusia interrupts him. "Thanks to these Volksdeutsche lists it is also easier to identify our own people, those trustworthy ones."

Dad looks at her, not quite sure what to say. "I hope you are right, my dear."

Gienio has been observing Danusia intently. Her determined face ornamented with meticulously curled brown hair attracts his full attention. "Dear Miss Danusia," he says gently, "if someone is not on the Volksdeutsche list this is certainly a good sign but this is only the first step. Please remember that everybody should be observed, scrutinized, and carefully tested. And even then, there is no guarantee of safety. Germans continue widespread, day and night arrests of those considered as carriers of Polish identity. The Gestapo tortures them pitilessly in order to get information about our members and our operations. We have warnings that they have developed such sophisticated tortures that no one can withstand them. That is why we recommend working in small groups of absolute confidants. This strategy assures that in the event of being captured, an individual can't endanger many others. Remember, these days we don't want to know much. We only need to know the bare minimum that is absolutely necessary to carry out our mission."

Gienio doesn't stay long. He must leave before the curfew. His big brown bag puts him at risk on the street. But he doesn't seem to worry. He is calm and friendly. Mama blesses him for the trip.

"But where is Zbyszek?" she suddenly realizes. "Where is he? It's getting late." She walks between the door and the kitchen window back and forth, then grabs her jacket and rushes out.

"*Panie* Gara, *Panie* Gara! Did you see Zbyszek?"

"No, not yet. I will be locking the gate soon. That's the new rule. He better show up soon."

They stand at the gate with old Gara checking his watch every other moment. With the new bosses, he doesn't want to be accused of not following the rules but he sincerely worries about Zbyszek, too. It's already five minute past the hour and old Gara starts closing the gate. "Don't worry. I will be here waiting for him anyway, " he assures panicking Mama. As he is about to turn the key, Zbyszek's breathless face appears around the corner. The gate opens up quickly and Zbyszek sneaks inside like a cat.

"Thanks, Mr. Gara," Mama shakes his hand with gratitude.

At home Dad is angry. "Where have you been? Don't you understand you can be arrested and no one will ever see you again?"

"I am sorry. I am really sorry. But I was at Andrusiak's house. You know these twin boys down the street, my classmates? Their mother invited me in."

"Don't they have a watch?" Mama snaps angrily.

"No, it's not that.... We just forgot ourselves in this discussion about *Komplety*. Have you heard about *Komplety*?"

"What's that about?" Dad throws up his hands.

"That's the Polish Underground School." Zbyszek is mesmerized by the name. "It is being organized right now and the two Andrusiak boys will be going."

"Yes, I heard something about it," Mama says. "They call these classes *Komplety* or flying classes because the classes are held in private homes, mostly at the teachers' houses, and in very small groups. But to assure safety it is recommended that the children also attend schools approved by the Germans and attend *Komplety* in addition."

"You know Jasia, I thought about it." Dad looks at her decisively. "Today it is critical to have proper identification documents. You must be engaged in officially approved activities. That's your best protection; it's your security. Otherwise you can be rounded up any moment and you can disappear without a trace. That's why I think Zbyszek should go to this German trade school; they call it the Ressler School, I think. This way he will get a student ID that will protect him. The same with you!" He turns to Danusia.

"Yes, I know, I know." Danusia's face shows deep frustration. The trade school is out of the question. She doesn't like to sell stuff.

"You either go to this trade school or get a proper job. In fact, I was already talking with Nowak about a job for you at the mint. We lost so many people that there are plenty of positions vacant and they are looking for some entry level workers." Dad pats her on the back. "The mint is an excellent place to work. It is a strategic business for the Germans. All your friends, Wanda, Janka, Danka, and Marysia will go to word at the mint, too."

"Okay, if you want, you can sign me up." Danusia drops on the sofa with resignation. "But how about *Komplety*? I want to try *Komplety*, too."

"Well, one thing at a time. Let's first get settled with the proper papers so that you can move around safely," he replies.

"Zbyszek, then I will sign you up for this trade school tomorrow," Mama declares.

Time passes by quickly and winter approaches. Every day Danusia awaits the mail, looking anxiously for a letter from Julian but the mailman doesn't even come every day and no one receives letters from Eastern Poland.

Instead, every day brings more appalling German announcements. The Poles must turn in all the radio sets. The possession of a radio is forbidden and will result in immediate arrest. Alek turns some of his radio sets in but not all of them. He places a tiny but powerful radio in a small opening under the floor in the corner of the family room. Occasionally, he takes out the radio and tries to catch his favorite stations from Lwów or Wilno, but with no success. He easily catches the German and Soviet stations and turns them off quickly.

"Nothing, absolutely nothing, no news, what's going on out there?" He worries. He has already written several letters to his brother, Vince, but there is no reply from Vince either.

Gienio comes frequently. His *Bulletin* becomes the primary source of information. Occasionally the *Bulletin* publishes reports about Polish soldiers who responded to call to arms in September and went east hoping to join the reorganized Polish Army.... Some of them managed to come back home, some were taken prisoners of war by the Soviets and transported into Russia, some escaped through Rumania and Hungary south and from there to France and Great Britain. The reports reveal the drama of the defeat but also renewed hopes for the future. The Polish Government in exile addresses the Polish people. High-level international negotiations are taking place. Efforts are being made to resurrect the Polish Army in the West.

Gienio becomes a close family friend. From time to time, he brings gifts, most often some food but occasionally presents like bonbonnière or flowers either for Danusia or Jasia, and even a pocketknife for Zbyszek. He takes great pleasure in watching Danusia and always tries to strike up a conversation with her. She accepts his presence but is totally disinterested in him and blatantly ignores his gestures of interest. Gienio is short and chubby, nothing like her handsome Julian. It doesn't matter that he is a rich, good-hearted, and reliable man, courageous patriotic Pole, caring and loving son. She just ignores him. But Dad can't stop praising Gienio for everything. It's always Gienio this, Gienio that, Gienio will come, Gienio will say..., etc, etc.

Finally one day Mama says, "You know, Danusia, I think that Gienio is in love with you, what do you think?"

"That's fine, but I am not. And let's not talk about it anymore, PLEASE!"

Mama is not happy with her answer. "That's a shame. Think about it and give him a chance. He is such a good man. Oh, by the way, aren't we going to the wedding of your friend, Basia, this weekend?"

"That's right!" Danusia exclaims. "I almost forgot about it. This is this wedding that was first scheduled for October in the Church of Our Lady. But the church has been destroyed. I think they rescheduled it in one of the churches in the Old Town. I have to check which one."

Two weeks later, some brighter moment awaits them—Basia's wedding. The boys don't go. They are not interested. But for Danusia this cold Saturday afternoon is the first occasion since the beginning of the war to dress up and possibly have some fun. With great effort Mama arranges for a small bouquet of white and red carnations meticulously decorated with white and red ribbons. The white and the red—the Polish national colors. Mama is proud. Everybody looks at the bouquet with admiration.

"But be careful with it. Cover it with paper," Dad warns.

Danusia wraps the flowers in ugly brownish packing paper. "It's awful, but better than the newspaper, I guess," she observes with disgust.

In front of the church a small group of guests awaits the ceremony. Danusia searches the crowd but finds no familiar faces. The bride is already in the church. Her long white gown with an elegant veil was bought before the war, back in August. Today August seems like another era. There are not many weddings nowadays. But people are in good spirits. The city is almost cleared from the rubble and Christmas is fast approaching.

However, the groom hasn't arrived yet. That's all right. Transportation is still a problem. He can't take a taxi and not many electric trams are operational. Most likely he had to take a *britzka*.

It is already two o'clock, but the groom is nowhere to be found. The bride is very nervous. The priest stands by. The guests are anxious, too. Even the cameraman is ready. But there is no sign of the groom. It's already fifteen minutes past the hour and the groom doesn't show up. People start whispering. The bride is terrified. Such a shameful situation. Something must have happened to him. Danusia observes her friend. Basia's face is red and very tense. She tries hard to hold back tears. Her family comforts her.

"This is rather embarrassing," Danusia thinks. Fifteen more minutes of watching the agony of her friend in front of the wedding guests, then Danusia gets up.

"Mama, let's go. This jerk will never show up."

Mama picks up the bouquet and gets up as well. "Right, that's enough," she declares and they head to the door. Outside, they vent their frustration.

"Such a terrible situation. Poor Basia. I saw this groom once. He has such a crazy name, Herring or something like that, and he is short and bald."

"So, she must be taller than him because she is rather big," Mama observes.

"You know, Mama, if I were to get married I would line up five guys like that Herring just in case one chooses not to show up." They laugh.

"Good afternoon, ladies," an attractive baritone voice reaches them from behind. They come to an abrupt stop. A young handsome man joins them. Danusia carefully examines the intruder. Oh, this is this guy she met at the club, the priest to be. What's his name? Quickly, she tries to recall his name.

"It's nice to see you again, Miss Danusia. I am glad to see you in good health after all this horror we have been through lately."

"Nice to see you, Józek." She recalls his name at last. "Mama, let me introduce my friend, Józek."

"Nice to meet you," Mama says.

He bows and kisses Mama's hand. "Nice to meet you, Madam. I saw you ladies in the church. So, I decided to say hello. It's been quite a while."

"That's great. But do you know Basia, the bride?"

"No, not really. My landlord was going to the church, so I thought I would join him to see how a wedding looks like these days."

"Apparently, it doesn't look that great," Danusia replies in a dreary voice.

"Yes, and I understand you plan to line up at least five grooms to assure your wedding is not spoiled like that," he looks at her amusedly.

"That's right! Precisely!" she laughs as they walk together.

"So, how did you survive the attacks on Warsaw? Did you stay in the city?"

"Yes, we did. The State Mint is very solid and we even have a bunker there. And what about you?" Danusia asks. "What did you do?"

"Oh, I wasn't in Warsaw in September. I went home to Koło for vacation. As you know, the fall semester doesn't start until October."

"So, you are from Koło?" Mama asks.

"Yes, Madam."

"Oh, that's the Reich now," Mama stops abruptly. "They incorporated you into Germany."

"Unfortunately yes, Madam. It causes us a lot of problems. I had a hard time to arrange for permission to come back to Warsaw. It takes a lot of effort to get the papers."

"Where are you staying? Do you have any family here?"

"No, Madam, I don't. I came back to the same place I was renting in the spring. I was hoping the University would reopen soon. But so far it doesn't look like any university will be reopening."

As they walk down the street, Danusia tries to joke while Mama keeps asking questions. Soon they stop in front of the mint.

"Please visit us one day." Mama extends her hand.

"Thank you Madam, thank you very much. I will, with pleasure." Bowing politely, he sends Danusia a smiling look and leaves.

"A very nice young man, this Józef," Mama comments.

"And good looking, too," Danusia adds.

Christmas approaches quickly. Danusia starts working at the mint while Zbyszek goes to the trade school. Still no letter from Julian and no letter from Uncle Vince. Gienio visits them almost every day but each time he shows up Danusia finds some excuse to leave. "Time for Christmas shopping," she explains. At last she earns some money and can make her own shopping decisions. This year there is not much to buy for Christmas though, but at least she can go for a walk with Józek. Of course, he is this fellow who doesn't want to get married but still he is much more interesting than the clumsy Gienio.

She talks with Mama and manages to invite Józek home for the evening. During the visit, Józek is stiff and official while Dad is surprisingly aggressive. The situation becomes tense.

"I don't like this guy, Józek. He is rather arrogant," Dad later declares.

"Oh, he is not arrogant, not at all," Mama protests. "He has very good manners."

"Maybe for you but not for me. And besides, he doesn't have any money."

"That's okay, you didn't have any money when I met you, either."

"You talk about him as if he were a contender for Danusia's hand."

"Oh, I thought you started talking that way...."

Over the next couple of days, Danusia fights with her parents about the New Year's Eve party. She wants to go with Józek to his friends but Dad doesn't want her to go anywhere. Alas, their dispute will be easily resolved.

On December 27, horrifying news hits Warsaw. A day before, violence erupted in the suburban district of Warsaw known as Wawer after a sporting event. In the riots, a German soldier was killed and another wounded. Seeking revenge, that night the Germans hunted down over one hundred Polish men and boys, dragging them from their beds in their pajamas out to the freezing cold streets. All together one hundred and seven men and boys were shot dead outside their homes that night.[17]

Warsaw is in state of shock. Warsawians are once again traumatized to the core. Around noon Dad comes home. The graphic artist, Sowiński, comes with him. Dad puts a bottle of vodka on the table.

"Jasia, listen to this!" he says forestalling her protests.

Mama quietly sits down.

"Tonight the Germans killed his friend."

Mr. Sowiński is totally wrecked. All he can do is cry.

"The man was of a mixed Polish–German origin," Dad continues, "and spoke fluent German. Apparently, the Germans gave him a chance. This fellow had to state that he was a German. We don't know what he said, but...they killed him out there, just like that, in his pajamas!"

Mr. Sowiński covers his face; his shoulders erratically heave up and down in silence. "I can't take it anymore," he sobs. "I just can't!"

Mrs. Sowińska must be even more devastated. That man was her closest friend. Their parents were old friends back in Austria years ago. Through him, Mrs. Sowińska met her husband. For years, they were the best of friends. Sowiński knows that his wife needs help but he is unable to console her now. He needs help himself.

Mama realizes the situation. "Alek, you stay here, but don't drink much! You still need to go back to work! I have to go upstairs."

In the afternoon, Danusia stops by home. "Daddy, they are looking for you, they need you to do something!" she shakes him.

"Okay, okay, Danusia." Dad is visibly drunk. "But you must stay here with *Pan* Sowiński."

"No, no, I have to go." Sowiński gets up. "Thanks for everything." He looks at his sweaty hands. "Can I just wash a bit?"

"Sure." Dad pours cold water into the bowl.

Sowiński plunges his hands into the icy water, splashes his face, and energetically shakes his head with relief.

"Dad, please drink a glass of milk," Danusia orders.

"No, no," he protests. "That is for you."

Milk is very precious and Mama reserves it only for the children. But Danusia insists and Dad finally drinks the whole glass. With considerable effort, Danusia puts both men back into shape and sends them to work.

The workday never ends. That's another way to exploit the Poles, to make them work to death.[18] Everybody is expected to work overtime. Sometimes overtime goes for another full shift. Once the tension increases, overtime is immediately imposed ensuring that people don't have time to think and talk. First of all, people must be tired, very, very tired. That's the best method to prevent unrest.

In the evening, Gienio comes with the *Bulletin*. Some of the names of the Wawer victims are listed there, among them the name of the Sowińskis' friend. Dad stares at the list with disbelief. What is going on?

The New Year's party is no longer an option. The city is in mourning for its latest victims. But Danusia can invite Józek home for New Year's Eve. With great hopes, they will welcome the 1940 New Year together at home. The war must be over soon. The Allies will finally show Hitler his place. Poland will regain its independence and life will go back to normal.

Mama even agrees to prepare a bed for Józek. He won't be able to leave until the morning. Of course, Dad is upset. He would rather invite Gienio. But Gienio has to leave early. And besides, his parents want to spend that special night with him.

New Year's Eve in Poland is called Sylvester. Literally it means Saint Sylvester Day but informally it simply means the New Year's Party. It is a centuries-old tradition to have big parties that evening. But this year, not only the parties are forbidden but even Polish music is prohibited.

Danusia meets Józek around six o'clock near the Destiny Movie Theater, a remainder of their first date. Together they go to Danusia's friend next door. Later they will go to Danusia's house.

Gienio drops by with the *Bulletin* a little earlier. He inquires about Danusia in vain, leaves flowers for her, and rushes home. Dad is furious at Danusia. "Where is she?" he hollers.

"Any good news today?" Mama changes the subject.

Indeed, there is some good news in the *Bulletin* today. General Sikorski, the Polish Prime Minister in exile, nominates General Sosnkowski as the Commander of *Związek Walki Zbrojnej* (ZWZ). In November, General Sikorski issued a decree creating ZWZ, a new organization of the Polish armed forces. General Sosnkowski will direct the operations of ZWZ from France. The newly formed organization will operate both in Poland and abroad.[19]

Dad's mood improves just in time for Danusia's arrival. When she walks in with Józek, he hides the *Bulletin* and greets the guest politely. Zbyszek joins them. Dinner tonight is very special: *pierogi* with different stuffing, *pierogi* with either meet or cheese or potato, or onion and cheese, and the delicious dessert—*szarlotka*—a very special apple pie.

The conversation at the table is awkward. Dad doesn't trust the visitor. What does this quasi-student do now? Why doesn't he go back to Koło, to his family? "So, how is your family in Koło these days," he asks.

"Not very well," Józek replies. "There have been several mass executions in the nearby villages lately, starting right after the German troops moved in.[20] The villages were burnt to the ground and hundreds or maybe even thousands of villagers were executed. People are terrified. And because we have been incorporated to the Reich, it's much worse than here. The Germans talk about deportation, eviction, and property confiscation. I am looking around here to see whether I could bring my mother and sister to Warsaw or at least to the General Government."

"Well," Dad sighs heavily, "you see what's going on here. It's neither better nor safer here, I am afraid."

"Yes and no. Here at least people still speak Polish."

Dad looks at Józek in a friendlier way, his heart warms up considerably.

"Don't worry, boy, don't worry," he puts his heavy hand on Józek's shoulder. "The Allies must act, I am sure they will finally put their acts together and do something about this mess. Our government in France will make sure that our interests are protected. We just have to wait a little longer."

"Yes, but in the meantime innocent people in the thousands are killed every day," Józek observes bitterly. "Danusia, do you know this Herring, the groom who didn't show up for his wedding?"

"Ouch, something happened to him?" she asks anxiously.

"Well, my landlord told me that the Gestapo arrested the man at his home about two hours before his wedding. No one can find him now. Most likely he was taken to Pawiak."

The dead silence sets in. Dessert doesn't really taste the same anymore. Danusia takes up a cup of tea and slowly sips the hot liquid. She remembers making fun of the man. Such a shame...how could she? Poor Basia. She must be devastated.

"We are approaching midnight," Zbyszek announces.

Indeed, the big clock on the wall shows three minutes to twelve.

"Let's get ready for the New Year!" Mama rushes from the kitchen. "Get up! Get up! Glasses, candles, money, you need to hold money in your hand, wishes, make a wish quickly, trumpets and small buzzers, you need to announce the beginning of the New Year. You must be ready." The big clock strikes. "Happy New Year to all!" Mama proclaims ceremoniously.

Wishes. What kind of wishes might they have...? In the next-door apartment the German occupants also celebrate the New Year. What kind of wishes do *they* have?

Józek kisses Danusia's hand and her two rounded cheeks. "Happy New Year," he whispers. Danusia is delighted. She senses his affection. They slowly sit down.

A reflective mood sets in. The memories of those killed in the war come back. The memories of those arrested or lost without a trace come back. too. With his eyes fixed on the candle, Dad talks in vain. "We still don't know what's happening with my dear Vince and the rest of them down there in the east. I wonder what's going on out there at Dryświaty and in Brasław? I already sent them so many letters."

Danusia drops her eyes. There is no letter from Julian either. But she no longer awaits his letters with the same eagerness. He must be busy and doesn't have time to write. Obviously, he must have forgotten her. She fidgets about in the chair. Julian wasn't really on her mind in her New Year's wish....

13. Partition of Poland 1939-1945

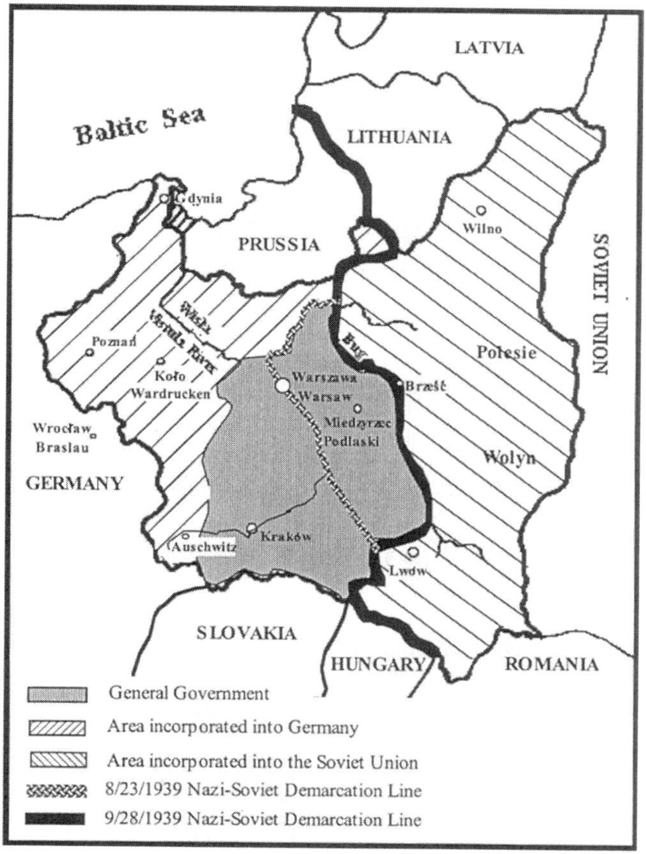

14. Marshal Józef Piłsudski, 1867-1935

15. General Władysław Sikorski, Prime Minister of Poland and Commander-in-Chief of the Polish Armed Forces, 1939-1943

6

Far away, in a remote fortress about three hundred kilometers south of Moscow, a group of Polish soldiers gathered around a tiny candlelight to welcome the New Year 1940. They are not the regular soldiers, they are the Polish elite captured by the Soviets during the Soviet invasion on Poland, mostly officers, several generals, doctors, lawyers, and government officials. Among them is Julian Sierżant—a 28-year-old lieutenant from Zbaraż. In reverie, he watches the twinkling candlelight while his mind relentlessly ventures back to the recent past.

Danusia is very much on his mind. How is she? Warsaw suffered such terrible destruction. "She must have survived," his subconscious tells him. "But is she all right?" There is no way he can find out, he can only pray that she is all right. Leaving his home in Zbaraż near Tarnopol, he had to calm down his mother and sisters, organize his unit, and plan the action. In the chaos of the moment, he left Danusia's address at home.

Heading towards Lwów, he learned that the Polish Army was withdrawing from the original defense lines to regroup and that the Polish Government was about to leave Warsaw to direct the counter-offensive from the east. The lack of any news about the allied support and finally this horrifying Soviet invasion from the back devastated the Polish soldiers. His detachment met the Soviets near Lwów. After a brief fight, his unit was surrounded and captured by the Soviet armored division.

Taken as a prisoner of war, he spent over one month in a transit camp in central Russia. At the camp, he met another lieutenant named Michael who fought the Soviets in the battle of Grodno. Michael was older than Julian, an attorney by profession. The two men became good friends. At the beginning of November, Julian and Michael were both withdrawn from the transit camp and, together with other Poles of higher ranks or "bourgeois tendencies," were sent to Kozielsk.

The camp in Kozielsk is located in an old, gigantic monastery turned by the Soviets into a heavily guarded prison. Despite its grim appearance, arriving at Kozielsk is like coming to a miniature Poland, an unforgettable, uplifting experience. The place welcomes the newcomers like the homeland welcomes its brave sons returning from the battlefields, with cheers and handshakes.

Inside the camp, the cross-section of the Polish elite from all parts of Poland is in high spirits and already well organized. There are over four thousand Polish men, mostly high-ranking reservists mobilized at the beginning of the war—professionals, intellectuals and officers. Among the prisoners are four generals of the Polish Army, many university professors, several hundred attorneys, judges, and representatives of the legal profession, hundreds of medical doctors including Poland's most outstanding surgeons, hundreds of engineers and school teachers, many journalists, writers and businessmen.[1] To them, losing a battle or even a war in the face of overwhelming adversity is not a defeat. To the men of Kozielsk and their colleagues incarcerated in Starobielsk and Ostashkov, victory is defined by the triumph of honor over shame, dignity over humiliation, and endurance over submission. To all these men brought up on the legacy of the great Marshal Piłsudski, the insidious attack on Poland in violation of all civilized norms and the dramatic defeat in overwhelming adversity became a uniquely Polish triumph, the triumph of trust in ultimate justice despite all adversity.[2]

After registration, Julian and Michael are directed to the barrack. Equipped with electricity and radiators, the place is warm and decent. The newcomers receive mattresses, blankets, some extra bread, and are warmly greeted by the barrack residents. Their barrack is much better than other camp accommodations, most of them larger, more crowded, and without a proper heating system.

The main bedroom of the camp is located in the old Orthodox Church. Some 500 men are squeezed there on the three or five-tier bed-like shelves. The place is popularly called the Circus. Going to bed and getting up or climbing down is a life-threatening experience. At the Circus, Julian meets some teaches and doctors from Zbaraż and Tarnopol. Michael also finds some familiar faces from Grodno, his hometown. In addition, many famous people and celebrities including scientists, actors, and musicians could be found there.

Soon life at the camp develops a rhythm of its own. Reveille before dawn. For breakfast, soup and fresh bread is served. Before noon the prisoners perform cleaning, washing, some repair jobs or kitchen duties. In the afternoon, large groups are assigned to various projects on nearby farms or at the railroad station. Dinner, consisting mostly of a potato or barley soup, is served around 6 p.m. After dinner, free time.

In the evening, the camp life bubbles with activities.[3] Endless discussions dissect the political situation of Poland at the outset of the war, the defense campaign, the strategy of the Allies, the Soviet invasion, and the chaotic nature of the situation in Eastern Poland ranging from organized self-defense in Lwów and Grodno to the enthusiastic welcoming of the Soviets by the Polish minorities. A variety of lectures are offered in various parts of the camp by leading authorities in their fields: history lectures, language classes, even anthropology sessions and discussions of the genesis of the Jewish, Slavic and Arian races, lectures about the Nazi policy to germanize the Poles, about the strategic significance of the city of Gdynia on the Baltic Sea, about the colonies and power of Great Britain. Many prisoners play chess and bridge.

Around All Saints Day, Michael falls into a depression. He doesn't know what has happened to his beloved wife and a baby daughter, Ala. In all likelihood, they don't know anything about him either.

"I wonder whether they lit a candle in my memory today," he whispers from his bed.

"Don't worry. I am sure they already know about you. We have asked so many people to pass a message to them. I am sure that somehow they already know." Julian tries to sound assuring.

There are a lot of discussions, a lot of speculation, a lot of rumors. Finland is the focus of the latest Soviet news. Soviet territorial claims to Finland in the middle of October remind everyone of Hitler's claims to Gdańsk and the corridor. Sorting through the Soviet propaganda, the Kozielsk prisoners evaluate the situation with a critical expert eye. Obviously Stalin is a quick learner. He closely follows and quickly adopts Hitler's dirty tricks. He has taken over Estonia and Latvia, imposing on them a "mutual defense agreement" which bears a striking resemblance to Hitler's peaceful resolution in Austria and Czechoslovakia. Now, he flexes his muscle against Finland. At this moment of trial, no one understands the Finns better than the Poles at Kozielsk. The Finns know, like the Poles three months earlier, that yielding to the tormentor once will only bring about more demands. Like the Poles a few months earlier, the Finns try to buy time. But the Soviets are not in the mood to play games. On November 26, the Soviet press announces that the Finns have launched an unprovoked attack on the Soviet Union. The stage for invasion is set. The men at Kozielsk bitterly laugh at the news. Stalin's imperial drive is an eyesore to them. Hitler's provocation in Gliwice is too fresh in their memories.

On September 1, 1939, at dawn, men dressed in Polish uniforms stormed the radio station in Gliwice. Subsequently, a Polish voice calling for uprising against the Germans was broadcast to the sound of pistol shots. The men storming the radio station were in fact German convicts dressed in Polish uniforms. The German SS immediately gunned them down during the attack. Before the night was over, the Germans announced to the world that Poland had launched an unprovoked attack on the Third Reich. That is how German and international public opinion was preconditioned for the attack on Poland.

Even though the bodies of the German convicts were soon found, properly identified as Germans in Polish uniforms, and the provocation was exposed, the world didn't care. The German provocation, carried out to provide a justification for the invasion of Poland, was trumpeted throughout the world and served its purpose of offering the appeasement lunatics a desperately desired argument. After the war, Naujock, the German leader of the Gliwice provocation, admitted at the Nuremberg trial that Heydrich had ordered him to attack the radio station and make the inflammatory speech in Polish.[4] It was only many years later that international public opinion had no choice but to face the truth.

Within less than three months after the Gliwice provocation, the world is ready for another brutal attack in violation of all civilized norms. On November 30, 1939, the Soviet land, sea, and air forces descend on Finland without any declaration of war. The Finns stage a desperate defense. Some 120,000 Finns oppose 300,000 Soviet troops backed up by 800 aircraft.[5] The following days don't bring any news about the Soviets' swift victory in Finland. In fact there has been no follow-up on Finland whatsoever. The men at Kozielsk pray for Finland.

The guards at Kozielsk receive reinforcements from the NKVD. The political agents start systematic interrogations of the prisoners. The interrogations take place almost around the clock. The NKVD calls Michael for his so-called "interview" at 11 PM. He comes back at dawn. Julian hasn't been called yet and wants to know everything.

"What did they ask?"

"Well, first they ask about your address, education, profession, religion, your family background, and whereabouts of your closest relatives. And then they have this strange line of questions that I am not sure what it really means."

Many other friends from the barrack gather around Michael. A lawyer by profession, he should give them a professional assessment of the purpose of these interrogations. But Michael himself is puzzled.

"You know, they asked me, for example, what is it that I would do if they sent me home. Or for example, if one day they would show up at my door whether I would welcome them and offer them a shelter."

"And what did you say?"

"Oh, I certainly don't want to see them at my door. I just gave them some kind of an indirect vague reply."

"Yes, yes, they asked me the same question," one of the men says. "They also asked me whether I would report them to the Gestapo if they visit me one day."[6]

"Where are you from?" Julian asks.

"I am from Kraków. That's apparently the so-called General Government now, under the German protectorate."

"Right," Michael replies. "You see, I am from Grodno. That's under Soviet occupation now. But I wonder what is it that they are looking for in these interrogations. It seems as if they test our loyalty to them."

"I bet you're right," the inmates agree. "All these movies, newspapers and pep rallies are their attempts to convert us into loyal communists. That's obvious."

"But at least they talk about our release. It must be coming soon," Michael observes.

Every day the men at Kozielsk await their release. Some write petitions to the NKVD requesting that they be sent home, some write that they don't want to return to a Poland occupied by Germany and request to be sent to France or Great Britain. Those from the Soviet-occupied part of Poland face the most uncertainty. The Soviets are their masters now. They do not consider themselves Soviet citizens but they are told they are no longer the Polish citizens either.[7] According to the Soviet propaganda, Poland doesn't exist anymore. Michael and Julian are from Polish territory occupied by the Soviets. But Julian copes with the discomfort of this limbo much better than Michael, who grows more impatient every day.

He worries about his beloved wife and a baby daughter, Ala. He left them in Grodno at the beginning of the war. It's been already more than three months. How are they doing in these dangerous times? What has happened to them? Just recently, the prisoners were allowed to send letters home but only one letter per month.[8] No one at the camp has received any reply yet. Michael spends more and more time dreaming about his loved ones. His mood improves only when he talks about his dreams. Mary and Ala often visit him in his dreams. Then he awakens and spends hours looking at their picture that he keeps close to his chest. Initially, he liked to talk about his dreams but as time passes, his anguish grows, and his dreams are not that bright any more. His sunny dreams gradually turn into dark nightmares. Churches, cemeteries, mourning, and his loved ones, more and more elusive and more and more distant. It's hard, very hard to cope with this separation and uncertainty.

But he is not alone. Most of the men in the camp left behind their wives with small children. They all agonize in solitude over the fate of their loved ones left vulnerable and lonesome far away in the eye of the storm.

Fierce debates take place in the camp every day. France and Great Britain are favorite topics. The Allies did not attack in September but they must be preparing for the spring campaign. The Polish government-in-exile probably negotiates with the Soviets for the release of the Poles. The French and British must be interested in strengthening their army with Polish soldiers. Most of the men at Kozielsk, especially the younger single men, want to join the allied forces in the West. Julian is among them.

Before Christmas, Julian is called for interrogation. Despite countless discussions and debates, no one at the camp has a clue what the real purpose of the questioning may be. In the meantime, the NKVD agents systematically build files on each and every man. To complete the files, two pictures of each prisoner are taken, one forward facing and the other a profile. The NKVD agents keep inquiring about the addresses of all the relatives, collect them meticulously, and write down selective statements from the interrogations.

Realizing that the prisoners are evaluated ideologically, Julian is cautious with his words. He provides his address in Zbaraż but does not reveal other addresses of his relatives. He doesn't manifest his loyalty to the Soviet Union but he doesn't criticize the Soviets either. He only states that he wants to fight against Germany. His interview goes well. At the conclusion, the interviewing *politruk* even offers him a cigarette.

As Christmas approaches, the first letters start arriving at Kozielsk. Every few days, lists are posted with the names of the lucky ones who have received letters. Julian is very anxious to hear from home but Michael becomes insane with worry about Mary and Ala. Every time the names are posted, he is sick from stress. His name has not been posted yet. As days go by, he becomes obsessed with a letter from home. He loses his appetite, doesn't care about his appearance, and doesn't want to talk, play or read. Only when the names are posted, he rouses himself from his apathy. Frequently he talks to himself as if he would talk with Mary. Julian tries to reach him but without much success. Michael spends most of the time in bed either sleeping or day-dreaming. When he wakes up, he says "Good morning" to Mary and Ala, and when he goes to sleep, he says "Good night" to them.

With great anxiety but also with great hope, the men at Kozielsk celebrate Christmas. Their spirits improve considerably. Rumors are again spreading that the Allies are preparing an offensive and negotiating the release of the Polish prisoners. Julian and Michael celebrate Christmas Eve with other inmates in the barrack. A table is covered with a white cloth and a small Christmas tree and a candle stand in the center. The most senior officer delivers an uplifting speech. Next, the people share traditional *opłatek*, best wishes, greetings, hugs, and tears. Christmas carols are forbidden but quiet singing resounds throughout the camp nevertheless. On the official table, a holiday meal is served. It's a special treat—small sandwiches with fish, some fruits, and thimbleful of vodka for everyone. Emotions run high and everyone struggles not to fall apart....

The next few days are quiet. The men contemplate their grief and anxiety about their loved ones in the seclusion of their plank beds. Just before New Year's Eve, inmates from the Circus drop by looking for Julian. "Where is he?" a tall man hastily searches the beds.

"What's happened?" Michael asks.

"He has a letter!" the visitor exclaims.

Michael jumps out of bed, his face white and tense. "He has kitchen duty today. Let's go! Here, this way."

A group of men rushes out through the courtyard to the kitchen. "Julian, Julian!" they yell to him from the distance. But Julian already knows because he only waves to them, rushing towards the office.

Michael is shaken to his bones. He is happy for Julian and anxious to know what kind of news the letter brings. At the same time, he worries even more about Mary and Ala. Are they safe? Are they okay? Why don't they write?

Slowly, Julian emerges from the crowd with the letter in his hand. It's from his mother, from Zbaraż.

"Any news from Zbaraż? Any news about the neighbors, any names, what's happening in Zbaraż?" a self-proclaimed camp reporter intrusively inquires. He tries to put together a camp newsletter based on the information received from the latest correspondence.

"No names, Sir," Julian replies. "Only some comments that the Soviets took over the town and that the people talk about possible re-settlements."

"Resettlements? What's that? Doesn't sound good," people in the crowd repeat with concern. "Smells like a new buzzword for the old-style Siberian deportations."

At the barrack, Julian retreats to the seclusion of his bed and reads the letter over and over again. "My Dearest Juleczku!" his mother writes. She worries about him very much. A package with warm underwear, dry sausage, vitamins, and dry fruits is already on its way to Kozielsk. His sisters are doing fine although they have some problems with the Soviets.... Julian bites his lips, speculating what that means. At the bottom of the page there is this sentence that intrigues him very much. Apparently, a letter from Danusia came. His mother didn't open it. It means that Danusia is fine and he can even get her address. Julian is delighted. Eventually he will find her. His imagination races. The war must be over soon. He will go home, take his mother and his sisters into his arms. And maybe he could even see Danusia again. He looks forward to the New Year with keen hope.

For New Year's Eve, the central table is set again, another candle is lit, and more greetings are shared. On January 3rd, news breaks out that the Soviets have negotiated with the Germans for the exchange of POWs. Julian and Michael do not like the news. The exchange could apply to the prisoners from those parts of Poland incorporated to Germany. It is unlikely it would apply to them. But the news about any exchange quickly dies out.

In the middle of January, Michael receives the desperately longed-for letter from Mary. His girls are fine. The letter is very short though. Mary and Ala are in good health, but there is not much beyond this basic information. Michael is excited but nervous. He wants to know more, much, much more. The laconic content of the letter is not a coincidence. Apparently, there are plenty of problems that Mary doesn't want to write about. He worries even more.

Julian tries to calm him down. "Mary knows that if she writes too much, the Soviets may throw out the entire letter. She just wanted to make sure that her letter would reach you. Think about your own letters. How many times you write and rewrite these few words to make sure it would pass the Soviet censorship."

Indeed, everyone can write one letter per month. The prisoners are expected to write very brief letters, with only good news and only positive thoughts. They are not allowed to write about the camp conditions, or how they live, what they eat, or what they do. Michael writes and rewrites his letters endlessly. He tries to write how much he loves and misses his lovely girls, but he hates the thought that some *politruk* would read these precious, deeply personal words. The letter-writing process becomes an agonizing experience.

At the beginning of March, news breaks out that the Soviets have defeated Finland, but there are not many details. What sort of oppressed minorities the Soviets defended this time?, some cynically wonder. It took the Soviets surprisingly long to score that appalling victory. A depressed mood grows among the prisoners and plenty of new rumors about transports and transfers from Kozielsk spread throughout the camp again.

Easter approaches quickly. With considerable effort prisoners manage to arrange to have Easter eggs. Most of the Catholic priests have been withdrawn from the camp. Those who are still around are busy hearing confessions and granting absolution. They work around the clock despite the blatant prohibition of any religious activities in the camp. Easter, like Christmas, passes quietly in sorrow and with plenty of tears.

Suddenly at the beginning of April, the rumors about transfers turn into reality. The Soviets call a group of generals and the highest ranking officers, ask them to gather their personal belongings, and round them up for deportation.[9] Excitement rages through the camp.

"Liberation!" Some cry.

"No, they will send us to the transition camps. From there, some of us will go home, some would be turned over to the Germans," others speculate. "An international commission of French, British and Soviets will decide which officers would be sent to the West," others believe.

Julian and Michael are excited, too. They go to the clubhouse to say farewell to their departing friends. Some with suitcases, others just with blankets, the departing men proceed to the clubhouse for a thorough search. Knives and all sharp objects are confiscated. Everything else is fine. Next, the group is offered a good meal and each man receives provisions for the journey—bread, sugar, and one herring wrapped in a decent piece of paper. The prisoners are impressed. The Soviets apparently want to make a good lasting impression before the non-Soviet authorities assume custody of the prisoners, the common wisdom goes.[10]

A few days later, new rumors abound: Germany has invaded Denmark and Norway. What does that mean? How does that affect their destiny? Consternation reigns among the prisoners. But it appears as if the events in Denmark and Norway have no impact on the destiny of the men at Kozielsk at all. The deportations continue in orderly fashion.

Every day between two and three hundred men are called and rounded up for transfer to an unknown destination. Every morning, their names come directly from Moscow via a special telephone line.[11] As the deportations continue, personnel changes are made at the camp. Regular guards are gradually withdrawn and replaced by NKVD agents. But hardly anyone notices these changes. Everybody wants to leave the camp as soon as possible. Some people, Michael among them, desperately want to go home; others like Julian want to go to the front to fight the Germans. Everybody is anxious to find out where they are being sent. And it turns out that this is the most guarded secret of all. No one knows.

In the middle of April other news comes: the Germans have taken over Denmark and Norway. What will happen to Sweden, people wonder. And how about the United States? Some statement from the United States regarding the current developments are expected soon.

But Michael doesn't care about any statements any more. He has washed his underwear, fixed his shoes, and is ready for his departure. He hasn't received any further letters from Mary and that's the only reason why he still hesitates to leave. He would prefer to go after receiving another much sought-after letter. But that will not happen.

One sunny spring day his turn comes. He hugs Julian, shakes hands with the prisoners, takes a bag with personal belongings and eagerly moves on. "Remember to write your destination on the side of the wagon," his friends remind him.

The round-ups and deportations have been continuing already for about two weeks and no one knows yet where the prisoners are being sent. So those who depart are asked to write the name of their destination on the side of the train.[12] The speculation is that they are sent west. The NKVD guards seem to confirm this speculation. To the men at Kozielsk, to go west means only one thing—to go home. For many, that's all what they want to know.

After waving farewell to Michael, Julian returns back to the barrack and disappears into bed. He doesn't feel well. Despite the exuberant cheers and excitement outside, he feels as if he has just lost his best friend. They have been together for many months. Michael became everything—father, mother, and brother—to Julian. Even in his moments of despair, Michael tried to find warm and comforting words for Julian.

"Am I going to see him again? What's going to happen now?" Julian ponders.

He doesn't have to wait long. Two days later, his name comes from Moscow. He is ready. But sadly no letter from Danusia and no letter for Michael either! Farewell to his friends, the search procedure, the meal, provisions for the trip, the marching order, the long line of cheering inmates, and Julian, together with another two hundred or more selected companions, leaves through the gates of the Kozielsk camp.

A short distance from the gates, a new squad of NKVD guards takes over the group of deportees. The new guards are strikingly unfriendly, even frightening. With truncheons, machineguns, attack-dogs, and grim faces, the new guards order the deportees into nearby trucks. "Why such a heavy escort?" everyone wonders. The truck ride is short, just to the train station where a train with windowless prison cars awaits the deportees. This doesn't look good. Julian becomes frightened.

"Get off and onto the train!" the guards order.

The NKVD guards brutally push the men to their train prison cells. With every minute, the deportees become more apprehensive. Some drag their feet and hesitate to board the ugly train. A guard pushes the man next to Julian. The man swears and kicks the guard back. Without blinking an eye, the guard pulls out a truncheon and hits the man full force in the head. The man sways, his face bloodstained. Julian and some others grab the collapsing man. The furious, confused, and terrified deportees are pushed to the train. Six men are packed into small three-person compartments. The man hit by the guard, a teacher from Brześć, is badly wounded and needs help. The guards pay no attention to repeated requests for medical assistance. Julian is outraged. His companions have the same uneasy feeling about these developments. The train starts moving. The wounded man bleeds profusely. With considerable effort, Julian and his other companions manage to stop his hemorrhage.

The train moves slowly, jerking, often stopping, and rumbling. As evening sets in, the rays of light inside the cell indicate that the train is moving west. To the Kozielsk deportees it means only one thing—Poland.

But the night is very uncomfortable. Everybody is cold, exhausted, traumatized, and hungry. With the first rays of daylight, the train stops for good at a small station. It's Gniezdovo, a small town not far from Smolensk. "Is this our destination?" people wonder.

Yes, the train will be unloaded here, they learn. To their dismay, there is nothing to eat or drink. The NKVD guards equipped with fixed bayonets and assisted by attack-dogs load the first group of prisoners directly into an ugly black prison van.

"How scary," Julian thinks. In an effort to cover his feelings, he assumes a more arrogant posture, plunging his hands into the pockets of his pants. His fingers nervously move around different objects in the pockets. Impatiently squeezing and pawing everything there, his hand suddenly senses the familiar shape of a tiny book. This is his most precious companion—Słowacki poems! He withdraws to the back of the wagon and slides to the floor. It looks like the unloading will take some time. Closing his eyes, he tries to calm down, reciting in his mind his favorite poems. The poetry of Juliusz Słowacki is born from the national drama, from the deaths and unimaginable sufferings of generations of Poles fighting against the Russian oppressors for independent Poland throughout the nineteenth century. His favorite lines come from the most dramatic poem, "My Testament." How strikingly similar! He gets up fast. "No, no, I need something else." His mind frantically searches for more positive thoughts.

His friends at the steps of the wagon are becoming frenzied. "We are the next to go," someone tells him. The black van unavoidably backs up to their door.

"These bastards are going to kill us here!" one of the men says as the rest breathlessly watch the black coffin approaching. "Just like that?" another voice asks in a strained pitch. "No, they will hand us over to the Germans here," another energetic voice counters.

The guards don't waste time. With savage brutality, they grab the men and push them into the van. Julian doesn't want to be pushed. He kicks the rough hand that tries to grab his shirt and steps into the van passageway. On both sides, low doors lead to dreadfully rotten one-person cells with small grated windows painted black. Tension grows as the NKVD guards push confused people one by one into these small burrows of torture. Julian, painfully hit in the stomach, lands in an awkward position in one of the cells in the middle of the van, the doors rapidly locking behind him. Soon all thirty or so cells are loaded and the van starts moving.

The ride is short, only a couple of minutes or so. But for the men inside it is an eternity. Some pray and cry, some curse and swear, some kick and scream. Julian, in a hunched position, keeps his hand on the tiny book and prays: "Our Father.... I believe in one God...." But his blurred mind mixes the prayer with Słowacki's poetry. Suddenly, the van stops; the screaming and kicking stops, too. Everybody listens attentively. What's next?

The prisoners from the front cells are taken. Seconds later, a horrifying scream pierces the air, changing into the sound of a struggling fight and ending with the sound of a clear single pistol shot. The men inside break into a cold sweat. Now they know! There are no Germans or French or British here, not even human beings here. There are only cold-blooded NKVD murderers awaiting them outside.[13]

As the terror-stricken men agonize in their last moments, a powerful voice resounds from one of the cells: "Poland is not yet lost…!" and the Polish national anthem bursts throughout the van. The next cells are opened and the next men are taken. "Long Live Poland!" the men shout between the pistol shots.

As his turn approaches, Julian's mind ventures back to 1830—the tragic Polish uprising against the Russian oppressor. As his ancestors did one hundred years ago, Julian embraces his fate. His soul and mind embody his destiny, his lips proclaim his mission. The verses of "My Testament" written a century ago become his calling...

I lived with you, suffered and cried with you
Every honorable man always mattered to me,
Today I leave you and I go away to the shadow of death
And as if happiness was here – I depart in sadness.

He steps outside. It's a sunny spring day. He raises his head: fresh green woods, its fragrance in the air, and a sharp blue sky above.

I do not leave any heir behind
Neither to my name nor to my talent
My name has passed like a lightning
And will endure as an empty sound for generations.

He proceeds along two rows of NKVD guards. A man in front of him struggles. With one piece of white cord, the murderers tie a knot around his neck, wind the cord around his hands behind and tie another knot at his neck. "Long Live Poland!" the man tries to shout. The slaughterers throw a greatcoat over his head, tying it with another cord at the prisoner's neck.[14]

But you, who have known me, in your tales recount
That I dedicated to my country my youth.
And as long as the battleship was fighting – I was on the mast
And when sinking – with the battleship I went.

Another pistol shot. A huge pit...bodies down there. His turn. Two murderers tie his hands as the third one reloads the pistol.

But one day, reflecting upon the tragic fate
Of my unfortunate country – the honorable man will admit
That the coat on my spirit was not that of a beggar
But the noble one – great in the glory of my ancestors.

"Poland Now and Forever!" Julian proclaims. Another pistol shot...abyss and oblivion.

My friends should meet in the night
Burn my suffering heart in aloes,
And return it to the one who gave me the heart
That's how the world repays the mother – return that heart!

* * * *

Sixty years later, Danusia moves around the Ohio suburban house busy with housework when suddenly she recognizes the familiar phrases.

My friends sit down with the beaker cup
And drink for my funeral and your misfortune.
If I am the restless spirit I shall appear
If God releases me from suffering I shall not come.

"Konrad, come, come quickly, look! This is 'My Testament,' this very famous poem by Słowacki." On the TV screen, in an elegant living room decorated with antique furniture, a young man dressed in the romantic nineteenth-century loose-fitting white shirt with a dashing turned down collar recites "My Testament" with burning eyes. Konrad already knows the poem by heart but now he can watch it performed on TV. He stares at the screen in silence.

But I adjure – you, the living, don't lose hope!
And carry the awareness light in front of the nation
And when called upon – in step proceed to death
Like stones thrown by God on the battlement.

Konrad freezes. The powerful image burns in his imagination.

As if for me – I leave tiny friendship here
Those who could fall in love with my proud heart;
Let it be known that I fulfilled severe God's service
And I agreed to have the un-moaned coffin here.

"This is my Julian speaking to us." Danusia holds back tears.

Who else like so without the world applause would agree
To go forward... have such indifference for the world as I do?
Be the steersman of the boat full of souls
And depart as quietly as a flying away soul.

The camera zooms in on the face of the young man on the screen. The image of his tense lips sharpens, his burning eyes stitching through the audience.

However, I will leave behind that force fatal
Useless to me – the living, merely adorning my forehead.
But after death it will press you invisible
Until you, the bread eaters, will transform into angels.

Danusia cries.

"Grandma," Konrad starts slowly, "have you heard that in Baltimore the 44-foot bronze Katyń Monument has been erected this year."

"Yes. And I also heard about the one in Jersey City across from the World Trade Center, one in Australia and another in Sweden. It is only now, after the demise of the Soviet Union, that these memorials are being allowed. In Great Britain, where many of the families of the Katyń victims eventually settled, any memorial to the memory of the Katyń victims was strictly forbidden for almost half a century."

"As I understand, Grandma, this crime was disclosed to the public a long time ago, back in 1943 when the Germans invading the Soviet Union stumbled over the Katyń graves."

"Yes, yes, how ironic, isn't it?" Danusia shakes her head. "It was back then when the representatives of the International Red Cross clearly identified the timing of this massacre and its perpetrators. But you see, the Soviet Union unleashed a propaganda war, blaming the Germans for the crime and for half a century successfully denying any responsibility for this crime. It was not until April 1990, when Mikhail Gorbachev acknowledged to the Polish Government that the NKVD had murdered all Polish prisoners held in the camps at Kozielsk, Ostashkov, and Starobielsk.[15] The murders were carried out during the six-week period in the spring of 1940. Today, this genocide is known as Katyń Murders. Not many people realize, though, that in Katyń only about 4,100 prisoners from Kozielsk are buried. No one knows yet for sure the final burial place of 3,920 prisoners from Starobielsk and 6,500 prisoners from Ostashkov.[16] But we have some leads as to the fate of the remaining ten thousand or more of Poland's best and brightest men. Do you remember when Germany invaded its fateful ally, the Soviet Union?"

"Yes, in June of 1941, only one year after the Katyń Murders." Konrad eagerly replies.

"Weren't these Katyń Murders a nonsensicality of global proportions?" Danusia's whole body tenses and shakes in convulsion. She sighs. "You see, the Polish government-in-exile was initially based in France and subsequently operated from London. Through its government-in-exile, Poland was a founding and very important member of the Allied coalition. It became obvious back then, in 1941, that Polish acceptance of the Soviet Union as its ally would not only improve the poor international standing of the Soviet Union but more importantly would help foster the realignment of powers towards a stronger anti-fascist coalition. Under pressure from the British Government, General Sikorski, representing the Polish Government-in-Exile, decided to sign a new treaty with Stalin.[17] In his broadcast to Poland in the summer of 1941, General Sikorski announced that the agreement with the Soviet Union offering amnesty to all Poles located in the Soviet Union would enable the Polish people to form the Polish Army from the Polish prisoners of war held anywhere in Russia. In his words, the treaty restored freedom 'to all Polish citizens located in the Soviet Union, whatever the pretext for their detention could be'."[18]

"That treaty would have returned freedom to those fifteen thousand Polish officers from Kozielsk, Ostashkov and Starobielsk slaughtered a year earlier. Oh, how dreadful!" Konrad exclaims with sore disbelief.

"But, unfortunately, this is not the end of the dirty face of this chapter of history," Danusia continues. "Half a year later, in December of 1941, General Sikorski met with Stalin and asked about thousands of missing Polish officers. To him, the terms of the amnesty had not been fulfilled because the most valuable Polish soldiers were still in the Soviet prisons. Stalin replied that all of the Polish officers had been released but probably hadn't returned home yet."

"That was when Pearl Harbor was attacked and the United States joined the Allied coalition, wasn't it, Grandma?"

"You are right. Soon after Sikorski's discussion with Stalin, the United States joined the war. Overnight the balance of power on the international scene had changed. Great Britain was no longer in isolation, thus the significance of the faithful Polish allies had rapidly diminished. The United States became the leading force in the Allied coalition and without delay reached out to the Soviet Union.

"Despite the changing dynamics on the political scene, Sikorski never gave up his search for thousands of his officers. The tension in the Polish–Soviet relations reached its climax when the German Army in the Soviet Union tumbled over the Polish mass graves at Katyń. As a result of the German announcement about the Katyń graves, Polish–Soviet relations were irreparably ruined. The Katyń Murders became such a contentious issue that the unity of the entire Allied coalition was at risk. The issue was swept under the carpet though a few months later, together with the tragic death of General Sikorski who was killed in a bizarre airplane crash in July of 1943. Only the pilot survived that crash."

"Was there any investigation of this accident?"

"The British conducted some investigation but kept the results secret. I only remember the German tabloids triumphantly announcing the death of General Sikorski in the airplane crash over Gibraltar. We were devastated beyond imagination."

In her mind, Danusia goes back to this dramatic day back in the summer of 1943 when Poland was plastered with the sinister death notice of General Sikorski to the delight of the German oppressors. With Sikorski's death, the Polish government-in-exile lost forever an influential, effective, and powerful leader. No one would ever match the international stature of General Sikorski, and Poland was never able to regain the position of influence adequate to its military contribution to the Allied cause. From that point on, the role of the Polish government-in-exile began to diminish. In the meantime, the Soviets were busy concocting their own "Polish" communist government that would be willing to approve all Soviet territorial gains made during their September 17, 1939 invasion pursuant to the vicious Ribbentrop–Molotov pact.

"But what about the leads as to the Ostashkov and Starobielsk victims, Grandma?"

Danusia raises her eyebrows. "That's right, I am getting there. You see, as a result of the June 1941 amnesty, many Poles managed to return home. Among them were those returning from Siberia and from other remote locations in the Soviet Union. Those returning from the Kola Peninsula area reported that in the spring of 1940, a boat bearing Polish prisoners had been towed into the White Sea and sunk with artillery power.[19] This information was corroborated later by the oral accounts of the local Russians who claimed to have seen two barges containing thousands of the Polish prisoners towed from Arkhangelsk and sunk."[20]

"But I also read that NKVD high-ranking agents in Kalinin and Smolensk conducted mass killings of the prisoners from Ostashkov and Kozielsk, non-stop for several weeks, about 200 to 300 killings per night."[21] Konrad chooses the words with some effort.

"You may be right. Apparently, it is not clear yet how and where the prisoners from Ostashkov and Starobielsk were exterminated. Some sources point out that the prisoners from Ostashkov were first sent in large groups to Kalinin and from there transported in small groups for extermination to a village Miednoje, about 30 kilometers from Kalinin. It is believed that the NKVD built a villa on the graveyard of the Polish victims in Miednoje."

Danusia reaches for a tissue. "One thing is very clear today," she continues, blowing her nose. "We know for sure that on March 5, 1940, Beria, the Soviet Commissar for Internal Affairs, submitted for Stalin's approval a top-secret document pursuant to which '14,700 Polish officers and government officials kept in prisoner-of-war camps and 10,685 Polish landowners, factory owners, former Polish officers and government representatives, and other spies and counterrevolutionaries kept in the Soviet prisons in the former Polish territory should receive the supreme penalty: death. [...] The cases should be examined by a three-person tribunal[22] consisting of the top NKVD officials.' According to a report prepared for Nikita Khrushchev in 1959, all together

21,857 Poles were executed pursuant to this order in 1940.[23] Polish prisoners of war of the officer rank and all other 'carriers of the Polish identity,' the best and the brightest among Poland's citizens overrun by the Soviet Union, perished without a trace during the spring of 1940, and only about four thousand bodies found accidentally by the Germans in the Katyń forest have been accounted for."

"These murders seem to me not only tragic and cruel but simply stupid," Konrad's distressed voice reaches Danusia.

"Well, this was a senseless, irrational crime ordered by a totalitarian madman and meticulously carried out by the totalitarian system that does not tolerate any dissent. There is, however, this question that often lingers in my mind. Why weren't the Katyń victims sent to the labor camps and just worked to death—the standard Soviet approach at that time? There must be only one answer to it, I think. The Katyń victims were the part of the Polish elite, their loss translated into irreparable harm to the Polish nation. Obviously, Stalin was determined to destroy Poland once and for all. His decision to exterminate all those considered the carriers of the Polish identity meant the genocide of the Polish nation. To me, the Soviet slaughter of the Polish intelligentsia was a deliberate decision to eradicate the entire ethnic group with its culture and heritage.

"His vision was short-lived, though. In his blind hatred, he didn't realize he would badly need the Poles just one year later. Also he didn't realize that by committing this atrocity, he immortalized the Katyń victims and transformed them into national martyrs and Poland's eternal heroes. We are determined never to forget. To us, the Katyń victims became our dearest heroes sacrificed on the altar of freedom and independence. They embody all those hundreds of thousands of Poles slaughtered by the Soviets in World War II."

"I wonder, Grandma, why weren't these mass murders ever investigated after the war? No one was ever brought to justice for this atrocity. To me this was the crime against humanity."

"Ha!" Danusia pauses. "Listen to this. In the Summer of 1945, four victorious countries, the Soviets, Americans, British, and French, met in London to decide upon methods of 'the prosecution and trial of the major European war criminals.'[24] The four victors divided amongst themselves the areas of responsibility. The United States chose to prosecute the war of aggression. Great Britain chose crimes on the high sea and treaty violations, and the Soviets chose to prosecute 'crimes against humanity,' sharing that responsibility on a geographical basis with the French.[25] Thus, the perpetrators of the Katyń crime became be the prosecutors at the Nuremberg trial."[26]

Konrad opens his mouth, trying to catch his breath. "And why!?" he exclaims. "Why did the Allies agreed to that?"

"Well, Konrad, the leaders of the new world once again decided that the Poles had to be sacrificed in order not to upset the Soviets."[27]

"And look, Grandma, isn't that symbolic that in the end, it was Poland that destroyed the Soviet Communism, the Polish Pope, the Polish Solidarity Movement, and the Polish first non-Communist government melted down that tip of the Communist iceberg, making the whole Soviet empire to crumble and fall apart." This part of history Konrad knows the best. The Solidarity struggle is the reason why he is in America today. It is the integral part of his parents' life, and a vivid image in the memory of his older sister.

His mother walks into the room and catches Konrad's last comments. "Right, son. Today many rush to claim credit for destroying Communism. President Reagan and Mikhail Gorbachev are frequently mentioned, East Germans and the falling Berlin Wall become the symbol of the demise of Communism. The truth of the matter is that it was not Gorbachev, not Reagan, and not even the East Germans who risked their lives to fight Communism and regain dignity, but once again, it was the unruly people of Poland, united in the Solidarity Movement, who struggled relentlessly against the Soviet domination and once again put their lives on line to regain that precious independence, liberty, and freedom." Konrad's mother energetically drops a package of mail on the table and goes through the envelopes at random.

"Oh, another one!" she picks up one of the letters and tears wide open an official envelope. "Ha, another voter identification card for me. I wonder why I am receiving the second ID card and no one else receives any."

Dinner is about to be served. She switches the channels and the CNN news reporter brings the latest shouting match between presidential candidates George W. Bush and Al Gore.

"Mae, would you take me to the polls?" Danusia asks with a dose of urgency in her voice. She remembers her first elections in Poland back in 1946. Those critically important elections were stolen by the Communists back then and for the next forty-four years Poland had only phony elections with predetermined rubber-stamped results. Going to the polls under the Communist regime meant selling your soul and betraying your country. But in the United States, Danusia treasures that priceless feeling of personal dignity. As an individual with full rights, she feels as though she can make a difference, as though her existence has meaning and value, her voice and her opinion count and can be heard. After years of Nazi terror and despicable disregard for human rights and dignity, after decades of Soviet oppression and indoctrination, the respect for the rights of the individual has been a priceless treasure for Danusia and the main source of her fascination with America.

"Of course I'll take you." Mae smiles taking of her formal jacket.

"We already had the elections in school." Konrad says with pride. "We even discussed the issues."

"So, who won your elections?" Danusia asks.

"George Bush, of course."

"Why do you say 'of course'?" His mother asks.

"Because he looks nice and seems to be a cool guy, that's what everybody's saying. The kids think that Gore is stiff."

"And how about the issues?" Danusia asks.

"Frankly, no one really cares about the issues. Hardly anyone votes on them."

"That's very, very dangerous," Danusia shakes her head with disappointment. "But you still have some time to learn to vote on the issues. I hope by the time you are eligible to vote you won't vote on appearances."

"Oh, I have to check why is it that I am the only one who has received this voter identification card." Mae picks up the phone.

"Yes, Ma'am, your husband is on our lists but your mother-in-law is not," the election official informs her.

"So what can we do to make sure she can vote?" Mae asks, bewildered.

"At this point there is nothing you can do. She simply cannot vote." The election official replies.

"I am sorry, but that's ridiculous. We all voted in the last elections and I am getting two ID cards, my husband doesn't get any, and

Grandma doesn't even make it to your lists. This is clearly your fault and you are telling me you can't do anything about it?"

"That's right, Ma'am."

Mae gets up. "Please understand. She is 78 years old and I cannot simply tell her not to vote. This is too important to her, she never ever missed any elections here, and how am I supposed to explain to her that she can't vote?"

"Well, Ma'am, I understand. What you could do is to take her to the polls and let her vote as a 'walk-in.' Her vote will not count but at least you could calm her down." The election official advises her.

"So, you want me to cheat her?"

"I am sorry but that's the best you can do under the circumstances."

Mae furiously hangs up the phone. Eventually she pulls herself together and doesn't say a word. Election Day is busy and tense. People rush to make it to the polls and still catch up with the daily chores. Roads are crowded; occasional drizzle slows down the traffic. But the turn out for the elections is high. In all polling locations, people stand in long lines eager to make their personal statements regarding the future of their country.

Mae takes Danusia to the polls early in the morning. "I am not going to take my oxygen equipment with me. It's not that far and it shouldn't take that long," Danusia decides.

At the poll located in the nearby church, people eager to vote form long lines. With some effort, Mae arranges for a chair and Danusia slumps into it. The election workers confirm that Danusia's name is not on the lists. Thus, her name and address is placed at the last page of the big election book and a glaring green ballot is given to her. Mae takes Danusia to the voting booth. Breathing with exhaustion, Danusia tries to punch a hole through the green paper. "Oh!" a grimace shows on her face. It hurts. Her swelling fingers twisted with arthritis lost their grip. The pen slips out.

"That's okay, let me help you." Mae takes the pen and punches the paper as Danusia points the names of her candidates. It is a long process, the president, the state officials, the local officials, and the issues.... Whew, she hardly catches her breath and has to sit down quickly. Mae returns the ballot and hurriedly takes Danusia back to the chair. "Relax now."

With satisfaction and sense of pride for well-fulfilled duty, Danusia returns home. Throughout the day, she closely follows the election news. In the evening, the family gathers at the dinner table when first election results start coming in: the agricultural states mostly for Bush, the industrial states mostly for Gore. At around 9 PM, the TV networks call All Gore as the winner in Florida. He scores a major victory there. But the race is very close. It becomes obvious that the West Coast states will have a final say in this unfolding election drama. It doesn't look like the end will come anytime soon. Mae turns off the TV and the house falls asleep.

In the morning, they find out to their amazement that the presidential race is still too close to call. They also learn that later in the night Florida went to Governor Bush but subsequently, while Vice President Gore was on his way to give the concession speech, Florida was taken back from Governor Bush and was again put into the toss-up column making the race too close to call. The presidential race hinges on the Florida results.

Several weeks later, Konrad rushes to finish up a present for his Dad. It's Dad's name-day today. He prepares *laurka*, a special greeting card with hand-painted flowers. All Polish children write name-day greetings for their parents on *laurkas*. The table is set for celebration. Grandfather in his wheelchair is waiting in the dining room. Danusia brings flowers and presents. Konrad at the piano starts playing the very special name-day song *Sto Lat*. Everybody joins in the singing. Pictures are taken as Dad is loaded with presents.

In the middle of the celebration, the CNN reporter announces that the Supreme Court of the United States stopped the counting of the Florida under-votes in the contested presidential race. Everyone rushes to the TV room. A day before, the Florida Supreme Court ordered a statewide hand-count of all ballots rejected by the computer. Now the highest court in the land comes back and stops the hand-count of the Florida votes.

On the screen, the supporters of George Bush cheer the decision. The Bush campaign reporter, Candy Crowley, announces that the Bush team exhibits subdued exuberance. The Democrats are cautious. For the past month, their opponents have demonstrated power at every step of the process. "We are covered everywhere. No matter what the Democrats do, we are determined to stop them," the Republicans declare.

Danusia stares at the TV with fear. "But I don't understand," she says quietly. "Why is it that so many votes are not counted, invalidated, or disregarded? Doesn't that jeopardize the fundamental rights of each and every one of us? To me this race sets a precedence to disregard the will of the people, am I getting this right…? Why do the people allow for the rules of the jungle?" Danusia keeps asking.

Her son shrugs. "And what should they do? They are powerless."

Danusia's eyes are getting round. "They should protect their rights," she raises her voice. "If the system loses its democratic safety net, the people will pay a steep price to restore it." Her eyes are burning. "Why the people don't respect their fundamental rights? They don't value them because they have never experienced life without them. What they are really saying is that they don't care about the will of the people as long as their candidate is winning. That brings back some of my worst memories, I must say."

"Grandma," Konrad says. "Have you heard about this astrological prediction from Pennsylvania about the assassination?"

"It's insane." Danusia gets angry. "It would be like John F. Kennedy or like our president Gabriel Narutowicz in 1922." She sighs. "Fanatic hatred and drive for power at any cost…. And all this propaganda, it's called 'spinning' these days. A new buzzword for the thousand-year-old propaganda machine that promotes hatred and prejudice. It's not good. It's very unhealthy and dangerous."

16. Unearthed mass grave of the Polish officers in Katyń Forest

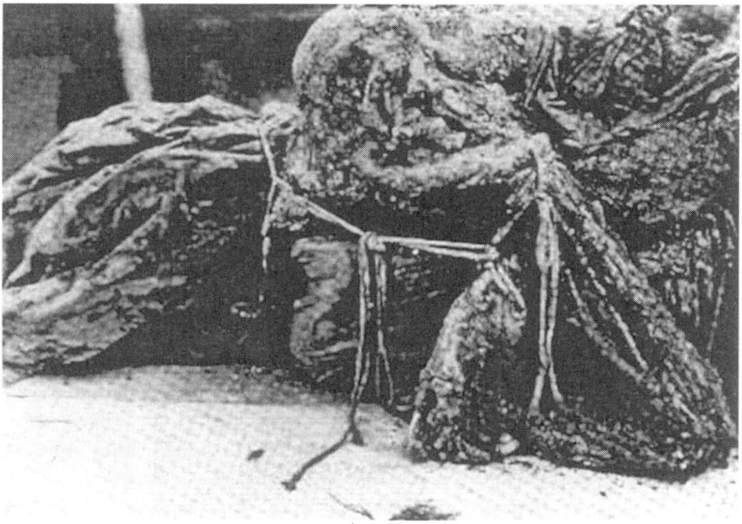

17. Katyń victim: greatcoat tied over the head, at the neck, passed down, around the tied hand, and tied again at the neck

7

The curfew approaches and old Gara is about to lock the gate.

"Good evening, Mr. Gara," Danusia's resonant voice reaches him.

"Hi, Dad!" Maya waves to him in a weary gesture.

He looks with apprehension at the two girls emerging from the shadow of the mint production building. "Jesus Christ, you two look like revenants."

"Right Dad, we had to work twelve hours without rest." The girls are pale. With dull looks on their pretty faces, they hardly shuffle with their feet, unable to take pleasure in the refreshing charm of the spring evening.

"Not only today," Danusia complaints. "It has been like that all the time. And it's only getting worse."

Gara energetically wrestles with the heavy gate. "I know, I know. We have to do something about it."

"And what's even worse is that not everybody has to work overtime. Some girls are simply treated better." Danusia kicks the gate with fury. "We must do something about it!"

"Yes, yes." Maya Gara echoes with resignation. "Bye, Danusia!" She waves leaning heavily on her father.

"Bye, Mayą, have good dreams!"

At home Danusia drops dead on the sofa, stretching her legs high up.

"At last you are back!" Dad explodes. "We were afraid they might work you overnight!"

Smoothing over Danusia's soft hair, Mama shakes her head. "We must do something about it. I know! I must talk with Mrs. Sowińska. As a German she has a special status now and all these shopping and traveling privileges. She has become very influential lately. And after all, she is my faithful customer and good friend."

"I am not sure whether that's going to work but I will talk with her husband," Dad declares. "He is a decent man and he also became more influential lately because of his Austrian wife. I know how bad he feels about all the persecutions. He is one hundred percent Polish and has been firmly anti-Nazi since the killing of his good friend in Wawer."

"I have a feeling that if Mrs. Sowińska could talk to the Director General that would be the only chance to put this problem to rest once and for all." Mama is fiddling affectionately with Danusia's fine hair. "Oh, by the way, both Józek and Gienio were here today."

"Oh, really?" Danusia opens her eyes. "And what?"

"Gienio brought a very interesting issue of *bibuła*," Dad says.

"And he left some flowers for you," Zbyszek pointing out to a vase with fresh daffodils.

Danusia fleetingly glimpses at the flowers and turns her penetrating eyes on the mother. "And how about Józek? What did he say?"

Dad shakes his head in discontent, grabs the *bibuła*, and disappears in another room.

"He said he would stop by over the weekend," Mama replies trying to sound casual.

"How about if I invite him for dinner on Saturday?" Danusia presses Mama.

"Well...," Mama hesitates. "I guess, that's fine."

"But then make sure you invite Gienio, too," a comment comes from the other room.

"That's a good idea," Zbyszek adds. "Gienio always brings some goodies."

"Okay, then you invite Gienio," Danusia angrily glares at Zbyszek.

"No problem. He is here with *bibuła* every day. But I know he would much rather prefer to be invited by you."

"Too bad. I am not going to invite him!" Danusia growls.

The next day Danusia catches Józek in his apartment and invites him for Saturday dinner. The curfew approaches rapidly and Józek walks her back. Risking arrest he has to sneak through the back yards on his way back.

On Saturday, Danusia works in the morning. After lunch, she rushes home to help in preparation of the special dinner: pork chops with mashed potatoes and sauerkraut, and a cheesecake for dessert. Soon Gienio shows up with the latest issue of *bibuła*, a bonbonnière for Danusia, kiełbasa for Mama, and a bottle of vodka for Dad. He is dressed more officially than usual, in a white shirt and a jacket. When he drops by with the *bibuła* during the week, he is energetic, considerate, and full of jokes and optimism. But today he is tense. In Danusia's presence, he loses his animation and becomes shy. She welcomes him politely and continues preparing the table. He follows her every move with covetous eyes.

Fifteen minutes later, Józek arrives. He is also officially dressed, in a dark blue suit and a white shirt. With his dark blond hair combed back, high forehead, and intelligent deep blue eyes, he looks like a dignitary. Danusia welcomes him eagerly. Józek hands her a bouquet of red tulips, politely kisses her mother's hand, and shakes hands with Dad and Zbyszek.

"Mr. Eugeniusz Pawłowski, Mr. Józek Fijałkowski," Dad introduces the two men. They carefully scrutinize each other. Neither understands the role of the other man. Neither likes the other. The hosts don't rush with explanations. Gienio sits quietly and observes Danusia as she places a crystal vase with red tulips on the white tablecloth in the center of the table. Dad tries to strike a conversation with him but Gienio is tense and visibly uncomfortable. Danusia beams; her dark curly hair enhances the beauty of her pale childish cheeks and adds depth to her sparkling brown eyes. She doesn't pay much attention to Gienio but radiates with joy talking with Józek. But Józek is tense too. He senses the cold reception from the parents and Gienio's covetous eyes fixed on Danusia. She tries hard to loosen his stiffness but without success.

Dinner is served. Dad carefully checks a bottle of vodka from Gienio and smacks his lips in great content. "White Label Vodka!" he exclaims with delight. "This is top quality stuff, it's impossible to buy this vodka now. Where did you get it?"

"Oh, I've got it from one of my clients."

With fascination, Dad pours the crystal liquid into glasses. "Just a little please," Józek asks. Danusia, Mama, and Zbyszek don't drink at all.

"To your health!" Dad raises his glass, strikes Gienio's glass first, then turns to Józek, and drains his glass to the bitter end.

"To your health!" they reply, wetting their lips with the fiery liquid. Gienio drinks more than half of his glass but Józek is way behind. Dad starts filling up the glasses again but Józek covers his glass and signals that he can't drink any more. With great concern, Danusia observes the developments. Dad insists and Józek firmly resists. Danusia realizes that Józek has just failed an important test to become Dad's bosom buddy. Indeed, Dad makes some disappointing gesture and a ruthless comment about Józek's restrained drinking habit, and turns abruptly to his other companion. Gienio is not a heavy drinker either but his half-full glass is filled up again and thus Dad's glass gets filled up too. With every other glass, Dad's mood improves; his voice grows louder, his arm lands on Gienio's shoulder.

"So my friend, have you heard about our submarine—*Orzeł*? It's incredible what our boys are doing these days!"

"What is it, Dad?" Danusia tries to bring the other half of the table into the discussion.

"Our brave submarine sunk a huge German transporter *Rio de Janeiro*," Zbyszek explains proudly.

"That ship was carrying the German Army to Norway," Dad adds.

"But what's also interesting about it," Józek cautiously joins the discussion, "is that this incident took place one day before the German invasion on Norway. After exposing German intentions, *Orzeł* sent an urgent message to the Allied forces alerting them to the impending German attack on Norway. Apparently, someone chose not to act upon this message and the Allied forces were once again taken by surprise the next day."[1]

Dad sends Józek a careful look. This fellow actually knows something. But who knows what his affiliation is. So, he turns to Gienio, his trusted advisor.

"My friend, tell me more about this Podhale Rifle Brigade that has been sent to fight the Germans at Narvik. How many men do we have there?"

"I don't know that much." Gienio tries to play down his underground background. "But I heard they have about five thousand men under the command of General Szyszko-Bohusz."[2]

"I understand that General Sikorski is in the process of forming several more divisions of the Polish Armed Forces in France." Dad adds.

"Yes, but this Podhale Brigade is the first Polish military formation abroad that actually went to combat against the Germans. So, in this sense it is an important step for us," Gienio says.

"Apparently, the formation of the Podhale Brigade began already back in 1939 when the Soviet Union attacked Finland." Józek follows up. "Back then, the allies decided that instead of sending British or French forces to Finland it would be politically advisable to send the Poles and preserve a neutral standing towards the Soviets for as long as possible. That's when they started the formation of the Podhale Brigade. But by the time the brigade was ready for action, the Finns have signed the so-called peace treaty with the Soviets."[3]

"The so-called treaty?" Dad interrupts. "I gather you don't believe in this peace treaty...." He sounds sarcastic.

"Of course not." Józek replies firmly and at the same time gets a solid kick under the table. Danusia jumps into the conversation. "How about our other ships that escaped to London at the beginning of the war? What happens to them?"

Gienio slightly bends over the table and lowers his voice. "I understand that most of them including our destroyers *Grom*, *Błyskawica*, and *Burza* together with three transporters *Sobieski*, *Batory*, and *Chrobry* are also taking part in the Narvik campaign. "

"That's great!" Dad pours more vodka and before long switches to singing.

Dessert is served. Józek talks quietly with Danusia. From time to time, Mama asks some questions about his family in Koło. But he only has bad news from Koło and doesn't even want to talk about it. Before dessert is over, Józek gets up and apologetically announces that he has to leave. Danusia also gets up and explains that she will walk him to the gate. To her great disappointment, Gienio also gets up and decides to leave with them. Dad asks him to stay longer but Gienio is determined to leave with Danusia and Józek.

"See you tomorrow, Gienio," Dad amicably waves to Gienio.

The three of them leave the house and walk down the street in silence, Danusia walking between the two of them. At the nearest corner Józek stops.

"I am going in that direction," he points out to a nearby apartment building. "I will leave you here because I take a shortcut through this backyard."

"Bye, Danusia, I will call you later," he leans forward and slowly kisses her delicate hand, then bows officially to Gienio, and walks away. She stands still watching him disappearing behind the apartment building.

"Miss Danusia," Gienio says in a shy and quiet voice, looking at her with sad admiration, "I was hoping very much that one day you would marry me," he starts in a shaky voice. "But today I've realized that Mr. Fijałkowski is very much on your mind. I am convinced that, but for Mr. Fijałkowski, you would marry me. I only want to say this: Please beware because he is a ladies' man and you may regret your decision one day."

Danusia kicks some stones with her shiny shoe, then scrapes her foot back and forth. Finally she raises her head and fixes her almond eyes on Gienio.

"Sir, I am very sorry but I don't know whether I would marry you or not but I do know one thing...." She ponders for a moment then turns her big dark eyes on him. "I know that I don't love you," she says apologetically.

He grabs her hand. "I know that. But I very much believe that I could win your heart. Life is not a honeymoon, especially now. I could offer you my unconditional love and security for you and your family."

Danusia is overwhelmed with his passionate plea, his big blue eyes gazing at her imploringly. Unconsciously, she takes a step back. "I admire you and I respect you, but I don't love you." She takes a deep breath. "And I don't think I would ever marry you.... I am sorry."

"You believe you can't marry me because you met Mr. Fijałkowski." He swallows hard. "But I will be always waiting for you, Miss Danusia."

* * * *

At work Danusia stages a big fight. "I am not going to work overtime again. They pay close to nothing and I can't even see Józek. I can't even talk to him. No way!"

During the break, she talks to Maya Gara. Together the girls go to their supervisor and declare that they can't work overtime; it is too hard for them.

Supervisor Nowak doesn't want to hear about it. "You either work overtime or you don't work at all," he replies, shooting down any argument.

"Fine! Then I don't work at all!" Danusia snaps back, bursts into tears, and runs out without waiting for Maya. "I quit!" she announces at home.

Mama panics. The mint is the safest place to work. It offers good papers and security. She already talked with Mrs. Sowińska about Danusia's work problem but she hasn't heard anything back from her yet. There is no time to waste; she must talk to Mrs. Sowińska immediately. In great hurry, she rushes upstairs. This overtime prevents Danusia from enrolling in the underground *komplety* program. But she must get her high school diploma. She already lost one year. She must start *komplety* this year. Something must be done about this work schedule. On the stairway, Mama runs into Mrs. Sowińska.

"Jasia! Did Danusia quit?" Mrs. Sowińska yells.

"Yes and no," Mama replies. "She didn't give any formal notice. She just had an argument with Nowak and left."

"Is she home?"

"Yes, she went to sleep." Mama replies.

"That's bad. Looks like she may be depressed. You know, I did talk to the Director and he promised me to look into this matter. I told him that she was not even of legal age and that she should be treated like a child. Actually both of them, Danusia and Maya, are formally under age."

"But I am afraid because of this argument with Nowak, it will be more difficult to do anything about it now." Mama folds her hands.

"We'll see. Let me check right away. Just wait." About an hour later, Mrs. Sowińska comes back with a mysterious look on her face.

"Where is Danusia?"

Mama goes to the other room and literally drags Danusia out.

"Leave me alone, I have had enough of all this!" Danusia cries.

Mrs. Sowińska gently hugs her. "Listen my child, everything will be fine. I already took care of the big problem but now you must help me."

"Did you, really?" Mama is ecstatic.

"I hate that job, I hate that man, and I hate everything!" Danusia storms, weeping.

"But listen to me first!" Mrs. Sowińska's patience starts running out. "You will be released from the overtime duty but first you have to go to Nowak and apologize for your behavior in the morning."

"There is nothing to apologize for. I didn't offend him. I simply told him I would not work overtime." Danusia revolts.

"It doesn't matter whether you offended him or not. What's important is that he feels offended. Therefore you must apologize. And remember, he already promised me that if you apologize he would not give you any overtime."

Danusia looks at Mrs. Sowińska suspiciously. "But what if he doesn't keep his promise?"

"If he doesn't keep his word then you will tell me about it. As long as this Director General is around, you will be fine. But now, my dear, you comb your hair, wash your face, and let's go. We must take care of this little apology now."

Mama hastily tries to fix Danusia's hair. "Get up, get up! Do you see what Mrs. Sowińska has done for you! You should be grateful!"

"And what about Maya? What happens with her?" Danusia asks.

"She will be excused from the overtime, too. But she is not such a hot-tempered person as you, young lady, so she doesn't have to apologize."

"But I don't want to apologize, there is nothing to apologize for." Danusia drags her feet.

"Danusia, you must be reasonable. Remember, you must have that job back, you understand?" Mama stares straight into her eyes, squeezing her hands with full force.

Mrs. Sowińska puts her arm over Danusia and leads her gently towards the door. "Wait for us Jasia and don't worry. Everything will be fine." She sends Mama a knowing look.

Right after they leave, Dad comes home. "Where is Danusia? I heard there are some problems with her! Someone said that she was fired."

"It's all right now. Mrs. Sowińska is involved and I hope everything will be fine." Mama tries to assure him but she herself is still shaken. Who knows what other craziness is still on Danusia's mind. Certainly she is not in the mood for apologies.

"Where is she?" Dad yells.

"She just went with Mrs. Sowińska to see Nowak."

"Oh, then I have to go there."

Mama grabs his arm. "No, you better stay here." Dad hates Nowak and could even beat him up for Danusia. Then they both would lose their jobs for sure. With great effort Mama holds him at the door. As they debate, some steps resound outside. They stop arguing and hold their breaths.

Mrs. Sowińska enters first, her face focused but friendly; Danusia follows, her face distressed but contained.

"Everything is fine," Mrs. Sowińska declares. "Danusia was brave and apologized."

Dad takes Danusia in his arms. "What did you do, my *molodiec*? There was so much noise today about your disobedience."

Mama tearfully embraces Mrs. Sowińska. There is no end to the thanks and cheers.

Finally they are alone. Dad checks the door carefully then calls Danusia to the table with certain sense of urgency.

"Remember, baby, there is no mercy here. What you did today will be remembered. Some will consider you a hero; others will view you as a rebel. You must be extra careful. Someone may be watching your every step."

The next day, Danusia goes back to work with aversion. At the outset she is directed to another group and doesn't work for Nowak any more. In her new position, she finishes work at 4 PM and has plenty of time to see Józek.

They meet frequently at the park near the Vistula River. This is the same park where they met for their first date just less then two years ago. Today, those distant days appear so remote and unreal. And the park is not the same either. It's not a park anymore but more of a graveyard with simple graves and wooden crosses everywhere, with bomb craters, knocked down trees, and ghastly stumps. The bank of the Vistula River is ragged with craters and all sorts of rubble and debris. The nearby Kierbedzia Bridge lies in ruins. The people in the park seem to be different too. No one feeds pigeons anymore. An elderly woman kneels motionlessly like a permanent fixture near a simple grave. No one pays attention to her. The fearful passersby are mere shadows of those park visitors from before the war. Their faces are gray, their eyes hollow, and their clothes wretched.

As if in defiance of this abhorrent human destruction, the water in the river flows as before and the nature around slowly wakes up from the winter morass. Here and there lilies, spring catkins, daffodils, tulips, lilac bushes, and majestic chestnut trees breathe new life.

Suddenly, a Gestapo patrol with an attack dog emerges at the other end of the pathway. The three SS-men, armed to their teeth, with a deep sense of mission on their faces, are on a zealous hunt for more victims. Danusia and Józek abruptly turn back and subconsciously run towards Danusia's house.

At home, Mama welcomes them. With every passing day, she becomes more apprehensive about leaving home, about going outside the mint complex, about just being on the street. More and more people talk about surprise round-ups on the streets and in public places. Innocent passersby, young and old, men and women, are hunted like animals and transported in trucks into the unknown, disappearing without a trace.

Unfortunately, staying home is not a solution either. Since the official dinner, Dad dislikes Józek even more. Gienio doesn't come around any more. As a result, Dad receives supplies of *bibuła* with considerable delays. For the time being, Dad holds his tongue but Mama knows his patience is running out. However, she also knows that Danusia is hopelessly in love with the high and mighty Józek. In less than a month, Danusia will turn 18 and will be in the position to make her own decisions no matter how irresponsible or unreasonable they may be. While the tension grows, Józek tells Danusia that he has to leave Warsaw for a couple of days to take care of some business and will be back the next week.

The atmosphere at home instantly improves. Dad pulls out his beloved radio, joking and playing around with it while Danusia and Mama relax. One day returning from work, Danusia finds a visitor at home.

"You have a guest," Mama informs her.

A corpulent woman in her late fifties with gray hair and a good-looking face watches Danusia intensely. Rather surprised, Danusia approaches the woman with curiosity. For me? She debates in her mind. What for? I don't know this lady. Mama quickly withdraws to the kitchen.

"Miss Danusia?" The woman gets up and extends her hand. "I am Mrs. Pawłowska, Gienio's mother."

Aha, that's who she is. "How do you do." Danusia greets the woman politely. What does she want? Why is she here? Mrs. Pawłowska has visibly red eyes and hides a small handkerchief in her hand. Danusia starts feeling uncomfortable.

"I came here because I can't watch my son suffering so much," Mrs. Pawłowska explains in a quiet, shaky voice, her eyes instantly brimming with tears.

"Please sit down." Danusia gently touches her. They sit down on the sofa without a sound. After a while, Mrs. Pawłowska clears her throat.

"He loves you so much. He would do anything for you. You would be very happy with him."

"Mrs. Pawłowska, please understand." Danusia swallows hard. "I don't love him," she says with disarming frankness.

"My child," Mrs. Pawłowska takes her hand. "I am sure you will fall in love with him. He is such a good, gentle, loving, and caring man. You will fall in love with him just for his virtuous soul and his golden heart. I am sure you will! Just give him a chance—please! He suffers so much...."

"I am very, very sorry, but I can't. I really, truly can't!" Danusia's voice grows desperate. She wants to get out, out, leave immediately. She jerks back her hand with her whole body.

Mrs. Pawłowska realizes she hasn't gained ground for her cause. She can't press any more; she needs to take a step back. "Miss Danusia, I understand. I only ask you to give him a chance, to reconsider. That's all I am asking for." She blows her nose, wipes tears, and gets up.

"God be with you, my child. Please, give him a chance...."

Danusia remains silent. Deep inside, she is sincerely shaken by this motherly plea. At the same time, though, she feels threatened. Her fervent love is challenged once again; her treasured image of happiness is endangered.

Mrs. Pawłowska slowly moves towards the kitchen. She pulls the door and takes one more look at Danusia.

"Please give him a chance!"

At last the door closes, the handle slowly returns to the rest position, and Danusia finds herself alone.

Oh, how awful. She is the cause of suffering. And she can't help it. Józek is her most precious treasure. She can't give him up, she won't give him up, and she cannot even pretend to reconsider her decision. In any case, she must be quite attractive.... With an increased sense of self-worth, she stretches her legs on the couch and slowly closes her eyes. A headache, a terrible headache knocks her down and takes away her worry.

"Danusia, wake up! Or...maybe not.... There is nothing to wake up to, anyway." Dad heavily falls on the chair. "This is insane! Jasia, have you heard what's going on?"

"What do you mean?" Mama asks edgily while putting a pot of soup on the table.

"Today, the Germans invaded Belgium, Luxemburg, and the Netherlands. Can you imagine, all three at once, just like that!" he snaps his fingers in the air.

"Jesus Christ!" Mama wrings her hands.

"Another devilish victory. All three Low Countries have been taken almost overnight!" Dad bursts with fury. "And the Allies do nothing. Even worst than that! Apparently, Chamberlain has been fired and Great Britain doesn't even have a government in place."

Zbyszek bursts home dirty and sweating but with several loaves of bread and a bag of potatoes.

"Dad, do you know what's going on? All the German tabloids trumpet this blitzkrieg victory in the Low Countries. Do you have our information on this?"

"Unfortunately I do. But you may not want to know what this 'information' is about."

"Oh, gee! Is it worse than what I know?"

"In Great Britain, Chamberlain resigned," Dad snaps cynically.

"Well, that may not be such a bad news after all. Maybe a new guy will have guts to actually do something rather than just talk. Let's take out the radio, Dad. Maybe we will catch something."

"Zbyś, you know what?" Mama sends him a furious look. "I don't like this radio business. You're just inviting trouble."

"Don't worry, Jasia. We will be very careful," Dad assures her. "Zbyszek, curtain off the windows!"

After a quick dinner, Dad with Zbyszek's assistance carefully dismantles the floor and takes out the radio. For a while, only whistles and noises fill out the room.

"Lower the volume!" Mama panics.

"What are you looking for, Dad? Any particular station?" Zbyszek asks as Dad browses through the airwaves.

"We need anything in Polish or Russian, unless you can understand German."

"No, I don't, not yet," Zbyszek replies.

"And what about English or French? Can anybody get that?" Dad asks a rhetorical question.

After considerable effort, he zeroes in on a Russian language station. A voice of a Russian broadcaster is engaging but only Dad can understand it. The distant voice comes and goes, jumps louder and completely fades away in the whistling noise of outer space. They wait and listen in tense quietness until the broadcaster's voice is replaced by the rhythmic tunes of a revolutionary song. Dad turns off the radio and starts summarizing the news.

"Apparently, a man named Churchill was chosen to replace Chamberlain. It's interesting. This new guy started his political career as a conservative, later switched to the liberals, and now is back with the conservatives. But for his new cabinet, he chose many labor leaders and liberals. Maybe that's good. He must be more of a centrist." Dad sinks into a reverie.

"But what about the invasion? What do they say?" Zbyszek pokes him urgently.

"They don't say much but apparently the Germans are advancing towards France."

"France?"

"That's right, Son, towards France.... Well, it's enough for today. Let's put the radio back to its cage."

"Right, there is no point to bother with radio just to get even more depressing news," Mama states forcefully.

The time goes fast. No one talks openly about Mrs. Pawłowska's visit although they all somehow wonder about it. Danusia is determined to avoid the subject. Only Józek is on her mind. He will be back on

Sunday. She can't wait to see him and spend time with him but how to meet and where? To her delight, it turns out that her parents go out Sunday evening. The name-day for Zofia approaches and her parents are invited by their old friends for Zofia name-day party. There are many *Zofias* in Poland and all of them celebrate their name-day this coming weekend.

After the Sunday mass, Danusia rushes home, leaving behind Mama and Zbyszek.

"*Panie* Gara, was there a phone call for me?"

"No, my dear, not that I know of."

"I will be home now. Please let me know if there is any phone call for me."

The telephone system is not yet fully operational but in certain parts of the city repairs are completed and recently Józek was able to call the mint from his apartment building.

Around 3 PM, her parents leave and Zbyszek disappears with his friends. Danusia stays home. There hasn't been any phone call yet. She grabs a book and starts reading—a romance of course. The day is warm and beautiful. Streets are full of people heading for Zofia name-day parties with pastel bouquets of flowers. Danusia also has many Zofia friends and could visit them today. It is not even necessary to have an invitation. On the name-day every Zofia expects the unexpected. But Danusia is determined to wait. At last, an hour later someone knocks at the door. She jumps out and opens the door forcefully. A bouquet of flowers springs up in front of her nose.

"Happy non-name-day!" Józek laughs heartily.

"Welcome my non-name-day guest!" She grabs the flowers with delight and laughs. At last she is happy, very happy. Józek is back safely and as planned. She takes him to the room, puts the flowers to the vase, makes some tea, and asks about the trip. But he doesn't want to talk about it.

"There is nothing interesting about the trip," he insists. "I am glad I am back." He treads the room from end to end, shooting furtive glances at Danusia. Her slender figure full of energy and grace, her playful dark eyes, and beautiful pale face so distinct and yet in great harmony with curly brown hair captivates his imagination. Tea is ready.

"Tell me more, what did you do?" Danusia insists. "Why can't you tell me where you went? I feel as if you are hiding something."

"I am sorry, but you must understand," he says. "We live in such perilous times. It is not safe to say too much and it is not safe to know too much. And above all, I want you to be safe. You must understand that, and you must trust me, please."

"But you should trust me, too," Danusia continues to argue.

"Darling, I trust you with all my heart." Józek slowly takes her elfin body in his arms.

"I have something very special for you." He reaches to the pocket, takes out a small leather box, and opens it with caution.

"A diamond ring!" Danusia whispers.

He takes out a small ring with a shiny crystal clear diamond and in silence and with great care slides it into her slender finger. They kiss. It's a long and affectionate kiss.... But he doesn't have much time. In fact he is in a hurry. He must leave immediately because he has to take care of some very important business. "Danusia, don't worry. I'll be back soon, I promise."

"Will you be back tomorrow?" she asks in despair.

"I'll try," he replies and in no time is gone.

Danusia walks back to the table. Two cups of tea, half full, are steaming. The white tablecloth, the flowers, the ring, and the kiss.... It's like a dream. For all this waiting, for all this anxiety, he was here just for a brief moment, only a moment, without saying much. She looks at her hand. It's like a fairy tale. He left a ring and disappeared. He didn't even say the sacred 'I love you.' This could be an engagement ring but he didn't say that. He didn't say anything about the ring or about his intentions. "Apparently, it's just a ring. But at least a very nice one...."

Her parents return home late in the evening. Mama is in a great mood but Dad is not thrilled. He is too sober and grouchy. "Oh I see! Some flowers. You didn't waste time. I bet it's that fellow of yours, right?"

"Well, Dad, I told you that Józek was traveling and he just came back today," she pretends as if nothing unusual happened.

The upcoming week brings more challenges and more trouble for Danusia. Józek visits her several times. Mama tries to be polite but she is mopish and visibly unhappy. Once or twice Józek stays long enough to cross paths with Dad. But it's not a pleasant encounter.

Towards the end of the week, Mama takes Danusia aside for a serious talk. "Danusia, you must finish this business with Józek. Dad cannot tolerate this situation any longer. Józek is much older than you. He is not your school friend or your neighbor. Why is he coming here? What is his role or intention? If he is interested in you he should have some courage to say so."

Danusia freezes. She feels the same way. Why isn't he saying anything? Is he serious about me or is this just a bluff? On one hand she is upset, uncertain, and wants to leave him but on the other hand she desperately wants to see him, to be with him, to see his deep blue eyes smiling to her....

"Mama, give me some more time, please.... If he doesn't say anything soon I will break up with him, I promise."

"Danusia, it might only make matters worse. He doesn't seem interested in making any commitments. What does he think? I don't understand." Mama shakes her head. "And you are taking a risk that Dad will throw him out the door. I am just telling you. Dad's patience has already run out. He has told me that if he sees Józek again at home or with you, that will be it. And you know that he means it."

Danusia starts weeping.

"Here you are," Mama gives her a handkerchief, a piece of paper, and a pen. "Write him a letter. That's the best way to do it." She pats Danusia on the back giving her some encouragement and retreats to the kitchen.

Danusia closes her eyes. Józek, the handsome, mighty Józek. He is merely playing with her. He comes and goes, he says nothing, does who knows what, goes who knows where.... He is much older, already in his late twenties. For all these years, he must have played with many girls. He may be even seeing other girls now. Danusia gets angry. But he doesn't want to marry. That's right. He told her that up front, on the first date, and he hasn't changed his mind. Danusia wipes her tears, bites her lips, grabs a pen, and starts writing.

> Józek!
>
> My parents don't want you to visit us any more, and they don't want me to see you any more. I thought a lot about us and I concluded that

my parents are right. It will be better for both of us not to see each other any more. And that is why I am returning this ring to you.

Danusia

With great care she takes off the shiny ring from her slim finger. The beauty of the flashy diamond is enormously tempting. How about if she throws out the letter or just sends the letter without the ring? How about if she just keeps the ring? No, she must be strong! With great pain, she puts the ring into a small handkerchief, thoroughly folds the fabric several times, and diligently ties the corners together. She then addresses the envelope: "Józef Fijałkowski, Chmielna 34, Doctor Kiszkiel's Apartment." With the letter and the bundle in her hand, she rushes out.

"Zbyszek, Zbyszek," she shouts. "*Panie* Gara, did you see Zbyszek?"

"I think he is with Bruno and the other boys in the basement."

"Zbyszek, Zbyszek!" she yells.

Zbyszek's head curiously shows up. "What's up?"

"Zbyś! I need you to do something for me right away!" she declares with drama in her voice.

"I don't have time. Not now," he objects flatly.

"Zbyś, I need you to go to Józek right now! You must return this ring to him." She shows him a white bundle. "And this letter too." Her eyes glisten and she is about to burst into tears. "It's very urgent." she repeats in a shaky voice, trying hard to hide her emotions.

He looks at her astounded. "Well...," he slowly replies, taken aback by her demeanor. "It's really serious, I see. Hey guys, I'll be back," he hollers to his friends. "Looks like some kind of a big deal here." He grumbles. With reluctance, he takes the letter and the small bundle with the ring. "Exciting ending, like in the movies, right from some sort of a love story.... At least Dad will be happy," he mutters to himself.

"But be very, very careful with it. You must give it only to Józek. Remember! Don't leave it with anyone else, only with Józek, and don't lose it, be very careful with it," she instructs him again and again.

At the gate, they run into Danusia Staniszewska and Wanda Tołłoczko. Since their fathers were rounded up and deported to the concentration camp, the two girls have became inseparable friends. In the morning they work together at the mint and in the afternoon they always disappear together.

"Hi, Danusia," the girls wave to her.

"Hi," she replies apathetically. Danusia is no mood to talk. But they don't talk much either. These days, people don't talk much. It's safer that way.

On the one hand, Danusia sympathizes with them over their fathers' tragedy. On the other hand, though, she hides certain bitterness towards them. She knows very well that the girls return from school, from the Polish underground school—*komplety*.[4] Danusia also wants to go to school. She also wants to attend *komplety*. But this year she couldn't attend *komplety* because of the mandatory overtime requirement. At the same time, though, the two girls, for some inexplicable reason, have been exempted from overtime. The summer approaches and Danusia knows that the two girls are just about to complete the school year while she has just lost that year.

"That's it. I am going back to school right away," she decides. "No more Józek, no more distractions, I have to try to catch up with school." Without looking after Zbyszek, she returns home ready for the new beginning.

Her brave attitude doesn't last long, though. The next day she comes home from work with one and only one thought. Can she see Józek today, will he show up...? Over the past months, they have been meeting at 5:30 PM on a regular basis. As the scheduled time approaches, Danusia's anxiety grows. Would he come? Zbyszek gave him the letter without saying anything and Józek didn't say anything either. Maybe he will come!

The clock ticks slowly past 5:30 PM. Danusia sits at the table and bites her fingers. He must come. He must show up. She cries inside. "We can't go our separate ways just like that, without saying a single word." But the clock mercilessly moves beyond 5:30 PM, it reaches 6:00 PM, and 6:30 PM. Danusia cries. She has just realized how lonely she feels. It's as if she has lost her purpose in life, the bottomless emptiness has filled up her heart. She cannot imagine life without Józek.

"Danusia, I have an idea!" Mama tries to help her cope with the grief. "Your 18th birthday is next week. How about if you invite your girlfriends for Saturday? We will arrange for a small party at home."

"Thank you, Mama, but I don't want any party."

"Oh, stop lamenting. Everything will be fine. I will prepare the party. Zbyszek and Dad will help me. You just go ahead and invite your friends."

"I don't have any friends." She cries.

"No, that's not true. Invite your friends from school and from the neighborhood. You'll see it will be great!"

Over the next couple of days, Mama draws Danusia into the preparations for the party. She makes suggestions as to whom to invite, she debates the menu, and asks Danusia to do some shopping. She even tries to find out what presents Danusia would like, knowing very well that she can hardly afford any. Danusia demonstrates total indifference to all these efforts but reluctantly goes along with the preparations.

Saturday afternoon arrives and Danusia's girlfriends come for the party. Plates with small sandwiches are prepared, a cake is baked, and some delicious drinks are stacked up on the table, among them Danusia's favorite cocoa with meringue. Mama and Dad greet the guests and soon leave the house. Zbyszek with a group of neighborhood boys drops by to taste the food. But Danusia is disinterested in the party or in the guests. This is her 18th birthday. From now on she can make her own decisions. As 5:30 PM approaches, her patience is running out. She has to see Józek. He must be thinking about her today. Maybe he will come to the park as always. Yes, that's right! He must be waiting for her in the park. Quickly, she spots Maya Gara among the guests.

"Maya, I must leave for a moment." She looks at her friend imploringly. "Please take care of the guests for me. Ask Zbyszek if you need any help, okay? I'll be back soon."

"And where are you going?"

"I must check something. I'll explain later." Danusia throws her a knowing look and runs out the door like a hurricane only to slow down outside the gate.

As she walks through the streets towards the river, her heart pounds, her legs are shaky. Is he there? He should be there. He must be there! But where? Her mind works feverishly.

Suddenly, at the other end of the street, she spots a familiar silhouette. Her heart almost stops; her legs feel numb. It's Józek! For sure it's Józek! He is coming towards her. Suddenly she becomes scared, very scared, and nervous. Although she wanted to see him so much, she didn't really expect to see him. It's like her dream come true. But now, when he really approaches her, she is paralyzed, she doesn't know what to do, doesn't know what to say, where to turn. She is terrified and confused.

Józek walks fast with his sharp blue eyes boldly fixed on her. His face is determined as he reaches her. Without stopping, he takes her hand and hides it under his arm.

"Let's go!" he says decisively and takes her with him like a father takes home a disobedient child. They walk in silence towards the Traugut Monument. Down there, on the slopes of the Vistula bank, a small quiet bench in the lilac bushes welcomes them.

"Would you like to sit down here," he asks in a low, soft voice. Obediently, Danusia sits down. Another uncomfortable moment of silence. Slowly, Józek moves his hand and takes out a small envelope from his jacket.

"Here you are, Danusia. This is a letter I wanted to send to you. But ultimately I decided to give it to you...."

With shaking hands she takes the envelope and gently unfolds the paper.

> My Beloved Danusia!
>
> Please forget for a moment everything that divides us. In my dreams, I kiss your heavenly lips. I miss them so much in my own special way. I have been thinking about us very seriously for a long time. It was my sincere intention to ask your parents for your hand on the day of your 18th birthday.

Danusia can't believe her eyes. She goes back and reads the sentence again and again. "Józek, you really want to marry me?" She can't hold that question back any more.

"How could you think otherwise!" he replies indignantly.

She takes a deep breath and continues reading. "It is so hard for me to accept the fact that I wasn't even worth a phone call from you." She reads, feeling a lump in her throat. Her eyes glitter.

He takes her in his arms and they fall into a long passionate kiss. Their bodies tremble with emotion, their hearts yearn for each other, their sense of reality disappears. The extreme happiness veils them for a brief moment. They wake up to the realization how much they have been longing for each other and how much they have been suffering over the last days without each other.

"Józio, darling," Danusia starts. "So, you will come to talk to my parents?"

"Yes, Danuś, I will come and ask them for the permission to marry you, and for their blessing."

"Oh, darling, I love you so much," she whispers.

"How about if we plan for the next Saturday?" Józek is anxious to move ahead.

"That's good. But I need to talk with them first. I have to prepare them for the occasion."

It's getting late. Danusia's guests are abandoned and her parents may be returning home soon. They slowly walk back.

"On Saturday, let's meet at the Saint Francis Church and from there we will go together to your parents, how is that?" Józek suggests.

"That's great!"

They walk in silence holding hands. Before the mint, Józek turns back and Danusia returns to her birthday party with a stone face. Some guests including Maya are still around. Some ask suspicious questions, others send her strange looks, but she doesn't care. She has her Józek back and that's the only thing that counts.

That evening, before going to sleep, Danusia quietly corners Mama. Her face emanates with joy, her eyes shine and spark.

"Mama, Józio wants to ask for my hand!"

"Oh, no, he is back again?"

"But Mama, you have to help me now! You know how much he means to me! You can't let me down. He wants to come to our house on Saturday and ask both of you for the permission to marry me."

"This coming Saturday?" Mama is in shock. The situation looks more serious than she anticipated.

"Yes, this coming Saturday. And then we will be officially engaged! Wow, isn't that wonderful…?" Danusia grabs the flounces of her skirt and starts dancing.

"Be quiet," Mama cautions her. "We have to think what to do with Dad. I guess I have to talk to him first." She is rather unhappy about this prospect.

Over the next days, bad news from the western front prevents Mama from bringing up the sensitive subject with Dad. France is falling apart. The Polish Armed Forces in the process of formation in France are in danger of being dispersed before the formation process is even complete. German controlled tabloids trumpet German continuous successes. The people in Warsaw grow impatient. They are in a desperate need of some breakthrough, some hope, some shred of a good news.

It is already Wednesday and Mama cannot wait any longer. "Alek, I need to talk with you about Danusia." She sits down in front of him and looks straight into his eyes. "It's serious," she declares bluntly.

"What is it?" he asks with apprehension.

"Józek wants to marry Danusia."

"Whaaaat?"

"He wants to talk with us about that on Saturday," she continues, trying not to be distracted by his reaction. "Listen, don't make any noise. Danusia is crazy about him; you know that. We must be careful and reasonable about this thing."

"I don't want to see him!" Dad starts yelling. "I can't stand this fellow. I told you that already."

But Mama starts yelling even louder. "I don't care what you want or what you like!" she shouts, getting up. "The welfare of our child is at stake and you must act responsibly. This young man will come here on Saturday and you must treat him properly. You simply do it for Danusia!"

He looks at her surprised. "Do you really want to approve this marriage?"

"Well, we must be prepared for it. If you think there is a better solution, then tell me now."

"Let me think about it," he realizes the seriousness of the matter, lights a cigarette, and starts walking back and forth.

When Danusia comes home she gets a long awaited signal that Dad already knows about the Saturday plan. Slowly she puts the shopping bag on the kitchen table, pats her hair into place, clears her throat, and walks into the room.

"Hi, Daddy."

He sits on the sofa with a cigarette and watches her carefully. His precious little girl slowly walks to him with a gentle childish smile and slips onto his lap. He puts the cigarette away and embraces her.

"You know already?" she whispers. "Oh, Dad, I am so happy!"

"I worry about you, Danusia, I very much worry about you, darling." In an unusual outbreak of emotion, he cuddles her to his chest, shelters her with his arms, and presses his head over her soft curly hair as if trying to hide her.

"Everything will be great." Danusia sounds assuring and convincing. "Please don't worry, Dad. You will see. It's going to be wonderful!"

By Saturday, the situation is under control. Dad is pacified. Mama is somehow supportive, only Zbyszek is still a wildcard but she knows how to win him over. Józek will have a present for him. When the time comes she puts on her church dress and goes to the Saint Francis Church.

The day is pleasant. The trees bloom; the birds twitter. Only the people around are gray and cheerless, and vicious posters with ugly swastikas shout at her from every corner. But she looks right through them without seeing anything and flies straight to the church.

In the twilight of the splendid nave, she notices Józek standing near the altar with a big paper bundle under his arm. As she creeps up on him, she notices a big piece of kiełbasa sticking out from under his arm and starts choking with laughter.

"Józek! You are just about to lose your kiełbasa!" She covers her laughing mouth. He turns around trying to catch dropping kiełbasa and smiles. "Look what I have!" Unfolding the paper, he proudly puts the tasty treat under her nose. That's a real accomplishment these days and the best evidence of his ability to provide for the family. It entails considerable risk and demonstrates his skills to adapt to the new circumstances.

At home, the greeting goes well. Dad is polite and restrained. Mama is tense and concerned. The tasty present is well received. Zbyszek is not around, thus a box of cards is set aside for him.

"Thank you for having me today," Józek starts, ill at ease. "First I want to apologize for the wrong impression I made, but I have been thinking about Danusia very seriously for a long time."

"You see, we are not the Holy Ghost to know what you think," Dad snaps at him. "You are a grown up man and you know what you want."

"Yes, Sir," Józek replies standing in the official upright position. "I certainly know that I very much want to marry Danusia and I hereby ask both of you for her hand."

The parents look at him in silence with their faces at a loss.

Danusia moves closer to Józek and takes his hand. "We love each other very much," she adds in her childish but determined voice.

"Okay, young man," Mama finally says. "Please sit down." She invites him to join her on the couch.

"I have already written to my mother and sister in Koło. I wrote to them that I have met beautiful Danusia and that I want to marry her," Józek continues.

"But I am afraid that neither of you understand the consequences of your decision," Mama starts. "Think about it. We are in the center of the worst human catastrophe the world has ever seen. People are being kidnapped and killed on the streets and in their homes every day in the thousands. People are persecuted, deprived of all their rights and means for making a living. And in this hell on earth you want to start a family, possibly bringing to this world another human being while you can hardly provide for yourselves? And Danusia is only 18. She is still a child!" Mama's tender voice breaks.

"And look what's going on around!" Dad follows. "The West is falling apart. It means we will be in this mess for a long, long time."

"I understand very well everything what you've just said, Sir," Józek raises his voice slightly. "I have been struggling with these questions for a long time. In fact, because of these concerns I didn't come to you earlier. But today, I have no doubts. Looking at where we stand, I don't see any light in this tunnel of madness for at least a couple more years. But our lives must go on regardless. And we want to capture at least some semblance of happiness even in these devilish times because we may never have another chance at it...."

The parents listen to his driven, ardent voice and watch his sparkling, desperate eyes with sad sympathy. Now they understand. They understand how much he loves her; they feel his pain; they see his passionate struggle. Upon exchanging unspoken words, the parents give up.

"Danusia," Dad approaches them, "and Józek." He looks at the young man in a blaze of emotion. "We bless you both." Mama makes a sing of cross over their heads and kisses both of them ceremoniously. "God be with you, my children," she says holding back tears.

Józek and Danusia flush with joy.

"Danusia, please accept again this diamond ring as a symbol of my eternal love for you." Józek once again opens a small leather box, takes out the shiny diamond ring and gently puts it on her slim finger. From now on, their lives will never be the same.

"So how about the wedding?" Dad brings up the difficult subject.

"I was thinking that we could plan on it for Mama's name-day, the 24th of June," Danusia jumps in with an idea.

"That's in less than three weeks," Mama worries.

"We are not going to have any fancy wedding reception. I could rent a wedding dress in a week and we don't need anything more. What do you think, Józek?"

"I would like to have the wedding at Saint Mary's Church." He replies. "One of my best friends from the Seminary, Father Kowalski, is there. I would be happy if he could celebrate our wedding mass. But I don't know whether he can schedule our wedding on the 24th."

"Also, I assume you would like to invite at least your mother and sister from Koło," Mama inquires.

"Yes, and I don't know how much time they need these days to obtain all the papers and authorizations to come here. In my experience, they should be able to arrange for everything in three weeks but with the latest harassments, who knows?"

The loud noise of the slamming front doors interrupts them and Zbyszek crashes through the door like a blizzard. He glances at their faces and takes a step back.

"Oh, I am sorry, I guess I'm interrupting something."

"That's quite all right," Dad says. "It's good you came because we were discussing an important matter.... Your sister is getting married. Mr. Fijałkowski is here to ask for her hand."

"Holy pierogi!" Zbyszek of course heard some discussions about Danusia's engagement but didn't pay much attention to it. And now he finds himself in the middle of the engagement ceremony. Suddenly, he becomes very uncomfortable and doesn't know what to do or what to say. But Józek gets up and quickly solves his problem.

"Here, I have a little present for you, Brother." He gives Zbyszek a friendly pat on the back, handing him the box of cards.

"Thank you and best of luck." Zbyszek shakes his hand and kisses Danusia. "So, when is the wedding?"

"We will be trying for the 24th, Mama's name-day," Danusia says proudly.

"Wow, that fast? Does that mean I will have the bedroom just for myself in three weeks?"

"That's what it means." Józek replies firmly.

The parents look at each other rather feebly. Danusia also seems to be uneasy about this realization.

"That's great!" Zbyszek feels the tension and quickly pulls out a piece of paper from his pocket.

"Did you see the recent *Bulletin*? Here is some good news at last. Look!" He unfolds a tiny piece of the blotting paper and starts reading dense print:

Victory at Narvik!

> After the heroic nine-hour fight, the Podhale Brigade successfully broke the German defense lines at the Ankenes peninsula and took over control of the land access to the town of Narvik. The successful attack of the Polish forces enabled the Allied forces to take over the strategic port of Narvik. Two Polish Navy destroyers and three transporters take part in the Norway campaign.[5]

"What is the date of your *Bulletin*?" Dad asks skeptically.

"The second of June."

"Apparently you don't have the latest. Actually, you would be better off not to have it," Dad comments with ironic fury and pulls out another piece of paper.

"Here is the latest." With disgust, he drops the paper on the table. The headlines on this one read: *Allied Forces Defeated!*

"Oh, no! What's that?"

"That's the latest news," Dad replies cynically. "You see, even though the Allied troops took over Narvik, they were ordered to withdraw from Narvik and from Norway all together because of the dramatic situation on the French front. All the Allied forces simply left Norway and are on their way back to Great Britain." Dad pounds his fist on the table. "And here, listen to this." He turns the page and points out to another headline: *Evacuation at Dunkirk!* "You know what that means?" He looks around the room to make sure that everybody is listening. "It means that the British and the French have been defeated in France and are evacuating, or rather escaping, to Great Britain!"

Deathly silence sets in. Mama hides her face in her wrinkled hands. "This is catastrophe for us," she sobs quietly. "What's going to happen to us? God, please help!"

"Don't worry, Mama. We have survived hundred years of partition, we will survive this madness too." Zbyszek tries to console her.

"I am wondering what is happening to our military forces in France." Józek looks at Dad. "General Sikorski has been working since January on the formation of the Polish Armed Forces in France. Apparently, we have hundreds of thousands of our men there."

Dad nods. "Yes, we do have a large portion of our army in France, but I understand there have been endless obstacles to the formation of the Polish military forces in France. So far they were able to finish the formation of two infantry divisions and one panzer division under General Maczek. Many of our units are not under the unified Polish command but instead are spread throughout the French Army and can be completely dispersed in this situation."

"Dad, where are these Polish divisions right now, do you know?" Zbyszek asks.

"As far as I understand there are no Polish military forces at Dunkirk. They are located further west, more towards Brest.[6] It looks to me that our boys will have to leave France and jump across the Channel. Our pilots should be able to make that move easily. But as to the infantry, who knows?"

"They can try to evacuate from, for example, Marseilles in the south," Józek observes.

"Yes, but to where? To Africa? What sense does that make?" Dad asks.

"Yeah, what sense does that make...?" Józek echoes him with apathy.

Mama belatedly gets up. "How about if we eat something now?"

Soon dinner is served and the discussion shifts back to the wedding preparations. The mood at the dinner table improves. All previous animosities and the tension related to the engagement ritual gradually disappear. The decision has been made and they all are now committed to make the most out of this special wedding occasion.

Over the next few days, Danusia and Józek work like bees. First, they talk with Father Kowalski. He is delighted with the news and makes arrangements for the wedding mass, as requested, on the 24th of June. Three priests—Fathers Kowalski, Sztajner, and Stefankiewicz, all Józek's former colleagues from the Seminary—will concelebrate the wedding mass.

Danusia is thrilled. She immediately starts inviting guests for the ceremony. Everybody at the mint is invited, her friends from school and from the neighborhood, too. She also writes letters to her cousins near Brasław.

The entire eastern part of Poland has been incorporated into the Soviet Union after the Soviet invasion of September 17, 1939. Very little is known about the fate of the Polish families in these territories. Unconfirmed rumors indicate grave persecutions on a mass scale but there are no details whatsoever. Danusia writes to Gienia in Brasław, to Uncle Vince and to Uncle Józef. "Please come to Warsaw for my wedding," she writes without even knowing whether the cousins are still alive. It has been almost a year since her memorable vacation in the east and there hasn't been a single letter from any of them.

While there is absolute silence from the families in the eastern part of Poland, at least communication with the families in the western part of Poland incorporated to the Reich is relatively good. Within a couple of days, a reply letter arrives from Koło. Józek's mother sends her blessing for Józek and Danusia. She is very moved and enlivened by the news. Unfortunately, she won't be able to travel to Warsaw because of her poor health. But Józek's sister, Marysia, will come for sure. "Don't buy the wedding rings," the mother writes. "Marysia will bring you my wedding rings. Don't worry about clothing. We will send you money to rent the wedding attire." Józek and Danusia write back expressing great thanks and sending them some photographs.

The next week, Józek takes Danusia to the rental warehouse to choose the wedding dress. The place is huge and the selection is mind-boggling. An old Jew in a yarmulke and traditional black attire invites them in and leads them through numerous rooms, explaining in great detail the latest fashion trends and pointing out to the latest arrivals. Danusia tries on different dresses. Never before had she the opportunity to try on so many beautiful dresses, never before had she the opportunity to underscore her beauty so effectively, never before had she the opportunity to shine so powerfully in front of the adoring eyes of her admirer. Two professional women assist her. The dress, train, veil, gloves, shoes, brooch.... Józek takes care of everything and pays at once.

The ride to the church is their next problem. The Poles are forbidden to drive a car. But Danusia wants to drive to the church by car because her fancy dress requires that kind of transportation. The Director General of the mint not only has a car but he also has a private driver at his disposal. She decides to ask once again Mrs. Sowińska for help. And once again Mrs. Sowińska takes care of it. The director's private driver will take Danusia and Józek to the church in the official black limousine.

The wedding day approaches quickly. Mama makes last-minute preparations for a small reception at home. Only two or three guests will be joining them for the modest party at home: Danusia's godfather, Kostek Śniadecki, with his wife, and Józek's sister.

The situation in Warsaw worsens with every passing day, though. More and more night arrests are carried out, more and more street round-ups, and more and more executions are announced every day. The crack down on the Polish underground intensifies.

Three days before the wedding, horrifying news strikes Warsaw: in Palmiry, a small town near Warsaw, the Germans carried out a mass execution of prominent Poles. Approximately 360 well-known public figures were executed in the Palmiry forest, among them political leaders, professors, lawyers, doctors, and sport celebrities such as Janusz Kusociński, the Polish gold medallist from the Los Angeles Olympics.[7] The Palmiry slaughter casts a dark shadow on the fast-approaching wedding ceremony. On top of it, the German tabloids announce that France is about to sign the capitulation act, yet another heavy blow to the spirit of the Warsawians. Nonetheless, the wedding will go on.

On the eve of the wedding, the first guest arrives. Marysia, Józek's sister from Koło, manages to get through the heavy border guards and arrives safely in Warsaw. She is traumatized but in the end quite happy. She has successfully smuggled through the border a wedding present: two wedding rings hidden in her mouth have arrived safely and just in time for the wedding.

Marysia is a tall, good-looking young lady with thick dark hair and big blue eyes. Unlike Józek , she is very straightforward and outspoken. Older than Danusia but younger than Józek , she immediately becomes everybody's good friend.

"Józek, where did you find such a beauty?" she declares up front.

"You see, I am lucky," he replies with pride.

The evening before the wedding is very hectic. They all gather at Danusia's house. Marysia receives a welcoming reception from the parents and gets involved in the last-minute preparations. Józek's tuxedo needs ironing. His shirt also needs attention, as well as the bows—the big bow tie and a small bow on his lapel, too.

The house pulsates with activity. Curious neighbors stop by, some bring home-made goodies from their very special reserves, marinated mushrooms or stewed plums. Others just come to take a look at the wedding preparations. Eventually, everybody leaves and the hurly-burly dies down. And only then Danusia notices the gray, stooping shadow of a man sitting quietly in the darkness of her bedroom. Noiselessly she bends over him. "Dad?" she asks softly. In the dusky moonlight, she notices her father's face etched with pain and senses tears on his cheeks. "Daddy," she whispers in shock. "Daddy, my dear, I am so happy and you are crying? You don't want to share with me my happiness?" she asks with frustration.

"I am sorry, darling, your happiness is the most important thing. But, yet, there are other things that you can't understand. But don't worry, darling.... I'll be fine. You'll see." He wipes his face with the sleeve and tries to smile.

"Oh, Dad, I love you so much." She gently slips onto his lap and together they stare at the moon.

On the morning of the wedding day, all attention is on Danusia's hair. From the early morning hours, the styling is under way. Mama outdoes herself in her creative, meticulous effort to match Danusia's hairstyle with the wedding attire. Józek and Marysia show up early and observe the ritual with great interest. Around noon they start dressing up. At 2:30 PM, the driver shows up. It's time to go.

Outside the church, a small crowd gathers while the black limousine splendidly arrives in front of the church; the driver opens Danusia's door, helps her with her dress, and hands her over to Józek.

"I'm glad I don't have to wait for you," she smiles formally and mutters under her breath.

"I am glad you don't have five bridegrooms lined up," he reciprocates, gently squeezing her hand.

"The celebrants are ready," Zbyszek reports.

"But let's wait for the parents, we have to wait for them," Marysia orders.

For a few minutes, they stand in the doorway of the church. Danusia's parents, who have to walk from home, should be joining them momentarily. Gracefully holding a bouquet of white lilies, Danusia shines. The whole crowd is mesmerized with her beauty. Józek in the tuxedo, with white bow tie and characteristic intellectual glasses, also makes a very good impression. "Such a lovely couple," onlookers comment.

The breathless parents finally reach the church, the organ resound, and the wedding ceremony gets under way. The old church, heavily damaged less than a year ago, delights the visitors with its renovated majestic arches and a beautifully restored altar buried in pastel flowers. The three young priests pray with devotion in their splendid surplices with richly embroidered and carefully arranged stoles. Danusia and Józek kneel on the small faldstool in front of the altar. This wedding ceremony is as splendid and as impressive as any other wedding ceremony held in this church years before the war and years after the war, as beautiful and as elegant as your wedding or mine, but yet, so much different as to the hopes, expectations, and fears of the celebrants and so much stronger in its meaning.

After the wedding, Danusia and Józek receive greetings. Marysia and Zbyszek stand behind them ready to collect flowers. A long line of family and friends slowly passes in front of the young couple. First, the parents, the family, and the older guests proceed with their best wishes. Towards the end of the line, the youth, friends from school and from the mint, among them Maya Gara with her brother, Zenek, and four sisters, finally Wanda Tołłoczko with Danusia Staniszewska. In a white dress with a long red rose in hand, each girl looks like a matching flower of the other. Moving closer and closer in line, they scrutinize with girlish fascination Danusia's wedding gown and her handsome, intelligent husband.

As the girls pass by, the next guest in line makes Danusia break into a sweat. It's Gienio! With a bouquet of red and white roses, Gienio approaches Danusia with his head held high. While handing her the bouquet, he looks deeply into her eyes. "I sincerely wish you all the happiness in the world," he says quietly and quickly moves on to shake Józek's hand. It is a tense moment for all of them, but Gienio moves on.

"I think he sincerely wishes us well," Józek observes.

A few more kisses, hugs, handshakes, flowers, and the line of guests comes to an end. Danusia and Józek return to the limousine and drive away for their photo appointment at the nearby atelier.

A handful of guests walks from the church for a modest reception sat home, among them Danusia's godfather, Konstanty, with his wife. Konstanty, or Kostek as everybody calls him, is Dad's dear old friend. Many years ago, they sailed together. Like Dad, he comes from the eastern part of Poland, and like Dad, he has the same melodic Vilnius accent. Dad loves his company. They always joke about the good old days and tell frightening sailors' stories.

At home, Mama makes last-minute preparations for the reception while Dad enjoys the company of his comrade. Another friend from the memorable sailing expeditions lives in Warsaw these days—Mr. Tukacz. But lately they've lost contact with him.

"I hope the Tukaczes are okay," Dad wonders.

"I am sure they are fine but we should check with them anyway," his friend replies. "I think the last time when we all got together was exactly one year ago. That was for Jasia's name-day party, before the war, remember?"

"It seems like another era," Dad observes melancholically.

Meanwhile, the black limousine arrives at the mint. Danusia and Józek get off and parade with confidence and pride in front of many curious eyes.

"They've arrived, they've arrived!" Marysia announces.

Mama grabs a silver plate covered with a white cloth, places a round loaf of delicious bread and a saltshaker on it, and heads to the door.

"With bread and salt, I welcome you, my children, into this home," she proclaims the centuries-old greeting with great emotion in her voice.

The euphoric newlyweds take the plate and with rapt attention walk into the house for the first time as husband and wife.

"Such a beautiful and felicitous couple!" Kostek extends his arms towards them.

"That's right," his wife echoes. "I have heard many comments in the crowd about how good looking you both are. And you know what, Danusia? Many people thought that you married a German."

Danusia is stunned. "Why?" she asks.

"The Poles can't drive cars these days. So, people concluded that Józio was a German."

"Stupid...," Danusia bursts with anger.

"I am a German?" Józek asks laughing.

"Well, you could certainly pass for a German," the woman replies.

Indeed. Józek is fluent in German and his blond hair and blue eyes meet the test of the Aryan race. Being born in Koło, he could easily get the German citizenship. If he only wanted to, he could easily get on the *Volksliste*. Just a simple declaration, and in a blink of an eye he can move from the underclass to the privileged class. The future for both of them would be so much brighter.... Tension builds in the air. The sole notion of being considered a German instantly invokes the highest emotions.

"You know what we should do with those Poles eager to become Germans?" Józek asks the woman. "For high treason, we should kill them outright, no questions asked, in the name of Poland." His dark eyebrows rise; his bright eyes flash dangerously.

"That's right, young man, that's right." Kostek is pleased with Józek 's reaction. "You're a smart young man. Poland is proud of you!"

"It's easy to say so, but you really have to be very careful with making such statements these days," Marysia challenges her brother. "You haven't been home for a while, Józek. You cannot even imagine what's going on in Koło these days. The official German policy towards the Polish lands incorporated to the Reich is simple. The Poles must be either germanized or deported or exterminated.[8] Those are the only choices we have. And you know what has happened to our cousin, Aniela? She and her four young children were expelled from their house overnight and deported to the General Government somewhere near Kraków."

"Are you serious?" Józek exclaims in distress.

"I didn't want to tell you earlier, but we have to help them quickly because Aniela and her kids must be struggling to survive."

"Józek, you have to look for them immediately," Danusia says in an alarmed voice.

"Don't worry, Danusia. We have it under control. We will talk about that tomorrow," Marysia calms her down.

"So, how is it that they deported your cousin but they left you alone?" Kostek's wife sends Marysia a provocative look.

"We are lucky because my husband works as an accountant in a factory that was taken over by the Germans. They need him in the factory and that's why they've left us alone for a while."

"But as I understand, even if they didn't deport you, they are about to seize your home, is that correct?" the woman keeps asking.

Józek's eyes zoom in on his sister.

Tongue-tied Marysia tries to invent a quick answer. "Don't worry," she says looking at Józek timidly. "As long as Kazik works in the factory we can stay at our house."

"What do you mean *stay at our house*?" Józek follows up. "Do we still own our house?"

Marysia clears her throat. "According to the Germans, we don't. To them, we own nothing; they have decided that we don't have the right to own anything."

"It seams to me that you would be better off to pass for a German now out there," Kostek's wife observes bluntly.

"It's our centuries-old dilemma," Dad says. "Should we put our heads down and wait for the right moment to strike back…."

"Or should we embrace death for the cause…," Józek finishes his thought.

18. Danuta and Józef, Summer 1940 Wedding

19. Danuta and Józef, Summer 1940 Wedding

8

Danusia's transition to a new life is very different from the wedding experience. With just one bag of clothing, she moves to a small room that Józek rents out from Doctor Kiszkiel. Her new home is about half-an-hour's walk from the mint. The landlords, an elderly couple, are friendly and quiet people, but the entire building is old and shabby. The apartment does not have a central heating system and the dilapidated bathroom doesn't have a bathtub. Overall, the living conditions here are much worse than in the modern apartment building of her parents.

And yet, they have to strive hard to pay the rent. Danusia didn't receive any dowry and Józek doesn't have any estate either. Danusia continues working at the mint but nowadays she has to commute to work quite a distance and her monthly earnings are less than the monthly rent. In the first year of the war, inflation has reached several hundred percent while the salaries of the Polish workers remained frozen at the pre-war level.

Józek lives frugally and watches money very carefully. Every day, he leaves for work early in the morning but Danusia doesn't know where he goes or what he does. She is supposed not to know, she can't even ask. She only knows that Józek frequently works with his old friend from Koło, an engineer Szewczykowski, who now lives at the outskirts of Warsaw. From time to time, Józio visits his other friend, Kamiński, who runs a butcher's shop on the other side of the Vistula River. After visiting Kamiński, Józio always brings home a big bag of kiełbasa and the next day Danusia sells the kiełbasa at the mint.

After work, Danusia likes to visit Mama. She often stays for dinner and returns to her new home in the evening. Her parents are happy to see her home after work. Mama cooks dinner for everybody and occasionally Józek stops for dinner too.

Within less than a week after the wedding, a special letter arrives at Mama's home. The long-awaited letter from Uncle Vince finally comes. The letter contains wedding greetings for Danusia and Józek. Apparently, they have not received any earlier correspondence from

Warsaw and were delighted to learn, after all this time, that everybody in Warsaw was fine and that Danusia's wedding was about to take place. Apparently, Uncle Vince and Bolek wrote to them already several times, the last letter they sent in the spring was for Easter. It appears as if only now the postal service has resumed delivery from Eastern Poland.

Despite its joyful tone, Uncle Vince's letter brings disturbing news. In vague language, Uncle Vince alludes that his cousin, Uncle Józef, is no longer alive. His wife, Aunt Michalina with Wila and Felek were sent east.... Also Lodzia, their elder daughter, together with her husband were "taken away." Danusia is in shock. Her favorite Uncle Józek is dead. She remembers him so well as he played cards with her and sang her favorite songs during the hot summer's hammock siestas. Less than a year ago he took her for a once-in-a-lifetime "buy what you wish" shopping spree in the village and went hunting with Zbyszek and Felek. Back then, Uncle Józek was in perfect health and good spirits. What could have happened to him?

Dad is the most disturbed. He didn't visit his cousin last year but he was anxious to see him the next time. Zbyszek is also shaken. The best time he has ever had was his hunting experience with Felek and Uncle Józef last summer. And what happened to Felek? They were "sent east...?" Is that an indirect way of saying they were simply deported to Siberia?

Uncle Vince couldn't write much. Letters are randomly screened and censored. But from the Polish underground press everybody knows that killings, mass deportations, and expropriations have been under way from the moment the Soviets invaded eastern Poland. In some areas local ethnic minorities eagerly cooperate with the Soviets in pointing out the more prominent Polish families to their new bosses. The Soviets are destroying everything: Polish landowners, nobility and petty gentry are their primary targets. Private farms are turned into kolkhoz, churches and museums into warehouses, and private homes into public apartments. Because of his wealth, social status, and ethnic background, Uncle Józef was an obvious target for the Soviets.

Danusia wipes tears from her face. "We must find out what has happened to dear Uncle Vince." She grabs a piece of paper and starts writing.

"Yes, and what happened to Felek and the rest of them," Zbyszek adds.

"That's good," Dad says. "I will add a couple of words, too. We have to write back to them immediately before there's another breakdown in communications."

"What do you mean, Dad?" Zbyszek looks at him curiously.

"Oh, nothing in particular. But if the Germans decide to invade the Soviet Union or the other way around, that is likely to cause another breakdown in communications."

"What are you talking about, for heavens' sake?" Mama freezes, her mouth wide-open.

"I'm just speculating. The world is so delirious today that anything can happen. The West is pretty much done. Soon the time will come to spread the fascist empire further east. Why not? It's going to be fun. Or the Soviets with their messianic message may decide to save the West. They already tried before, and why not? It would be a lot of fun, too. The hunger for power never ends. It can only grow stronger."

"You may be right, Dad." Józek just walks in with a bag of kiełbasa. "What we are hearing from Koło is not only scary but rather insane. The Germans decided to mandate military service for all the Poles from the Polish territory incorporated into the Reich. They try to grow the German Army with their greatest enemies. It means only one thing—they are desperate for manpower."

"Soon they may want to do the same here," Dad observes.

"But not for a while at least. There is too much resistance in the Government General. They wouldn't be able to enforce anything like that here, I hope," Józek sighs.

"You never know what they are capable of doing," Dad replies.

"I know for sure that they have more draconian rules in Koło than here. Do you know, for example, that to get married in Koło you must be at least 25? We would not be able to get married in Koło, can you imagine! That's how they try to limit the growth of the Polish population," Józek flares up. "It's yet another tool for the biological extermination of our nation."

"Don't worry, son. The more they persecute us the more resistance we put forward. Did you hear about the latest decree issued by General Sikorski?"

"I only heard that our Government safely moved from France to London."

"You see that's really important. And a couple of days ago, General Sikorski issued a decree to form the Central Command Post in Poland to coordinate the resistance movement throughout the country."[1]

"Great!" Zbyszek jumps. "I have to check with the Boy Scouts. We may be actually doing something again!"

Mama sends Dad a furious look and quickly says, "Danusia, I need to visit my cousin in Milanówek—you know, 70-year-old Aunt Lila. I want to take Zbyszek with me. It may take us about two or three days over the weekend. Why don't you come over and take care of Dad while we are gone?"

"I don't need a babysitter," Dad protests.

"But Dad, we could have some fun together." Danusia sends Mama a knowing look. She knows Mama's intentions. When left alone, Dad likes to invite friends for tippling. Now more than ever, he will be inclined to drown his sorrow in vodka. She needs to watch him carefully. But how to do it with Józek around? To have fun with the two of them together is quite impossible.

Sunday morning Danusia is nervous. First she must fight with Józek to convince him to go. "Józek, I would like to go for a picnic to the park. And we could take Dad with us, how is that?"

"Picnic? In the park? That's not the best idea." He is less than enthusiastic.

"Look, I'll make sandwiches. Why don't you pack some fruit? We'll take a blanket and go to the Vistula River. It's such a nice day today."

"Sitting on the blanket, that doesn't sound like fun," Józek grumbles but reluctantly goes along.

At home, a group of Dad's trusted companions are already stationed at the table with several bottles of vodka in front of them. Danusia walks in energetically and announces that she needs to take Dad with her, thus the guests are requested to leave. With some disappointment, the comrades slowly get up and leave one by one.

"Dad, let's go! Look, I've prepared a picnic basket."

"Okay, okay, but wait a second. I have to take something with me." He turns around and grabs the bottle from the table. "We must have something to drink, right?" Hastily, he stuffs big pockets of his vest with a bottle of vodka, small metal cups, and a pack of cigarettes.

Józek observes these developments with outrage. He doesn't drink and he doesn't smoke. The whole idea of going for a picnic with a blanket and a bottle of vodka sounds disgusting. But he knows he has to go through this dubious entertainment for Danusia. With some effort, they manage to get outside. The day is hot and peaceful. It's harvest time in the countryside. But here on the streets of Warsaw everybody dreams of water. They walk leisurely towards Vistula and decide to sit on the hillside of the riverbank.

Danusia opens the picnic container and hands them the sandwiches. Dad takes the bottle and starts filling up the cups.

"Not for me." Józek takes away his cup.

Dad looks at him with resentment.

"Dad, I will drink with you." Danusia rushes forward with her cup instead.

"Well, okay," he mutters.

They sit and eat and drink without saying much. Danusia keeps lifting her cup as if drinking. In fact she doesn't. She hates drinking vodka. She hates the taste, the smell, and the very idea of drinking vodka. But she loves her Dad greatly and doesn't want to hurt him. They all must compromise a little. She lifts her cup, wets her lips, and watches Dad instantly drinking the whole cup at a draught. Józio can't wait to end this libation. He moves back and forth impatiently, finally he gets up and starts walking around. Danusia, mindful of his discomfort, decides to take away the bottle of vodka and packs the picnic basket.

"Let's go for a walk," she orders and reaches out for Dad's hand. "This is terrible," she thinks. "How am I going to survive with the two of them?" Slowly, they pick up their things and walk along the river in silence. Józek is uptight, gloomy and even angry. Dad seems disappointed and frustrated. Danusia walks between the two of them with great discomfort.

"Józek, brother! How are you?" A man coming towards them suddenly shouts from the distance.

"Peter, my dear!" Józek immediately shakes off his uneasy demeanor. "I haven't seen you for centuries," he roars and the two men embrace each other warmly.

"Peter, please meet my wife, Danusia, and my father-in-law," he turns around, making introductions. "This is my good friend from the Seminary. I guess by now I can call you Father Peter, right?"

"Yes, as a matter of fact, I work in this church on the hill. And I invite you all to my church now. You must come with me. We are just about to have a get-together with our old friends. You haven't been with us for a long time, so you really have to come," Peter insists.

Dad observes the discussion and slowly retreats. Danusia notices his withdrawal and looks at him, her eyes turning severe. Józek holds Danusia's hand tightly.

"Danusia, you go with them. I have to go home," Dad says.

"No, I am not going anywhere without you, Dad!" she declares.

Józek looks at her impatiently. "Danusia, you have to go with me. If Dad wants to go home, let him go. You are my wife now, we have to be together."

Danusia stands between the two of them, torn in half and ready to burst into tears.

"If I may be of any help," Father Peter interrupts, "the Bible says that one day you will leave your father and you will go with your husband." He looks authoritatively at Danusia.

"Go with them my dear, go!" Dad says. "It was nice meeting you, Father. So long." Dad turns around and moves away. Józek instantly pulls Danusia towards him. "Let's go!" They start walking towards the church.

Danusia is enraged. She feels as if she has betrayed her beloved father. She doesn't want to go with this newly discovered friend. It's not her friend, after all. She doesn't have anything in common with this man or with Józek's other friends from the Seminary.

But Józek shines. He talks with Father Peter eagerly, waves his arms vigorously, laughs and jokes. It's not the same Józek any more. He is never so comfortable and conversational in her presence. He is always serious and paternalistic towards her. With her, he doesn't talk much, doesn't discuss anything. He treats her as if she was a baby. True, he is almost ten years older but yet, she is an adult, too.

At the rectory, a room is ready for the guests. Nuns in long heavy robes walk around preparing the table. Soon other priests arrive. Danusia is the only woman among the guests. She sits quietly and observes the rest of the crowd. Józek is the center of everybody's attention. His friends pat him on the shoulder, shake his hand, and look at Danusia as if she was a painting in a gallery, just an object of curiosity and admiration. Hardly anyone talks with her. After all, what is there to talk about? It's better to watch her.

Józek notices those curious glimpses at Danusia and his male ego thrives. He knows he has a beautiful wife and is very proud of it. His friends joke and laugh, someone starts playing piano and they all start singing. Strong tenor voices resound throughout the old building. Danusia also likes to sing. She has a strong, colorful voice too. But she doesn't feel like singing. The image of her father walking away is painfully stuck in her memory. The group of strangers rejoicing in front of her eyes angers her.

At first, Józio sings with the group but soon he walks to the piano and starts playing. He plays some popular songs and more sophisticated piano pieces. Danusia watches him with astonishment. She didn't know he played the piano, she couldn't imagine he would sing so well, and she couldn't imagine he would be the life and soul of the party. She almost jumps in to join him in singing but some inexplicable anger makes her resist the temptation.

Why is he so cheerful here? Never before he has been so thrilled. He would never play or sing with her friends or with her family. Only now she realizes how different their worlds are. Can they ever find common ground? Maybe it was a mistake to marry him. Her father suffers, she suffers, and Józio will ultimately suffer, too.

Józio is aware of her uneasiness but decides not to deal with it until they leave the rectory. Only on the way home, he embraces her tightly and lectures her gently about the meaning of marriage and the sacrifices it requires. His soft voice, his gentle caring touch, his pledge to be more considerate to her father slowly breaks the ice.

"I have to travel this week." He finally says. "I have to find Aniela, this cousin of mine who was deported from Koło to the General Government, remember?"

"That's fine," Danusia replies. "But when do you have to go?"

"I have to leave on Monday and I should be back before the week is over."

At any other time, Danusia would be upset but this time she doesn't mind. Aniela needs help. But also Danusia will be able to spend more time at home with her Dad, as before.

On Monday morning, Józio kisses her and takes off. He will be traveling south towards Kraków. That's how much she knows. He should be back no later than Friday.

After work, Danusia goes home. Mama and Zbyszek are safely back. They bought a lot of food in Milanówek and despite strict prohibitions, smuggled everything successfully to Warsaw. Everyone rejoices as they unpack fresh fruit, bacon, and aromatic tomatoes. Danusia stays home that night. It's so much more convenient to go to work from Mama's house.

By Wednesday, she starts worrying about Józek. He may be coming home tomorrow. She goes shopping and plans to cook something special for his return. On Thursday she doesn't go to Mama's but instead rushes home from work. Their apartment is on the third floor. A heavy cage-like elevator slowly takes her up. Creaking and screeching, it comes to a stop on the third floor. Loud grating noise reverberates through the building as she pushes the heavy, metal sliding door full force with both hands. The door to the Kiszkiel apartment stands ajar and some commotion is going on inside. Hastily she tries to close the elevator when Józek shows up at the door.

"Józek, my love!" she throws herself upon him. They can't stop kissing each other as he carries her into the room. Standing in the hallway, Mrs. Kiszkiel shakes her head with indulgent smile. The charm of youth....

The evening goes by quickly. Danusia has thousands of questions and Józek tries hard to answer them. He talks about Aniela, about her children, how they all struggle in a poor village near Kraków, how the local people help them, how the children understand the situation and help their mother, and how happy Aniela was to see him.

"And the trip, how was the trip?"

"It wasn't pleasant. Many patrols, endless controls, German police everywhere."

Next, it's Józek's turn. He wants to know what happened in the meantime, how was she doing, did they get any letters from Koło?

"There have been some round-ups around here lately. People are captured on the streets and sent to Germany for slave labor in the military factories," Danusia brings him up to speed. "The Red Cross sends warnings to be careful and watch for street round-ups."

They look at each other with great admiration and Józek takes her in his arms. "Let's forget about all this for a moment." They are together again and just want this moment to last.

"I hope you aren't planning any more trips for a while."

"No, not at all. And next week I will be working only part-time."

"You know darling, I have to go to work tomorrow but maybe I should take a couple days off from work next week," Danusia dreams. "This way we could spend more time together."

"That's a great idea, Danuś!" Józek passionately catches her in his arms and fervently carries her to the couch....

Over the next few days their spirits are as high as the temperature outside. They visit her parents over the weekend. Józek and Dad chat amiably with no sign of tension between them. Danusia is finally at ease with the two of them. Mama is in a good mood and quite friendly towards Józek.

"Mama, I'm taking three days of vacation this week. We want to go to the club to relax on the Vistula beach. That's where we met the first time."

"Good idea. It's so hot that we all should go to the club," Mama replies.

"But I am afraid there are some restrictions for us to use the club now. You may want to check what's going on," Dad advises.

It turns out that the club is no longer available to the Poles. Thus, Danusia and Józek decide to spend most of her vacation time together at home. The thick walls of the old building provide a nice chilly shelter from the scorching summer heat.

Danusia rejoices. She sleeps late into the morning. Józek gets up early and prepares breakfast. They spend a lot of time listening to music from a fancy gramophone borrowed from Mrs. Kiszkiel. Danusia recalls her movie school experience. In the evening, they dance to the quiet sounds of the tango.

On her last vacation day, Danusia doesn't want to wake up. Józek gets up quietly, puts his white jacket on, and heads to the door.

"Where are you going?" she asks drowsily.

"I'm going to buy some milk and fresh rolls for breakfast."

She turns around and falls into sleep again just to wake up about an hour later. While she is wondering what time it is, the doors suddenly open with considerable noise and Mrs. Kiszkiel bursts into the room.

"Is Mr. Fijałkowski home?" she asks in a most alarming, shouting tone.

"No, he left," Danusia replies, trying to collect herself.

"Oh, my dear! Why did you let him go? For God's sake, why did you let him go?" the old woman taps her forehead and starts crying.

"But why? Mrs. Kiszkiel, I don't understand..... What are you talking about?" Danusia jumps out of bed.

"Look my child, just look through the window! The round-up, you see!"

Danusia rushes to the window, her heart skipping a beat. "Good God!"

Down below, groups of civilian men with their hands in the air are lined up along the street. Heavily armed SS-men, with machine guns ready for action and attack-dogs at their side, guard the terrified and confused men. Wehrmacht regular soldiers help the SS-men.

Holding her breath, Danusia glances at her watch. Józio should have been back a long time ago. Fear and panic paralyze her. Her stomach ties in a knot. "Józio, where is Józio? Why isn't he back? Oh God, it looks like these beasts hunt only men." In a mad rush, she tries to put on some clothing. An overcoat, the white light overcoat is easy to put on. Suddenly they hear knocking on the front door. With one shoe on, Danusia jumps to the door ready to throw herself into Józek's arms.

"Good morning," she hears an unfamiliar voice. "It's not Józek! Not Józek!" she screams inside. A tall, elegant woman walks in. Her gray hair is neatly tied in the back. She has the white and red pin of the Red Cross on the lapel of her gloomy blue dress. The grave-looking woman asks for Mrs. Fijałkowska. Danusia's legs buckled under her, her eyes held spellbound by the small Red Cross pin.

"Yes?" she whispers timidly.

The woman focuses her penetrating eyes on Danusia and says: "Mrs. Fijałkowska, your husband has been caught in the round-up."

Danusia starts sliding against the wall but squarely-built Mrs. Kiszkiel grabs her tiny, supple body and holds her up.

"Madam, your husband needs your help," the woman's firm, low voice penetrates Danusia's consciousness. She comes to life instantly and collects herself at once.

"Help! He needs help! My help! I must get him back!" Urgent, chaotic thoughts overwhelm her.

"Please find his passport and go to the military base near Łazienki. He should be there." The woman bows politely and heads to the door. Danusia doesn't pay any more attention to her.

"Passport, where is his passport?" she panics. She doesn't know where his passport is. "Mrs. Kiszkiel, do you know where he keeps his passport?" she yells frantically.

"No, darling, I don't!" Mrs. Kiszkiel hovers about her helplessly.

"Oh God, help me!" Danusia goes wild, turning the room upside down.

"Wait, wait, I know where it is!" Mrs. Kiszkiel's maid comes to rescue. "Please relax," she says. "I know that Mr. Fijałkowska keeps his documents in the couch." She lifts up the top of the couch and stretches her hand groping the side wall of the wooden base.

"Here you are." To the great applause, she pulls out a pile of documents.

"The passport! Here is the passport!"

Danusia grabs this ticket to heaven acquisitively and runs out. The elevator is ready. She jumps in and shuts the door. The cage moves down sluggishly. The ground. She runs out the door. How to get there? It's too far to walk. The tram, she needs the tram, but which one? She rushes to the tram stop at Marszałkowska, the main street in Warsaw. Here comes the tram. She runs with all her might but she misses it. What to do now? Run or wait for another tram? How long will she have to wait? It's too far to run but it's better to run than to be stuck here forever—she struggles with herself. Suddenly, her heart turns faint. A large group of men march down the street towards her. The civilian men, marching in rows of fives, are surrounded by the heavily armed Germans with their bayonets fixed and rifles ready for action.

To her horror, she recognizes her beloved Józek marching in the front row of the group with his head proudly held up. Impulsively, she dashes straight at him with her eyes fixed on him and her hand with the passport stretched out. She doesn't see the fixed bayonets or rifles. She doesn't hear a sound. In wild despair, she only aims at Józek. In a split-second, she pushes through the cordon. Her desperately outstretched hand reaches him. The passport changes hands. Her quick, bold action surprises the guards. They shout and push her aside while she screams, cries, and dashes back to Józek. The guards aim the bayonets at her but she doesn't care.

"Józek! Józek!" she yells at the top of her lungs while a stranger's hand from behind grabs her white overcoat. A woman stops her, grabs her hand, and holds her tightly.

"Stop, stop, you must stop!" the woman yells at her and tries to drag Danusia away from the guards. Another woman joins in the struggle, and another one, and another one. Together, they drag Danusia to the sidewalk while the men march away.

Danusia looks at them in shock. She cries, staggers, and shrieks "Józek! Józek!" The women try to calm her down. A few minutes later, Danusia comes to herself and the passersby slowly leave. They, too, worry about their love ones.

Half numb, Danusia watches as the departing men turn into the central square near Świętokrzyska Street. Slowly she walks in that direction. The gate to the central square is crowded. Countless groups of men under heavy guard pour into the square from all directions. The huge, well-fenced field normally serves as a central bus station. But today there are no buses. Instead, the field is packed with over one thousand men and more are flowing in. The scene is insane. Some cry, some scream, some laugh. Outside the fence, many women either stare helplessly or cry, shout and scream. They will take them to Germany for hard labor, the rumor goes. But why such a large round-up? There were no such huge round-ups before. And such a heavy guard. "What is going on?" people wonder.

Danusia leans against the fence near the gate and cries bitterly. Crowds of people flow through the gate, among them some high-ranking Germans. One of them looks at her tiny silhouette shaking in convulsions and stops.

"Don't cry," he says to her.

She wipes her eyes and looks at him worshipfully, as if seeing an angel.

"Is your father there?" he asks.

She strains her ears to catch the German words and looks at him imploringly. "My husband," she replies stuttering.

"You already have a husband?" the German asks in disbelief and thinks for a moment. "Okay, show me your husband," he says, making an inviting gesture towards the gate. She looks at him gratefully and walks bravely onto the packed field. But where is Józio? How to find him? Hundreds and thousands of men around. Her German may lose patience any second. She looks around hastily.

"Danusia!" the familiar voice reaches her and Józek's had touches her shoulder.

"Here, here he is!" she pulls Józek towards her angel.

The German examines Józek carefully. "Documents, please," he finally says.

Józek hands him the passport.

"What do you do?" the German asks.

"I am an artist, I paint," Józek replies instantly.

Danusia sends him a curious look. An artist? Why artist? This is the first she has heard of it.

"Okay, you two, you may leave," the German says. For Danusia these words mean more than the whole world. She looks at her angel with boundless gratitude and the three of them start moving towards the gate.

At this very moment, a big black convertible limousine drives in, stops perpendicular to the gate, and effectively barricades the exit. A very high-ranking German, his chest decorated with medals from top to bottom, gets up and looks harshly at Danusia's angel.

"Why is this woman here?" He points his finger at Danusia.

The tall German hesitates. "This woman...was very distressed," he stutters. "I checked her husband's papers and decided to release him," he finally replies.

The General in the limousine looks straight into Danusia's eyes and says calmly, "You don't cry. Just leave now and don't worry. Your husband will be home tomorrow." His tone is convincing, powerful, and inspires confidence. "Just leave now and don't worry," he repeats reassuringly. "Everything will be fine."

The tall German spreads his arms helplessly and Józek's voice whispers to her ear: "Leave, Danusia. You have to leave, darling!" She looks at him in despair and slowly passes through the gate as the limousine with the top official moves inside. The gate closes behind her. She walks down the street without turning back. One second, just that one second and we would be out the gate. Why didn't we move faster? Why did we talk that long? One second, only one second, we missed everything by only one second. That one second becomes her obsession.

At home, Mrs. Kiszkiel welcomes her at the door. "Danusia, did you find him? Where is he? What happened?"

She sends Mrs. Kiszkiel a strange look. "One second! We have missed it just by one second!" she mutters with resignation and goes to her room, leaving a wondering Mrs. Kiszkiel behind.

With some effort, she takes off her overcoat, drops it on the floor and falls on the bed. She sleeps for the rest of the day and wakes up in the evening. Her stomach is empty but she doesn't really want to eat. She takes several bites of an apple and falls back asleep. Except that this is no longer sleep. It's more of a daydream or nightmare. But what if the high-ranking German simply cheated her? What about if Józio won't come home tomorrow? She should have insisted more upon his release. She should have not believed that official. They are not trustworthy. They are so cruel. But then, he sounded so honest and assuring. For sure he meant what he said. How could he lie to her like that...?

She struggles through the night. At dawn, she gets up and puts her white overcoat on. The woman from the Red Cross said the men would be taken to the barracks near Łazienki. Danusia decides to go there and check. She can't wait any longer.

She leaves the house quietly. This time she catches the tram, changes to a bus, and gets off near the stadium. In the chill of the early summer morning, she walks towards the barracks. From the distance, she observes that the vast wooded terrain is empty. Only here and there a few workers sweep the ground cleaning as they would normally clean up after a big soccer game. Clearly, Józek is not here. She walks towards the fence. "Excuse me," she calls one of the men. "A large group of men was sent here yesterday. Do you know what happened to them?"

"They left," a middle age man replies brusquely without interrupting his work.

Danusia reviews the situation. It looks like they were released, as promised. Józio must be on his way home. She clears her throat and asks again. "But do you know, by any chance, where they went?"

The man continues sweeping without looking at her.

"Please tell me what happened to them, were they released?" She asks in her childish, delicate voice.

Apparently stricken by her words, the man abruptly stops sweeping. "No, they were not released," he grunts without raising his head.

"They were taken to the train station," he adds after a moment's thought.

"The train station! And...when did they leave?"

"Late in the evening." By now the man is irritated by her questions and walks away.

Danusia slides down to the ground leaning against the fence and feels nothing, simply nothing. She doesn't cry, she doesn't scream, she doesn't feel anything. She just stares ahead without seeing.

As time passes by, more and more women gather around the fence. "Where are they? What happened to them?" the women ask. The cleaning crew has disappeared altogether and the wide field is strikingly empty. A beautiful young woman with long blond hair and shining blue eyes approaches Danusia. She must be just a year or two older than Danusia.

"Hi," she says timidly. "Do you know anything?"

Danusia raises her heartsick eyes and the woman takes a step back as if she can't bear to hear the answer. "They took them to the train station," Danusia bluntly replies, gets up, and walks away. She doesn't want to look at the woman, doesn't want to hear her voice, and can't stand any questions any more. Deep inside, she still harbors some hope though. Maybe Józio is already waiting for her at home. Maybe he has just returned. She desperately entertains that thought, her last hope, her last chance. Yet, her subconscious jeers at her, telling her loud and clear that he is not waiting for her at home. Indeed, the Kiszkiel apartment is very quiet. No one waits for her there. "That German lied to me! Pure and simple, he lied straight to my face!"

In shock and panic, she runs to Mama. From time to time, her lips mechanically repeat over and over: "One second, just one second." At the gate, old Gara welcomes her jovially but she passes him quickly. Struggling to hold back tears, she takes refuge in the staircase. She then waits for a while and slowly knocks at the door. Mama opens up and looks at her apprehensively. At that moment, Danusia falls apart. She bursts into tears and throws herself into Mama's arms.

"Józio! Józio!" she sobs hysterically.

"Did they take him?" Mama immediately asks.

Danusia merely nods.

"Oh, God! Doctor Petrynowska was right!" Mama doesn't know what to do. Dad nervously rushes in and takes Danusia to the room.

"Be quiet my darling, be quiet." He tries to comfort her. "We were afraid of this. Doctor Petrynowska came over late last night and was asking about him. She thought she saw him in on one of the groups in the round-up."

They all sit down and Danusia cries and cries while Dad snuggles her to his broad chest. She won't go to work today. But Dad has to go. On his way out, Mama stops him. "What should we do? What's going to happen now? We must do something about this."

"You know what's going to happen," he replies harshly. "Józek will never come back. No one has ever come back from any round-up. Be honest with yourself." He violently grabs his tool bag and shuts the door.

20. Street Roundup in Occupied Warsaw

21. Execution near Warsaw, 1940

22. Podhale Rifle Brigade Before Departing for Norway

23. Polish Submarine „Orzeł"

9

The round-up of August 12 in which Józek was caught was the first mass round-up in Warsaw. People all over town are shaken. More than a thousand sons, fathers, and husbands disappeared in that round-up without a trace. The news about Józek quickly spreads. Many stop by Mama's house to express their sympathy.

One day, Zenek Gara comes by and asks for Danusia. Zenek is a handsome young man about three years older than Danusia. He has just received a new underground newspaper, *Polish News*. The newspaper reports on the round-up of August 12. Zenek is anxious to share the article with Danusia. Dad invites him in. "Can you show me the article?"

The young man takes out a thin piece of paper. *Prisoners of August 12 Round-Up*, the headline reads. Dad grabs the paper; his eyes quickly skim through the text, zooming in on one and only one phrase—*concentration camp*. Immediately, he realizes the gravity of the situation. It's worse than he thought. He has already heard about the concentration camps. The *Information Bulletin* recently reported on the formation of so-called concentration camps throughout Poland. No one knows for sure what the real purpose of the camps might be, but one thing is certain—the people in the concentration camps are treated worse than the prisoners of war and worse than those kidnapped and shipped to labor camps in Germany. He folds the paper and remains motionless. Only the wrinkle on his forehead deepens.

Zenek waits in discomfort. A few minutes pass by. At last Dad realizes his presence and hands him back the paper. "I would like to ask you to do me a favor, could you?"

"Anything for you, Sir," Zenek replies eagerly.

"Please don't tell Danusia about this article. You see, she worries so much. But we don't know anything specific yet. We can only speculate. It won't help her."

"I guess you are right, Sir." Zenek puts his head down.

"But please, don't get me wrong," Dad adds. "This subject is very, very important for us. Please follow up on any news about the round-up and let me know if you find anything. We must know as much as possible, but for now I just want to spare her the pain. So just talk with me about it, please."

"I understand," Zenek replies politely.

"So, tell me what other news you have gotten there in this new paper of yours. I only read the *Bulletin*."

"Except the round-ups, nothing in particular today. But about a week ago, there was this news about Lithuania, Latvia and Estonia. Apparently all three countries were officially incorporated into the Soviet Union."

"Yes, yes, I read about that. It's very bad news. A lot of persecutions and a lot of terror out there too," Dad shakes his head.

"And of course this battle for England. I am sure you heard about that," Zenek adds.

Dad shakes his head. "Not much, really. Just that Luftwaffe attacked selected British targets. And this radar business, of course. The Germans are spreading the news that they have destroyed the secret British radar system along the British coast."[1] The radar technology is Dad's great fascination. He closely follows all reports about this latest electronic wonder of the world.

"According to my newspaper, the damage to this so-called radar system was not that significant," Zenek replies. "But what is very important for us is that many of the Polish pilots made it through the Channel to Great Britain and are in the process of forming Polish Air Force squadrons there. Our sources say that General Sikorski, on behalf of the Polish Government, signed an agreement with the British Government to form the Polish Air Force.[2] Let me see. There is a follow-up article about our pilots in this issue." He checks the tiny pages of the *Polish News*. "Oh, here it is, on the second page."

> In accordance with the bi-lateral agreement, the Polish Air Force will be recognized as a sovereign military formation and will swear allegiance to the Polish Government only. The Polish Air Force is expected to include at minimum four bomber squadrons, two fighter squadrons, and one army support squadron, all with their own reserves. More squadrons can be formed in the future. With respect to the organization, training, equipment, discipline, promotion, and operational use, our squadrons

> will be under unified RAF command. Our fighter squadrons are currently training on the British Hurricanes and are expected to go to combat any day....

Dad listens with bated breath. "Those Hurricanes are pretty good machines even though they were introduced back in 1936. It's a simple design with a good Rolls-Royce engine, if I remember correctly. They are almost as fast as the German fighters but supposed to be very efficient and more maneuverable."

Voices resound in the hallway and Danusia with Maya Gara appear at the door. "Zenek, what are you doing here?" Maya looks at her brother suspiciously.

"The same that you're doing here. I'm visiting my neighbors," Zenek laughs, discreetly putting the newspaper into his pocket. "You don't have a monopoly on visiting our neighbors."

Danusia's inquisitive eyes immediately turn to Dad. "Have you heard anything?"

"No darling, nothing."

"Okay, I'm going home then."

"But wait a moment," Mama protests. "First, you must eat dinner."

"No, I can't eat anything. I feel queasy."

"Danusia, you must eat now. You haven't eaten all day," Maya gently pushes her to the table and sits down with her. "Don't worry and don't be so impatient. You'll go home soon."

"But what if he waits for me already?" Danusia replies with great urgency in her voice.

"Then he doesn't have to wait long," Maya assures her. "You will be back in less than an hour."

Dad observes Danusia with a sorrowful heart, then takes out a small paper box from his tool bag, and gives it to her. "I have something for you, Danusia. Look."

She recognizes the present just by looking at the box. Éclairs! A box of delicious éclairs, her favorites from before the war. She hasn't seen them for a year and has dreamt about them often. But this time the éclairs don't excite her. Even worse than that. She doesn't feel like eating them at all. Smiling slightly, she takes the box. "Thank you, Dad. Thank you very much. But how about if I take them home. It would be a nice welcome for Józio." She looks at Dad gratefully. "If you don't mind, of course," she adds quickly.

"No, not at all." Dad replies, swallowing hard.

The days pass by in tense anticipation of some news from Józek. Danusia keeps coming to Mama's after work just for a quick meal and rushes home with great anxiety, hoping to hear from Józek. She can't sleep and she can't eat. She feels sick and falls into a depression. At work she doesn't do much. With great care, Maya watches after her, trying hard to keep her alert and cheer her up a little. She often walks her home to Mama's and later walks her down to Mrs. Kiszkiel's apartment.

One day, though, when Danusia comes to work, Mr. Gara doesn't welcome her at the gate and Maya is not at her desk either. Danusia feels a certain emptiness around but doesn't ask, rather, she quietly sits down and starts counting the pile of freshly printed banknotes. She doesn't pay any attention to a commotion around her. Her co-workers whisper, gesticulate vividly, and glance at Danusia from time to time. During the break, Danusia takes a cup of tea and turns to Wanda Tołłoczko. "I wonder what's happened to Maya today? She's always here."

"You don't know?"

"No...," Danusia replies with worried curiosity.

"Zenek was rounded-up yesterday," Wanda says, lowering her voice.

"Oh, no!" Danusia puts her teacup on the table and slides into the chair. "I haven't heard of any round-up yesterday," she tries to argue.

"He was not taken from the streets but from the café."

"You mean they were dragging people out from private places?"

"Yes." Wanda's horrified eyes require no further explanation.

"I must go." Danusia abruptly ends the conversation and heads straight to the Gara apartment. In front of their door, a group of women is engaged in a heated debate while trying to keep their voices down. Danusia pushes through the crowd to the door.

"Danusia don't go there! Leave them alone," one woman tries to stop her.

"But I have to talk to them!"

"Old Gara is devastated. He needs to be left alone," another woman says.

"Let me go, let me go!" Danusia gets angry.

"Let her go!" a powerful voice dominates the clamor. "If anybody, she should be the one to go and talk with them." Everybody looks at Danusia. "That's right!" Other voices support the idea. The woman slowly steps aside. Without knocking, Danusia rushes inside.

"Good morning," she says.

With all five daughters at his side, Mr. Gara sits in the armchair like a statue. He looks but doesn't see, he hears but doesn't listen. Maya sits on the couch with her long blond hair disheveled and her delicate face more pale than usual. Her other four sisters wander about. Noticing Danusia, she stretches out her hands in a welcoming gesture.

Timidly smiling to everybody, Danusia slowly walks to her best friend and hugs her affectionately. She feels her pain deeply. Zenek is the pride and the shining star of the entire family. A talented artist, he graduated from the nearby Graphics High School and has been working in the mint as a banknote designer. A very bright and articulate young man, he has also been an active member of the Polish underground. Most of all, he was a caring and devoted son and brother. Old Gara was especially fond of his son. He admired his only boy and laid all his hopes and life's ambitions on this bright and handsome young man.

"Maya, honey. You shouldn't worry," Danusia starts. "I am sure they will release Zenek. He has such good papers. He works at the mint and they need him here."

Old Gara looks at her bitterly and seems about to say something, but on second thought falls back into his apathy.

"Had Józek had such good papers as Zenek did, I am sure he would be released," Danusia continues. "They need people like Zenek. I am sure they will release him," she keeps repeating.

But her message isn't well received here, quite the contrary. They have already learned that the greatest, the brightest, the famous, the influential, the rich, the powerful, the respected, the indispensable—all are being killed every day, and no one, no human power on earth can save them. Danusia sticks around for a while but she is not at ease with her own message. More and more, she feels the unspeakable load on her mind and heart. Upon reflection, she becomes even more frightened. Trying to hide her growing fear, she once again hugs the girls and leaves in a rush.

With this new burden on her shoulders and without Maya around, Danusia becomes very sick. She becomes feverish; her stomach hurts; she can hardly eat anything. For the next few days she stays in bed. Under the watchful eye of old Mrs. Kiszkiel and with Mama's help, she eventually recovers and is ready to go outside.

The day is cloudy but warm. The sorb apples on the trees along the sidewalk start turning red. Wondering whether she can find anything to buy, she rambles along the streets and finds herself on Nowy Swiat. Every Warsawian loves this place. The most elegant street in town, with wide sidewalks and picturesque, luxurious apartments, brings back happy memories. A long time ago, her mother had a hair salon on this street. She recalls her wonderful childhood days.

Nowy Swiat means "New World" in Polish. This captivating name carries with it certain unspoken strength and appeal. Danusia reads the name with admiration. In other parts of Poland the Polish names of towns and streets have been replaced with either German or Russian names. Koło is no longer Koło. It's Wardbrucken or something like that, a name that Danusia can hardly pronounce, let alone write. But here in Warsaw the Polish names of the streets still can be found.

Walking down the street towards the Old Town, she suddenly notices a loudly sobbing woman with a little girl and a package from the post office in her hand. The woman cries openly and bitterly. The scene grieves Danusia's heart. She approaches the woman and anxiously offers her help. The woman leans against Danusia's shoulder and bursts into tears with new strength.

"My husband, my husband!" she sobs desperately.

Danusia feels shivers run up her spine. She holds the woman in her arms and asks gently: "What happened to your husband?"

"They killed him! These beasts killed him!" the woman screams.

"What do you mean?"

"They caught him on the street, took him to Auschwitz, and simply killed him there! Like that, just killed him, for nothing!" The woman hysterically shakes her head. "Look! Look here! This is a package from the so-called Auschwitz Concentration Camp. Do you know what's in this package? Do you know?" she screams wildly. "This package contains the ashes of my husband!" she pronounces in a half-laughing tone with a weird look on her face. "That's right! They sent me back his ashes! Oh! It's so considerate of them!" She laughs and cries.

Danusia's eyes grow round as she looks at the small package stamped all over with red and blue imprints.

"When," she tries to clear her throat, "when did they catch your husband?" she finally asks with a sinking stomach.

"On August 12, during this big round-up," the woman wipes her tears.

All of a sudden, Danusia starts swaying and the distressed woman tries to hold her up.

"Gracious God!" Danusia stammers out.

The woman stops crying and watches Danusia keenly. "Did you have anyone in that round-up?" she asks cautiously.

Danusia nods her head; her huge eyes bore into the woman urgently. "Where…?" she stutters again. "To where, did you say? They took your husband?" she finally chokes out her question.

"Auschwitz Concentration Camp," the woman hesitantly replies. "It's our Oświęcim near Kraków," she adds softly. "They renamed Oświęcim into Auschwitz. It's the Reich now."

"Do you know…," Danusia tries to catch her breath, "whether everybody from that round-up was sent to that place?"

"Yes, everybody," the woman boldly replies.

Danusia's eyes are getting even bigger and she visibly pales.

"But whom did you lose?"

Danusia shakes her head in despair. "My husband," she whispers, staring straight in the woman's face.

Horror-struck, the two gaze at each other in silence.

"I am sorry, I have to go." Danusia tries to hold back tears.

They embrace each other and walk in different directions. At first, Danusia doesn't care where she goes; she just has to walk away from that woman, as far as possible and as quickly as possible. She can't stand the image of that woman with that package…. Home. She has to go home. She has to let Dad know where Józio is. They must get him out quickly. She turns around and hurries home. Mama is happy to see her.

"Is Dad home!!"

"No, not yet. What happened? Where have you been? Why are you so nervous?"

"Because I already know where Józio is. Have you heard of Auschwitz?" She looks at Mama with keen scrutiny. "That's a concentration camp in Oświęcim near Kraków."

Mama has already heard the name. Dad has already told her about that place. But they didn't want to share this information with Danusia. Dad has been talking with his friends at the mint about various options to get Józek out. Apparently many people have already been trying to get their loved ones out of this dreadful place but to date no one has succeeded.

As she talks to Mama, Danusia gets red flashes and rushes to the bathroom. The old feeling of sickness comes back and she starts vomiting. Mama runs after her.

"What is going on with you? This stomach upset should be gone by now. It has been bothering you too long," Mama looks at Danusia suspiciously.

Danusia hardly walks back to the room and drops on the sofa.

"Give me something to drink, please."

Mama hands her a cup of hot tea and covers her with the blanket. "Danusia, you know what I think?" Mama slowly says after mulling over some thoughts. "You have to go to the doctor. We have to check what's going on with you."

"Oh, no! I don't want to go to the doctor. I'll be fine, don't worry."

"But listen. You know Doctor Petrynowska. There is nothing to be afraid of."

"Mama, tell me what you really think about this?" Danusia suddenly puts Mama on the spot. "I have a feeling you have your own diagnosis, haven't you?"

Mama takes a deep breath. "Yes, that's right. I am afraid that you may be pregnant," she confesses, her eyes searching the floor.

Danusia doesn't say a word. She lies down, her face expressionless. Deep inside, she's already thought about this possibility. But this is such a strange idea. She doesn't know whether to cry or to rejoice. It's such a foreign concept. It has happened to others but somehow it was not supposed to happen to her. A baby, a child? She's not ready for any baby. She is a baby herself. She needs care and attention. How can she take responsibility for another human being in this hell on earth? But the baby—that's Józek's baby. That's so important for both of them; that's their love. "Okay," she says finally, "then let's go to the doctor."

Doctor Petrynowska is the general doctor at the mint. She takes care of all the employees. A middle-aged widow and a mother of two, she works around the clock, frequently rushing to emergencies in the middle of the night. Everybody at the mint appreciates and admires her devotion to her patients and respects her wisdom and judgment.

Danusia knows her mostly by sight. Luckily, besides vaccinations, Danusia hasn't been in need of much medical help. But her best friend, Maya, has had many health problems. As a small child, Maya badly injured her leg and the resulting infection ate away part of her bone. Danusia spent many hours at Doctor Petrynowska office accompanying Maya to her regular visits.

Sitting in the waiting room, Danusia feels awkward. This time she is a patient and Mama is her companion. With a warm smile, Doctor Petrynowska invites Danusia into her office. Sensing a comforting atmosphere, Danusia gets up, leaving Mama in the waiting room.

The door closes and Mama finds herself alone in the simple quiet waiting room. She rubs her tired hands and plays with her fingers. There is not much expression on her weary face. She just waits as the big clock over her head counts off passing seconds and minutes. When the door finally opens, Mama notices a strange look on Danusia's face, the kind of a look that Danusia gets very rarely, only when shaken to the core. Mama recalls that look from a year ago when Danusia learned about her teachers killed in the bombardment. Doctor Petrynowska looks at Mama with some concern.

"Yes, Jasia," she says, "Danusia is pregnant. It's the second month."

Mama looks at Doctor Petrynowska, not quite sure what to say. "Thank you, doctor," she finally whispers, embracing a confused Danusia.

Mama walks in silence while Danusia struggles with her thoughts. What to do now? What to tell Dad? He will be mad. And how about Józek? He may be happy.

"Mama, don't tell Dad anything yet. Just give me some time to think about it. I must find out more about Józio."

* * * *

It's the holiday season in Ohio—Christmas 2000 and the end of the second millennium or the beginning of the third millennium, if you will. Danusia commandeers the kitchen. Not many guests are coming, only her two granddaughters. But the traditional cooking must take place: borsch with *pierogi*, herring in vinegar, carp, special mushroom doughnuts, poppy seed cake, and many other delicious dishes. Tradition requires at least thirteen dishes for Christmas Eve. The guests arrive early. Everybody crams into the kitchen. The granddaughters are also eager to cook. They try to follow Grandma's directions but add their own twist to the recipes. They argue for more salads and want more fresh vegetables.

When the first star appears in the sky, the Christmas Eve feast starts. This is a special feast, no meat is allowed, only fish and vegetarian food. For Polish stomachs heavily dependent on beef and pork, this is an extraordinary challenge. Danusia begins serving borsch with unique *pierogi* called *uszka*. It's a ritual. She always worries whether there will be enough *uszka* for everybody. But this time there is plenty of *uszka*, no need to worry. The traditional sharing of *opłatek,* holiday wishes, Christmas carols, and finally, after the feast, the time comes for presents.

Konrad can't wait. Colorful boxes are stacked up under the Christmas tree. Without wasting time, he distributes the presents. At last he can open his boxes. This is the year for Lego sets. He gets several big boxes of Lego including the biggest one—the Knights' Castle set. But he also gets a scooter. Scooters are popular this year, too.

After the gift extravaganza, it is time to go to church for Midnight Mass. It's a traditional Polish mass called *Pasterka*. For this occasion they will drive to the Polish church in Cleveland. But Danusia won't go; she is too tired by now.

Pasterka Mass entails a special celebration. On average, three times more people attend *Pasterka* than any other mass. The priest welcomes the newcomers. And the music! The music is very special that night. The Polish carols carry so much meaning, so much emotion, and so much power. The enthusiastic, thunderous voices shake the Gothic church to its foundation. The people are mixed: young and old, tall and short, some already Americans, some Polish-Americans, some purely Polish—the new arrivals.

The time comes for the Holy Communion. A long line forms in the center aisle of the church. One by one, people proceed to the steps of the altar. Different faces slowly move through the spotlight. But these are not so happy faces. These are tired faces with a certain sense of resignation and insecurity. These are struggling faces of simple hard-working people. No dignitaries here, not many leaders either, very few businessmen, very few faces of academics and intelligentsia. Where are they, one may wonder. What happened to that powerful, noble, and proud nation, a visitor from two hundred years ago would inevitably ask. Are they really gone?

Christmas Day is quality family time, as Konrad likes to call it. A videotape from Poland has arrived. This movie is mandatory. Danusia's oldest son, Andrzej, recorded the latest family events. First of all, the video shows his cute three-year-old Maciuś—Danusia's and Józio's first great-grandson. Andrzej is absolutely crazy about his lovely grandson. The video shows Andrzej serving as a horse for Maciuś, playing ball with Maciuś, playing hide and seek with Maciuś. Danusia can't believe her eyes. Her Jędruś, the one who didn't want to get married at all…!

In the second segment of the video, Zbyszek's grandson, Przemysław, enters the priesthood. The occasion is very special. The entire family attends the ceremony. This event is considered the equivalent of a wedding—when a young man makes his commitment for life. Przemysław is one of many young Polish men who choose the priesthood these days. Pope John Paul II is the most powerful role model for the young Poles. Too many young Polish men answer the call of God these days, many more than the country can absorb. As a result, at the outset of the third millennium, Poland became the leading world supplier of Catholic priests. Przemysław, too, most likely will be sent abroad to serve the spiritual needs of some distant community.

The videotape ends. Everybody gets up, ready to continue the Christmas feast. Finally, they can catch up with their meat—all this ham, smoked and boiled, and kiełbasa, and sausage patties, and *kabanosy*, a very thin dried and smoked pork sausage—it's so delicious! The intense, smoky aroma spreads throughout the house.

"Is Przemysław going to enter any particular order?" Konrad asks.

"What do you mean?" his mother looks at him, surprised.

"I don't know, a Franciscan Order or Bernadine Order, or...you know, something like the Teutonic Order for example?"

"Oh, I see what you mean," she laughs. "I don't think so, but who knows?"

Over this holiday, Konrad together with his dad reads one of the greatest Polish historical novels, *Teutonic Knights* by the Nobel laureate Henryk Sienkiewicz. Knight Zbyszko, in pursuit of the kidnappers of his beloved Danusia, takes the readers back to the beginning of the fifteenth century. The novel vividly depicts the relationship between the Kingdom of Poland and the Teutonic Order half a millennium ago.

The Teutonic Order was founded as a charitable organization in 1190 in Palestine by the German crusaders. Only eight years later, the order assumed a military character and upon the invitation of the Hungarian King, Andrew II, the order moved from the Middle East to Hungary to help fight the invading pagans there. In 1225, Andrew II expelled the aggressive Teutonic Order from his country. Subsequently, a Polish Duke, Konrad Mazowiecki, struggling with his pagan Prussian neighbors in the north, asked the Teutonic Order for help. Over the next fifty years, the Teutonic Knights exterminated most of the native Prussian population. In 1263, the Pope released the Teutonic Knights from the vow of poverty and allowed them to engage directly in trade. The Teutonic Order quickly monopolized the lucrative grain trade from Prussia and Poland through Baltic Sea to Western Europe. By the beginning of the fourteenth century, the Order had firmly established its control over Prussia, cut off Polish access to the sea, and begun its expansion east towards Lithuania. Throughout the fourteenth century, the Order had been exploiting and invading all surrounding lands, steadily building its military strength and creating a new state with its capital in Malbork (Marienburg). Malbork Castle became the most powerful military center of the Medieval Europe.[3]

In 1409, the Order invaded Polish territory near Dobrzyń and reached out for Samogitia (Żmudź) near Lithuania. At that point, military confrontation with Poland and Lithuania was inevitable. Over the winter, all sides made preparations for war and engaged in intense political campaigns in Rome to assure the Pope's support. Although Poland was baptized back in 966 and Lithuania converted to Christianity in 1386, the Teutonic Knights portrayed Poland and Lithuania as barbarian pagans that posed a threat to Catholic Europe, and the Polish King, Władysław Jagiełło, as a false Christian.

In July of 1410, the army of Teutonic Knights under the command of Grand Master Ulrich von Jungingen met the Polish and Lithuanian armies under the command of King Władysław Jagiełło at Grunwald near Dobrzyń lands. At the battle of Grunwald, the Teutonic Knights were decisively defeated, Grand Master Ulrich von Jungingen was killed, and all the flags and military insignia of the Teutonic Order were captured by the Polish–Lithuanian forces and deposited for safekeeping at Wawel in Kraków.[4]

As a result of the Grunwald defeat, the Teutonic Order returned Dobrzyń lands and Samogitia. More importantly, the battle at Grunwald marked the beginning of the end of the military might of the Teutonic Knights. By 1466, the Teutonic Order was forced to return most of its lands to Poland, and the Grand Master became a vassal of the Polish King. Subsequently, Grand Master Albrecht von Hohenzollern decided to convert to Protestantism, dissolved the Teutonic Order in Prussia, and transformed its lands into a secular duchy of the Kingdom of Poland. In 1525, he paid homage for his new duchy to the Polish King at a ceremony in Kraków.

The sixteenth century found Poland at the summit of its power. The Kingdom of Poland was undeniably the largest state in Europe. In political union with Lithuania, the country stretched from the Baltic Sea to the Black Sea, from the Oder River to Smolensk. Within its vast territory, a variety of ethnic groups and religions flourished. Catholics, Orthodox, Jews and Muslims lived in peace and harmony together. At the time of the Counter-Reformation, Poland welcomed all kinds of heretics and religious refugees—Anabaptists from Holland, Catholics from England, Czech Brethren, or Italian Unitarians. With the Calvinist-dominated Senate, the Polish Parliament adopted the most progressive statute of its times, the epoch-making 1573 Statute of General Toleration, assuring permanent and universal tolerance to all ethnic and religious groups, making Poland the prime European haven of tolerance.[5] The legal guarantee of tolerance that dates back to the sixteenth century is the primary reason why Poland became the home of the largest Jewish settlements in Europe.

The Kingdom of Poland or *Rzeczpospolita*, meaning Commonwealth, was governed by the joint Polish–Lithuanian elective monarchy and by a joint *Sejm*. In this aristocratic-democratic system, the ruling noble class—*szlachta*—played a leading role in electing kings, hiring them like contractual managers.[6]

The Polish *szlachta* has no precedence in history. At times reaching as much as 15 percent of the entire population, *szlachta* was by far the largest noble class any country ever had. At the same time, however, *szlachta* represented an incredibly diverse group consisting of the most powerful magnates in Europe as well as the so-called petty gentry working on their land like peasants. The most powerful families, such as the Czartoryski, Poniatowski or Lubomirski, possessed vast estates, private armies, and income larger than the king. The petty gentry possessed above all their noble blood, their honor, their coat of arms— *herb*, and their inheritable privileged legal status. For centuries, this noble culture became the leading ingredient of the Polish identity. Throughout Poland's darkest years of partition, it was *szlachta* who zealously guarded and cultivated the national culture and identity. The Soviets would later persecute and oppress the Poles, labeling them as the nobility or *Pany*, in other words the greatest enemies of the masses.

The Christmas holiday in Ohio passes quickly. In the evening of Christmas Day, the family gathers in the TV room to watch a movie. This year, they will be watching *Teutonic Knights*, a Polish movie based on the book of Henryk Sienkiewicz. As portrayed in the movie, Danusia is a sensational blond 16-year-old beauty, a daughter of the powerful Polish nobility—Jurand from Spychów. She becomes a lady-in-waiting to the Queen of Poland. Using deception the Teutonic Knights kidnap Danuśka from the Queen and using blackmailing tactics, summon Jurand to their castle in Marienburg. Upon his arrival, Jurand is badly humiliated. After losing his temper and killing several adversaries, he is most awfully tortured. His eyes are put out, his tongue is wrenched out, and his right hand is cut off. After all this torment, he is set free. Near death, he is miraculously found by his people and survives. Eventually Zbyszko wrests Danuśka from the Knights, but she dies in his arms on the way home.

While rescuing Danuśka, Zbyszko takes several prisoners. Discovering Danuśka's heart-rending conditions, Zbyszko is about to kill her oppressors. But his old friend, Maćko, stops him. "You will do harm to yourself by killing your prisoners," he says. "Remember, you are a Knight. The reason you are a Knight is because you value your honor. It is your honor and your moral strength that makes you a Knight. If you kill defenseless people you will bring dishonor and infamy upon your name forever."

The Teutonic Knights had just invaded Żmudź and Dobrzyń lands. The battle of Grunwald looms on the horizon. In the meantime, the Pope in Rome orders Poland and the Teutonic Order to exchange prisoners. The reports of compliance are sent to Rome. But there are striking differences in the reports of the two sides. It turns out that the Polish side releases mostly warriors while the other side holds very few warriors. Instead, it releases mostly women and children kidnapped like Danuśka through deception and fraud for ransom or revenge.

"We didn't make much progress since those times," Danusia's son observes. "To the contrary, deception, fraud, and killing of defenseless populations became more popular than ever. All the mass exterminations throughout five long years of German occupation.... As a civilization, we made clearly regressed in this respect. Honesty, morality, and honor, those are liabilities today viewed by the majority as the weakness...."

"Yes," Danusia sadly nods. "How naïve I was back then, during the war.... I remember very well this round-up, and this distinguished high-ranking German officer telling me so honestly and convincingly that my Józio would come home tomorrow.... Stupid me—I trusted that monster...!"

10

The door of the cattle wagon opens with a drawn-out screech. The morning sunlight blinds the men inside. Józek and his sixty or so companions, worn out by the long journey, emerge into the daylight.

Raus! Raus! Strident voices greet the terrified men. Helping each other, the men leave the wagon. For a brief moment, the train platform is swarming with dazed human shadows, hundreds of them.

"*Raus! Los!*" Heavily armed SS-men shout, push, kick, and herd the men to a distant gate.

Scared and confused, the people are rushed towards a big sign "*Arbeit macht Frei.*" Józek looks at the sign. "Work...freedom...? How strange...." But there is no time to ponder. Behind the gate, a long alley of SS-guards with horsewhips ready to strike awaits the newcomers. One by one, the captives are pushed into the corridor of beating and lashing. People are falling, crawling, howling with pain, losing their bags and belongings. Józek is numb. He must do something. His mind searches feverishly for a solution. Yes, that's right, he must run as fast as he can. His turn. But the alley is not clear yet. "*Raus*!" the order comes. He glances at a big SS-man. A hat bearing the death's head emblem, strong legs in long shiny boots spread apart. Unknown hands push him into the alley. He starts, runs full speed. Drubbings...sharp pain.... He still runs. Another blow...he trips, loses control, and falls forcefully into the pile of barbwire at the side of the lashing line. "*Raus! Raus!*" A guard with the death emblem is about to hit him. He jumps up and runs away. Only now he feels a growing pain in his calf. He glances at it—his right leg is bleeding heavily.

The terrorized men, many of them wounded, some already bleeding, are ordered to form a squad in the center of the yard. They stand speechless, awaiting the next blow. A short, skinny, middle-aged, higher-ranking SS-man holding a big whip jumps on an upturned barrel and calls for a translator. Several hands go up, he chooses one.

"This is the Concentration Camp!" he croaks out. "No one will get out of here alive! You Poles, remember! You don't have your Poland anymore! Your homeland is behind these barbwires now! For us, the Germans, you are not human beings, you are just mere dunghills. You are the enemies of the Reich. There is no pity for those like you. Forget about your wives, children, and families. You will die here like animals! You have no more than three months to live! Understand?"

Stunned, Józek and his companions stand mute when suddenly heavy truncheons fall on their already swelling shoulders.

"*Jawohl*!" the column instinctively replies. The men got the message....

The short SS-man leaves the barrel and another young and haughty SS-man takes his place.

"Now you will undress and make a bundle of your clothes. Also, you must take off your shoes."

Horrified, Józek bites his lips. The pain is growing, numerous cuts are deep; his leg is bleeding heavily. He undresses with difficulty. Registration is next. One by one, the men approach long tables hurriedly set up in front of them.

"Name and profession?" a prisoner behind the table asks, fills out a form, and hands Józek a card.

"This is your number," he says in a subdued voice.

Józek looks at the card. From now on, he becomes KL Auschwitz Number 3088. To date, 3087 men were brought to Auschwitz and thousands more are yet to follow. Józek puts the card in his pocket while being pushed over to another table for medical exam. A tall, bold doctor checks his ears, eyes, and mouth, and takes away his clothing, his watch, his wallet, his passport, and the wedding ring. All his possessions are placed in a paper bag clearly marked as 'Number 3088' and carried away. Even though Józek pleads for help, his bleeding leg is of no interest to the self-assured doctor.[1]

"Later, later. You have to move on," the doctor hurries him.

The line must move on to the next station. Naked, barefoot, and bleeding, he is led to another section of the camp where he receives underwear and a bizarre pajama consisting of pants and a shirt in blue-gray strips. That's his new outfit.... Next, he receives a metal bowl and a half-liter cup. His leg stops bleeding.

Eventually, the Warsaw transport, as they are being called here, gets something to eat. It's a liquid of indeterminable color and some potatoes. After the meal, Józek is sent to Block 4, later renumbered as Block 12.

The Warsaw transport that arrived in Auschwitz on August 15, 1940, consisted of 1153 civilian men caught in the street round-up and 513 political prisoners from the Warsaw heavy security prison known as Pawiak. The prisoners from Pawiak consisted mostly of political and religious activists, lawyers, doctors, and officers.[2]

At the time of Józek's arrival in Auschwitz, German criminals operated the camp. The very first prisoners arrived there in May of 1940. The first transport consisted of the German criminals carefully selected from the Sachsenhausen camp in Germany. They became the first functionaries in Auschwitz, in other words the helpers of the SS-men. Their main task was to supervise the prisoners and maintain discipline.[3] As the camp grew, the functionaries were recruited from prisoners of all ethnic backgrounds. Subsequently, the camp underground movement made every effort to assure the promotion of their trusted people to the functionary positions. It was a matter of life and death.

After the arrival of the Sachsenhausen prisoners, subsequent transports consisted primarily of the members of the Polish resistance movement from Silesia. This strongly industrialized region, rich in coal and other natural resources, had been hotly contested by Germany before the war, and like Gdańsk, intensely infiltrated by the aggressive German nationalist movement. The Nazi fear of the growing Polish resistance movement in Silesia was the foremost reason for the creation of the Auschwitz camp. According to the initial plans, the camp was to hold about 10,000 Polish underground activists.[4]

Every day, the camp bell rings for a long time just before dawn and the light in the block is turned on. Crammed together, the recent arrivals rush to make their beds and dress. Józek's leg hurts even more. A functionary called a "room-man" bursts in and drives everybody out with a riding crop. Józek is too slow, thus a sharp whip lands on his head. Drips of blood shroud his glasses.

After having a cup of hot liquid, supposedly coffee, the prisoners are summoned for roll call. Every Block Senior, a functionary responsible for the block, arranges and counts his people in front of the block. He then reports his number to the Block Chief, this time the SS-man in charge of the larger squad who, in turn, reports his numbers to the SS-officer in charge of the roll call.

One of many ways to torment the prisoners is the roll call. Under normal circumstances, the roll call lasts one or two hours. In the event of an escape, the roll call lasts interminably. The longest recorded roll call in the men's camp—some 20 hours—took place in July, 1940, after the escape of Tadeusz Wiejowiejski.[5] This time, the morning roll call lasts just over 2 hours.

After roll call, training begins. The *capos* train the new arrivals to form rows of five, snap to attention, make turns, line up, etc. Poor execution of a command results in a fit of rage with a beating of anyone nearby. Józek moves with difficulty. His leg is swelling badly. He's kicked and beaten and ultimately falls down. A haughty SS-man with an attack dog at his side orders him to get up. But Józek does not jump up. Instead, he points to his hurting leg. And that is his grave mistake. The puffed-up superior human being sets his bloodthirsty dog right on Józek. Long, sharp fangs sink into the tender flesh of Józek's thigh. Pain, fright, and in the end, infinite blackness embraces him.

The next day, Józek wakes up in the infirmary. He battles a high fever for several days. Caring hands of other inmates help him recover but his leg is badly swollen and sore. He cannot walk. While he recovers in the infirmary, a new transport of about 100 German criminal and political prisoners arrives at Auschwitz.[6] They will become the new *capos*, the rumor goes.

During his stay, the infirmary is in the process of being transformed into a camp hospital. A high-ranking SS doctor will oversee the transition. Hans Bock, a German criminal number 5, one of the earliest Auschwitz arrivals, becomes the senior functionary in the hospital. His deputy will be Peter Welscha, number 3207, a newly arrived German with a number "younger" than Józek. The new managers select several Polish doctors to work for them. Among the chosen ones is the bold doctor with whom Józek has been developing a good relationship. Slowly, Józek starts walking. Thanks to this doctor, Józek is not sent immediately back to the block but instead is given time to regain strength.

Soon after the arrival of the new German transport, a frenzy breaks out in the camp. The occasion is very special—the first anniversary of the German invasion on Poland. The camp Deputy Commander calls all the prisoners out and announces that, from now on, all camp activities shall be performed not by walking but by *Laufschrit*—running. He then turns the prisoners into the hands of the newly arrived oppressors.

That day there is no end to the sadistic tormenting. The prisoners, like animals in training, are kept jumping, running, turning around, rolling, hopping, and doing push-ups. Some climb the trees while the oppressors pursue them with sticks and riding crops. The Deputy Commander walks from one group to another, inciting the new oppressors in their rage. People fall like flies. Several dozen of heavily beaten bodies have to be removed from the yard afterwards by those who withstood the ordeal. This task has to be performed running, of course.[7]

Miraculously, Józek escapes this ordeal by remaining in the hospital. He is sent back to the block the next day. But he also lands a job as a nurse's aid in the newly formed hospital. For Józek, his first job is a blessing, not much physical effort, occasionally some extra food, and a relatively safe and warm working environment. In 1940 the hospital was still in the business of offering medical treatment to its patients. But in 1941 its focus would shift towards so-called "routine selections" for the gas chamber and mass murders by phenol injections.

Several of Józek's friends from the Warsaw transport, mostly Jews and Catholic priests, ended up in *Strafkompanie*—the penal company. One of the newly arrived German criminals, Eric Krankemann–Number 3217, is appointed a Block Senior of the penal company. He begins his career in the camp by hanging another German prisoner. The next day, he selects a group of older people from his block and forces them to push a huge ram roller, at least two meters in diameter, forcing them to level the main square of the camp. Fat as a pig, Krankemann stands at the shaft of the roller like a warrior on a military chariot, whipping the swaying men in front of him with a long riding crop. The rest of the camp watches this bestial demonstration.[8]

"Look at this monster," a man next to Józio whispers, pointing at Krankemann. "That's what a victim of Fascism looks like...."

One of the men falls. Krankemann cheers and forces the others ahead. The man on the ground is slowly pressed down and run over by the roller. The spectators clench their fists....

By now Józio is bold like everybody else. His picture is taken in three poses, face on and two profiles. He is even permitted to write a letter home but first he has to register his home address on a special form.

"Why do they need to register our home address?" he wonders.

"You don't know?" the inmates are ironically surprised. "They have to know where to send a death notice."

"Or to take your loved ones as hostages in case you dream of escaping from here," others add, laughing viciously.

Shivers run through Józek's body. But it is pointless to worry about it. He already gave Danusia's address for the records. Now he has to write a letter! But what to write? "Don't worry," his friends advise him. "They will tell you what to write...."

Indeed, the first letter is straightforward. The block-man brings a big blackboard and special forms on which the letters will be written. He then prints the pre-approved text on the blackboard. The text, written in German, is as follows:

> Dear (so and so):
>
> I want to let you know that I am in the KL Auschwitz. I am healthy and fine. I hope you are healthy and fine too. In the camp, we have a shop in which we can buy food and cigarettes.

The healthy, sick, and the dying had the right to write such a letter. Asking for money was forbidden, though.[9] Official instructions on the standard form letter informed the addressee that the prisoner could receive two letters per month with each letter not exceeding fifteen lines per page. Sending anything else was prohibited and was subject to confiscation. Petitions for release were not accepted and visits were forbidden.

On September 22, another huge transport arrived from Warsaw. It consisted of 1,139 men from the street round-up and 566 Pawiak prisoners. Among them Józio recognized many familiar faces including Zenek Gara from the State Mint and Witek Pilecki. Witek was one of the senior officers of the Secret Polish Army. In the camp, Witek was known as Tomasz Serafinski–Number 4859. After the war, it was revealed that Witek voluntarily joined one of the groups caught in the Warsaw street round-up in order to develop underground resistance structures in Auschwitz and link them with the outside world.

* * * *

In the meantime, Danusia interrogates everybody in Warsaw about Auschwitz. She reads the underground press, talks with the people at the mint, visits churches and confers with many priests. But she doesn't talk about her pregnancy with anyone, not even with Mama.

Returning one day to her apartment, she notices Mrs. Kiszkiel anxiously awaiting her at the door.

"Danusia!" the old woman exclaims. "You have mail. A letter from Józek!"

With reverence, Danusia reaches out for the small piece of paper. *Konzentrationslager Auschwitz* in large print on the front jumps at her. And a bright red stamp—*Deutsches Reich....* The letter is written in German though and she can't read it. In despair she turns to Mrs. Kiszkiel.

"Can you read it?"

"Not really, my dear, but maybe my husband can. This text is very brief, so maybe he can help."

Mr. Kiszkiel, a gentleman in the old grand style, is in his armchair and, as always, with a cigar, his cane and a top hat nearby. He is reading something. When approached, he takes the letter and looks it over with great curiosity.

"Rather brief and laconic. Hmm.... I bet they censor it pretty well. Let's see. But you know, I am not that good in German." He pauses, correcting his eyeglasses.

"My Dearest Danusia!

"I am in good...health.... Don't worry." He stops and cleans his glasses. "Please write and...and let my mother...know about me." He snorts and wheezes. "I will write... to you...two letters...per month. Love, Józek."

He looks it over again. "Oh, here is his address, his...'Gef. Nr...,' I wonder what that is.... Maybe it's like...like a prisoner number, and his block number," he points to the front of the envelope. "You may ask someone else to translate it again. I think I got it right but I am not sure." He looks exhausted.

But Danusia is ecstatic. Józek is alive and well. Now that she has found him, she has to get him back. But first, she has to write back. She has to write immediately to let him know about the baby!

"Thank you Mr. Kiszkiel, thank you! I am wondering...," Danusia continues with hesitation, "I must write him back and I am wondering whether you could translate my letter into German?"

Mr. Kiszkiel inhales the cigar. "I would prefer not to. Only if needed...."

"Whom should I ask?" Danusia brainstorms her options. "Oh, I know! Maybe Mrs. Sowińska will help. After all, German is her native language."

"That sounds like your best option." Mr. Kiszkiel is relieved.

Danusia goes back to her room and examines the letter in great detail. One half of the front of the envelope is covered with small print in German. It starts with these big letters *Konzentrationslager Auschwitz* and looks like some sort of official instructions. The date on the envelope is only half legible. Looks like September 16. It means the letter has been delivered within just a few days. It also means that her letter could reach Józek quickly and that, at last, she could let him know about the baby! She has to write immediately.

Early in the morning, she rushes to Mrs. Sowińska without even stopping at Mama's house. Mrs. Sowińska, in her long dressing gown, opens the door. Trying to catch her breath, Danusia hands her the letter through the door. Mrs. Sowińska glances at it and invites her in while reading the brief text and translating it simultaneously. The translation is in essence the same.

"Mrs. Sowińska," Danusia says, "could you please help me write a letter to Józek? I am afraid it has to be in German."

"Let's see...," Mrs. Sowińska focuses on the small official print next to the addressee. " Yes, I guess you are right. It says here that you can write back no more than fifteen lines per page. It has to be in German, I think."

"Can we do it now?" Danusia begs her.

"Well, I was planning..., but if you are ready...then let's do it now."

Danusia swallows hard and tries to concentrate. With her eyelids half closed, she begins dictating. But how to squeeze everything in? What to say? She tries hard to calm down.

My Dearest Józio!

I have just received the first letter from you. We all are very happy that you are in good health. I already wrote to your mother and sister in Koło. I will write to them again today. We all are in good health and miss you very much.

Danusia stops, somehow troubled. A dark blue pen swings in Mrs. Sowińska's hand. "You can write more. We still have plenty of room. Go ahead."

"I also want to let you know that...I am pregnant."

Mrs. Sowińska drops the pen. "Are you sure?" she asks in a shaky voice.

Without raising her eyes, Danusia nods and tries to continue. "The doctor has said that this is the second month." She dictates without looking at Mrs. Sowińska. "I very much want to have this baby.... But if you think otherwise, I will terminate this pregnancy. Please let me know what to do. With love, Danusia."

"You can write more. There is still room." Mrs. Sowińska says.

Danusia looks at the page with several blank verses at the bottom, looks at Mrs. Sowińska, and at the page again. "No, I don't have anything else. Maybe next time." She sinks heavily into the chair, her hand pressed against her temple.

"It looks like you have a headache." Mrs. Sowińska observes. " I would give you a headache pill but I don't know whether you can take it now."

"Thank you, you are so kind. I will go to Mama now. She has a special warming ointment that always helps me."

"But wait, let's address this envelope." Mrs. Sowińska carefully copies the address.

"I will write the return address myself. This way he will see my handwriting," Danusia says.

"Very good. And take care of yourself!" Mrs. Sowińska hands her the envelope and warmly pats her on the shoulders.

"Thank you very much." Danusia rushes out.

"Mama, look! A letter from Józek! He is in Auschwitz but he is fine!"

Standing in the doorway, Mama stares at the letter.

"But, Mama, I will come home later, after work. Now I have to run to the post office. Mrs. Sowińska has helped me write my reply. See you later."

"Danusia…!" Mama tries to say something but Danusia is long gone. "A reply. I wonder what sort of reply…," she ponders, closing the door.

After work, Danusia comes home exhausted. Her head is about to explode. Her stomach hurts badly. She lies down on the sofa while Mama gently puts a cold pad on her forehead and carefully applies the magic ointment on her temples.

Dad comes home and energetically drops his tool bag on the floor. "Danusia, what's wrong with you?"

"I am just tired, Dad. I will be all right, don't worry."

"She got a letter from Józek today…," Mama says. "From Auschwitz," she adds timidly.

"Where is it? Show it to me!"

Danusia points out to her handbag. "It's in German but Mrs. Sowińska translated it for me. It doesn't say much and I already wrote him back."

Dad hurriedly inspects the letter. "What did you write?" He asks absently with his attention fully focused on the letter.

"That we are fine…and that I wrote to Koło…and…and…."

"And what else?" He glances at her somehow impatiently.

"Dad, I must tell you that, too…I guess…. I am pregnant…."

"Whaaaat?!!!!" Dad's horrified roar cuts through the air like thunder. In desperate fury he turns to Mama. "Is that true?"

"Yes, Alek. That's true. But calm down, please!" Mama grabs his hand but he jerks it away.

"That's insanity! That's the worst joke I ever heard! All we need now is for her to have a baby! The man is in a death camp and she is going to have a baby in the middle of this cannibal feast! That's wonderful!"

"He is not in a death camp!" Danusia jumps up and faces him. "Józek is alive and well, and I will get him back! I will, for sure, no matter what!" She screams, yells, and cries, all at once.

"You two sit down, *NOW*!" Mama pushes herself in between them.

"Go to hell! All of you!" Dad raises his hands in grief and walks away.

Mama takes Danusia in her arms. "Be quiet, Danusia, be quiet. You know his choleric temper. But he will calm down." She gently carries the trembling and crying Danusia to the sofa. After waiting some time, she finally asks: "So, what did you write about the baby?"

"I...simply asked him...whether...whether he wants me to...have this baby," she chokes out, sobbing.

"Well, you left this decision to him, then."

"Mama," Danusia raises slightly her head, "I want to have this baby," she says forcefully. "But if he tells me 'no,' then I may decide...not to...."

"Okay, my dear, okay. Why don't you sleep now?" Mama covers her tenderly with a blanket, glances at her with sorrow, and walks out on tiptoes.

"Alek! I have to have a serious talk with him. This is unacceptable." She looks around the house but he is nowhere about. He must have gone out. She looks through the window and goes out. To her amazement, she notices Alek, as gentle as a lamb, talking quietly with Mr. Chyżyński, one of the Polish quality control inspectors at the mint.

"It's not the same Alek." She observes and curiously approaches the men from behind. "I wonder what is it that calms him down so effectively?"

Even though the two men didn't see her, they instinctually sensed her presence and fell silent at once.

"Hello, Mr. Chyżyński," she says, trying to cover up her intentions. "I need him if you don't mind."

The quiet man looks at her with his deep intense eyes. "He is all yours, Madam." Bowing politely, he sends Alek a strange categorical look and walks away.

"What did he want?" Jasia can't resist asking.

"Oh, nothing special, just business."

She looks at Alek also categorically. "We need to have a serious talk about Danusia."

"What is there to talk about? She must get rid of this baby business right way. There is nothing to talk about. And I understand you will take care of it. Otherwise I will step in."

"Don't be silly. This is not the end of the world. She wants to have this baby, you understand!"

"Oh, sure she wants it because she knows we will take care of everything. That's not fair. It's not fair to you."

"But I don't mind," Jasia looks at him provocatively.

"But don't you understand? She will totally ruin her life and jeopardize her chances to survive this madness. Honestly, Józek doesn't stand any chance of surviving this insanity. Can you imagine a nineteen-year-old widow with a child in the middle of this hell on earth? I can't!" Alek gesticulates furiously.

"Well, first we have to think about her immediate well-being. She is sick and depressed. I believe she should move back home and give up this apartment at the Kiszkiels. You have to stop your hysteria and be nice to her. She wrote to Józek asking him what to do. If he writes back that she should not have this baby, then she would probably get rid of it. But for now, we have to wait."

"Do you believe that this man on death row will tell her to abort his baby? No way, especially a former candidate for a priest. Now, he struggles to survive. And her interest is at best a distant thought to him. Isn't that obvious?" This time Alek looks at her provocatively.

"But you must understand also that having a baby will make her more cautious and more careful. She won't volunteer for any suicidal mission as many of our young people around are longing for. Look at Zbyszek, you know how difficult it is to keep him out of trouble today."

Alek shakes his head. "But the baby will put her in trouble anyway, you'll see."

"Instead of causing trouble, you should try to find out how to get Józek back!"

"And what do you think I am doing? I already did more than anyone else could. Do you know that Zenek Gara is also in Auschwitz? The director of the mint will try to get them back but the chances are very slim. It may be easier with Zenek because he has a long work history at the mint, with Józek it's much tougher."

* * * *

Around October 10, Danuta's first letter arrives in Auschwitz. With shaking hands and pounding heart, Józek tears the envelope apart. The letter is short but the message is astounding and overwhelming. Danusia will have a baby, his baby, and he will be a father.... This is the most powerful message anyone could ever get in this kingdom of death. He puts down the piece of paper, looks around as if he were in a bad dream, and bursts into tears. He can't control his emotions any more. His closest inmates don't rush with questions but watch him with concern.

People don't ask questions. There are too many tragic stories around here. Every prisoner carries within his tragedy. The most dramatic ones are those of the political prisoners who came to Auschwitz through the Gestapo prisons like Pawiak. The images of bestial tortures and killings are engraved in their psyches. Their night terrors only grow stronger and stronger. Imaginary orders shouted out by angry voices wake them up in the middle of the night. Shaken to their bones and sweating, the prisoners agonize in solitude. Every night, mad screaming and quiet crying resounds in the block. The prisoners have to get used to it. Above all, they try to survive....

A child.... That strange concept sticks in Józek's mind like a permanent fixture. In the night, in the morning, at roll call, at work, and during the meals, it's always on his mind. God sends him the child. It means that God will also give him the strength to survive. He will survive. He must survive! His reply to Danusia is ready. The standard language has to precede the most precious words. But the message is loud and clear—he badly wants this child. His only path to survival is through this child.

* * * *

Over the few next days, Danusia stays at Mama's house but she doesn't want to give up the Kiszkiels' apartment yet. Józek must know about it. The atmosphere at home is heavy, though. Dad tries to keep quiet but deep inside he feels like a wounded beast. His dear, defenseless girl is hurt. She suffers and inevitably will suffer even more. He either keeps quiet and doesn't talk at all or explodes with great fury. "Get rid of that baby now!" he yells and cries from time to time, scaring everybody around.

In the middle of October, the long-awaited reply from Józek finally comes. It's a real two-page letter in his own handwriting!

"Prisoner Number 3088, Block 17, Auschwitz, October 13, 1940." Danusia manages to read herself. But with the rest, she needs help.

"My Dearest Beloved Wife!" Mrs. Sowińska reads while Danusia devours every word.

> Thank you very much for your letter. I am healthy and fine. I was delighted to hear from you. You are very brave and very smart. I love you even more. I already know your letter by heart. You wrote: 'I want to have this child,' and this message pleases me more than anything else. If God wants us to have this child, it's wonderful. God will help us and will protect us. I hope I will be able to return home soon. I really hope that I will be able to live happily with you and with our baby. Please write back quickly and write a little more this time. I am sending you a hundred kisses.
> Your husband, Józek

"He wants to have this child!" Danusia proclaims. "Now I am convinced that he will come back. He must come back!"

* * * *

It is already mid-October but the prisoners still walk barefoot. The mornings are piercingly cold. The days are already rainy and windy. As winter approaches, Józek's job at the hospital, away from freezing rain and harsh fields, becomes even more attractive.

But many of his friends work outside in the sticky mud clearing off the area around the camp. The local Polish population has been expelled from the vicinity of the camp. A radius of a few dozen kilometers has to be cleared from the buildings. Demolition proceeds at a furious pace.

Back in July of 1940, the Camp Commandant, Rudolf Höss, wrote to the head of the regional SS authority that "the local population around the camp is fanatically Polish and—as determined by intelligence sources—prepared for any action against the hated SS camp. Every prisoner who manages to escape from the camp can count on their help as soon as he reaches the first Polish farm." In response to this letter, the regional authority designated the 40 square-kilometer area surrounding the camp as the so-called Auschwitz Concentration Camp Zone of Interest.[10] Despite all efforts to prevent them, the escapes from the camp continue. Prisoners escape through the barbwires and under the machineguns, but most frequently while working outside the camp.

On October 28, at around noon, the SS discovers that a prisoner in Block 8 is missing. Immediately a punitive roll call is ordered. All the prisoners must stand at attention and wait for the results of the search. They can be dispersed to the blocks only after the search crew returns. At about 4 PM, it starts to rain and snow. The prisoners, dressed in light denim clothing, without caps and coats, stand like mummies in the endless rows of five. Two days before this horrific roll call, wooden shoes or so-called *holenderki* were distributed. But not everyone has receive them yet and a good number of people stand barefoot.

All of a sudden, an older man faints and falls down. One of the SS-men jumps at him and starts kicking the man with his heavy boots, ordering his victim to get up. But the poor wretch never gets up. The enraged SS-tormentor throws indiscriminate blows. His fist lands on the shoulder of a nearby prisoner, and something strange rustles under the prisoner's blouse. The SS-man stops, gives a man a bestial look, and orders him to undress. To everyone's horror, the SS-man discovers that the prisoner's thorax is neatly wrapped around with thick packing paper. The SS-man jumps at the prisoner shouting, cursing, and kicking him. Other SS-men join in the melee. The most senior SS-man orders the entire first row to undress. It turns out that sixteen prisoners have wrapped themselves with paper from cement bags. Their numbers are registered. Severe punishment awaits them.[11]

At around 9 PM, the missing prisoner is found dead in the cellar. The roll call ends after nine agonizing hours in the freezing cold. Over 120 dead, fainted, and sick prisoners are removed from the yard.[12] But Józek is not among them.

All Saints Day takes its toll. Last year, Poland was saying farewell to her brave defenders killed in action. This year, it's a farewell to the defenseless, brutalized and tortured civilian population dying by the thousands every day everywhere.

The Germans are eager to celebrate All Saints Day. On November 1, *Reichsführer* SS Himmler issues an order to execute forty Polish prisoners from Katowice as a punishment for so-called assaults on the

SS officials in Silesia. On November 22, during the lunch roll call, the forty victims walk through the square with their hands tied behind their backs with barbwire. The execution squad under the command of SS Second Lieutenant *Untersturmführer* Tager consists of 20 outstanding SS-men carefully selected from the camp guard squad.[13] For twenty minutes, the entire camp listens to rhythmic shots in regular intervals. The bodies of the victims are burned in a brand new crematorium, the first of its kind. This is the first mass execution at Auschwitz and the "grand opening" of the first camp crematorium.[14]

During the evening roll call, camp Deputy Commandant Fritzsch warns the prisoners. "If you try to escape," he shouts, "you better think about it twice and remember! Many people from your town or village will be killed immediately!"

December comes and Christmas is around the corner. The Archbishop of Kraków sends a written request to camp commandant Rudolf Höss asking for permission to celebrate Christmas Mass at the camp. Höss denies the request but permits instead that anonymous food packages not exceeding 1 kilogram each be sent to the camp. On December 27, the Prisoners Assistance Organization from Kraków delivers six thousand food packages to the camp. Each package consists of a piece of bacon, a cake, cigarettes, and holiday wishes written in Polish together with a traditional thin piece of bread *opłatek*. "A piece of Poland," people comment tearfully.[15]

Józek is particularly lucky Before Christmas he received a package from home, or rather two packages, both larger than 1 kilogram, both from Danusia. When an order was issued that the prisoners could receive one Christmas package not exceeding 1 kilogram, everybody wrote home about this new order[16] but Józek didn't write anything. He didn't want to cause Danusia any trouble and didn't expect anything. So, he was even more surprised when long before most of the other packages started to arrive, he received a Christmas package with food and an extra package with warm clothing. Under the circumstances, these packages were unheard of and truly sensational. Sent according to a special permission of the Camp Commandant, each package was officially stamped dozens of times and painted in red all over. Warm underwear hand-quilted with cotton, warm socks, gloves and earmuffs arrived in one package, *opłatek*, bacon, kiełbasa, lard, sugar, chocolate, tea, and a cake arrived in the other.

Józek couldn't believe his eyes. And all this accomplished by his little tiny and childlike Danusia? Most of his famous, prominent, powerful and rich friends don't get such packages. And everybody knows that those are not ordinary packages, those are life-saving necessities. So much tragedy and yet so much happiness.... "This is a sign from God. I must survive." Józek is convinced.

But the world that surrounds him laughs at his fantasies. This doomed place has its rules. Only the greatest villains can count on a brighter future. The biggest sadists are offered the most prominent careers. The camp is managed in accordance with a simple rule: the most deaths with the least effort. People die every day, everywhere. Human shadows hover with suppurative wounds, with frostbite, with hunger diarrhea and swelling. In resignation, they await their ultimate destiny. Deprived of human dignity, they perish in all kinds of barbaric ways. They are sentenced to starvation, killed on the spot and during tortures at *Stehbunker*, under whips, sticks, heavy boots or ram rollers, during work and in the blocks, burned alive, decimated by typhus spread by sucking lice, subjected to cruel medical experiments, and finally gassed in the gas chambers and burned in the crematoria.[17]

Each death translates into extra bread for the functionaries. And bread in the camp is everything—it's life, it's the only moment of peace, it's the object of the greatest human desire. The most awaited moment of the day is the distribution of bread. This exciting moment takes place after the evening roll call. Everyone receives 250 to 300 grams of bread per day. The prisoners are expected to leave some of it for breakfast. But it never happens. The omnipresent feeling of hunger is so strong that the prisoners eat the daily ration of bread, crumb by crumb, chewing it as long as possible to prolong the soothing feeling.

Józek's food package generates unthinkable emotions. Not only that he wants to share the food, he *must* share the food. Otherwise it will be stolen in a blink of an eye. He tries hard to preserve *opłatek* and chocolate for Christmas Eve. His block-man promises to save it for him. After all, there are some decent functionaries.

More packages start to arrive. A young country boy from south-east Poland receives a package with 1 kilogram of salted bacon. He hides his trophy and disappears. This delicious homemade salted bacon turns out to be deadly for his starved body, though. The next morning he is found dead in his hiding place together with his emptied can of bacon.[18]

Right after Christmas a new order is issued. Packages are no longer allowed. Everybody must write home to let their families know not to send any more packages. But they can send money—no more than 20 Marks per month. The so-called *cantina*, or a cafeteria, offers cigarettes and sauerkraut. A functionary, upon appropriate commission, occasionally can purchase one of these things for the prisoner.[19] Józek's mother and sister from Koło send him the money on a regular basis.

Danusia doesn't write very often now. Her due date, the end of April, is fast approaching. She wants to know whether Józek has any preference for a boy or a girl. On February 5, 1941, Józek writes:

> To your question as to a boy or a girl, I don't have a real answer. I like little boys as much as little girls. I think about you, long for you, and hope to return soon and live happily with you for a long time. The weather here is beautiful, the sun is shining, and spring is awakening. I hope I will be going home soon. I am waiting patiently for the day when I will see you, our baby, and my mother.

That hope to go home becomes Józek's obsession. In every letter, he writes over and over again about going home soon. He believes with all his heart that he will be going home soon. On March 9, 1941, he writes:

> My Dearest Wife, Danusia!
>
> From the bottom of my heart, I thank you for every word you wrote.
>
> Your letters give me hope, strength, and courage. I am so happy that you are healthy and thank God I am also healthy. I long for you and think about you every day. My greatest wish is to be with you. I am anxiously awaiting the birth of our baby. Thank you so much for your birthday present. I already imagine seeing my picture over your bed. I hope I will be able to thank you in person soon.
>
> Please send thanks to my mother for the money and also for her letter even though it was so short. It had only three lines. I cannot write to her because we cannot write to two different addresses. I am now able to buy a little more in the cafeteria, sometimes hot soup and salad. If you

want to send me 10 RM, you only need to show the last envelope with the address.

I kiss you a thousand times. Please send my regards to your family.

Your husband, Józek

Despite the hopeful tone of his letter, survival in the camp becomes more problematic with each passing day. On April 23, 1941, Camp Commandant Höss, with the assistance of his deputy Fritzsch, for the first time selects ten prisoners for death by starvation as a reprisal for the escape of a prisoner. During the punitive roll call, ten Polish political prisoners from Block 2 are chosen for a cruel death by starvation in the bunkers of Block 11. Among them is physics professor, Marian Batko, from Kraków. This elderly man, a high school teacher, "volunteers" for the selection in place of 17-year-old Mieczysław Pronobis, who will survive Auschwitz. Marian Batko will die in his cell on April 27. The other chosen prisoners will be fighting for their life to the bitter end, licking humid walls and eating insects. The last of them will die on May 26.[20]

As Danusia's due date approaches, Józek becomes very nervous and impatient. Every day he keeps inquiring, asking, and nagging for a letter thereby driving his block-man crazy.

"That's it! I have had enough! From now on you can only receive one letter per month. You must immediately write home and let them know not to send more letters than one per month," the *capo* orders. Thus, on April 27, 1941, Józek writes:

My Dearest Wife!

I worry about you. You are always in my thoughts, my beloved, and I am proud that I will soon become a father. I am awaiting your next letter with great anticipation but you must know that, from now on, you may only send one letter and receive one letter per month. You must observe this rule in the future.

On May 14, 1941, his most anxiously-awaited letter finally arrives. Józek has a son, a little baby son Andrew, nicknamed Jędruś! Danusia and the baby are fine. He cries with joy. On May 26, 1941, he writes back.

My Dearest Wife!

Thank you so much for your letter. I was awaiting this letter so impatiently and for so long. I am very happy that you are fine. I cannot even tell you how happy I am that God has given us a big and healthy son. In your next letter, please describe his cradle. You don't realize how much your letters mean to me. I think about you and Jędruś day and night and I am still hoping to come home soon. Your letters give me hope and courage. I work every day and I am well, thank God. In His hands lies everything....

Indeed, in God's hands lies his fate. Józek no longer works at the hospital. Instead, he works hard in the field. But by now he knows all the spoken and unspoken rules of the camp and knows how to cope with the adversities. He manages to repair his relations with the blockman and informs Danusia that, from now on, they can correspond again twice a month. His letter is optimistic.

"Don't worry about me," he writes on July 20, 1941. "In my free time, I listen to the camp orchestra, play games, and read the newspaper *Die Woche* (The Week)."

Die Woche has just informed the prisoners about the capitulation of the Yugoslavian Army and soon thereafter about the Greek capitulation. "*Deutschland über alles*!" the paper proclaims.

On July 29, Camp Commandant Rudolf Höss travels to Berlin for a high-level meeting with Himmler in order to discuss, in person and without witnesses, the so-called "final solution to the Jewish question." At the meeting, Höss receives an order to prepare a plan of mass extermination of the Jewish population.[21]

During Höss's absence, Zygmunt Pilawski, Polish prisoner Number 14156, located in Block 14, escapes from the camp. Höss's deputy, Fritzsch, following his boss's example, orders the punitive roll call.

In unspeakable terror, prisoners from Block 14 report for the roll call. Fritzsch inspects their rows with predatory satisfaction and slowly, methodically begins the selection for death by starvation. Among the selected men is Franciszek Gajowniczek–Number 5659, a husband and father of a number of young children. In great despair, Gajowniczek begs for mercy while Fritzsch laughs at his plea. All of a sudden, another prisoner steps forth from the rows of Block 14. Dead silence falls. The daring man in a clear and firm voice asks to be included in the selected group of ten in exchange for prisoner Number 5659.

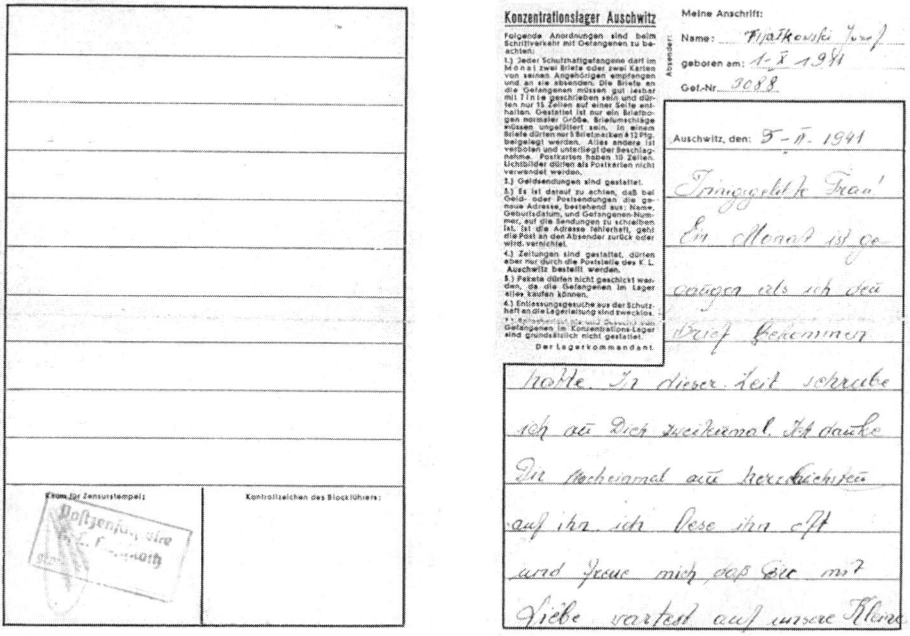
Raum für Zensurstempel:

Postzensurstelle K. L. [illegible]

Kontrollzeichen des Blockführers:

Konzentrationslager Auschwitz

Folgende Anordnungen sind beim Schriftverkehr mit Gefangenen zu beachten:

1.) Jeder Schutzhaftgefangene darf im Monat zwei Briefe oder zwei Karten von seinen Angehörigen empfangen und an sie absenden. Die Briefe an die Gefangenen müssen gut lesbar mit Tinte geschrieben sein und dürfen nur 15 Zeilen auf einer Seite enthalten. Gestattet ist nur ein Briefbogen normaler Größe. Briefumschläge müssen ungefüttert sein. In einem Briefe dürfen nur 5 Briefmarken à 12 Pfg. beigelegt werden. Alles andere ist verboten und unterliegt der Beschlagnahme. Postkarten haben 10 Zeilen. Lichtbilder dürfen als Postkarten nicht verwendet werden.

2.) Geldsendungen sind gestattet.

3.) Es ist darauf zu achten, daß bei Geld- oder Postsendungen die genaue Adresse, bestehend aus: Name, Geburtsdatum, und Gefangenen-Nummer, auf die Sendungen zu schreiben ist. Ist die Adresse fehlerhaft, geht die Post an den Absender zurück oder wird vernichtet.

4.) Zeitungen sind gestattet, dürfen aber nur durch die Poststelle des K. L. Auschwitz bestellt werden.

5.) Pakete dürfen nicht geschickt werden, da die Gefangenen im Lager alles kaufen können.

6.) Entlassungsgesuche aus der Schutzhaft an die Lagerleitung sind zwecklos.

7.) [illegible] von Gefangenen im Konzentrations-Lager sind grundsätzlich nicht gestattet.

Der Lagerkommandant.

Absender:

Meine Anschrift:

Name: Fijałkowski Józef

geboren am: 1-X-1941

Gef.-Nr. 3088

Auschwitz, den: 5-II-1941

Innigstgeliebte Frau!

Ein Monat ist gegangen als ich den Brief bekommen hatte. In dieser Zeit schreibe ich an Dich zweitemal. Ich danke Dir nocheinmal am herzlichsten auf ihn. ich lese ihn oft und freue mich daß Du mit Liebe wartest auf unsere Kleine

24. Józef's Letter From Auschwitz to Danusia

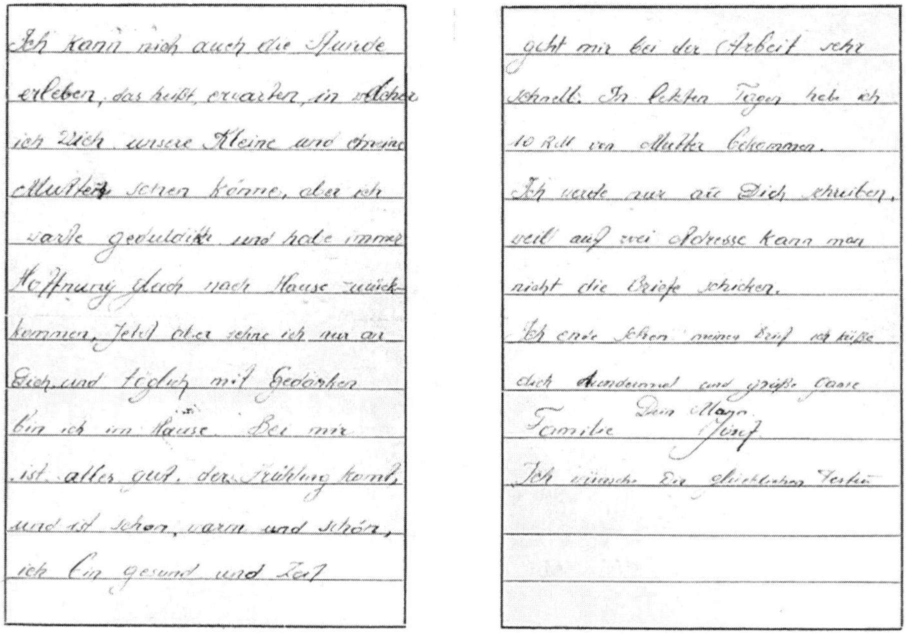
Ich kann nich auch die Stunde erleben, das heißt, erwarten, in welcher ich Dich, unsere Kleine und meine Mutter sehen könne, aber ich warte geduldikh und habe immer Hoffnung gleich nach Hause zurückkommen. Jetzt aber sehne ich nur an Dich und täglich mit Gedanken bin ich im Hause. Bei mir ist alles gut, der Frühling kommt, und ist schon warm und schön, ich bin gesund und Zeit

geht mir bei der Arbeit sehr schnell. In letzten Tagen hab ich 10 RM von Mutter bekommen.

Ich werde nur an Dich schreiben, weil auf zwei Adresse kann man nicht die Briefe schicken.

Ich ende schon meinen Brief ich küsse dich [illegible]mal und grüße ganze Familie

Dein [illegible]

Józef

Ich wünsche Dir glücklichen Festen

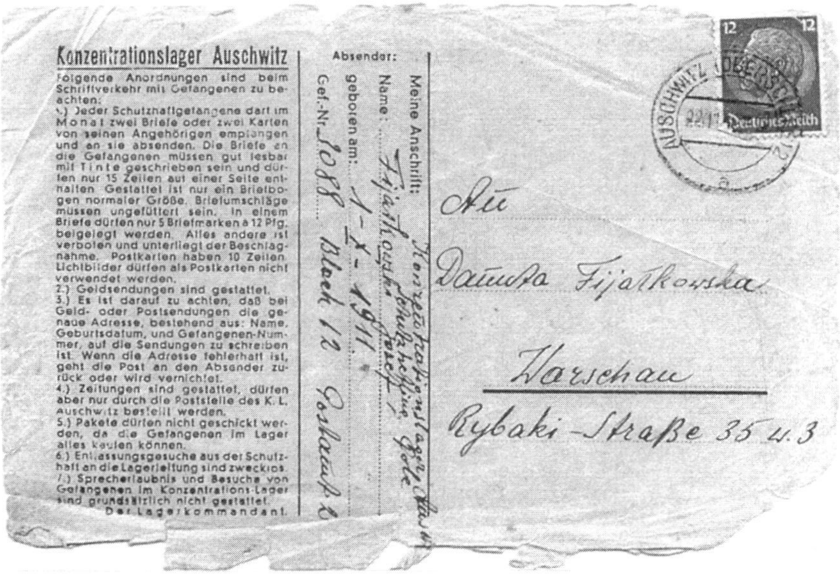

25. Envelope from Auschwitz

26. Danusia, Zbyszek and Jędruś, October 1941

Slightly surprised, Fritzsch asks the insubordinate man a few questions and without giving it much thought, accepts his offer. Maksymilian Rajmund Kolbe, a Catholic priest and Auschwitz prisoner Number 16670, is sent with other nine casualties of the day to the death block in place of Franciszek Gajowniczek, prisoner Number 5659.[22]

Arrested for production and distribution of an underground press in Niepokalanów monastery near Warsaw on February 17, 1941, Father Kolbe went through Pawiak and arrived in Auschwitz on May 29, 1941. He will survive his nine companions in the death block and after a two-week long agony will be killed on August 14 by phenol injection performed by Hans Bock, prisoner Number 5.[23] But Franciszek Gajowniczek will survive Auschwitz and will return to his family. Forty years later, the Polish Pope, John Paul II, will proclaim Father Maksymilian Rajmund Kolbe the Saint Martyr of Love.

Józek has been lucky, however. So far he has survived the selections and in the process did not lose hope or sanity. In mid-August, he was informed that his wife has requested permission to send him a photograph of his newborn son. But through a special order, Hitler personally forbade any pictures in the concentration camps. Thus, on August 31, 1941, Józek wrote:

> My Beloved Danusia!
>
> I am grateful for everything you all have done for me. I have seen your application regarding the photograph. But you may not send any photographs *directly* to me.... I kiss you and my little Jędruś one thousand times....
>
> Your husband, Józek

In his wildest dreams, he could not imagine the significance of these words.

* * * *

As usual, Danusia awaits Józek's letter with great eagerness and anxiety. She doesn't work any more. Instead she watches Jędruś and spends most of her time visiting all sorts of institutions and officials, and constantly sends letters and petitions requesting and appealing for Józek's release. She goes from one official to another; she wears smooth paths to the Brill Palace, Blanka Palace, and who knows where. She even writes to Hitler. Every day she works with Mrs. Sowińska who has become not only her advisor and translator but also her most trusted companion and caretaker, feeding Danusia on a regular basis. Food for the Polish people is rationed and very scarce. Danusia's family is on the verge of starvation. Enjoying the privileged status as German nationals, the Sowiński family has plenty of food and gladly takes care of fragile Danusia.

It was almost a year ago when, with the help of Mrs. Sowińska, Danusia wrote her special letter directly to the Auschwitz Camp Commandant. Upon finding Józek's whereabouts, she desperately wanted to send him something, even just a chocolate bar, more as a symbol of her love and remembrance than anything else. So she wrote to the Camp Commandant requesting permission to send Józio a package. And she received a reply! And what a reply it was! No one in the whole world ever received such a reply. It was the greatest victory of her life: a special permission issued by the Camp Commandant in her name to send not just a chocolate bar but a real Christmas package and warm clothing. She then went to the jewelry store and without a moment's hesitation sold her engagement ring. The old Jewish storeowner looked at her with sadness and offered to put the ring on hold.

"Don't hold it for me please," she replied firmly. "I would never be able to buy it back."

It took her about one month to prepare the packages. When everything was ready, she called a *britzka* and drove to the post office.

"I am sending these packages to the Auschwitz Concentration Camp," she said to a woman behind the window.

"What? Are you joking?" the woman looked at her ironically. "You can't send anything there! Don't you know that?"

"But I have a special permission from the Camp Commandant," Danusia replied and unfolded an official paper holding it firmly in her tiny hand.

The woman examined the paper and said: "Wait here! I have to call the manager."

A tall and elegant German, twice as big as Danusia, came out, asked for the paper, inspected it carefully, shook his head in disbelief, and said in a ruthless but friendly voice:

"*Gut, gut, kleine kinder.*"

Danusia reached out for the paper.

"Oh, no, no, I can't give it back to you. I have to glue it to the packages." He then stamped both packages all over, tied them together, and took them to the back. Danusia had accomplished the impossible!

Almost one year later, Danusia holds her little Jędruś in her arms and desperately wants to have Józio back. At the very minimum, she must show her charming little Jędruś to his father. Thus, she decides to write again to the Auschwitz Camp Commandant asking for permission to send a photograph of the newborn baby.

* * * *

Sixty years later, Danusia tells this story with the same passion and the same intensity as if it had happened only yesterday. The events of those cruel times from over half a century ago are engraved in bold in her mind. Sitting at the table in her suburban Ohio house, she recalls with unthinkable precision all the details from that remote, dark past.

"I wrote in my letter that I was only eighteen years old when I got married, and that six weeks after the wedding my husband was rounded up on the street and taken away to the concentration camp. I also wrote that the Commandant once allowed me to send a Christmas package to the camp. And that is why I decided to ask whether I could send a photograph of my newborn son so that my husband could see his son at least in the photograph.

"Mrs. Sowińska translated my letter into elegant literary German. On the front of the envelope, she wrote in capital letters: DON'T THROW THIS AWAY WITHOUT READING!"

Danusia ponders a long time then slowly continues. "Maybe it was intriguing to them that someone would write such a thing on the envelope. I don't know…. Anyway, this letter ended up in the hands of one of the officers with the death head emblem…, oh yes, yes, an SS officer," she corrects. "Apparently someone read this letter, it must have touched someone's heart, although no one had any heart there any more…." She shakes her head at a loss. "But nevertheless…. Anyway…they responded to me once before. So why wouldn't they respond this time…?"

* * * *

It's September 1941. On a golden afternoon, Mrs. Gara rushes to Danusia with a green-blue envelope that has just arrived from Auschwitz. A letter from Józek! Danusia runs straight to Mrs. Sowińska, tearing the envelope apart on the way. Mrs. Sowińska reads the letter carefully. But she stops from time to time, looks it over and over again, and ponders.

"I see you have a problem." Danusia's sharp eyes scrutinize her every facial move.

"Well, you see...he writes here: *I have seen your application regarding the photograph. But you must not send the photograph directly to me...* and I am trying to figure out what he is really trying to say."

"If I cannot send it directly then obviously I must send it indirectly!" Danusia doesn't have any doubts.

"Right! But what do you mean? How do you want to send it indirectly?"

"Well, I will just send it to the Camp Commandant, like before!"

From now on, she only thinks about the photograph. It must be the most beautiful photograph in the whole world. This may be her only chance to reach, though indirectly, Józek's eyes, Józek's heart, his mind and imagination. It may be their very last chance to meet on this earth....

She plans the photo session with great care. It will cost a lot of money but it doesn't matter. After all, money is not that important. Two weeks later, she puts on her favorite white coat, the same one she wore on the day of Józek's round-up, puts her little Jędruś in the baby carriage, and at the pre-arranged time shows up in the best photo atelier in town. From among several takes, she selects two. On the first photograph, Danusia holds little Jędruś in her arms. In the second photograph, a naked Jędruś on his tummy smiles from the fur rug. He is such a darling....

With the pictures ready, Danusia sits down with Mrs. Sowińska and for several days the two wrestle with a letter. Finally, it's ready. The letter is addressed directly to the Camp Commandant and is full of appeals and pleas to make the pictures available to Józek. It is already October 1941, and winter approaches quickly.

* * * *

The German invasion of the Soviet Union is in full swing. For the past several weeks, the Auschwitz camp has been flooded with the Soviet prisoners of war.[24] Thousand of them arrive every day. The mortality rate among the Soviet POWs is the highest of all. The camp resources are strained to their very limits. Food rations shrink as the living and breathing space shrinks, too. The race for survival heats up.

For several months, Józek stays in Block 18a. He considers himself lucky because many of the functionaries of this block enjoy a good reputation among the prisoners. But his luck is short-lived.

On October 27, 1941, the camp is boiling: "Escape!" the whisper goes. To his horror, Józek discovers that the escape is from Block 18a, HIS BLOCK! A punitive roll call is ordered.

"Selection!" Józek thinks instantly. "Selection from my block!"

Yes.... As always, ten people will be selected for death by starvation. They will count to ten. Just to ten, just like that: one, two, three.... Those counted as *tens* will be selected. It's that simple.

Counting...! Józek is in great danger. He has already survived one count. He was then the lucky *eight*. But it was close, terribly close. Not much time to think, though. Now everything depends on his place in the miserable rows of five.

"*Raus! Raus! Los! Los!*"

The horrified rows of five leave the block. SS-men like vultures swarm around his group anxious for their prey. The Deputy Commandant finally arrives. The Russian roulette starts from an unpredictable place into an unpredictable direction.

It is beyond human genius to put into plain words what is happening in the minds and souls of these gray shadows standing in rows of five in their blue-gray *pasiaki* in the center of this vicious theater. Stricken by this degree of terror, people are not capable of thinking or feeling. Many lose any sense of being.

And yet, standing in one of these gray rows of five, Józek watches every gesture, every eye movement, and every breath of the oppressors. It has started. The first victim is selected, an old man from the relatively recent transport. In his mind, Józek desperately tries to outrun the count. But no...! He quickly stops. It looks as if he stands in the zone of serious danger.... But he must survive this one. He has to survive it for Danusia and Jędruś. They need him. After all, God wants him to survive... Now he can only pray.

Another two strong and skilled workers are selected. The count approaches. It's in his row. It looks as if he may be the *tenth*.... He shakes, shrinks, and bends down in an effort to hide, escape, and disappear.

"NINE!" The count goes.

A good friend of his, also named Józef, is selected. Number nine is speechless, unable to move, to emit a sound or to glance at his already half-dead friend—number TEN.

The selection ends. Ten brutalized human specters are taken away. They all have numbers "younger" than Józek. They all are Polish political prisoners. They all are his good friends. Many of them are beloved sons. Several of them are beloved husbands and fathers. Stefan, Franciszek, Henryk, Paweł, and Józio too—Józio Tomczak–Number 21373, the latest arrival to the block. Fate handed them such a cruel joke. Józio Tomczak, together with Franek and with the old man, would continue their ordeal in the starvation cell the longest. In the end, they will be killed by a pistol shot.[25]

But one of the doomed men will survive. Henryk will be released from the death block two days later. Subsequently, it will be reported that one of the higher functionaries of the camp has been successfully appealing for his release.

Camp life slowly goes back to its routine. The work in the fields becomes more difficult as the winter approaches. Every day, Józek prays for the strength to survive his ordeal and for his return to beloved Danuta and little Jędruś. One day, a *capo* with the attack dog comes to Józek's block and calls his name.

"*Raus! Raus!* Come with me!" he orders.

Józek follows the *capo* obediently. He doesn't dare to ask any questions—no one here dares to ask any questions. They pass through the camp along the heavily guarded electric fence. "What is it? Execution? Maybe interrogation or transport...." Feverish thoughts fly through Józek's mind. Something awaits him. But what? "Oh, God, please postpone this inevitable destiny, just postpone it, please!" Unspeakable fear chokes him.

It's a pleasant sunny day. Józek looks at the clear blue sky in unimaginable pain. He is only twenty-nine and his life could be so wonderful with his beloved Danusia and Jędruś. But this is undoubtedly his last journey. He will most likely die today.

"Are they going to torture me?" he wonders. "Hopefully it's going to be quick.... But if they are going to kill me, why do they drag me this far...? They should do it right here, right now." Józek's mind is racing, his soul is screaming.

"Maybe it would be better to kill myself and deprive these beasts of their pleasures." He looks at the electric fence not that far from him, just a meter or so. Many of his friends threw themselves on those wires and ended this shameful existence with dignity.

"Maybe I should jump at it and end this agony once and forever." The notion of death has been his daily companion for over a year now. But what he really fears the most is torture. He is not capable of enduring torture. The barbaric beatings, dog bites, wounds, starvation, and these selections for death by starvation left permanent scars on his psyche. He just can't take it any more.

Suddenly, he wakes up from his desperate thoughts. His *capo* proceeds all the way to the main gate. To Józek's astonishment, they leave the dreadful camp with its ugly buildings and horrible smell of death behind and continue in the unknown direction.

"What does this mean? Is this good or bad?" he fervently wonders.

A few minutes later, he knows! They are approaching the residence of the Camp Commandant, the man – fate, the ultimate murderer of hundreds of thousands of terrorized, abused, tortured and trashed people brought here from many different countries conquered by the superior being of the human race – Adolf Hitler.... Józek is scared.

"Will they torture me...? Will they perform some experiments on me?" He doesn't know what to think. "But at least it means they won't kill me outright, or at least not now, not here, not yet!"

The Camp Commandant sits behind the desk. A relatively young man, maybe ten years older than Józek, he is not very big, just of average size. As every good Aryan should be, he is blond, with a high forehead, thick nose, and sharp, rather small eyes.

Józek sits down in front of him. The eyes of the two men meet. The Commandant watches Józek intensely. Instinctively holding his breath, Józek drops his gentle eyes.

"Your number?" the ruler asks.

"3088," Józek replies in perfect German.

"How long have you been here?"

"Since August 1940."

"Why did you end up here?"

"From the street round-up."

A series of brief questions ends and the commandant ponders for a while, snapping his fingers against the desk and observing the prisoner with restrained eagerness.

"Your wife sent some photographs here..." he says slowly, his eyes penetrating Józek curiously. "As you know, we cannot give you these pictures...." He stops and looks at Józek enigmatically. "But... I will show them to you," he finishes his thought deliberately.

Józek is in shock. From deep despair, his mind shifts to unbearable joy. Thousands of thoughts rush again through his mind. He must not rejoice! He must be very careful. There must be a cruel trick in all this. That's right! This sadist will now observe his pain and will relish in his anguish. Oh, no! With full force, Józek clenches his fists.

"I am not going to cry! You'll see, you beast! I won't cry. I won't please you with my pain!" he pledges to himself. "Oh, God! Give me strength for this trial!"

The ruler takes out a yellowish envelope. Holding it in one hand, he then slowly pulls out the first picture. In the palm of his barbaric hand, Józek recognizes a delicate profile of his heavenly beautiful Danusia with a little baby in her arms.

His heart pounds, his teeth and fists clench, he starts to sweat.

"No! No! I am not going to cry! No!!!" But his eyes are already veiled and big tears disobediently pour down his face. He is ecstatic and furious at the same time.

"After all, why should I care about this monster.... I have my beloved Danusia and Jędruś in front of my eyes. The image worth life...!"

But the moment is short. The cruel hand pulls back the photograph. Józek closes his eyes. The image of Danusia and Jędruś stays in his imagination for another brief moment.

"Here is another one," the commander says, taking out the second picture.

A plump big baby smiles to Józek from the fur rug. "Jędruś, my beloved son!" Józek bites his lips, his nails cut into his flesh.

The merciless hand puts the photograph back.

"Fritz!"

"*Jawohl!*" a short fat SS-man comes in.

"Take his number for quarantine," the master of life and death orders.

"*Jawohl!*"

"Quarantine...quarantine!" The word reverberates like a thunder in Józek's battered mind. He sends the commandant an inquiring look. Two pairs of intense blue eyes meet again for a split-second. In that misty window of time, Józek catches a faint flicker of an eyelid.

"3088," he loudly pronounces his number.

Fritz writes down the number and Józek is out the door. Gradually he regains his sanity and starts putting chaotic thoughts together. "Danusia...more beautiful than ever! And Jędruś, such a darling...! Quarantine?" Here it means one and only one thing—FREEDOM. Pure and simple FREEDOM! But he is fearful to entertain this thought so not to ruffle, thwart or frighten this miraculous chance to survive the death camp.

His friends in the block welcome him warmly. "We were worrying about you. What happened? What did they do to you?"

But Józek is careful, very careful. At first, he doesn't share his secret with anybody. But he is anxious to write a letter. For some time, he hasn't received any letters from Danusia. It is now her turn to write. But he can't wait any longer, certainly not now.

> My Dearest Wife!
>
> Even though I have not received any letter from you lately, I want to write to you whenever I can. I have read a thousand times your last letter about my son who can already say *tiatia*. When my son calls me, it means I have to go home. For this I am always praying to God.

He puts down the pen and debates with himself. Should he write about the photographs? Some sadistic functionaries may choose to give him a special treatment for this pleasure. But he is too excited, he can't resist. "I have seen your photograph," he continues. "You look beautiful. I am closing here...."

From now on, Józek intensely watches the camp routine hoping to spot some indication that the process of his release has been set in motion. And indeed, one day he is called to the hospital for a blood drive. Another day, he is sent to the political department for a "discussion." Apparently, they want to make sure he is well rehabilitated and would become an obedient servant of the Third Reich once released. Now Józek is certain. He is slated for release!

Slowly, he shares his secret with the closest friends. They all are astounded and sincerely moved. They all share his joy. Releases are unheard of around here, some isolated instances, mostly upon intervention of the highest German officials. As the time goes by, Józek gains more confidence. The release process has been set in motion and by itself already gives him some protection. The functionaries are uncertain as to his connections and begin treating him with suspicious respect. On December 7, 1941, Józek writes with even greater confidence.

> My Beloved Wife, Danusia!
>
> I am so glad that you, my dearest, my Jędruś, and the whole family is fine. I have seen the photographs that you sent here, those of you and Jędruś. You look very beautiful. When I saw you last time, my darling, you were a young girl. Today, you are a beautiful young woman, like a movie star. Once I have seen you in this picture, my dearest wife, my longing for you has been even greater.... My Jędruś is such a handsome boy! Please send these photographs to my mother and sisters in Wartbrucken. I kiss you a thousand times.
>
> Your husband, Józek

27. Danusia with Jędruś—Photo sent to Auschwitz

28. Jędruś, October 1941—Photo sent to Auschwitz

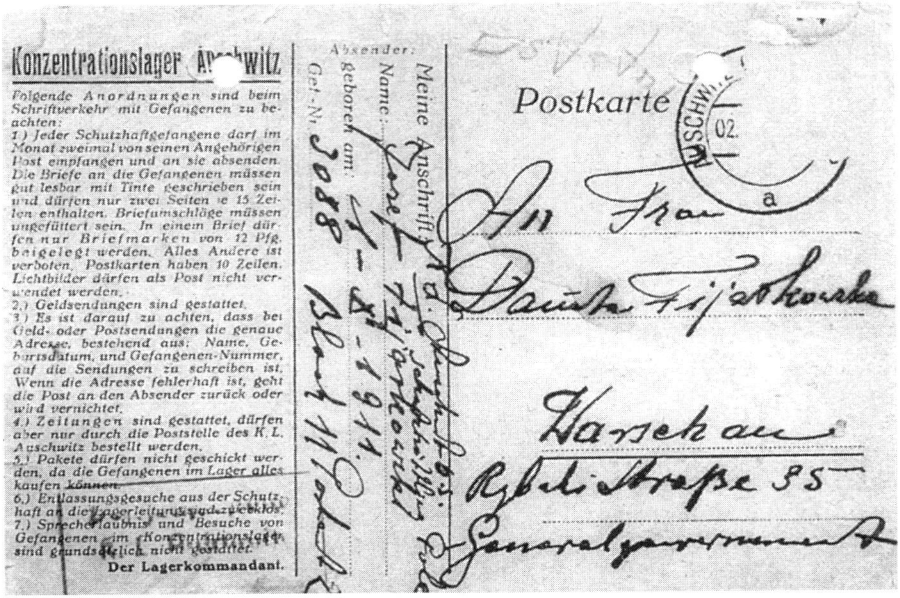

Konzentrationslager Auschwitz

Folgende Anordnungen sind beim Schriftverkehr mit Gefangenen zu beachten:

1.) Jeder Schutzhaftgefangene darf im Monat zweimal von seinen Angehörigen Post empfangen und an sie absenden. Die Briefe an die Gefangenen müssen gut lesbar mit Tinte geschrieben sein und dürfen nur zwei Seiten je 15 Zeilen enthalten. Briefumschläge müssen ungefüttert sein. In einem Brief dürfen nur Briefmarken von 12 Pfg. beigelegt werden. Alles Andere ist verboten. Postkarten haben 10 Zeilen. Lichtbilder dürfen als Post nicht verwendet werden.

2.) Geldsendungen sind gestattet.

3.) Es ist darauf zu achten, dass bei Geld- oder Postsendungen die genaue Adresse, bestehend aus: Name, Geburtsdatum, und Gefangenen-Nummer, auf die Sendungen zu schreiben ist. Wenn die Adresse fehlerhaft ist, geht die Post an den Absender zurück oder wird vernichtet.

4.) Zeitungen sind gestattet, dürfen aber nur durch die Poststelle des K.L. Auschwitz bestellt werden.

5.) Pakete dürfen nicht geschickt werden, da die Gefangenen im Lager alles kaufen können.

6.) Entlassungsgesuche aus der Schutzhaft an die Lagerleitung sind zwecklos.

7.) Sprecherlaubnis und Besuche von Gefangenen im Konzentrationslager sind grundsätzlich nicht gestattet.

Der Lagerkommandant.

Absender:
Name: Józef Fijałkowski
geboren am: 5-IV-1911
Gef.-Nr. 3088 Block 11
Meine Anschrift: K.L. Auschwitz O/S

Postkarte

AUSCHWITZ 02. a

An Frau
Danuta Fijałkowska
Warschau
Rybaki Straße 35
Generalgouvernement

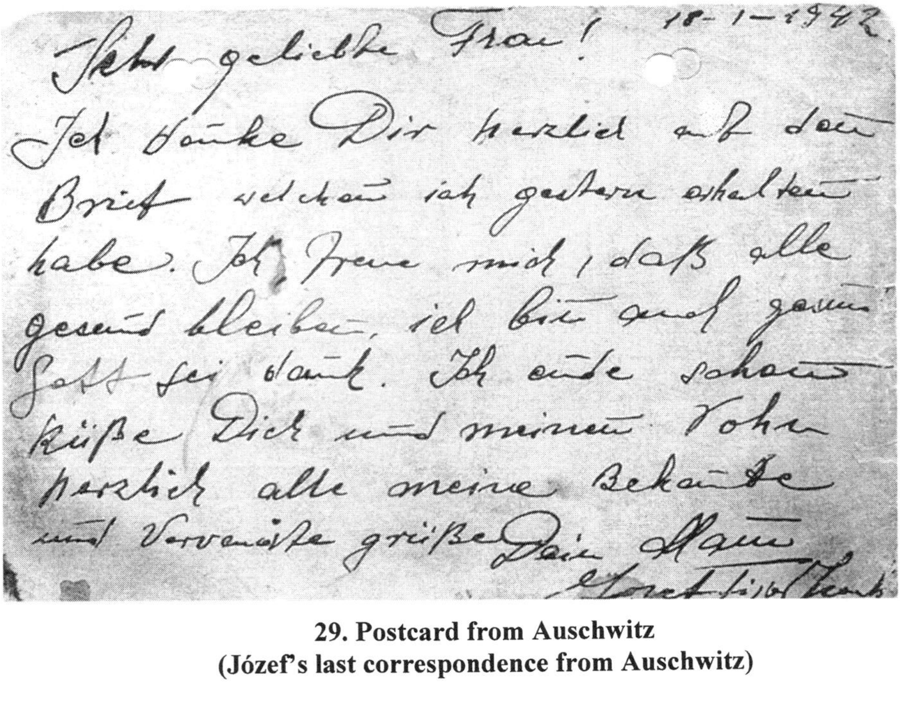

18-1-1942

Sehr geliebte Frau!

Ich danke Dir herzlich auf den Brief welchen ich gestern erhalten habe. Ich freue mich, daß alle gesund bleiben, ich bin auch gesund Gott sei dank. Ich ende schon küße Dich und meinen Sohn herzlich alle meine Bekannte und Verwandte grüße Dein Mann

Josef Fijałkowski

29. Postcard from Auschwitz
(Józef's last correspondence from Auschwitz)

11

A subdued pounding at the door awakens Jasia. It is 2 AM on a frosty January night. Shaking with terror, she wakes up Alek. The knocking continues in steady intervals. "Germans!" she chokes out to Alek. Nocturnal visits from the German police have been frequent occurrences in Warsaw. They almost certainly bring tragic endings. Without showing any sign of distress, Alek sits up and asks Jasia to open the door. She creeps with inquietude. "Who is it?" she asks.

"It's me," a male voice replies quietly, "the Auschwitz prisoner."

Stunned, Jasia hurriedly wrestles with the door lock. A familiar face shows up in the darkness of the hallway. "Józio!" She utters a cry and throws her arms around him. Alek is overjoyed, too. He shakes Józio's hand, pats and kisses him ardently. Zbyszek jumps out of bed and embraces the visitor. Only Danusia doesn't jump. Instead, she sits on the sofa like a mummy, unable to emit a word.

Józio's eyes are searching for her desperately. "Here she is! His beloved Danusia; real Danusia!" He walks to her slowly. "Danuśka, darling, it's me!"

She looks at him, unable to speak or even make a gesture. He pats her gently on the cheek. "Wake up! You see? I am back!" He takes her in his arms and the world starts whirling with them. We will start a new life, darling, a new life! With you and Jędruś!"

She smiles through tears, takes his hand, and leads him to another room where his eight-month-old son is calmly asleep in the cradle. With Danusia in his arms, he stands in the darkness of the room gazing at his beloved son for the first time. Jędruś is serenely asleep.

"Józio darling, how did you get out? Who released you?" Danusia asks quietly.

"My son released me!" Józio firmly replies and gently touches his son's forehead. Jędruś slightly raises his hand as if saying hello but doesn't awaken. They creep out of his room.

"Danusia, I am sorry, but I have to write down something quickly. Please give me a pen and a paper." Józio grabs the paper and immerses himself in writing for a couple of minutes to the amazement of the rest of them. "I am sorry for that.... Those are the addresses of the people I have to contact," he finally explains. "I didn't have any paper in the camp so I had to memorize all these names and addresses that my friends kept giving me. Now I have to meet with all these people and let them know about their loved ones in the camp." He jots down at least twenty names. "But those are not all.... I must have forgotten someone," he worries.

Józio's return is widely celebrated. The entire mint community is stunned. Old Gara is the most astounded. He was the one who opened the gate for Józio in the middle of the night and couldn't believe his eyes.

"*Panie* Józek! Did you see my Zenek there? Is he going to come back? Please tell me whether they will release him. Dear *Panie* Józek! Tell me please whether I will see my Zenek again!" Old Gara can't stop asking Józio about his beloved son.

"You will see him, *Panie* Gara. You will see him. Zenek will come home. I have seen him in the camp and he is doing fine. Zenek paints a lot and makes portraits for the SS officers. They like him for that. I am sure he will be coming home soon," he tries to console the old man.

Of course, Józio doesn't have a clue whether Zenek would come home or not. Knowing the reality, it is highly unlikely that Zenek would ever come home but who knows? On the day of Józio's release, all together thirty-eight people were released from the camp. But that was the first and the only group released thus far this year.[1]

During the entire year 1941, about seventeen thousand civilian prisoners and about ten thousand Soviet prisoners of war had been brought to Auschwitz while more than twenty thousand lost their lives either through executions or from starvation and exhaustion. About three thousand prisoners were transferred from Auschwitz to other camps, and only about three hundred were released.[2] But even those counted as released are not really true releases. The so-called release always comes with heavy strings attached....

Formally Józio is free, but for all practical purposes he is still on the SS-leash. His Discharge Certificate issued by the *Sturmbannführer* of the Auschwitz Concentration Camp contains unequivocal conditions: "Until further notice, you must report to the city police in your place of residence," the general instruction reads. An additional typewritten instruction follows: "Report at once to the office of the Security Police and Gestapo in the District of Warsaw, Police Street 25." In other words, Józio has to report to the Gestapo immediately.

But first and foremost, he has to get some clothing. On the day of his release, the camp officials returned to him the same paper bag in which he deposited all his personal belongings eighteen months earlier. Everything in the bag was in perfect order. Nothing was missing. Except that his summer clothing looked strangely at odds with the harsh January weather. It was only through the efforts of many good friends in the camp and thanks to complete strangers at the train station that he managed to get some warmer clothing on his way home. Ordinary people on the train station helped him the most. Out of nowhere they arranged for a winter coat, warm boots, gloves, and a hat.

When he first walked into the house in the middle of the night, he made a good impression on everybody. He looked healthy, his clothing looked fine. But the next day Danusia realized how deceptive that good-looking image was.

Due to prolonged starvation and exhaustion, his face and his body is visibly swollen. Hunger swelling! She has never seen a man swollen from hunger.... Józio's leg and hip show the scars of a deep dog bite, and his eyes are chronically infected. He is in a desperate need of convalescence. But first he has to report to Gestapo.

"Police Street 25. That's Aleja Szucha!" Danusia realizes in horror. That's where the Germans kill and torture hundreds and thousands of Warsawians every day. The name raises deathly fear. And Józio has to report to that cave of torture at once! Danusia decides to go with him. She is determined to protect him no matter what. The guard at the gate stops them, check the papers, and lets Józio in.

"You must wait outside!" he says to Danusia. "Don't worry, darling. I'll be back...."

Waiting outside the building, Danusia walks back and forth along the tall metal bar fence. There are not many passersby here. Warsawians avoid this street. Only now and then some individuals timidly come to the gate and imploringly talk to the guard. Some try to pass packages; others try to get in. They all have frightened eyes, distressed and meek faces. The guard is not anxious to deal with them and ignores their pleas.

Danusia keeps walking faster and faster as if she would try to outrun this excruciating wait. It's already been 10 minutes. How much longer? She needs to know. Every minute is like an eternity. But the guard doesn't respond to her inquiry.

"Just wait!" he orders flatly and turns back. A few more agonizing minutes and Józio comes out. His stony face doesn't reveal anything. "Let's go!" He energetically grabs her arm and pulls her away from that frightful place.

"What did they say?" Danusia can't wait to find out.

Józio takes a deep breath and tightens his arm around her. "From now on, I have to report here every third day." He throws out the news all at once.

"Oh, my God!" Danusia utters a cry. Their dreamed-about new life suddenly looks more distant and much bleaker.

Over the next few weeks, Józio travels a lot, trying to contact all the families from the memorized Auschwitz list. Every third day he makes the trip to the Gestapo. Danusia always goes with him. Upon returning from this wellspring of evil, Józio likes to play with Jędruś. He likes to hold the baby in his arms, rock and dandle Jędruś on his knee. He tries to sing him lullabies but he doesn't remember many. Instead he sings church songs, and to Danusia's amazement, he sings them in Latin. His paternal efforts are rather amusing at first and even worrisome at times. Most of his songs are inappropriate for a lullaby. They are solemn and serious—some, like *Mise Recordi*, are depressingly grim.

After months of being fed the German propaganda, Józio is starving for even the smallest bit of brighter news from the Allies. He scrambles for every shred of underground news and spends hours talking with Alek about the latest developments.

By far the best and the brightest news thus far is the memory of the Battle of Britain. A tiny brochure entitled "Squadron 303," written on thin *bibuła* paper, made its way from Great Britain to Poland via underground channels and instantly became an underground smash hit.[3] The powerful speech delivered by the newly elected British Prime Minister in the House of Commons is on everybody's minds. The famous Churchill words: "Never in the field of human conflict has so much been owed by so many to so few,"[4] are deeply engraved in the consciousness of every Pole. This is because among those few were so many Polish fighters. Every eighth RAF fighter pilot in the Battle of Britain was Polish.[5] During the decisive six-week fighting period, the Polish Squadron 303 achieved the top score for any RAF fighter unit: 126 confirmed kills, despite its delayed introduction into action, while losing nine of his own pilots.[6] Named "City of Warsaw," Squadron 303 consisted of combat veterans coming from two Warsaw *eskadras*. The top ace of Squadron 303 was Stanisław Skalski with 18 individual kills, 4 shared and 2 probable kills, and 4 damaged planes.[7] A Czech pilot flying with Squadron 303, Joseph František, recorded 17 confirmed kills and one probable kill before losing his life in action in October of 1941.[8]

Among the Polish fighter pilots, about 60 achieved ace status in the Battle of Britain, recording five or more kills. Many of them recorded more than ten kills and some, like Witold Urbanowicz—18 kills, Bolesław Gładych—17 kills, and Eugeniusz Horbaczewski—16 kills.[9]

During the Battle of Britain, the Polish pilots flying in different RAF squadrons definitely destroyed 203 enemy fighters, most probably 35 planes, and damaged 36 enemy planes. Those numbers represent about 12% of all planes lost by the Luftwaffe over Great Britain in this historic battle.[10] Twenty-nine Polish pilots lost their lives in that battle. But the effectiveness of the Polish pilots was the most impressive. While on average one RAF casualty claimed four Luftwaffe kills, in two Polish Squadrons one RAF casualty claimed nine Luftwaffe kills.[11]

* * * *

Konrad arrives home and yells from the door: "Grandma, look what we have!"

"Oh, finally you are back. It's so late, I was worrying about you."

Danuta's son wearily walks in. "Dayton is not that close. I told you it's going to be a long trip. It's about four hours each way."

"But look what I have here." Konrad proudly hands her a small book.

"Polish Aces of World War II," the title reads. Konrad and his dad have just visited the US Air Force Museum in Dayton, Ohio. The trip was great. They saw first airplanes designed by the Wright Brothers, the World War II fighters, the latest B-1 and B-2 bombers, and some passenger airplanes that in the past served as planes for United States Presidents.

"You know, Grandma, one of those presidential planes was so narrow inside that Dad could hardly walk through. I wonder how the President could move around."

"Probably he was on a diet and I am not." His dad looks with concern in the mirror. "But this book is very good. Finally we found an English language book about the Polish contribution to the Battle of Britain." The tiny book is just one of the titles in the *Osprey Aircraft of the Aces* series but it's still something! Most of the bookstores in Konrad's neighborhood don't carry any books on this subject.

Danusia is delighted. She takes the small book and looks it over with reverence. Printed in Honk Kong. How strange...but nicely published.

"I remember reading about these great victories of our pilots in the underground bulletin back then in the fall of 1940. You cannot even imagine what those stories meant to us back then, in Nazi-occupied Warsaw." Danusia gazes blindly into space.

Konrad examines the drawings and photographs with great interest. "Our pilots were flying those Hurricanes and Spitfires."

"Do you know what was our greatest day of victory in this battle?" Danusia asks.

"Let me see...," Konrad ponders.

"If I remember correctly," Danusia continues, "it was Sunday, mid-September, around the 15th, I guess. That was the peak of German attacks on London."

"Yes, yes, I remember now," Konrad exclaims. "I read about that in a Polish book. Wait, I have to find it." He runs upstairs and comes back with a book entitled *Poles on the Fronts of World War II*. "Here it is, Grandma. That day, September 15, the Polish pilots scored 26 confirmed kills for RAF while losing two pilots."[12]

"Right." Danusia pats him on the shoulder. "But remember Konrad, numbers by themselves don't mean much. They have meaning only if put in context. And that context is critical here. It was that day when the Battle of Britain reached its climax. At that time, the reserves of RAF were totally depleted and, but for the Polish contribution, could not have withstood the Luftwaffe attack. September 15th was the moment of truth for both Germany and Great Britain. Because of the losses suffered that day, the Germans concluded that the Luftwaffe could no longer afford any more losses.[13] The outcome of that battle led directly to the German decision to postpone the further attacks on Great Britain. As we know today, they discontinued their attacks on Great Britain indefinitely and for good. That is why this date, September 15, 1941, is considered the turning point in World War II."

"Maybe it was an important point, Grandma, but today we hear more often that World War II was decided on the Eastern front and not in the West."

"You are right that the decisive counter-offensive came from the East. But without engaging German forces in the West, the outcome in the East could have been very different. We should also remember that the RAF victory preserved the Allied base in Europe. That by itself had incredible psychological significance for the entire battered European continent, and ultimately attracted the United States to the Allied cause. As it was once said, without RAF preservation of the British islands the United States would never have intervened in the European War[14] and many non-Aryan races would have vanished from this earth."

* * * *

"Józio! Józio!" Mama rushes home, yelling from the yard.

"What is it?" Holding the baby in his arms, Józio shows up in the door.

"You know...? Zenek...! Zenek...!" she can hardly catch her breath.

"What happened to Zenek?" Józio grows nervous.

"Zenek has returned home!" she finally finishes. The cold air of the February frost flows to the room. "Here, give me Jędruś and go! You must go there, to the Gara's apartment." She grabs the baby, protecting him from the frosty draft.

Within seconds Józio is at Gara's door. A jubilant Maya welcomes him. "Józio!" She throws her hands at him. "Can you imagine? He is here! Can you imagine?" Old Gara hugs Józek without saying a word and leads him to another room. There, Zenek lies on the sofa, surrounded by his mother and four sisters. He smiles at Józek, trying to rise.

"No Zenuś, don't get up, please!" his mother begs him. Despite her objections, he gets up and the two men clasp each other in a big hug. The two former Auschwitz prisoners, the born-again humans, instantly become more than brothers to each other. The extent of their jointly experienced drama is out of reach for any other human being and instantly creates an unimaginable bond between the two men.

"You look good, brother!" Józek examines his friend.

"But you look even better," Zenek replies joyfully.

"So when did you get out and how did you come here?"

"They started the release yesterday. But there were thirty-five of us,[15] so you know, it took them almost all day."

"I know, I know. They let you out in the evening. And how about clothing? Did they give you anything warm?"

"Jesus Christ! He came almost naked. Can you imagine? To let someone out in summer clothing into snow two meters deep at the beginning of February?" his mother shrieks hysterically.

"But, Mama, I got a sweater and a scarf." Zenek tries to calm her down. "Don't worry, Mama. I will be fine."

"So tell me, how did you manage to get out?" Józek keeps asking.

"Well, you know, with them you can never be sure. But I think that one of the wives of those SS officers advocated my release because she was very pleased with a portrait I did for her and for her husband. I know for sure that she was trying. But I have just realized that the mint here was also appealing for my release. My dad tells me that the mint director sent several letters to Auschwitz requesting my release. I understand that he also wrote on your behalf."

"Yes, that is true. Director Reinhart gave Danusia a letter requesting my release even though technically I was not a mint employee. And you know Danusia. She herself sent about a dozen letters everywhere, to Hans Frank in Kraków, to Berlin, to Prince Czartoryski, to the bishop, everywhere. She left no stone unturned. But as you may have heard, the photographs of our newborn son in her arms turned to be the most effective.

"It's incredible, isn't it?" Maya sighs.

"We no longer have Director Reinhart at the mint," Mr. Gara says. "He was unexpectedly transferred out. Or at least that's the official version. We cannot even say thank you to him."

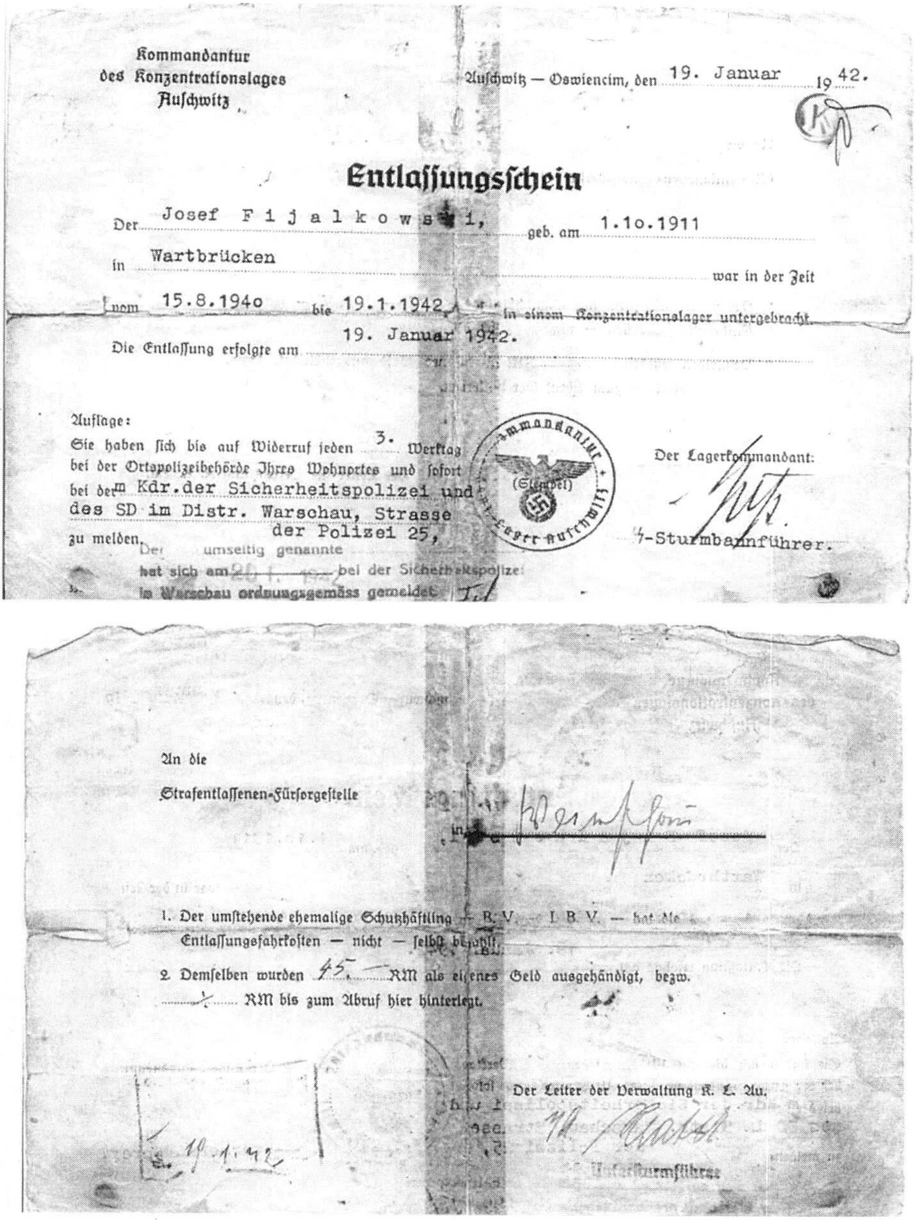
Kommandantur
des Konzentrationslages
Auschwitz

Auschwitz — Oswiencim, den 19. Januar 1942.

Entlassungsschein

Der Josef Fijalkowski, geb. am 1.10.1911
in Wartbrücken war in der Zeit
vom 15.8.1940 bis 19.1.1942 in einem Konzentrationslager untergebracht.
Die Entlassung erfolgte am 19. Januar 1942.

Auflage:
Sie haben sich bis auf Widerruf jeden 3. Werktag bei der Ortspolizeibehörde Ihres Wohnortes und sofort bei dem Kdr.der Sicherheitspolizei und des SD im Distr. Warschau, Strasse der Polizei 25, zu melden.

Kommandantur K.L. Auschwitz (Stempel)

Der Lagerkommandant:
SS-Sturmbannführer.

Der umseitig genannte hat sich am 20.1. bei der Sicherheitspolizei in Warschau ordnungsgemäss gemeldet.

An die
Strafentlassenen-Fürsorgestelle
in Warschau

1. Der umstehende ehemalige Schutzhäftling — B.V. — I.B.V. — hat die Entlassungsfahrkosten — nicht — selbst bezahlt.
2. Demselben wurden 45.— RM als eigenes Geld ausgehändigt, bezw. —/— RM bis zum Abruf hier hinterlegt.

Der Leiter der Verwaltung K.L. Au.
Untersturmführer

19.1.42

30. Auschwitz Release Certificate

31. Mjr. Stanisław Skalski, Polish Squadron 303, Battle of Britain

"Several men who were quarantined together with me told me that their families had to sign up for the *Volksdeutsch* list in order to get them out from Auschwitz," Zenek says. "Well, we are extremely lucky. But we don't know yet what's in it for us."

Józek saddens. "Do you have to report to the Gestapo?"

"Yes, as a matter of fact, I wanted to ask you about that. Do you have to report, too?"

"Yes.... But don't rush. You are entitled to recuperate for a day or two."

"And how is it? What do they want?" Mrs. Gara asks nervously.

All eyes turn to Józek. He looks visibly ill at ease. "You know, it's nothing pleasant. But thus far it goes all right. They are letting me out."

"But what do they want? What do they ask?" Mrs. Gara fixes her eyes on Józek intrusively.

"So far, not much. But, I am afraid it may get very ugly.... They are after our underground and you know what they do with the Jews.... It appears that they are about to intensify their persecutions. That's what I am afraid of...."

"So, what does that have to do with you?" Maya is confused.

"I am not sure, but it may have some relevance for us...," Józio drops his eyes.

They all look at him puzzled. "Do you know what's going on in the Warsaw Ghetto?" Old Gara asks. "It's almost like in Auschwitz. And it may get even worse."

"Yes, people are starving there," Mrs. Gara says in a shaky voice. "You know, before Christmas, a small child escaped from the Ghetto, a girl about four years old. The guards found her at the mint and took her to Director Reinhart. Oh, God, we were all so afraid he would order this child killed but he told the guards to take her back to the Ghetto. Before sending her back, we gave her a good meal and some food to take with her. She was so skinny. Just the bones and these charming huge dark eyes...."

A prolonged silence sets in.

"Well, Zenek, remember don't eat too much. Restrain yourself, you porker." Józek hugs Zenek again. "And try to enjoy life, my friend!"

At home, Danusia feeds the baby while Alek, standing above them, hums some rather strange marine song. "How is Zenek?" she asks.

"Oh, he is great. But his family is even better. They are thrilled."

"Hey, Józio! Look what I found!" Alek unfolds his tiny *Bulletin*. "Some information about our boys fighting in Africa! Amazing where these winds of war throw our people.... German propaganda ironically calls them Sikorski tourists. But they do a damn good job. Listen to this," he reads.

> The Karpaty Brigade was formed from the Polish soldiers who escaped the Germans in 1939 through Hungary, Rumania and Yugoslavia. The brigade was formed in Syria under the French command and subsequently was transferred to the British command. The Karpaty Brigade consists of over 4,000 soldiers. At the end of August of 1941 the brigade was sent to Tobruk to provide reinforcements to the Allied forces defending the Suez Channel against approaching Axis attack led by General Rommel. With the support of the Karpaty Brigade, the Allied forces withstood the enemy attacks on Tobruk and were able to preserve their positions until the successful British contra-offensive in December of 1941. Among all Allied formations, the Karpaty Brigade defended the Tobruk fortress the longest.[16]

"Four thousand men, that's a good size brigade!" Józio is thrilled.

"Okay, boys, I'm going for a walk with Jędruś," Danusia announces.

"Isn't there too cold to go out?" Józio worries.

"Look how warmly he is dressed. He needs some fresh air. You could go with us too."

"I'd rather stay home, my dear. I have had enough cold for quite some time. But let me help you with the carriage." Józek gives Jędruś a kiss and closes the door thoroughly. "Dad, I need to talk with you about something."

"Okay, but wait. I need my bottle. Now Jędruś has his bottle and I have mine." Dad tries to smile while taking a bottle of vodka and a glass. He will drink it himself and doesn't count on Józio any more.... The two men sit down in front of each other.

"I have some problems with the Gestapo," Józio says without any preamble. "So far they are letting me out but they want something in return...."

Dad's face turns white. "What do you mean?"

"Please don't ask about the details. I can't tell you. But you see, I am afraid that the time will come when I will have to chose between incarceration and going underground."

"Do they force you into collaboration?" Dad asks bluntly.

"Please don't ask." Józek tries to hold back tears.

A large crease cuts across Dad's forehead. "How much time do we have?"

"Not much, a month or so...at best."

Ding dong, ding dong. The two men look at the big clock over the front door announcing noon.

"Well then, you have to go underground," Dad replies without hesitation and drinks the whole glass of vodka at a draught.

"But Dad, do you realize the consequences of such a decision for all of us...?"

"Then we have to be prepared, too."

They ponder a long time. Finally Dad breaks the silence. "It means you all would leave Warsaw and stay with some peasant family in the countryside. I can stay here at the mint. They will not touch me here because they need me."

"Are you sure?"

Dad nods.

"Thank you, Dad. Thank you for your support. But I want to share with you one more concern of mine, if I may."

"Go on, Son."

"I believe the best way to protect Danusia is to keep as much of this information away from her as possible. First, I don't want her to worry too much, and second, I thing it's safer that way. As you know, she always says what she thinks. By nature she is so candid. In normal circumstances, this naïve truthfulness would be a great asset but not today. In case of arrest or interrogation, it would be immediately obvious if she tries to lie or hide something. That would be disastrous for her and for all of us. But if she doesn't know anything, I believe she is much safer that way."

"You are right," Dad nods sadly. "Not only that she is safer," he adds, "but she can be a great advocate of her cause. She can be very persuasive, convincing, and even clever in getting things done her way. But she needs to be above suspicion."

"That's right." Józio is glad they understand each other. "Frankly, I wouldn't even mention the underground press in her presence," he adds. "She would have a hard time lying even about that."

Dad sighs heavily. "Up until now, the situation wasn't that serious, so we could afford it. But now, it may be a good idea. We can talk occasionally about the news just not to raise her suspicions, but I agree, she shouldn't see anything. Being a young, charming, innocent mother with a baby may be her best protection after all."

The next day, Zenek comes down to say hello. He hugs everyone, wants to see Jędruś, talks vibrantly and laughs a lot. He looks good, not swollen as much as Józio was. With a sparkle in his eye, he grabs a chair and starts dancing with it. "I am starting a new life," he proclaims. "The spring is coming. We have to go for a nice daylong trip somewhere. What do you think?"

"Sure, but first you have to take good care of yourself." Józek replies.

Zenek's neck is wrapped around in a scarf and he coughs badly from time to time. "I must have caught some cold on the way home," he explains. "I even had a temperature yesterday. This trip to the Gestapo makes me sick when I think about it. Would they excuse me if I am sick, what do you think?"

"I don't know." Józio is puzzled. "But you better don't get sick. We don't want you to get sick."

By the next day, however, Zenek's temperature skyrockets. The news about Zenek's illness spreads around as quickly as the news about his return. The panicked family calls Doctor Petrynowska.

In her early forties, Doctor Petrynowska is a charismatic doctor highly respected in the community. She has two school age children but devotes a lot of time to her patients. Always busy, she visits patients at their homes, in the hospital, and wherever they need her. With short brown hair, small glasses, and a big black medical bag, her rather tiny and delicate stature inspires confidence and admiration. The Gara family welcomes her like a queen and looks to her like to God. She takes a quick look at Zenek, at his flaccid gray skin, his vacant eyes, and feverish raving. She checks his pulse and listens to his lungs.

"He needs to go to the hospital," she announces and immediately adds: "At once!"

The whole family freezes. These words strike them like a thunderbolt.

"Maybe the mint driver would take him by car." The doctor starts planning the transport. "If not then, we need to call a *britzka*."

"But, *Pani* Doctor...what is it?" Mr. Gara wretchedly cries.

"I don't want to give you any diagnosis yet. We have to check it first. Please help me make the necessary arrangements."

Over the next couple of days, the Gara family agonizes in uncertainty, taking turns watching Zenek non-stop in the hospital. Józek also goes to see Zenek in the hospital. Upon his return, he is devastated almost to the point of collapse and doesn't want to talk. It is only after hours of Danusia's gentle therapy that he utters a dreadful word: "typhus!"

By the following week, Zenek's life is entirely in God's hands. His weak, emaciated body struggles in convulsion, but his mind is strong, his desire to fight and survive is unquenchable. Towards the end of the week, the mint driver brings him home. Everybody wants to see Zenek, to say hello to him, to wish him speedy recovery, and to support him as best as possible in his deadly struggle. Zenek is alert and even attempts to smile.

"Don't worry, we will go for that trip this summer, remember?" he assures Józek.

But the next morning, Zenek is unconscious. The family rages in despair. Towards the evening, Zenek breathes his last breath. Zenek, the most beloved and the only son, the bright, gifted, and handsome artist, and best friend from Auschwitz, is dead at the age of twenty-five, less than two weeks after his happy return from oblivion.

The extent of their grief over his meek and peaceful body is unbearable. His father seems to depart together with Zenek's soul to the other world. He doesn't talk, doesn't recognize anybody, and doesn't care about anything anymore, his hair turning gray almost overnight. His mother and sisters sob hysterically. Dozens of neighbors and friends stampede the Gara apartment. They all are devastated by the news and need to express their grief.

In the crowd of mourners kneeling near Zenek's bed is Doctor Petrynowska. Together with others, she cries openly. Like Józek and the Gara family, she feels the pain of his loss in a very personal way. Her husband, also a respected medical doctor, was taken to a concentration camp at about the same time as Zenek, back in 1940. But he was not as lucky as Zenek and Józio. He was dead within less than a year. The loss of her husband didn't stop Doctor Petrynowska from risking her life for others, though. To the contrary, her devotion, especially to those who experienced the loss of their loved ones in the concentration camps, became uncompromising.

With each passing day, more and more families experienced the trauma of losing the loved ones in the concentration camps. Back in 1940, the families would be given back at least the ashes of their dead. Once extermination became the standard way of governing the conquered Polish lands, only notifications were sent out. As the Nazis' insane hatred towards the conquered nation intensified, the capacities of the concentration camps rapidly increased and death notification procedures couldn't keep up with the pace of deaths.

The concentration camps were legalized in Germany in 1933 by a decree on the protection of the German nation and the German state, and on the suspension of civil rights and liberties of German citizens. This decree allowed for limitless imprisonment of political opponents. All antifascists were considered the enemies of the German nation and the German state. The first concentration camp was built in 1934 in Dachau pursuant to a special directive of SS Chief Himmler. Up until 1939, about 170 thousand enemies of the Reich had passed through the concentration camps in Germany. They were mostly Germans, Austrians, and Czechoslovakians.[17]

With the outbreak of war in 1939, the number of concentration camps started to increase rapidly. Most of the new camps were set up in Polish territory. The new camps also took on new roles. In addition to, or rather on top of their traditional role of incarceration and hard labor, the new camps became the vehicles for exterminating undesirable ethnic groups and nations. In addition to Auschwitz– Birkenau, at least seven other hub-like concentration camps were built in Poland, each one with a wide network of sub-camps. The Treblinka concentration camp was set up for the Warsaw district. In 1942, Treblinka II, a new unit with 13 gas chambers, opened for business. It is estimated that about 700 thousand Jews lost their lives in the gas chambers of Treblinka II alone. In another camp, Majdanek, built in central Poland in 1942, about 350 thousand people, mostly Poles, lost their lives. The Stutthof concentration camp was built in northern Poland in 1939 to "serve the needs" of the Polish population in Pomerania. In addition to the main camp, there were 45 auxiliary Stutthof camps in the region.[18]

Some of the concentration camps built after 1941 relinquished the hard labor function altogether, focusing exclusively on the extermination function. Unable to quickly build the more sophisticated gas chambers, the Nazis mastered a technique of recycling combustion gases into big passenger truck containers. Loaded with enemies of the Reich, the truck containers were shut, and sent directly to the crematorium. On arrival, the enemies of the Reich were dead and their bodies, after meticulous extraction of any remaining valuables from their fingers, necks, mouths, and hair, were ready for cremation. One such camp operated, for example, in Chełmno, Pomerania.[19]

As the imminent Nazi defeat was becoming more apparent, the rage, hatred, and urge for revenge among the Nazis intensified. The killing sprees helped vent their frustration. In the winter of 1944, more camp prisoners were dying from starvation and exhaustion than before. Some prisoners, mostly those from northern Poland, many from the Stutthof camp, were packed on ships and subsequently sunk on the Baltic Sea, the technique developed earlier by the Soviets in the North Sea.[20]

Between 1939 and 1945, the Nazis built or set up about nine thousand concentration camps including main camps and their auxiliaries. It is estimated that about 18 million people from 30 nations went through these concentration camps. The enemies of the Reich consisted of Jews from all European countries, the Poles, French, Netherlands, Belgians, Czechs, Greeks, Yugoslavs, Norwegians, Dutch, Germans, Gypsies, and the Soviets, mostly Soviet prisoners of war. In Auschwitz–Birkenau alone, about two million enemies of the Reich from 29 different nations lost their lives.[21]

* * * *

Zenek's death has a devastating effect on Józek. He not only mourns the loss of his best friend but he also perceives Zenek's death as his oracle. He becomes more frightened and more agitated. The routine Gestapo visits also take their toll on his psyche. Each visits causes him sweats and stomach pain. His body is shaken, his mind is traumatized, and he can't eat for hours after each such encounter with the Nazi tormenters.

As his mental state worsens, the home atmosphere deteriorates as well. The family lives at the verge of starvation. Dad is the only breadwinner for the family. But these days his salary is less then the minimum wage. Jasia occasionally earns some money but spends most of her time helping with Jędruś. Józio tries to earn some money as a salesman but the penalty for illegal trade is simple—the concentration camp. Without a stable job and proper papers, he risks arrest at any time. Dad's drinking habits aggravate the situation. When drunk, he likes to pick on Józio's pious life style and quarrels erupt frequently. But little Jędruś, their angelic darling, always calms them down.

The beautiful spring arrives, warms their spirits, and breathes new hope in their hearts. However, the spring of 1942 is not as colorful as the rainbow of nature blooming all around them. It's only a halfway point in the cruelest war ever fought.

On one such blossoming spring day, Józio is on his way to the Gestapo for his routine check-in. As always, Danusia walks next to him holding his sweaty and shaky hand. "What time is it?" Józio asks impatiently.

"I just told you, it's about twelve," Danusia replies. "Calm down, please."

"But I need the exact time," he snaps while observing the street.

She checks her watch again. "Two minutes to twelve."

"Okay," he replies and tries to slow his pace.

Aleja Szucha is just a few blocks away. There are not many Germans on the street. The trams move noisily in different directions. Big blooming chestnut trees here and there beautify the wide sidewalk. The newspaper kiosks and announcement boards with screaming propaganda posters get in their way from time to time.

Suddenly Józio stiffens. Danusia detects this abrupt tension in his body and looks around with concern. A middle-aged man in a long light coat with a big round hat covering a large portion of his face walks towards them. Józio watches the man intensely. As the man approaches, Danusia catches a clear wink of his eye directed at Józio from under his hat. It's only a split-second and the stranger disappears in the crowd behind them. Józio slows down instantly. "Danusia, darling, I am not going to report today, I can't report anymore."

Danusia's legs buckle but he holds her tight and slightly pushes her forward. "Don't stop, darling. We have to walk as if nothing happened. Otherwise we will raise suspicion. We are going to check this store window up there and walk back." They leisurely approach a shoe shop.

"But, Józio, do you want to stop reporting all together?" she asks in frightened disbelief.

"We will see, darling. But please don't ask any questions. It's better that way…." They look into the shoe shop window but are unable to distinguish a single shoe. From there, they turn around and disappear into a small street.

32. Zenek Gara

33. Doctor Hanna Petrynowska (Rana)

12

At the train station, Mama talks to little Andrew with great affection while Danusia nervously rocks the baby carriage. Next to them, Józek and Dad are engaged in intense discussion.

"Don't worry about me. See, that's my *Ausweise*." Dad takes out a small document from his wallet. "Look, it says here that the owner of this document works for the Reich. But read here! *All relevant authorities shall provide assistance to the bearer of this document.* I'm covered. But with you, my son, we need more than this *Kenkart*[1] that I gave you. This is just an identification card. You should have some sort of an employment identification card, the *Arbeitskarte*,[2] as they call it, saying that you work for the Germans. That's the only thing that can really help you, Józio. I will think about it."

"Please don't worry. I'll try to arrange it through some of my contacts. Just take care of yourself. And don't take any more risks."

A train to Siedlce and Luków enters the station. The two men hug each other. "I'll be back in Warsaw in two weeks," Józek says.

Danusia hugs Dad with tears. "Take care of yourself and be careful."

"And remember to watch after Zbyszek," Mama cries. "Make sure he is safe and send him over to us quickly."

Dad kisses the baby as they board the train. A quick look at the train platform—no signs of SS or Gestapo. "Have a safe trip!" he yells as the train starts moving eastward. Józio finds good seats for all of them. Danusia puts Jędruś on her lap and snuggles him to her breast, her face wet from tears.

"Don't worry, Danusia," Józek tries to comfort her. "The summer is coming and Jędruś needs to be out there, in the countryside. It's better for him. He will have plenty of milk, better food, and fresher air. You also need a vacation, darling. You know the Czemierniki village from last summer, don't you?"

"That's right," Mama chimes in. "Only this time we will not stay at the same house but closer to the train station."

"But last summer we had more money," Danusia grumbles.

"I told you I would be working. I won't be able to stay with you long. Hopefully I will be able to earn some money."

The village of Czemierniki is not far from the train station, about an hour's ride by buggy. A half-finished room awaits them in a modest house surrounded by dense violet lilac bushes. The house is located on the main road leading to the central square. In their newly built room there is neither floor nor furniture yet. But the Musiałkowskis, their hosts, are busy building a bed for them.

Józio observes the process with mixed feelings. The so-called bed reminds him of the Auschwitz plank bed that he shared with two other stinking unfortunates. These images from Auschwitz frequently haunt him as nightmares and daytime specters. They cause him heart palpitations and heavy sweats. Tonight Danusia and Mama will sleep in the newly built bed and little Jędruś in the baby carriage. Józio prefers the hayloft in the barn. Tomorrow they will worry about another bed.

Instead of money, the hosts will receive rent in goods. Danusia brought with her some valuable items from their home in Warsaw—a small carpet, two lengths of fabric, draperies, and small china set. One length of fabric will serve as down payment.

The next morning, Danusia goes to say hello to all her friends from last year. She leaves little Jędruś with Mama and Józek, and takes off. In the afternoon, she comes back exhausted but happy with a big bag full of food and a large chicken under her arm. The chicken is alive, however, and no one knows what to do with such a present. As a result of a long and fervent debate, the terrified chicken joins his friends in the yard. In the bag, Mama finds potatoes, flour, eggs, and even a bushel of kiełbasa. They buy milk and bread from their hosts. The supper tonight is delicious. At last, no one goes to sleep hungry.

Józio is very uncomfortable, though. He knows he can't just sit and watch the women selling off their last possessions. He must provide for the family. From time to time, he nervously glances at the main road leading to the train station. Soon he will have to leave them and go out to earn some money. Besides, his friends are waiting for him. Deep down he knows, however, that one day he may not come back from such a trip.

Nevertheless, before long, he kisses Jędruś, hugs and kisses Danusia and Mama, and sets off on the journey.

"But be very careful," Danusia pleads. "It's so dangerous with these round-ups and constant inspections. We will be worrying terribly about you, darling."

"Don't panic, Danusia. I'll try to be back in a week."

"You must be back in a week," Danusia states firmly. "Otherwise we will be dying from worry."

"If I can't be back I will send you a telegram."

Danusia puts Jędruś into the baby carriage and walks with Józio to the outskirts of the village. There, Józio catches the buggy and soon disappears from view. The week seems to drag on forever. Danusia is impatient and irritated, watching the road all the time.

"Go and see your friends." Mama sends her out, hoping to cheer her up. "I will watch Jędruś."

Danusia likes to be with people. She easily makes friends and has already made friends with many local officials. The farmers respect her as a "lady from Warsaw" and ask her for advice or even for help in dealing with the local officials.

"Mrs. Danusia!" a bushy farmer calls her over. "My cow doesn't give milk. She must be sick. Ask the administrators to release me from the quota, at least temporarily."

All farmers are obliged to deliver a certain quota of their produce to German authorities because the Germans occupants and the German army must be well fed. The unreasonable quotas drive farmers into bankruptcy. Building materials and all farming necessities are rationed; the shortages of farming tools and other farming essentials are acute.[3]

Danusia talks with the farmers, talks with the officials, some of them Polish, some of them German, and quickly becomes a deal-maker among them. Everybody likes the charming, energetic Warsawian. They value her persuasiveness and great organizational skills. When asked for help, she always comes up with a solution. She manages to release one farmer from the milk quota, another farmer from the potato quota; she arranges for permission to buy building materials for one family and fertilizers for another. People are grateful for her help and reward her generously.

Before the week is over, Józio returns safely. He's exhausted and hungry but brings some money. He eats, rests a little, takes a couple of walks with Jędruś, and gets set to leave again. This time he will visit Dad and Zbyszek in Warsaw and should also be back in a week. This time, his departure is not as painful as the first one. After all, he came back safely before and this time he is just going home. He will check on Dad and bring them more things from home.

After his departure, Danusia plunges back into the village life while Mama watches after Jędruś. Occasionally, Danusia sends her some clients for a haircut or a perm. Jędruś gets a nice suntan in the early summer heat. He already walks, talks and tries to play with all sorts of cats, dogs and chickens in the yard, but the horses still scare him.

Before the week is over, Józio is back. To the women's delight, he arrives with Zbyszek. But the two men do not share the women's excitement. Their faces are grim. Even Jędruś's smiling face doesn't brighten their disconcerting sadness.

"What's happened?" Jasia asks.

"Well, Mama, we have a problem," Józio starts. "But please don't worry. Everything will be fine." He continues while his eyes search the floor.

"Alek!" Mama instinctively exclaims.

"Yeah...."

"What's happened to Dad?" Danusia asks.

"The Gestapo arrested him," Józio tells the bad news.

"Where is he?" Mama jumps up. "I have to go to him!"

"He is at Pawiak, Mama. They won't let you in...."

The word *Pawiak* paralyzes the women. No one gets out of Pawiak alive. Mama stares at Zbyszek in silence. "My Daddy, my Daddy!" Danusia bursts into hysterical tears. "They will kill my Daddy!" Mama doesn't cry. Instead, she energetically dries her hands on her colorful apron and proclaims in a tone that doesn't accept any opposition: "I am going to Warsaw." In a decisive gesture she takes off the apron and rushes to pack.

"I am going with you," Danusia announces.

"No!" They all protest at once.

"There is nothing for you to do there," Zbyszek assures her.

"You don't understand," Danusia shakes her head in despair. "I will get him out. I got Józio out and I will get my Daddy out, too."

"That's okay. You will go, my dear, but not now, later." Józio tries to wipe her tears. "First, let Mama go. We will see whether she will be able to get to him out. You will try later, okay, darling?"

"Yes, I'll go first and you will go later, if needed," Mama assures her. "You have to stay with Jędruś while I am gone. You're his mother. You can't just leave the baby like that."

Mama's argument convinces Danusia to concede. "So, why...?" Danusia ponders over and corrects herself. "Or...how did it happen?" she asks calmly.

"They arrested Dad at work," Zbyszek explains. "They said that he was arrested for sabotage!" Zbyszek looks rather puzzled. "Old Gara warned me at the gate not to even go home. Mama, before you go home please remember to check first with our people, you know.... They will tell you whether it is safe to go home and what to do next."

"I understand," Mama speaks briefly and unemotionally, just like an experienced member of the resistance movement. She leaves soon thereafter, trying to catch the last train to Warsaw.

With Mama's departure, a great emptiness and strange fear settles in their hearts. Danusia and Zbyszek suddenly realize that their parents are not here for them and they may not have a home anymore.... And Dad, their strong, courageous Dad who never feared anyone—Now he is in danger, he needs help, he is vulnerable. The future frightens them.

Józio tries to cheer them up. He asks about Jędruś, what happened in his absence, whether there have been any SS or Gestapo patrols in the area. But Danusia is not in the mood to talk.

Zbyszek paces back and forth like a caged lion. "I have to go back," he finally declares.

"You shouldn't go back now," Józio protests. "Remember what Dad wants you to do? He specifically wants you to stay away from there."

"I won't go home," Zbyszek says. "I will stay with my friends outside the mint, but I must go back to check on Mama and see what we can do for Dad."

Despite Danusia's protests and Józio's arguments, Zbyszek leaves for Warsaw the next day. Danusia is devastated. They are all in danger out there. And she can't help them; she doesn't even know what is going on out there. Józio does his best in helping her cope with the anxiety. He does the laundry, cooks, and gives her more time to play with Jędruś. He even postpones his next trip, realizing that he can't leave the low-spirited Danusia alone with the baby. First he needs to find some help for her. Through church channels he gets a recommendation. The woman's name is Becky. A former music student at the Kraków Conservatory, Becky is a very capable young woman. He tries out the idea on Danusia.

"But Józio," she says after listening attentively, "you understand that Becky is Jewish."

Józio takes a deep breath. "We don't have to know that. She doesn't look like a Jew at all."

"If you think it's safe…then okay. But if I know that she is Jewish then other people may know that, too."

"Well, then. It's your decision, Danusia."

She walks to Jędruś's cradle and gazes at his charming innocent face. "You know what they do with the Jewish babies these days…?" She turns to Józio. He instinctively shrinks into his shoulders. "They can stop a woman on the street, pull out a baby from her carriage and…hit the baby's head full force against the wall…in front of the mother. That's what they do in the Ghetto…." Her voice trembles wildly. She turns abruptly with a ferocious look in her fierce eyes. "Ask her to come! I want to see her."

"Thank you, Danusia darling. I knew you would agree. I have already asked her to come. She will be here tomorrow."

"Danusia! Mrs. Danusia!" A terrifying scream interrupts them. Mrs. Musiałkowska rushes in like a hurricane.

"Round-up! Round-up…! The Gestapo is coming! They are hunting all men. Jesus Christ, Mr. Fijałkowski, run! For God's sake, run!" Crying and yelling, she rushes to the next house.

They stare at each other in terror. Run? No! The attack dogs are smart. Józio turns white.

"To the hayloft!" Danusia orders. But Józio is paralyzed with fear, unable to move. She looks at him in despair, but he just stands there in the middle of the room like a mummy. Precious seconds pass by.

"Go!" Danusia pushes him full-force to the door. "To the barn!" she yells pushing and pulling him and dragging him in despair. "Faster, for God's sake, faster!"

"Ladder! Here's the ladder!" She pushes him up the ladder sweating from stress and effort. "Lie down!" She neatly covers him with hay, rushes down, drags the ladder to the nearby creek, and runs back home. Breathless, she checks on little Jędruś still sleeping serenely in his cradle when suddenly the heavy steps bang through the house. A cold chill runs down her spine. Wiping her forehead, she takes a deep breath and walks resolutely to the kitchen. Two big Germans in their shiny heavy boots stand in the kitchen with machineguns and truncheons ready for action.

"Are there any men here?" they probe Danusia carefully.

She looks straight into their eyes. How strange—they're just average men, like everybody else. Why does she fear them so much? Aren't they like all of us here...? Are those boots and guns making them different inside? Why can't she talk with them like with normal people? "Yes, there is a man here!" she replies doggedly and makes an inviting gesture towards them. "Let me show you."

The Germans look at each other suspiciously but follow her. *Tramp, tramp*, their heavy boots echo through the house. Danusia stops abruptly, turns to them, and puts her finger on her lips: "Ssh! Be quiet!" she orders.

The big soldiers look at her obediently and move quietly on their toes.

She leads them to the other room and points to the cradle where little Jędruś sleeps like an angel. "This is the man," she says to them.

The big soldiers look at her in consternation, slight smiles on their lips. "Quite a man," one of them says, nodding. "But where is your husband?"

"He's gone," Danusia gesticulates, trying to show that he is far away.

"Good, good." The two Germans stand near the cradle and smile. "How about if...if we come to you...this evening...for tea, how about that?" the taller soldier says in broken Polish. "Here!" he then points to the floor to make sure she understands.

Danusia swallows heavily but puts a smile on her face. "Yes, this evening, here, for tea...but what time?" She points to his watch.

"Six o'clock, okay?"

"Okay," she replies, bewildered.

The two big soldiers amiably smile back and walk out the door. She follows them with her eyes until they reach the street, then sinks to the floor numb from stress. Jędruś slowly wakes up but she doesn't have the strength to get up. Minutes pass by and Jędruś starts crying. With great effort, she pulls herself together, takes the baby in her arms, and walks outside. Old Mrs. Musiałkowska stands near the fence, watching the street. "They are almost gone," she announces.

Danusia walks towards the barn and says in loud voice: "They are almost gone. A couple more minutes...."

Indeed, a big truck called *buda* full of captured men closes its flaps and departs towards the station. The soldiers in a smaller car follow the *buda*. The round-up is over. Danusia puts Jędruś in the carriage.

"Could you please watch him while I get Józio?" Without waiting for reply, she runs to the creak trying to pull out the ladder. But by now the ladder is swollen with water and feels twice as heavy as before. And there is no help around. She pulls half of it out of the water and gives up. "He must jump then. It's not that high after all." She runs back. "Józio, get up, they are gone!" She yells but there is no reply from the hayloft. She keeps yelling and shouting for a long time until after several long minutes, Józio's half conscious face shows up from the hay.

"Finally," she sighs. "They're gone! Come down! You must jump because I can't get the ladder here!"

He looks at her as if not understanding, his eyes absent, his face is gray, his lips white.

"Jump, just jump!" she orders.

He slowly looks around, checks various beams, and with great difficulty lands on the ground. Only now she notices that Józio is shaking—his legs are shaking, his hands are shaking, and even his teeth are chattering. He is a nervous wreck. The experience of hiding in the hayloft has devastated him.

But there is no time to waste. "You must leave, you have to leave at once!" She urges him without even mentioning her evening appointment, at least not now. "You must leave because they may come back!" she orders flatly.

He eagerly agrees. "Becky will come tomorrow to help you and I will be back in a week, as always." He packs a sandwich, kisses Danusia and Jędruś, and is gone in less than an hour.

Now Danusia's mind is on the evening tea appointment with the hated oppressors. How strange.... How to handle it? She needs to make sure old Mrs. Musiałkowska will stay with her. Maybe she will help her prepare something to eat, like *placki*—potato pancakes with sour cream and sugar.

Mrs. Musiałkowska is terrified. "You mean you will host these monsters who took away our men? These oppressors, these beasts...!"

"But Mrs. Musiałkowska, I don't have any choice. They said they would be back. You can't leave me alone with them, you must be with me all the time, please."

Old Musiałkowska looks at the sublimely beautiful Danusia. Right. She can't be left alone with these monsters. If that's the case, then let's make sure they eat well and don't get angry. Together, they rush to make the *placki*.

At exactly 6 o'clock, the two Germans walk into the yard. This time they are without machineguns and without truncheons. Instead, each of them carries a package. Old Musiałkowska looks at Danusia with fear and hides behind the stove. Danusia sends her a knowing look and walks to the door to welcome the guests. The two men smile at her. "This is for you." They hand her the packages.

She invites them to the table, introduces Mrs. Musiałkowska, and starts opening the presents. There are chocolate bars and candies and coffee. The presents slightly calm down old Mrs. Musiałkowska. Danusia puts a pot of tea on the table while the older woman prepares *placki*. The men eagerly drink tea and pull out some photographs. One by one, they show photographs of their wives, children, and friends. They talk about their homes somewhere far away in Germany and how much they miss their families. Old Musiałkowska puts the *placki* on the table and sits down timidly in the corner. Danusia doesn't say much.

"So where is your husband?" one of the men asks.

Danusia feels cold sweat on her shoulders. "He is with my Mama in Warsaw," she replies in broken German, trying hard to sound casual.

"Are you from Warsaw?"

"Yes, my Mama is sick and my husband takes care of her...."

"That's nice, that's nice. So you are on vacation here, right?" The two men eat, drink, talk, and laugh. They are having a good time at this little country house in the middle of nowhere. For a brief moment, they are just like normal people having fun with their friends. But soon they will be back on their gruesome duty of oppressing, persecuting, and killing the local people in the name of their great leader.

In less than two hours, the strange guests leave. During the night Danusia tries to recover from the trauma of the day. Jędruś sleeps calmly in his cradle. It's so revitalizing to watch him asleep. The experience of the day puzzles her, though. She tries to sleep but the image of the two men sticks in her mind. How is it that the same two people were so cruel and unfriendly at first and so gentle and pleasant a couple of hours later? Totally different individuals and yet the same people.... Only first they were on duty and later they were off duty. How strange....

In the morning a young rather tall woman knocks at the door and asks for Danusia. Her name is Becky. Danusia greets her warmly. The two women quickly become good friends. Becky likes to talk about music, about her beloved violin, and about the magic of orchestra. Danusia tells Becky about her movie school experience. Becky easily wins Jędruś 's trust and quickly learns the baby routine. She stays with Jędruś all the time. Soon Danusia plunges back into her favorite "people duties."

Józio comes back as scheduled. He brings some money and good news from Warsaw. Dad was transferred from Pawiak to another prison at Mokotów. Józio is very pleased. He believes it will be much easier to get Dad out of the Mokotów prison. With Dad's transfer to Mokotów, it's safer to stay home and Mama returned to the apartment. She works a little and tries to send packages to Dad as often as possible. Zbyszek moves around a lot, sometimes staying at home, sometimes with his friends.

The summer quickly passes by. The unfinished room at the Musiałkowskis' serves them well in the summer but it's not adequate for the icy weather to come. They must find a better place for winter.

Danusia wants to go back to Warsaw but Józio insists on staying in the countryside. "It's too difficult to get food in Warsaw," he argues.

It's already late September and the nights are getting colder. Coming back from one of his trips, Józio announces that he has found a great apartment for them and has already leased it. It's in a small town of Międzyrzec, about thirty kilometers from where they are. A week later, they are ready to move. They arrange for the buggy, pack everything, say good-bye to their Musiałkowski hosts, to Becky and everybody else, and leave Czemierniki behind.

The day is cold and rainy. By late afternoon, the horse is exhausted. They all are wet, hungry, and chilled. In pouring rain the buggy passes through endless gray fields. The road is rough and there are no villages on the horizon. Drenched and frozen, Danusia begs the driver to stop at the first house. After several more kilometers in the windy autumn rain, the driver spots a house and turns the buggy towards it. A peasant shows up in the door and observes the buggy suspiciously.

"Can you give us shelter?" the driver yells.

"I don't know, let me check."

The peasant disappears and an energetic, corpulent woman comes out to inspect the buggy. "Jesus Christ! You have a baby here. Antek, help them with the horse! I need to take care of this woman and the baby."

Immediately, she takes Danusia and the baby inside, gives them hot milk and dry clothing, and puts the two little icicles into her own bed, covering them tightly with a heavy feather comforter. Half frozen, Danusia and Jędruś slowly thaw in the feather bed. It feels heavenly. With enormous gratitude, Danusia looks at the woman. She will remember that glass of milk and that feather bed on that dreadful October night to the end of her life.

In the morning chill, they leave the hospitable house and set out on the journey east, passing again through open fields, dense forests, and small villages. Another half a day ride to Międzyrzec is still awaiting them. At one point, the buggy enters a small town. As they pass through the town square, a bizarre scene unfolds before their eyes. On one side of the square several dozen Jewish women kneel in rows of five with their hands in the air. On the opposite side of the square,

Jewish men kneel in the same manner. The SS-men walk around and in between the two groups with machineguns and attack dogs at their side, kicking and pushing those who don't hold their hands high enough.

"What's that?" Danusia's jaw drops.

"Don't look, darling." Józio starts shaking. "That's how they torment the Jewish people before they send them to death. Let's get out of here." Józio turns pale, his hands shaking and sweating. "Faster, faster please!" He tries to speed up the horse. The buggy leaves the square full speed through a backyard.

"I hope Becky will be safe in that church in Czemierniki," Danusia sighs.

"I hope so, too. Father Albert takes good care of his people." Józio puts his arm around her. "The persecutions of the Jewish people have intensified lately. They are either held in the Ghettos or killed on the streets or deported to the concentration camps...."

"Sh!" Danusia puts her finger over his lips. "Don't talk about the camp, darling. I don't want you to relive it."

It starts raining again. This time Jędruś is warmly wrapped in the blanket but Danusia and Józio are getting cold. They have neither raincoats nor warm clothing. Everything was left in Warsaw. Finally, the buggy passes a road sign saying they are entering the town of Międzyrzec. There are no tall buildings, just small houses, cottages, and huts. Danusia is disappointed. "Józio, this is such a thoroughly forlorn place. How am I supposed to live here?"

"You haven't seen the apartment yet," Józio replies cryptically. "Wait until you see what I've found for us."

The buggy passes through the town square, turns into Warszawska Street, and stops in front of a small house just near the main square. "Here we are, darling, on Warszawska Street. I thought you would like to be on Warszawska Street."

Danusia is not excited about the house but is eager to get out of the buggy after long hours of the rainy ride. She stops in front of the house for a brief moment. "Nothing special," she thinks as they walk up the steps.

Józio proudly opens the front door and leads Danusia into the house. "See, darling, there are three big rooms in here and a nice large kitchen. In the back, there's another exit leading to a small private yard. See! We can even plant our own vegetable there." Józio is delighted.

The house reminds him of his home in Koło. He grew up in a small town house. Only his house in Koło was surrounded by a charming wide-open garden. Józio loved that garden with aromatic apple trees and wide-spreading cherry trees, blooming flowerbeds, and delicious tomatoes and crispy cucumbers hiding against the fence. But Danusia is more interested in the apartment itself. It's much better than Czemierniki but still nothing even close to her Warsaw apartment. There is no water or sewer system, no central heating system, just the stoves. A few pieces of old furniture are scattered throughout the house: an old bed, a falling apart armoire, one table and two chairs. She checks everything carefully.

"This is just something to start with," Józio explains enthusiastically. "Let me show you what I have in mind." He escorts her from room to room, talking about his vision of their home. "This location is excellent. The first room is perfect for a hair salon, for example. It has an easy access from the street, just near the corner of the market square. Think about it, Danusia. We can have our own business here. The other room may be for your Mama or anybody else who wants to stay with us, then the large kitchen and next to it this big and quiet bedroom for us. Look! Do you like it, darling?" He takes her in his arms, kissing her wet hair. "It will be our real home at last," he whispers in her ear.

They settle down in the new house quickly. Initially Danusia is busy with unpacking, organizing, arranging the house, and meeting her new neighbors. Józio works in the house and spends a lot of time with Jędruś. But soon it's time for Józio to travel again. The notion of being left with Jędruś alone in a new and strange place scares Danusia.

"I need Mama here. Please go to Warsaw and ask Mama to come. I can't stay here by myself," she complains.

In Warsaw Józio persuades Mama. "You don't need to stay here to send packages to Dad. Zbyszek can deliver the packages. I will make sure that he has everything that he needs to prepare the packages." Within a week, he is back in Międzyrzec with Mama. They bring more warm clothing and more things for the new home. Mama is anxious to see the new apartment and Józio is anxious to suggest to her the opening of a hair salon in the front room.

Before Christmas, a hair salon opens for business in the front room of the house. Mama is busy with clients while Danusia effectively spreads around the news about the hair salon. Józio arranges for and decorates the Christmas tree. A Christmas package with toys for Jędruś arrives from Koło.

Christmas Eve brings feathery snow and ringing frost. The traditional supper is ready but Mama is still busy with her clients. Jędruś plays with a new toy near the Christmas tree and Józio lights the candles. Danusia, dressed in a white formal shirt and dark skirt, her hair meticulously styled, decorates the Christmas tree. She reaches out and gently adjusts a big paper angel on the very top of the Christmas tree.

Józio looks at her with admiration. "You look very beautiful today, my Queen."

She kisses his cheek and pulls his hand. "Let's sit down here...I want to tell you something." They sit down in the flickering light of the Christmas tree and she plays with his hand. "I want to tell you something, darling." She looks into his gentle blue eyes with uncertainty. "I want to tell you that...that we are going to have another baby."

"Oh, really...? Are you sure, Danusia?"

"Yes, I am sure."

They remain silent. The fire crackles, spreading a delectable scent through the room.

"And...do you want that child?" Józio asks with uncertainty in his voice.

"Jędruś released you from Auschwitz. I believe this second child will also bring us good luck," she replies firmly.

"You're right, darling," he tries to convince himself. "I am sure we will have a beautiful little girl. That's really fantastic! That's great!" He takes her in his arms. Inexpressible joy overwhelms them.

"This gift of new life must be a sign from God," Danusia whispers. "It's like sunshine. We will be fine, Józio, we will be fine...." She holds him close.

"You know...," she saddens. "I have witnessed something inconceivable recently. It's so vivid in my memory.... It was here, in town. A Jewish woman with a baby in her arms walked down the street towards me. At some distance behind her, a big SS-man followed her. You know how they constantly hunt the Jewish people, they round them up, torture, kill or deport them.... Oh, God, how can you watch all this...! So, this woman knew she was being followed. She exchanged a desperate look with another woman in front of me and in a split-second, she threw her baby into the open arms of that other woman. They did it so quickly and so cleverly that the SS-man behind didn't notice anything. Can you believe it? Without words, without signs, without any preparation or hesitance, just that one look! That's how mothers communicate.... One block later, the Jewish woman was rounded up and led to her death....

"You know, Józio, I think about it all the time. To hand off your baby like that...just to a passerby.... Can you imagine? To be certain of your imminent death like that.... Can you imagine?"

"I know what you mean, Danusia. Many things are beyond our comprehension. But try to think about it this way. Death brings liberation from earthly suffering. This woman may be happier now, up there, with God...."

"I don't believe it. I just don't!" Danusia starts shouting, then lowers her voice. "I don't believe in eternal life. Look what happens to us after death. We turn into dust, just mere dust! And all those thousands and millions of people that are being killed every day in Poland...! What's left of them...? Just dust, nothing else." She walks to the window and presses her forehead against the frosty glass. "They are like those snowflakes, they exist for a brief moment, and they melt away instantly, just like that." She snaps her fingers. "Simply melt away...."

"Danuś, there is eternal life, I know that for sure. You just have to believe it...."

The doors open and Mama's tired face shows up in the darkness of the hall. They look at her with apprehension.

"Sit down Mama. You are completely exhausted." Danusia gives her a chair.

"Don't get up, just sit down," Józio says. "We have everything ready."

"Oh, how terribly my hands hurt," Mama looks at her swelling hands with many small burns. Hairstyling is done with a heavy iron these days. It causes frequent burns.

"I'll give you a towel with ice." Józio brings some snow from the yard. "Remember this good friend of mine, Kazik, who has a hair salon in Warsaw? I told you about him. He doesn't use this heavy iron anymore. Instead he uses a new tool, much lighter. I will ask him to come over here for a couple of days. He will bring this new iron and teach you how to use it."

"If you want, I can try." Mama is not excited about his idea. "I don't know whether I can learn this new technique. Probably it's not that easy."

"Sure you can, Mama. Once you try it, you will like it, I'm sure. And Danusia should try it as well."

Despite aching hands and swelling legs, Mama is content. "The business has been excellent these past couple of days. It's a good start for us. We made good money this week and people were very pleased with my styling."

The evening goes by quickly. They eat a little and talk about the new baby, talk about Dad in prison and Zbyszek in Warsaw, about Józio's mother in Koło who has been sick lately and his sister who sent the package. But exhausted Mama quickly falls asleep and the celebration is soon over. On the Christmas Day, they write to Józio's family in Koło sharing with them happy news about the second baby. "My little girl," Józio writes with unshakable confidence.

After Christmas, Danusia starts helping Mama in the salon.

"You must learn fast, Danusia, because I have to go to Warsaw to check on Dad and Zbyszek, and you have to be able to keep the business going." Mama quickly hires two more people, knowing that Danusia herself won't be able to do the job. But at least she can oversee the business and will manage the people.

After Christmas, Józio leaves for Warsaw and soon sends them a telegram. "Kazik, the hairstylist, will be arriving on Monday. Look for him."

On Monday before noon, a man urgently knocks at the door. "Kazik!" Danusia thinks.

The man at the door has a gloomy face. "Madam," he says officially. "A man named Kazik, who was getting off the morning Warsaw train, was caught and rounded up by the Gestapo at the train station. All passengers getting off that train were rounded up and most likely will be shipped to the concentration camp tomorrow."

The words *concentration camp* knocks Danusia flat. "Oh, God!" She whispers in horror. But there is no time to waste. "Where is he now?" She must get Kazik back before he is shipped out to oblivion.

"Everybody is held at the Gestapo headquarters here in town."

"We must do something immediately then," she says.

"The only thing you can do now is to talk to the Gestapo chief. His name is Dietel. If you're lucky you may find him in the local pubs, here in town. He is a tall fellow and always walks with a hound dog. Good luck!" The man lifts his hat and disappears.

In horror, Danusia grabs the coat and rushes out to look for the local monster. She inquires here and there, in local bars and in 'Germans only' pubs. "Come back later," someone says. "Look for him in the afternoon," another advises her. She comes home frustrated, warms up a little, and leaves again. After wandering around for several hours, she spots a big puffed-up German walking down the street with an attack dog.

"Mr. Dietel?" she heads him off.

"Ja?" The big man looks at her suspiciously.

"My friend was arrested today at the train station. He is only a hairstylist. He came here to teach me new styling methods. Please release him. He is innocent."

The powerful man listens to her with amusement. "A hairstylist you said.... Hmm...," he ponders. "What's his name?"

"Kazik, I mean Kazimierz Sowa," she quickly corrects herself.

"Ja, Ja, maybe." Dietel looks at Danusia with undisguised interest. "And you want him back, do you?" he asks provocatively.

Danusia senses his intentions and takes a step back. "Yes, Sir," she replies in a serious, grim voice.

"Well then...," he ponders, measuring her with his omnipotent eyes. "Then...come tomorrow to my office."

"Yes, sir. Thank you!"

The next day before the sunrise, Danusia is on her way to the Gestapo office. In front of the building she spots a big truck, the infamous *buda* always used for the round-ups. Shaking in her shoes, she walks to the building and asks for Dietel.

"He is not here yet. You have to wait."

She looks at the clock. It's very early. Suddenly it occurs to her that the prisoners could be driven away even before this Dietel shows up. She runs outside and finds a driver of the *buda* car. The driver is Polish.

"Please don't leave until I get my hairstylist back! Do something, I don't care what—flat tire, engine problem, gasoline leak, anything, but don't leave until I get him back, please!"

The driver nods. "Okay, okay, young lady. We'll see what we can do."

Precious minutes pass by and Dietel is nowhere to be found. Danusia bites her fingers, pacing back and forth like a dynamo. Suddenly, the back door opens abruptly towards the street and a large group of people, two at a time, emerges from the basement, walking out the door under heavy escort.

"It's them. They must be leaving!" Danusia screams inside. As she watches the procession in horror, the loud echo of heavy steps reaches her. She turns around and notices Dietel on the other side of the hallway. Her desperate eyes penetrate him like bullets.

"Hello!" she says imploringly. But he looks through her, articulates some kind of a cold sound, and walks into his office, leaving her behind.

"I need to talk to Mr. Dietel right now!" she almost screams at Dietel's assistant. He shrugs his shoulders in a helpless gesture. She agonizes in front of the heavy door for another minute or so while constantly checking the developments on the street.

"Come in!" Suddenly the door opens. She rushes into the room, her furious eyes stabbing at Dietel.

"I am sorry, but I can't help you. The names were already sent to Lublin." Dietel points out to the list of names on his desk.

Danusia looks at the list and uncontrollable rage overcomes her. "It's a lie!" she screams in broken German. "You must give me my hairstylist back!" She yells even louder, tears start flowing down her face. "You promised me!" she shrieks in a towering rage.

"That's enough! Enough of this!" He nervously tries to silence her. "Let's go, but be quiet!"

He walks out into the street. She follows him closely. A long row of the prisoners is about to board the *buda*. Dietel says something to the escort guard. As the prisoners board the truck, the guard calls a man to the side.

"That's my hairstylist!" Danusia's heart beats faster. She draws nearer him and asks:

"Kazik?"

"Yes," the man replies calmly.

Immediately, she grabs his arm and glances at Dietel. Rather unhappily, he beckons. "Let's go, but slowly," she whispers.

Stealthily, they move away from the *buda* heading desperately towards the closest street corner. It's not that far, right here, two more steps, here it is. Behind the corner, they quicken the pace and soon are running at full speed.

At home Mama welcomes them with a gray-green face. " I thought I would die here waiting for you!" she confesses.

"I couldn't believe they arrested me just like that!" Kazik is dizzy. "I thought they were looking for contraband and would arrest those who had some illegal goods. But when they put me back in the cell after interrogation I got really scared. I still can't believe they would round up people getting off the train and send them right...to the concentration camp."

"Well, now you will believe anything, I am afraid," Mama comments bitterly. "Anyway, thanks for coming...!"

Kazik stays for several days working diligently with Danusia and Mama and returns to Warsaw with apprehension but safely. Towards the end of January, Mama leaves for Warsaw, too. Józio, as always, comes and goes. Danusia takes care of the business and watches after little Jędruś. Winter is in full swing, more snow falls, and roads are icy. One of these snowy days Józio is ready for his next trip. "Tomorrow I have to go to Radzyń. I will take a bus in the morning and will try to be back in the evening." He looks at Danusia's unhappy face and adds. "I did some shopping today. You should be fine for a while." In the morning, he gets up early, dresses up warmly, kisses Danusia and Jędruś, and leaves. It's a sunny and frosty February day. The business is slow thus Danusia spends most of the day with Jędruś. In the late afternoon, the mailman knocks at the door and brings her a telegram from Józio.

Dear Danusia!

I can't be back today because I have to go to Warsaw. But don't worry. Take care of yourself and Jędruś. I will be back by the end of the week.

Love, Józio

She sighs and puts the telegram away. An hour later another man knocks at the door. "The hair salon is closed for the day," Danusia informs the stranger.

"But I must speak with Mrs. Fijałkowska," the man insists.

"I am Mrs. Fijałkowska," she answers the man.

"Can I come in?"

She briefly hesitates but opens the door. A middle-aged man walks into the room and looks at her in a strange way. "Madam," he starts officially, ponders for some time, then chokes out: "Your husband has been killed."

She stares at the man with her big almond-like eyes for some time. "No! You are wrong, Sir! You are mistaken!" She takes a step back. "My husband is on his way to Warsaw. I have just received a telegram from him. Here you are, you see!" She waves the telegram straight into his face.

"It is quite possible, Madam, that you have the telegram from him. Earlier in the day, he indeed was at the post office. But it is my sad duty to inform you that he was shot dead on the street in Radzyń, soon after leaving the post office."

Danusia stands still. "No! That's not true! That can't be true!" She keeps repeating quietly.

"You should contact Kristina in Radzyń," the man advises her. "She will help you." He bows politely and slowly heads to the door.

"Mama, Mama!" Jędruś runs to Danusia from the other room. She stands there and stares at Jędruś, not really comprehending his words, then grabs the boy and rushes out the door into the dark wintry night. Help! She needs help and runs to the closest neighbor. There she says that someone just came over and informed her that her Józio was...was... killed in Radzyń. This can't be true, of course, but she needs to go to Radzyń because something could have happened to him and he might be in danger....

Within minutes, people gather around her. Someone goes to her home and brings back her coat, someone else gives her money. "She needs to call her Mama in Warsaw," the neighbor decides and takes her to the post office. "Jędruś will stay with us once you go to Radzyń," another neighbor says. One of the local *Volksdeutsche* people takes her by car to Kristina to Radzyń.

Danusia watches everything around her as if watching a movie, with reservation and incomprehensible distance. "It's a bad dream, just a bad dream. Józio for sure is already in Warsaw. I need to wake up." She gets irritated. "When can I finally wake up from all this?"

Kristina greets her warmly. "Here you are, my dear, drink this tonic. It will help you." Later she gives her a glass of a homemade herbal concoction and puts her to bed. "Rest now and relax. Tomorrow we will go to the police to take care of everything." During the night, Danusia gets sick. Appearing unconscious she screams and wants to get out.

Early the following morning, Kristina takes her to the heavily guarded military police offices in the City Hall. From the darkness of the hallway, a guard directs them to a shabby room. A fat Gestapo officer looks at them edgily from behind a worn out desk.

"Her husband," Kristina points to Danusia, "was gunned down yesterday by the police. Please return her husband's money. She has a small baby and is pregnant with a second child."

Displeasure shows up on the functionary's face. "This *Polnische Bandit*!" he says with aversion.

Danusia steps forward in fury.

"Oh, be quiet, ma'am...," he says, stretching out his hand as if trying to stop her from making a scene. He then opens his drawer and takes out Józio's wallet.

Danusia stares at it. "It's Józio's wallet." She debates internally. "That's my picture there." Her mind works feverishly. "Why does he have all that?" She can't comprehend it.

The functionary opens the wallet thick with money, takes out three banknotes and throws them in a slapdash gesture across the desk towards Danusia. She looks at the banknotes, looks at the man again, and says in a wild voice: "I didn't come here for the money! I came here for my husband! Where is he? Where is my husband?" She raises her voice. "What did you do to my husband, where is he?" she yells wildly.

"Your husband was a *Polnische Bandit*!" the man replies with disdain. "We do not give back the bodies of *Polnische Bandits*. You will never get your husband back!"

Danusia raises her hand in an attempt to hit the functionary but Kristina pulls her back. "Can you at least give us back his clothing?" she asks politely.

"Okay, okay, enough of this! Come back in half an hour and you will get his clothing," he replies, showing them the door.

Kristina pushes Danusia toward the hall. "Wait for me here and be quiet!" she orders. "I have to run some errands and will be back soon." Thirty minutes later Kristina is not back but Danusia can't wait any longer and goes back alone. Without saying a word, the functionary points her to the corner of the room. There, on the floor, Danusia recognizes a pile of clothing—Józio's clothing: his hat, his coat, his pants and even his warm drawers, but no shirt or sweater. The coat has a bloodstain near the left sleeve. Danusia stares at the pile of clothing in silence. That's Józio, her Józio.... And that bloodstain...! They really killed her Józio...! She kneels down, gathers the pile meticulously, hugs everything to her chest, gets up with dignity, and walks out the door with her eyes fixed on nothing.

Only now she has come to the realization that her Józio is dead. Unbearable pain settles inside her, the kind of pain that makes breathing hard and every passing second a torture. She must end this pain; she must do something quickly to stop it. The lake! That's right! The lake is her salvation. She turns towards the bridge and quickens her pace, her eyes now fixed on the river. Quickly, she just needs to make it there and relief will come.... She is almost there...just a few more steps and her agony will end. There will be no more pain!

Suddenly strong arms grab her and a dear face heaves in front of her. "Danusia!"

"Who's that?" She doesn't understand. "Zbyś? It can't be him. He can't be here...no. He must be in Warsaw!"

"Danuś, my dear, I finally found you! I was looking for you in Międzyrzec and everywhere!"

"Zbyś! You came here for me?" She bursts violently into tears.

They stand there near the bridge united in their grief.

"Danusia, my dearest, don't cry." Zbyszek embraces her shaking and trembling body. "Don't be scared, darling. I will take good care of you and your children, I promise. I will look after all of you, always. I will be like a father to your children. You won't be left alone. I promise!"

Zbyszek's voice shakes but he doesn't cry. He's eighteen years old now, boyish looking still, but inside, he feels like a man. He holds her close and gently turns her back.

"They told me that you were staying at Kristina's. Let's go to her then." Tightly holding Danusia's arm, Zbyszek leads her to Kristina's house.

"Danusia! Where have you been? We were looking for you everywhere!"

"This is my brother. He just came from Warsaw," Danusia explains.

"Oh, that's very good." Kristina invites them in. "Listen! I spoke with a friend of mine. He works as a car driver for Hauptmann, the highest-ranking German in town. In the afternoon he will take you to his boss and you can ask this Hauptmann for the rest of the money and all the other things that they have stolen from Józio. But for now, be my guest, please."

Danusia obediently sits down. Kristina makes some tea. Zbyszek nervously walks around. At last he takes a deep breath and asks Kristina in a low voice. "How did it happen? Do you know?"

Kristina looks at Danusia with concern.

"Tell us everything, please!" Danusia asks calmly, wide-awake now.

"I don't know much," Kristina starts. "But I know that Józio met with some people in town that morning, then he came over to us saying that he must to go to Warsaw and wanted to let you know about the change in his plans. We helped him get the buggy that was supposed to take him to the train station. By buggy, he left for the post office to send you a telegram and from there he was supposed to go to the train station. Now when I think about it, I remember seeing two Gestapo men in front of our house when Józio was here...." She thinks for some time and continues: "But back then, I didn't realize that...," she sighs looking towards the window. "Apparently the Germans were after him. The driver told me that they waited for Józio on the street leading to the train station. They stopped the buggy, called Józio all sorts of names, hit him in the face, broke his glasses, and asked the driver to turn back to the police station. At the corner, Józio jumped out of the buggy and started to run while the Germans were shooting at him.... Someone told me...," she stops and lights a cigarette, "...that it was...when Józio slipped and tripped on the icy pavement that the bullet hit him in the chest...."

Danusia drops her head. Hysterical sobbing bursts from her chest.

Kristina takes out some of her magic potion and hands Danusia a glass of herbal liquid. "Take it once more before we go back there. But your brother must stay here. They have plenty of strange ideas when they see young Polish men these days. They seem to be more aggressive lately since the recent news about their defeats in Russia, you know, Stalingrad and everything else.... You better just wait for us here."

A dark limousine is parked in front of City Hall. Kristina's friend greets them from the limousine's window. "You stay here," he says to Kristina, "and I'll take her upstairs."

Danusia accompanies the driver into the gloomy building. This time they don't stop at the reception desk and don't ask anything of anyone. They just go straight upstairs. The driver knocks at the door and the baritone voice answers.

"Come in!"

Danusia walks in first. The room is long, rather dark, with a low ceiling and dark brown furniture. In front of them, against the window, a man sits behind the desk. Danusia steps forward and the man gets up. He is tall, around 45 years of age, with salt and pepper hair. Stretching his arms towards her, he has a mysterious look on his face.

"Dad?" Danusia's mind becomes blurry. She walks into his open arms, puts her head on his muscular shoulders, and bursts into tears.

"Charlotte?" he whispers, closing his eyes. "Charlotte, my dear...." He hugs her warmly.

For a brief moment, they stand there, in this strange embrace, the chief oppressor and his frail victim, united in their pain and suffering.

The speechless driver watches the scene from the distance. "This is the woman I told you about," he starts hesitantly. "Her husband was killed yesterday," he tries to explain.

Hauptmann eventually commands his emotions but can't take his eyes off Danusia. "When you walked into the room, I thought you were Charlotte, my daughter," he confesses. "You look exactly like her. But Charlotte is very far away.... She couldn't be here of course.... I haven't seen her for such a long time...," he sighs. "So young lady, what can I do for you?"

"She has a small baby and is expecting another one soon," the driver says in German. "She would like to get her husband's money back and all of his valuables."

Hauptmann calls the functionary from downstairs and calmly listens to his long speech. Once the speech is over, he gets up and pounds his fist against the desk so forcefully that the old phone jumps making a loud clanging noise. "*Warum....? Alles, Alles..! Raus... Raus!*" he yells. Danusia sits still and listens with apprehension, understanding only every other word

"Heil Hitler!" The functionary salutes, clicking his heels and rushes out.

"He will bring everything," the driver says quietly to Danusia.

Indeed, in no time the functionary is back with the wallet, the wedding ring, and the glasses.

"Is that all?" Hauptmann asks Danusia.

She glances at the objects. "No." she says. "The watch is still missing." The functionary rushes out and comes back with a golden watch.

"Is that all?" the boss asks again.

She nods and the functionary leaves the room with relief. "Sir," she gets up once the doors close. "I have one more request." She starts in broken German without waiting for translation. She walks to the desk with her urgent, expressive eyes fixed on Hauptmann. "I must have the body of my husband. Please give me back his body. It's not even so much for me as for my children. They won't know their father...." Her voice breaks down. "But at least...," her voice is failing now, "they will have his grave... Please!"

Hauptmann is visibly uncomfortable. Clearly, he is unable to say "no" to her. But she asks for more than he himself can deliver. "Well..., I will request permission to return the body. It will take some time, though. Please come back in three days."

"Thank you very much." Danusia once again wants to embrace the man but standing behind the gloomy desk, she realizes the distance, bows politely and leaves.

Hauptmann has a problem though. He cannot just request permission to return the body because the bodies of *Polnische Bandits* shall not be returned to their families. He needs to find a special reason why this body should be given back to the family. He meditates over a piece of paper for some time. He then calls the functionary and inquires further into the circumstances of the incident and the burial place of the victim. It turns out that the victim has been buried at the Jewish Cemetery. That gives him an idea. He will merely ask for the transfer of the body from the Jewish Cemetery to the Catholic Cemetery. That makes perfect sense and should not violate the *Polnische Bandit* policy.

Three days later, he hands Danusia the official document. Issued on the stationary of the District Captain, the document is addressed to Danusia and signed by the Chief of Police and by the representative of the Health Department. It grants Danusia permission to transfer the body of her "shot husband" from the Jewish Cemetery in Radzyń to the Catholic Cemetery in Międzyrzec. The last paragraph says that the exhumation procedure shall be conducted under the supervision of the police in Radzyń.

"I am very grateful to you, Sir," Danusia says tearfully.

"Why did he try to escape? I would have released him...for sure...."

"He was an Auschwitz prisoner...," she replies, biting her lips.

"Oh, I see...."

She leaves his room with the words "release" echoing bitterly in her mind. No, she can't fall apart again. Right now she has to get Józio back. And she must do so quickly before they change their minds. Equipped with the best possible papers, she goes downstairs and with a dose of satisfaction hands the document to the familiar functionary.

"Now you HAVE TO return the body of my husband. Tell me where he is!"

The functionary looks at the document, unimpressed. "You cannot go to the burial site. The guards said they wouldn't exhume the body in your presence. Send someone else."

"But you are ordered to exhume the body," she says.

"That's fine. But they won't do it in your presence. Send someone else." He hands her the document back and walks out of the room.

"What to do now? Zbyś! My Zbyś will go." She runs out of the building and is back with Zbyszek in no time. "He will go!" she declares.

"Okay then. Take him," he says to another guard.

Danusia looks at Zbyszek with apprehension.

"They need to schedule the time," the functionary explains.

In fifteen minutes Zbyszek is back. "Let's go, Danusia." On the street, Zbyszek embraces her. "I have to be there at 5 PM with the buggy. You have to go to Międzyrzec now and start making preparations for the burial. I should be in Międzyrzec no later than tomorrow."

Danusia says a quick good-bye to Kristina and takes a bus to Międzyrzec. At home, she finds some unexpected faces. Marysia, Józio's sister from Koło, and her husband, Kazik, were able to get the permission to come over here from Koło upon receiving the telegram. The neighbors welcome Danusia warmly and bring her some food. Jędruś is in good health and well taken care of.

Late in the evening, a stranger comes to the house. He says he is Józio's friend from Auschwitz and wants to donate money for Józio's coffin. "Józio shared bread with me in Auschwitz," he says. "You can't possibly understand what bread means in Auschwitz."

"I am sorry but I want to pay for my husband's coffin myself. You may be able to help me in some other ways."

"I understand..., Madam." He leaves in grief.

In the middle of the night, a buggy from Radzyń arrives. In the icy blackness, Zbyszek bring home Józio's stiff and frozen body. Zbyszek arrives not only physically exhausted but also mentally drained, and emotionally devastated. The experience of recovering Józio's half torn-apart and half-naked body directly from harsh winter soil, then cleaning and wrapping the body for the trip, and that interminable ride with his dead brother-in-law in the frigid, utter darkness of the ghostly night took its toll on young Zbyszek. By the time he reaches home, he is a wreck. But luckily Kazik is ready to take over his duty. Marysia convinces Danusia to stay with Jędruś, and runs out to assist Kazik. With God's help, they all survive this tragic night and in the morning the normal burial procedure takes its course.

Mama arrives from Warsaw after the burial. Without witnessing the drama, she is devastated nevertheless. They all are scared and confused. How are they going to survive without Józio and without Dad, with Jędruś and with this new baby on the way?

"Everything is in God's hands." Mama sighs feebly.

"Danusia, please give me Jędruś," Marysia asks. "You cannot even imagine how devastated my mother is. Józio is her only and very special son. And now, when Józio is gone, she has nothing left except this baby. Her days are numbered. Her health is rapidly deteriorating lately. Her greatest wish is to see Jędruś before she dies. You must let her see Jędruś, her only grandchild!"

"No way, I won't give you Jędruś!" Danusia's entire being rails against the very idea.

"But think about it, Danusia," Mama joins in persuading her. "We don't know how we are going to survive now without Józio and without Dad. Jędruś will have better food and better care in Koło. Marysia and Kazik don't have any children. With Józio's mother, they can take good care of Jędruś until we recover here."

"No, no!" Danusia cries violently.

"Think about it, darling," Marysia tries gently. "You are pregnant. You need to take good care of yourself. If you give us Jędruś even for a brief time it will be so much easier for you. And we can give you Jędruś back any time."

"No, no...," she cries, but less violently.

"We will be helping you as much as we can," Marysia declares. "We will be sending you money," she tries to sound reassuring.

"I think Marysia should take Jędruś to Koło to show him to Józek's mother," Mama concludes.

Danusia says nothing. The next day, Kazik and Marysia with little Jędruś on her lap depart by buggy to the train station. Jędruś's confused chubby face, his heavenly blue eyes, and golden hair sticking out from under his hat, sink deep into Danusia's heart. She sobs and cries bitterly while Mama tries hard to calm her down.

The drama of losing Józio leaves a permanent scar on Danusia's psychic. From now on, she is a pregnant widow in the middle of the cruelest war ever fought. Giving away Jędruś makes her suffering even greater. She has lost her husband and her baby almost simultaneously and finds herself alone with plenty of time for grieving and meditating. Surprisingly, the tragedy does not directly impact her pregnancy. The second baby has been growing nicely, giving her frequent energetic kicks.

"This baby will bring me good luck!" Danusia is convinced.

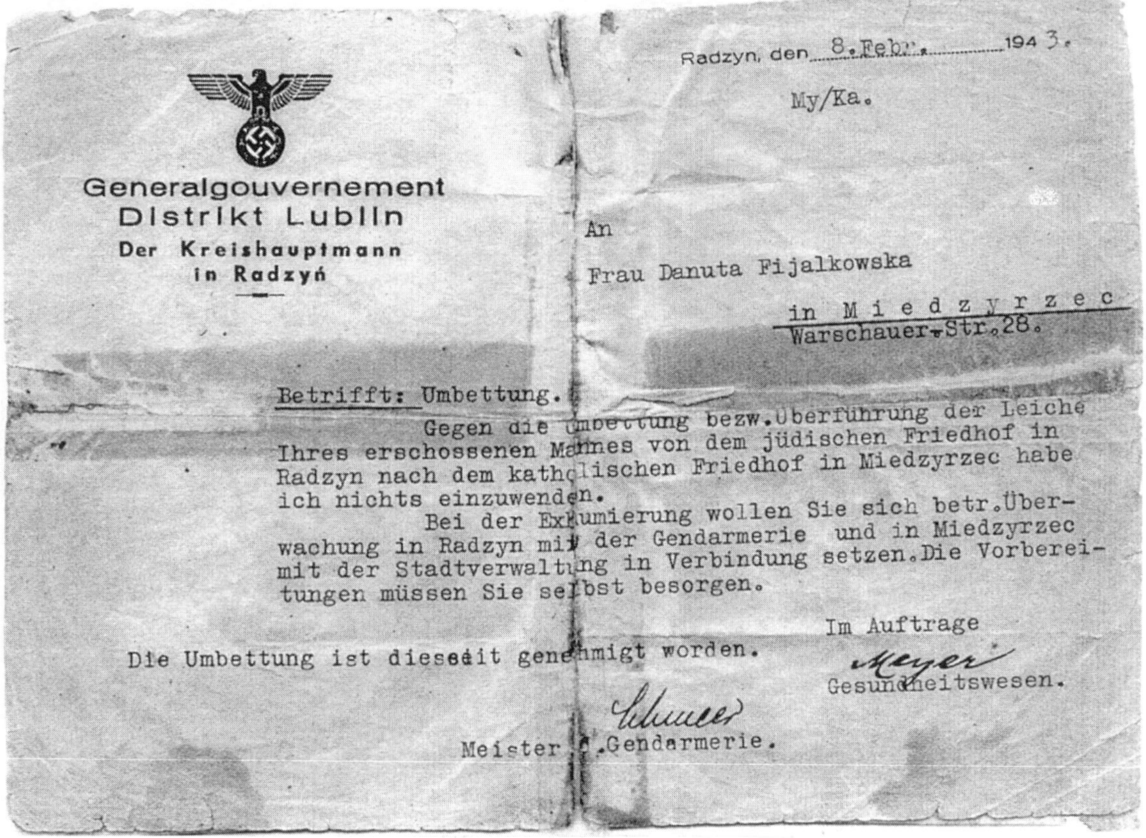

Generalgouvernement
Distrikt Lublin
Der Kreishauptmann
in Radzyń

Radzyn, den 8.Febr. 1943.

My/Ka.

An

Frau Danuta Fijalkowska

in Miedzyrzec
Warschauer-Str.28.

Betrifft: Umbettung.

Gegen die Umbettung bezw. Überführung der Leiche Ihres erschossenen Mannes von dem jüdischen Friedhof in Radzyn nach dem katholischen Friedhof in Miedzyrzec habe ich nichts einzuwenden.

Bei der Exhumierung wollen Sie sich betr. Überwachung in Radzyn mit der Gendarmerie und in Miedzyrzec mit der Stadtverwaltung in Verbindung setzen. Die Vorbereitungen müssen Sie selbst besorgen.

Im Auftrage
Meyer
Gesundheitswesen.

Die Umbettung ist diesseit genehmigt worden.

Schneer
Meister d. Gendarmerie.

34. Permission to transfer the body

35. Danusia at Józef's grave, February 1943

13

With Danusia's help, Mama runs the hair salon. Zbyszek frequently travels to Warsaw trying to earn money and take care of Dad in prison. Every other day Danusia goes to the cemetery at the outskirts of the town, about half an hour walk. She likes to go there, sit at Józio's grave, and be with him. After all, he didn't really die.... Spring approaches, the ground begins to thaw, and Danusia is eager to make some improvements to his grave. The simple wooden cross will stay but she can't wait to plant some flowers on his grave.

One day on her way to the cemetery, she hears loud German voices behind. The German language always frightens her. In her mind it sounds like barking or pistol shots—rough, mechanical, dry. The street is wide, with sidewalks on both sides, but very few people are around. The voices behind sound casual but commanding and self-assured. She glances back to check the situation. The scene behind turns her blood to ice. Two big superior humans, well-fed and well-dressed, in tall shiny boots with machineguns and attack dogs at their side, escort a small group of about six gray, ragged Jews, men and women of different ages. Apparently these people have been just caught and...and...! Oh, my God!

Danusia quickens her pace. They must be going straight to the cemetery. She looks towards the gray trees on the horizon. These people are being led to their deaths, just like that, casually! It's not a big deal for the representatives of the superior race to kill six sub-humans just like that. That's what the superior men are for.... And these poor souls...they've already given up; there is no escape for them in this world. They go like lambs to the slaughter, not only to their deaths, but straight to their graves. Oh, how horribly convenient!

Shaking in horror, Danusia turns toward the cemetery. This is the Catholic cemetery. They won't come here. They must be going to the Jewish cemetery on the opposite side of the street. She trudges to Józio's grave, drops down on a small bench, and falls into fervent prayer. Soon six clear pistol shots enter her prayer. She jerks with each shot as if her body were taking each and every one.

"Józio, my dearest, give me strength to continue living. I can't take it any more!" she cries. "It must be easier out there with you." She sits there for a long time too frightened to move or look around.

The actions of the SS-men frightened people for several kilometers around. No other human being is present. The place is deserted, only the dead, the graves, and Danusia...the elfin woman, mourning and shaking, but nurturing a new life within....

Before dark, Danusia gets up but can't force herself to walk the same way. She winds her way through the cemetery and later over the back roads. At dark she reaches home in pain and with a fever. After several days in bed, she recovers and returns to the hair salon.

"*Pani*, did you hear what happened near Zamość?" one of the clients whispers. "They rounded up entire villages, literally everyone, including the elderly and children!"

"They probably shipped all of them straight to the concentration camp," a corpulent woman says. "I heard that the families are separated like potatoes, fathers here, mothers there, children elsewhere. People say that in Majdanek the elderly and the weak are sent straight to the gas chambers."

The women shake their heads. It can't be true.

"I have heard that several cattle trains with thousands of little children from the Zamość region were sent to Germany to be raised as good Germans," another woman breaks the silence. "The children, some of them almost babies, are freezing to death in the cattle wagons in this weather. And apparently there are thousands of young children without food, drink or heat on the way to Germany."

"Aha, that's what Zbyszek was talking about." Danusia turns to her mother. "Remember, he was telling us about some cattle trains with small children. He said that in Warsaw people wait for those trains with food and drink, and try to retrieve the children."

"But no one knows what happened to the older children, ages 13 to 19," the corpulent woman says. "Oh God, how can you watch such a tragedy!"

"We may be next," a male voice makes an ominous observation. "It's so close. Zamość is south of Lublin and we are just north of Lublin. That's our district."

Suddenly, the creaky front door opens abruptly and a high-ranking German walks in. The conversation dies out instantly. People put down their heads in fear. Danusia looks around. No one is willing to handle the German. She takes a deep breath and trying to maintain her composure, walks to the visitor. "How can I help you?"

"Yes, I would like a manicure," the German replies.

Danusia's heart starts pounding. "But as you know, Sir," she stutters, "it is forbidden to perform manicures." She replies in broken German, pointing to a big sign: "Manicure Forbidden."[1]

"Please do it for me," he asks politely.

She hesitates for a moment and invites him to a small table. "Please wait, I have to prepare everything." She turns on a table lamp.

Mama looks at her with apprehension. "My God! What are you doing?" she whispers.

Danusia doesn't reply. Instead, she focuses her full attention on the task. If she cuts a nail too short or hurts his finger, she can be shot right here, on the spot. And why not? That's what the superior humans are supposed to do these days.... She works diligently, trying to remain calm. The room is completely silent. Everybody remains still. Only the buzzing of a fly mixed with Danusia's heavy breathing can be heard. Long minutes pass...it seems like an eternity.... No one dares to move. At last she is done!

"How much?" the officer asks.

"Nothing, Sir. I can't take any money for it," she replies firmly.

"Okay then." He takes out a notebook and starts writing something. "Here you are." He hands her a small piece of paper. "Go with this note to the depot here, on the Town Square, and you will get everything for the baby." He glances at her round figure and puts his hat on.

"Thank you," Danusia takes the note. The front door creaks, closing slowly behind the German, and the people relax instantly. Danusia, exhausted from stress, sinks into the chair.

"Show it to me!" Mama grabs the paper and tries to read it but without any success. No one in the salon can read the German's handwriting. Mama turns the paper up and down and against the lamp but she can't figure out what's there. "Maybe they will give you some diapers. You have nothing for the baby, my dear."

"But Mama...," Danusia sighs. "Those are the things that they robbed from the Jews. How can I take such things?"

"You have the moral right to take it, darling. The Nazis killed your husband! Soon you will have another baby. Do you know what that means?" Mama's eyes are blazing. She clenches her fists, looking at the door where the German disappeared.

"Danusia, you must go there," the heavy woman says. "Do you know that they are sending everything to Germany? If you don't take it, the Germans will get it. You better go there fast."

And so she goes. At the door she gives the note to the guard. He checks the note carefully and calls a higher-up who, in turn, calls a young Jewish woman from the depot floor.

"Give her everything for the baby," he orders pointing at Danusia.

The good-looking Jewish woman with thick dark curly hair and pale complexion takes Danusia into a huge storehouse and quickly piles up all sorts of things: cradle, carriage, table, diapers, clothing, even some toys. Danusia watches her with horror. This woman knows she will die soon. It's only a matter of weeks, or maybe even days. Most of the Jews in town have been already rounded up and sent to the concentration camps or killed at their graves. Only those who perform useful work for the Germans are still alive.

"Wait!" Danusia suddenly wakes up from her thoughts. "It's too much! How am I going to take all of this?"

"You must take it. The Germans killed your husband, I know, I know.... I am giving you the best things here. You have to take it!" The woman says urgently. "Do you have a buggy here?"

"No?"

"Then go and get one!" she orders.

Danusia quickly arranges for the buggy. When she comes back, the pile of baby goods is waiting for her but the Jewish woman is no longer there. Danusia looks for her but there is no time to speculate. "*Raus, Raus*!" The guard rushes her out. An hour later, she arrives at the house with a buggy full of baby goods.

Mama almost cries. "This is a miracle, Danusia!"

"That's my Józio, Mama. He takes care of me."

* * * *

Konrad comes home with a pile of mail. It's a chilly day in Ohio in the spring of 2001.

"Grandma! Letters from Poland!" he announces.

Danusia energetically gets up from her Lazy Boy recliner and rushes to the kitchen table. "A letter from Jędruś!" She tears the envelope open and starts reading. "Oh my God! Doctor Zalewska passed away!" She bursts into tears.

"Here you are, Grandma." Konrad passes her a box of tissues. "Calm down, Grandma, calm down." He gently touches her but she can't stop sobbing.

"You don't know, Konrad, what kind of a woman she was.... She saved your father from certain death when he was a baby, she saved so many children...." Danusia keeps wiping away tears. "Let me tell you about her." She chokes, clears her throat, and wipes away more tears. "Doctor Zalewska was in Warsaw together with my mother back in 1943 at the time when my first husband, Józio, was killed. Remember I told you about that?"

"Yeah."

"It was the beginning of February, a very severe winter that year. Since January, the Polish railroad workers had been sounding the alarm that thousands of young children were being transported in unheated cattle trains from the concentration camp in Majdanek westward, probably to Germany. The news spread with lightning speed. The Germans kept denying it but the cattle wagons with thousands of half-dead children were scattered all over the railroads leading to Germany. Some of those child cargo trains went through Warsaw. The women there made a fence with their bodies, stopped the train, and demanded the children. The convoy guards capitulated and the local people were able to rescue all the children from that transport. Doctor Zalewska was among them. She wanted to take a girl because she already had two boys. But one little boy, a charming four-year-old blond, begged her to take him home. She couldn't resist and brought the boy home. His name was Jarek. Around his neck he had a nametag. Jarek became her third and most caring and loving son. He later finished medical school and became a doctor. After the war, Jarek was able to find some remote relatives but he never found his parents. They perished in the gas chamber at Majdanek."

"I heard about the Zamość experiment, Grandma, and I read about Hitler's 'extermination for colonization' laboratory or something like that. Just recently, TV Polonia aired a documentary about it, reports and stories of those who survived the deportations by being selected for hard labor instead of the gas chamber. Wasn't that like an experimental killing program?" Konrad with bald-faced honesty admits some deficiencies in his historical expertise.

"We didn't know anything about this activity back then, during the war." Danusia admits. "Only years later, we were able to recreate the official policy of the Third Reich towards the Zamość region. In 1941, the Nazi government developed the so-called "Policy for the East" or *Generalplan Ost* ("GPO"). The objective of this plan was to resettle native Germans to the newly conquered lands in the east. After taking over the Russian territories back in 1941, Hitler ordered and Himmler began to implement a plan for the German colonization of the east. First, the territory to be colonized was defined. All Polish lands, Lithuania, Latvia, Estonia, Byelorussia and Ukraine, even going as far as Leningrad, Crimea and Dnepr, were designated as the colonization lands for the Aryan race. According to Himmler's data, the entire region was inhabited by about 5 million Jews and about 45 million so-called "foreign ethnicities." About 31 million inhabitants of the GPO region were destined for deportation to Siberia, a small percentage was scheduled for Germanization, and the rest was destined for extermination. Hitler intended to resettle ten million representatives of the Aryan race to this conquered territory.[2]

The Zamość region in the southeastern part of the General Government was selected as the experimental ground for the implementation of the GPO policy. On November 12, 1942, Himmler issued a decree designating the Zamość region as the first target for Aryan colonization. This experimental area spanned three counties, 297 villages, and consisted of over 110,000 Polish inhabitants, including at least 30,000 young children. The first round-ups in the Zamość region began in December 1942, and continued through the harshest winter weather until March 1943.[3] Thousands of Zamość children froze to death in the cattle trains. In one train found near Siedlce, the entire transport of over 500 children had frozen to death. In other transports, out of 100 children in one wagon, 20 to 30 were routinely found dead and thrown out from the train like garbage. It has been estimated that about four thousand "train" children made it alive to Germany and were delivered to German families for an Aryan upbringing. But the most horrible fate awaited the older children, especially boys ages 13–19." Danusia looks at Konrad with some concern. Should he know what happened to them...?

"I am afraid I know what happened to them, Grandma," he guesses her thoughts. "When I read about Auschwitz, I came across some notes about it. Those older Zamość boys were killed with phenol injections."

Danusia bites her lips. "They were too old to be germanized and too young to work well. So they were useless to the Third Reich.... The elderly were useless to the Third Reich, too. Thus, they were sent straight to the gas chambers in Majdanek near Lublin. The Third Reich afforded the inhabitants of the Zamość region a similar treatment as the one devised for the Jewish population. And that was just a pilot project to be later rolled over the entire eastern lands designated for the Aryan colonization...."

"But, Grandma," Konrad rivets his eyes on her, "I understand that the Peasant Battalions and the Home Army bravely defended the Zamość people. They organized self-defense, blew up bridges and railroads to stop the trains, and tried to rescue the transports."

"That's right. They were also attacking the German settlers who immediately began pouring into the Promised Land. Luckily for the human race, the Zamość experiment stopped in the spring of 1943 in connection with the Russian counter-offensive on the eastern front."[4]

The telephone rings. "It's for you, Grandma."

"Mundek, how nice of you to call...," Danusia sounds delighted.

"Hmm, Mundek, such a strange name," Konrad wonders. "Grandma has many friends with strange names. Interestingly enough, each such name carries with it an equally strange story. Why is it that my friends today don't have any exciting stories attached to their names?"

"Grandma, what kind of a name is Mundek?" he asks after she hangs up.

"I am not sure. I never thought about it. Mundek is an old friend of your grandfather."

"I bet you know some strange story about him, don't you?" Konrad looks at her expectantly.

She smiles. "As a matter of fact, I do have a fascinating story about him. Although it's not exactly about him but rather about his family."

"I hope it will have a good ending for a change..." Konrad grumbles. "Most of your stories have tragic endings. But here in America people like only happy endings. Can you find a story with some sort of a positive ending?"

"As a matter of fact, the Mundek story is very optimistic and it does have a happy ending. It's a very important story, I must say."

"Wow, I am impressed, Grandma, and I am real curious."

"You see, I didn't know Mundek during the war even though he was from Warsaw. I met Mundek only here in America, when I came to New York back in the seventies. In New York City, he had a house close to where we were staying. One day he went to the airport to pick up his mother who was coming from Poland. I went with him to pick up a package that she supposed to have for me. In the car, I met another man, a handsome Jew several years younger than me.

" 'This is my brother, Max,' Mundek introduced the man. 'Your brother? That's impossible!' I thought to myself. 'But you don't look like brothers at all,' I couldn't resist commenting.

" 'Because we are not related by blood...,' Max replied, smiling.

"I didn't want to be intrusive, so I didn't inquire further. At Kennedy airport, we waited for a long time in the anxious crowd. Back then every arrival from behind the Iron Curtain was a distressing experience with a lot of uncertainty up to the very last moment. Slowly, the passengers of the Polish Airlines LOT began to emerge one by one through the heavy security doorways. Among them was a small elderly woman in a scarf or rather a wrap on her head, in a gray coat and gray communist-style boots, with a multitude of bags and suitcases.

" 'Here she is,' Mundek said. But Max was already next to her. This big, elegant man, a real New Yorker by then, was on his knees there, in tears, in the middle of the exit path, kissing this poor woman's chapped hands. Crying with joy, she tried to hug and kiss his head. The scene was rather unusual in that people rarely demonstrate publicly so much respect and affection for their parents. Mundek finally joined them, kissed his mother, and the three of them moved away from the exit path towards me. Watching them from a distance, I was struck by the degree of affection between Max and Mundek's mother. So later on, I asked Mundek about it and here is what he told me.

"During the war, it was probably 1943, most of the Warsaw Jews were either rounded up and deported to the gas chambers or were still hopelessly fighting the losing battle in the Warsaw Ghetto. One day, Mundek's brother discovered his Jewish school friend, Max, hiding in a nearby park. At first Max got scared and started to run away but Mundek's brother called him up and begged him not to be afraid.

" 'They will kill me, they will kill me,' Max kept repeating in horror.

" 'But I won't kill you, I want to help you!' his school friend replied. 'I will take you to my mother. My mother is the best person in the world. She will help you, I am sure! She will protect you!'

"He brought Max home to his mother with complete and unshakable confidence that she would help Max. The woman was terrified. A widow herself with two young boys, she was struggling to survive from day to day. To help a Jew meant certain death for her and her boys. Huge notices aimed at reminding the Polish people about this inevitable punishment were plastered all over Warsaw. And Max was a archetypal Jew. Everybody could recognize his Jewish origin just by looking at him.

" 'But, Mama,' her son insisted, 'you are such a good person, you must help Max!' The boy had such a great faith in his mother that she couldn't say no. She tightly covered Max's head with a bandage and took the boy on a trip to her brother who was living in the countryside far from any village. It could very well have been their last journey. But they were lucky. They made it safely to the farm. Her brother was horrified but did agree to take the boy. There, hidden at the farm, Max survived the war. Later on, Max's relatives from New York found him through the Red Cross and brought him to America.

" 'I didn't do much,' Mundek's mother would later say. 'I just took him to my brother.'

" 'Yes, Mother, you didn't do much...,' Max would reply. 'You just risked your life for me.... And for that I am grateful to you to the end of my days.' "

"That's a great story, Grandma."

"But as always in life, there are plenty of good stories and plenty of bad stories," Danusia sighs.

"Yes, Grandma. You know, I just heard about the Jedwabne tragedy where the local Polish people under German command took part in the murder of hundreds of local Jews.[5] The PBS just aired a program about it. Is it really true?" Konrad raises his voice. "Grandma, is it true that the Polish people burnt 1,600 Jews in a barn in Jedwabne?"

Danusia reaches for his hand and looks deep into his eyes. "The way you put it, Konrad, is dangerous…it's a very dangerous oversimplification."

"Yes and no, Grandma! I know that the people dispute the number because no barn could hold 1,600 people. But whether we talk about 1,600 people or 400 people, it doesn't really matter. What matters is that we killed defenseless civilians."[6]

"Well, Konrad. Every action must be judged in its context. First you must know more about the Jedwabne killings in order to make an informed judgment."

"I don't care about the context. I've heard enough excuses that the Germans ordered the Poles to do it. The fact of the matter is that the Poles herded the Jews into the barn and burnt it. It was wrong, no matter what!" He gets up and heads to the door.

"Konrad!" Danusia shouts. "There are many things you don't know. So far no one told you the whole story. But it is your moral obligation to hear the whole story before making any judgment."

He looks at her reluctantly. "What do you mean, no one told me the whole story?"

Danuta smiles with a hint of sadness. "Let me tell you more about it, and then you decide for yourself, okay?"

"You know something about it that others don't?" he asks suspiciously.

She smiles sadly, her eyes looking absent. "Do you know where Jedwabne is?"

"Sure. It's almost on the Ribbentrop–Molotov partition line, but on the Soviet side. But why is that important?"

"Just sit down, please," Danusia says quietly. "First, you should know more about this region and its ethnic relations. Before the war, in small eastern towns like Jedwabne, the Poles held most of the administrative and governmental positions. Most of the doctors, lawyers, and teachers were Polish, the Jews ran businesses, and the Byelorussians represented mostly the working class. When the Soviets invaded Poland in 1939, the Poles were desperately defending their towns while most of the Polish Jews saw the Soviets as their saviors and welcomed them enthusiastically.[7] They greeted the invading Soviets with flowers;

some even kissed the Soviet tanks.[8] The Jewish youth spontaneously began to organize themselves into pro-Soviet militia groups. After all, the Soviets came to Poland to save the oppressed minorities. By eradicating the Poles, some of the Jews were hoping to make Jedwabne a purely Jewish town.[9] The invading Soviets found the local Jewish groups very useful in their infiltration of the Polish "Pany."

"I remember, I read about the Jewish militia groups fighting against the Polish Army in many places taken over by the Soviets," Konrad admits. "In Grodno, for example, the Jewish groups helped the Soviets take over the city."

Danusia nods. "In Jedwabne, the NKVD armed the self-proclaimed Jewish militia groups and gave them plenty of opportunities to settle old accounts with their Polish neighbors. The Soviets used the Jewish militia groups to annihilate the Polish population through killings, imprisonment, and deportations to the Soviet Far East.[10] The Jews were the ones who compiled the infamous deportation lists[11] and closely cooperated with the vicious Workers-Peasants Red Army, the so-called Cheka Operation Groups that followed the Soviet Army to organize the revenge of the "oppressed classes." The Cheka Groups in Eastern Poland had the same goal as the German *Einsatzgruppen* in Western Poland, namely to cleanse the land of the ethnic Poles. The Polish leaders were arrested and many of them executed in the local prisons. The Jewish minority had a lot at stake in collaborating with the Soviets. They immediately took over the administration of Jedwabne and assumed control over the assets and estates of the deported, imprisoned, or executed Poles."

Konrad grabs a handful of peanuts, crunching them loudly. "But, Grandma, how do you know all this?"

Danusia sights. "Remember, I lived in Międzyrzec Podlaski during the war. We moved to Międzyrzec in 1942 and stayed there until the end of the war. Międzyrzec was an interesting place because in September of 1939 the town was taken over by the Soviets. The people in Międzyrzec had vivid and bitter memories of the Soviet invasion and the response of their Jewish neighbors to the Soviet aggression. The Międzyrzec Jews welcomed the Red Army with open arms and manifestly celebrated the demise of the Polish State in front of their Polish neighbors. With the Soviet blessing, they immediately took control of the government in Międzyrzec and enjoyed their power tremendously. However, their festivities didn't last long. The Ribbentrop–Molotov deal was slightly revised after the Warsaw surrender and Międzyrzec was given to Germany. Thus, the Soviets left Międzyrzec and withdrew to the Bug River. About 2,000 local Jews fled with the Soviets to the East.[12] It is important to realize that the Poles considered this enthusiastic Jewish collaboration with the invading Soviet Army in Eastern Poland as high treason against the Polish State. The people in Międzyrzec were deeply hurt by the aggressive anti-Polish attitudes of the Międzyrzec Jews. Also, it's interesting to note that in Central and Western Poland the Jewish collaboration with the German oppressors against the Poles was not possible. Consequently, there was no widespread resentment against the Jews there."

Fixing her penetrating eyes on Konrad, Danusia lowers her voice. "You must remember that the Soviet occupation of Eastern Poland between 1939 and 1941 was marked by unspeakable terror and atrocities. The Polish intelligentsia was arrested, and many of them executed. Hundreds and thousands of Poles were loaded into the cattle trains and sent into oblivion in the Soviet east. Their Jewish neighbors led the NKVD squads under the cover of night to the Polish homes and later escorted the deportees to the train stations. They also took part in the executions of the Poles."[13]

Danusia takes a deep breath. "Now picture this," she pauses. "In June of 1941, the Germans take over Jedwabne on their way to Moscow. By doing so, they also free many Poles imprisoned by the Jewish militia in Jedwabne's prisons.[14] The released prisoners realize that their families are gone and their possessions are lost. The mass graves in the NKVD prisons, full of the murdered Poles, are still open, ready to claim more victims. The memories of unspeakable atrocities are painfully fresh in the people's minds."

Danusia closes her eyes. "The local Poles maintain that the Germans committed the Jedwabne murders because the Poles were not allowed to bear arms. They argue that German bullets were found at the crime site.[15] But the truth is that in Eastern Poland the Jews committed crimes against the Poles under the Soviet occupation between 1939 and 1941, the Poles retaliated against the Jews under the subsequent

German occupation, and the Jews prevailed again in Communist Poland. What really matters is that back then, power, force and violence was the only language and most of the people, regardless of their ethnicity, acted like the beasts."[16]

Konrad fidgets in his chair.

"Now make your judgment, Konrad. And remember this: Poland lost twenty percent of its population during World War II, over three million ethnic Poles and three million Polish Jews. Percentage-wise these are the highest losses among all the nations in the world. The United States, for example, lost less than a half percent of its people. Only about 123,000 of the Polish losses were due to military activities, while over six million losses occurred among the civilian population,[17] during 'peacetime,' if you will, as a result of the systematic extermination policy of a) the Third Reich towards both the ethnic Poles considered as a rebellious nation, and the Polish Jews, and b) the Soviet Union persecution of the ethnic Poles. It was the callous, intentional, well-organized, sophisticated, initially well coordinated, and always most brutal genocide of the entire civilian population of pre-war Poland.

"People like to point their fingers at each other—the Germans were evil, the Poles were the killers, too. Some of the worst concentration camp *capos* or NKVD *politrucks* were the Jews, the Ukrainians were bad, the Russian were barbaric, etc., etc. In times of catastrophe such as World War II, despair and confusion rein, civilized norms evaporate, and the worst human instincts thrive. By pointing fingers at each other, we all miss the most important lesson of this horrible war.

"The desire to dominate others and the climate of hatred is what I always fear the most. Once supported by radical ideologies, these human weaknesses lead to the greatest of human disasters. A few fanatics can easily create millions of criminal accomplices who willingly or passively accept their bosses' ideologies of hatred and blindly support their cruel drive for power."

Konrad turns on the television. CNN News reports from Jerusalem. "And this war in the Middle East, Grandma, these killings, suicide attacks, and constant funerals."

"There must be a lot of hatred there," Danusia nods sadly.

"And we just sit here and watch.... After all, what can we do?" Konrad sighs.

* * * *

The summer of 1943 is hot and dry. Danusia walks with difficulty as her due date approaches. At the beginning of July, the baby is ready to step into this vale of tears. Mama calls a midwife and a beautiful baby girl is born. Daddy's baby girl is slim and tall. She has Danusia's big brown eyes and Danusia's soft dark hair, a sharp contrast to Jędruś's blue eyes and thick, ash blond hair. The mother and the baby are doing great. The baby receives the name Elżbieta Maria and will be called Ela.

The whole town celebrates the happy occasion. People come to see the baby, some bring food, and others bring clothing. It's the middle of summer and many bring aromatic fresh fruits. Someone brings a basket of cherries; someone else puts a plate of big purple-red currants near Danusia's bed. She greedily tries everything.

"Oh, how delicious, so sourly sweet, just perfect," she takes a handful of currants and another one and another one.

In an hour she raves in pain. Her stomach is about to explode. Lying in bed, she groans and writhes in agony, her forehead wet from sweat. In a panic, Mama runs to the hospital and comes back with a bag of wormwood. Shaking from stress, she quickly prepares the bitter medicine. "You must drink all of it, my dear, at once!" she orders.

Danusia tries a sip and protests. "I can't, no way! I can't drink this nasty stuff, no way!" But frightened and determined, Mama forces Danusia to drink the whole glass, pouring the terrible acridity right into her throat. Two minutes later Danusia starts throwing up fountains of reddish stuff, sending them like flamingos meters away. After completely emptying her stomach, she lays down half-conscious. "Giving birth was easy but surviving afterwards was damn hard," she comments while fully recovered.

"No more cherries and currants for a while," Mama reminds her.

Zbyszek arrives from Warsaw with a letter from Dad who already knows about his new granddaughter. "Help me get out of here," he writes.

Mama is annoyed. "It's as if we didn't do enough," she complains. "Every second week he gets a package. And of course it's not only one package. It's always two packages, one for him and one for the guard who delivers the package. What does he think?"

"Next time, I want to go to Dad with the packages," Danusia declares. "I haven't seen him for such a long time."

In a couple of weeks, Danusia is on her way to Warsaw with two big packages of food. It's always a very dangerous journey. Germans frequently patrol the trains to Warsaw; confiscate the food, often arresting the people. But this time Danusia is lucky—no patrols. The packages are very costly and the trip is expensive, too. From the train station Danusia takes a *britzka*. At the prison gate, she introduces herself and talks with the guards. They seem friendly. After all, this is not a high-security prison.

"Oh, we know your father. He is a good electrician," the main guard, fat as a pig, comments.

She gives him one package and some apples to other guards. They eagerly take her to Dad. In ragged prison clothing, his cheeks sunk, his face gray, with bushy hair covering his lackluster eyes, Daddy opens his arms, crying, "Danuś, darling!" They hug each other for a long time.

Danusia stays longer than allowed but the guards don't mind. Dad told them about his special daughter and some of them even know her name. Danusia senses the positive climate around Dad and friendliness of the guards towards her. "I will be back soon," she pledges.

In a couple of weeks she is back with another set of packages and delicious apples for the guards. This time they wave to her and smile. Even Dad looks better. His eyes are brighter.

"Danuś," he says lowering his voice, "there is a chance they may release me soon. . . ."

Danusia is thrilled. "Oh, Dad! We pray for this moment every day. Look, Dad, I brought you a photograph of your little granddaughter. See how beautiful she is."

"How wonderful!" Alek exclaims. "But how different from Jędruś! He was blond and plump in that photograph, remember? And she is dark and slim. How strikingly different!" He puts the photograph into his pocket. "I have to show it to my friends here. They already know about Ela, now they will see this beauty." He pauses here and his face saddens.

"Danusia, how is Jędruś doing?" he glances at her. "Do you have any news from Koło? How much longer is he going to be there?"

Danusia grows deathly pale. Dad has just hit a very sore spot for her. It has been already nine months since Jędruś departed for Koło. She keeps writing letters asking for his return but Marysia keeps replying that it's impossible to travel to the General Government now. Instead, Marysia sends some money, trying to be helpful. But Danusia doesn't care about the money. She has plenty of food thanks to the local people. She only wants her son back. She has already asked several times for permission to travel to Koło but permission is given only for funerals. She asked Marysia to send Jędruś even with a stranger who would be traveling to Warsaw, but the child cannot travel without proper papers either, and Marysia claims she cannot obtain proper papers for Jędruś.

"I don't know how much longer." Danusia's eyes fill with tears. "No one is allowed to cross the border."

The next time Danusia visits Dad, it's already October. This time she brings pears and plums for the guards. They smile and wave amiably again. "Good news is awaiting you today," the main guard whispers to her cryptically. She walks to the visitation room where Dad is already waiting.

"What is it, Dad?" she asks.

Hugging her, he whispers in her ear: "They may release me today!"

A big guard walks to the room. "Wait here, they will bring your clothing," he says. After filling out many forms and papers, after reporting here and there, Dad is ready. Leaving behind eighteen months of incarceration, he walks out of the Mokotów prison into the golden streets of Warsaw with Danusia at his side.

First, they go to their apartment at the mint. Zbyszek is the only one living there now. After saying hello to old friends and neighbors, they find Zbyszek and together travel to Międzyrzec.

Mama cries with joy. Dad hugs her and rushes to the cradle with burning curiosity. Taking little Ela into his arms, he looks at the baby carefully. "She is even more beautiful than I thought. Look, these are my eyes!"

"And your hair too," Danusia laughs, looking at his bushy hair.

Christmas approaches quickly. They are still healing from the wounds of Józek's death but already look to the future with some hope. This past year the Germans suffered major defeats on all fronts. By

May 1943, the Allied forces had completely defeated the Germans in North Africa. In Italy, the Mussolini government collapsed and Italy declared war on Germany. In response, the German forces began occupation of Italy. Towards the end of 1943, the 8th British Army landed in Italy.

The Second Polish Corps under the command of General Anders became part of the 8th British Army. The Second Corps, consisting of 46,000 men, was formed from the Polish Army based in Palestine. Most of the men of the Second Corps left the Soviet Union with the Polish Army under the leadership of General Anders. They went through Tashkent, Krasnovodsk, Iran, and Iraq to Palestine, where in 1942 they met other Polish forces coming from the West. At that point a new Polish Army was born in the Middle East.[18]

However, the most significant developments took place on the Eastern front. The German defeat in the battle of Stalingrad at the beginning of the year, followed by another defeat in the battle of Kursk, and the subsequent Soviet offensive westward has been on everyone's mind. "The Russians are coming," people whisper. "And with them, the Polish Army is coming," others add with a strange gleam in their eyes.

Indeed, after the 1942 departure of the Polish Army from the Soviet Union under the command of General Anders, a Polish communist organization operating in the Soviet Union initiated the formation of another Polish military force from hundreds of thousands of Polish citizens still remaining in Siberia or Kazakhstan and from the Polish territories incorporated into the Soviet Union. In July of 1943, the first Polish military unit under the communist leadership was formed in Sielce near Moscow on the Oka River. The Polish Infantry Division named the Taddeus Kościuszko Division initially consisted of sixteen thousand men. Within just a few months, the Polish division was transformed into the Polish Corps consisting of forty thousand soldiers and by April of 1944, it became the Polish Army consisting of over one hundred thousand men. The Polish Army in the USSR under the command of General Berling came to Poland together with the Soviet Armies and subsequently took part in the storming of Berlin.[19]

While Polish soldiers were dying on the battlefield, fighting the Germans under the Soviet command, in Teheran *Grandpa* Stalin secretly negotiated with Churchill and Roosevelt the Soviet Union's territorial gains at the expense of Poland. Stalin was determined to get even with the old enemy from the time of the Battle of Warsaw and had the perfect opportunity to do so. His sinister plan to hold on to Poland's eastern territories which were invaded at the beginning of the war according to a secret partition deal with Nazi Germany, met no opposition from the two Western leaders of the Allied coalition.[20] To them, Eastern Poland was a minor issue in the scheme of their affairs.

In Teheran and later in Yalta, the 1939 Ribbentrop–Molotov criminal partition of Poland was given new life. The Ribbentrop–Molotov borderline was renamed the Curzon line and approved by the British and American leaders as Poland's eastern border with the Soviet Union. Almost half of pre-war Poland was officially given to the Soviet Union. The deal was made not only without regard to the Polish military contribution on all fronts of World War II, but also without Poland's participation and without even any consultation with the Polish representatives. The Soviet appeasement deal was kept totally secret. The vital information was withheld from the faithful Polish ally and, despite Poland's military efforts on the Allied side, the future of Poland was decided without Poland's having any say in the process. "The absentees don't have a voice," the old saying goes. "Never again about us without us!" the Polish saying goes today.

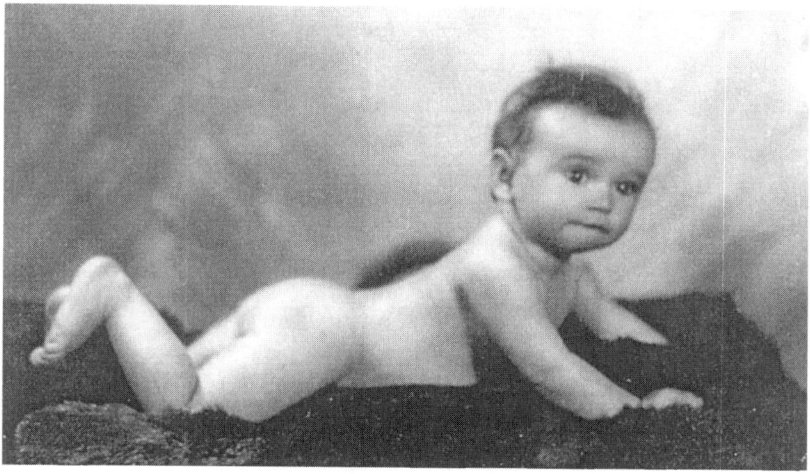

36. Ela, 1943

37. Danusia, Jasia, Alek, and Zbyszek. Międzyrzec, 1943

38. Danuta at Józef's grave, Spring 1944

39. 200,000 shoes of murdered Poles at the extermination plant in Majdanek

14

For the first anniversary of Józio's death, Zbyszek came from Warsaw. Also a letter came from Koło, letting them know that Jędruś was doing well. But the letter also brought the sad news that Józio's mother, Pelagia Fijałkowska nee Muchowicz, passed away at the beginning of the year. Danusia never met her mother-in-law but throughout the years she had received many warm letters and words of support from that woman. "The health of our mother rapidly deteriorated after Józio's death," Marysia writes. The news saddens everybody. But the letter enrages Danusia even more.

"They have stolen my Jędruś from me," she cries. "I have to go and bring him home even if I have to travel without any papers."

"Oh no, my dear, you are not free to commit suicide," Mama protests.

"Danusia, you cannot even imagine how dangerous it is to travel these days," Zbyszek supports Mama. "I hardly made it here. The Home Army attacks the trains on a regular basis. Railroads are destroyed and bridges are blown up.[1] Trains are derailed every day. From Warsaw I had to go through Lublin. The regular route was closed because the tracks were destroyed; and the Germans are now more aggressive than ever."

"The local people are saying that the nearby forests are in the hands of the Home Army," Dad adds with excitement. "Apparently thousands of well-armed partisans are stationed in this region. The Home Army has been attacking the German settlers who had moved to the Zamość region."[2]

Zbyszek looks at Dad cryptically. "Recently we have launched many more attacks. Some of them were truly spectacular. For example, did you hear about this latest attack on Kutschera? Have you heard about this one?" A triumphant look is painted on his face.

"A couple of days ago the Germans here were very agitated," Danusia says. "The people were saying that some sort of a high profile killing took place in Warsaw."

"That's right!" Zbyszek exclaims. "The Home Army Underground Court sentenced to death the SS and Gestapo Chief for the Warsaw district. General Franz Kutschera was given the death sentence for ordering and carrying out those countless mass executions in the Warsaw district. "Pegaz," the diversion unit of KEDYW [martial arm of the Home Army], executed the sentence on February 1, 1944. I know some of the plain-clothes female agents that took part in this action. Their pseudonyms are Hanka, Kama, and Dewajtis.[3] These girls are your age, Danusia. Some are even younger. It's incredible how courageous these girls are!" Zbyszek shakes his head with admiration.

"I haven't heard of any reprisals yet. But we can expect mass retaliation soon, I am afraid," Mama worries.

"There may be none," Dad replies. "The Germans are no longer so arrogant as they were at the beginning of the war. Back then they weren't afraid of anything. Today they are much more frightened. They already know that any retaliation will trigger another action of the Home Army."

"You're right, Dad," Zbyszek concurs. "The justice system that the Home Army runs is very effective. The death sentences on collaborators and perpetrators of genocides are carried out in such a way that the Poles, the Germans, and those who are sentenced and punished are informed about the verdicts."

"So how do you inform a General of the SS that he is sentenced to death?" Danusia is puzzled.

"The KEDYW officers must say to the convicts something like this: *In the name of Poland, you are sentenced to death.* Only after saying this formula, are they allowed to fire a shot."

"But it's more dangerous that way," Mama observes.

"But it has the greatest moral and psychological impact," Dad counters.

"I always wonder how the Home Army gets its weapons," Danusia marvels. "They must be getting those guns from the Germans."

"There are different ways to get arms." Zbyszek again sounds knowledgeable. "Sometimes it is possible to buy the guns. Sometimes entire shipments of arms are captured. But the most popular way is by ambushing and disarming German soldiers on the streets."

Mama looks at Zbyszek with alarm. "So, Zbyś, darling, I think you should stay here with us for a while. You don't really need to go back to Warsaw."

"Well, I can stay a little longer, but I really need to go back as soon as possible."

Dad looks at Mama. "You know, Jasia, that Zbyszek is working towards two degrees, one in the German trade school and the other one in our Secret Teaching Organization at *Komplety*. That's a very intense schedule."

"And very dangerous one," Mama replies angrily. "The Germans already know about the *Komplety*, and there have been many round-ups during these *'flying'* classes. I worry about him all the time."

"But Mama, next year I will get a Polish high school diploma!" Zbyszek replies proudly.

"Only if you are alive next year," she counters snappishly.

A week later, Zbyszek is on his way to Warsaw. Mama fearfully walks him to the train station and gently blesses his light brown hair for the journey. Since the arrest of the hair stylist at the train station, she panics over any train ride. But life must go on and she can't hide the 18-year-old boy under the mattress for God knows how long.

Spring is coming and with it more news from the Eastern Front. The Russians have been on an uninterrupted counter-offensive for several months already, destroying most of the southeastern wing of the German forces in the process except the 17th German Army that still exists but remains stranded in the Crimea.[4] Four million Soviet troops are spread over a 900-mile wide front, and the Soviets are engaged in the full scale planning of the final stage—the Byelorussian offensive.

Named *Bagration*, the Byelorussian offensive symbolically began on the third anniversary of the German invasion of the Soviet Union. Comprised of 1.4 million troops, four thousand tanks, and six thousand airplane fighters, the Soviet forces descended upon the German Army Group Center and by July 4, 1944, completed the encirclement of the German forces around Minsk.[5] The second phase of the offensive took place between July 5 and July 29. On July 13, the Soviets recaptured Vilnius, soon thereafter Grodno, and on July 27, after encircling another large German grouping, they took over Lvov and rode into Brest on the Bug River.[6]

The frontline is already less than half a day from Międzyrzec. Chaotic crowds of German military forces rush west. Flocks of military vehicles and fragmented infantry detachments crowd the roads. In the background, the horrifying echoes of the artillery hum and ghastly whistle from *Katiushas* resound day and night. Dad rushes to dig a hideout against bombs and shrapnel in the back yard.

"I think Zbyszek should be with us for this changing of the guards," Mama insists. "Who knows what kind of borders the Soviets will erect and where? We may end up on the opposite sides of some sort of sealed off borders again. God forbid another such problem, this time with Zbyszek!" She sounds the alarm.

Dad stops digging and straightens his back in pain. "But how are you going to get through to him?"

As always, Danusia has an idea. "I will go to the post office to call Mr. Gara. He will send Zbyszek here."

"Very good, my *Molodiec*!" Dad always calls her *Molodiec* when pleased with her. In Russian *Molodiec* means a young brave boy.

Leaving the house, Danusia notices two German soldiers near the front door. Their uniforms are slightly different from the frightening SS or Gestapo outfits. They must be from the Wehrmacht then. The two soldiers are no longer puffed-up or haughty but rather insecure and underfed. Their faces are stricken with fear. But what kind of faces are they? These are young boys, no more than sixteen years old, their delicate childish skin not even ready to grow a beard or mustache. One of them leans against the house, trying to catch his breath; the other is hiding in the bushes near the house and actually cries like a child.... The scene grieves Danusia's heart and she is about to invite them home but before she says anything the two boys run away like rabbits.

She walks down the street full of apprehension. The frontline is near the corner. The Soviets are coming. Is that good or bad? What is going to happen now? At least she can communicate with the Soviets better than with the Germans. Her Dad is fluent in Russian. That should help.

The streets are deserted, no Germans with attack dogs and no civilians either. People are busy building shelters and preparing for the siege. But the post office is still open.

"Mr. Gara! Dear Mr. Gara!" Danusia yells into the receiver. "Please tell Zbyszek to come here at once! It's an emergency!"

"*Pani*!" a postal worker says to her. "How do you want him to come? On foot? The trains don't run anymore."

At home the shelter is growing deeper and wider. Mama, with little Ela around, tires to cook and stock up some food. "Did you get through to him?" she asks in panic.

"I left a message for him. But apparently the trains aren't running anymore. I don't know whether he would be able to come at all."

By the evening, the shelter is dug out but Dad is totally exhausted. He lies down on the sofa, unable to move his arms or legs. It's already getting dark. The sound of gunfire grows louder though.

"We still have to fill the shelter with straw. And we must do it today because tomorrow may be too late." He gets up with difficulties and goes back to work. Danusia works with him.

As darkness falls, a big truck drives up to the front door. Mama runs out. The doors of the truck cab open and Zbyszek jumps out. "What happened? What's going on here?" He yells from the distance.

She runs to him, crying with joy. "Zbyś, Zbyś!" she kisses his hair.

"What's going on?" he asks nervously.

"The front is coming. It's near the corner. I wanted you to be with us. We must be together now."

"That's all? Is that why you summoned me here? Oh God! Mama! What did you do?" With frustration, Zbyszek turns around to the driver: "Okay, *Panie* Krupa! Everything is fine. It seems to be a false alarm." Krupa waves and drives away.

Danusia runs to Zbyszek with fervor. "You made it, my little brother, you made it!"

"Yes but for what?" Zbyszek asks coldly.

"We need to be together when the frontline comes. Otherwise you could be sealed off like Jędruś." Her voice trails off.

"Aha.... That's what this is." Zbyszek walks into the house. Dad is delighted to see him but Zbyszek is upset and tense. "You all don't understand! I belong to an organization...! I must be back in Warsaw tomorrow! Otherwise they will treat me as a deserter. I thought someone was killed here or something like that. I barely caught this Krupa delivery truck at the very last moment and...here you are! You just want to see me! How could you do this to me?"

"Okay, we'll talk about it later. But now let me show you something." Dad takes him to the back yard and proudly demonstrates his shelter. With Zbyszek's help, they quickly put some final touches on their construction and sit down, ready for a well-deserved supper.

"So what's up, Son?" Dad is anxious for the news. He hasn't received his *Bulletin* for a long time and he doesn't have his radio either. Recently, he has repaired some radios for the Germans and was able to catch some Russian stations but no news about Poland.

"A lot is going on, Dad. Have you heard about an attempt to assassinate Hitler? This one was unsuccessful but the next one will do the job for sure. But more importantly, did you hear about our victory at Monte Cassino in Italy? That's a story! Our 2nd Corps under the command of General Anders captured the German monastery fortress at Monte Cassino.[7] What's so exciting about this victory is that there were several major attempts to capture the monastery. I have a great article about it. Apparently it was an important strategic victory, the opening of the passage to Rome for all the Allied forces. Listen to this!" He pulls out *bibuła*.

> The Americans staged the first attack on Monte Casino in January of 1944 but were defeated within one month. Then the British went with carpet-bombing in preparation for a second attack by the New Zealand and Indian forces. Well supported by the British bombers, they staged two attacks but were unsuccessful. Suffering three defeats in a row, the Allies asked General Anders whether the Poles would like to try. General Anders had only a few minutes to make a decision. It was clear that a Polish victory at Monte Casino would advance the Polish cause on the world stage. Thus he took the risk. After one week of heavy fighting, the Polish Corp captured the Monte Casino fortress and, after six months of Allied struggle, opened the passage to Rome. It was a spectacular victory dearly bought with heavy losses in very trying circumstances. The terrain was very steep with artillery bunkers carved in the rocks, sophisticated mine fields everywhere, and the best German units of the Parachute and the Mountaineers Divisions firing at them from the fortress above. Our Corp first captured the monastery, next two nearby mountains, and moved on to the so-called Hitler line. They took over another German positions at Monte Cairo on May 25, thereby breaking the Hitler line. Those victories enabled the Americans to enter Rome on June 4, 1944.[8]

Dad nods. "Sounds like a spectacular victory that should strengthen our position within the Allies coalition, but I wonder what price we paid for it…."

Zbyszek folds the paper with passionate pride. "But you don't realize what all this really means!" He looks at them solemnly. "The Home Army is ready to call an uprising in Warsaw any day now. Right at this very moment, the uprising alert is in effect. This is why I have to be in Warsaw tomorrow, do you understand? I have to be there tomorrow!" he shouts with fury and gets up. "Anyway," he tries to calm down, "the victory in Italy means that Italy becomes another important location from which the Allies can send their air support to Warsaw."

"Let's go to sleep then," Mama softly suggests.

The night is very short though. Just before dawn, the terrible whistling of the Soviet *Katiushas* brutally awakens them. Trying to snatch some food on their way, they rush to the shelter. The bombing goes on and on throughout the day, a hundred times stronger than the familiar Warsaw air raids. For hours, they can't stick their noses out. Little Ela cries from exhaustion. In the afternoon, the attack subsides and Dad rushes to the house to bring more food. On his way back, the artillery goes back into action. The bombs are not directed at the town but rather at the outskirts and the surrounding villages. Huge bomb blasts and the towering flames of burning nearby villages persist throughout the day. Towards evening, the devilish whistling and uproar quiets down. They strain their ears. Suddenly, loud footfalls resound above their heads. Clearly, someone is approaching the shelter.

"*Kakij Germaniec jest*?" a Soviet soldier checks the shelter.

"*Germaniec niet*," Dad replies.

"*Nu vychadi*!"

"Let's get out!" Dad orders.

A tall angular Soviet soldier smiles at them. He is filthy and visibly exhausted. Big dark circles underline his blue eyes and blood trickles down his cheek. Danusia rushes into the house and comes back with hydrogen peroxide and a bandage.

"*Nie nada*!" the soldier protests, trying to wipe trickling blood with the sleeve.

"*Nada, nada*!" she replies categorically and dresses his wound.

"*Polskaja Armia prichodit*!"

"Really? The Polish Army is coming!" Danusia yells.

"Yes, I heard about that. I bet it's General Berling's Army, right?" Dad questions the soldier. "They must be coming from the Lublin side!"

"*Da, da. Kanieshno*!" The soldier confirms, pointing out to the road. "*Balshija Armia*!"

"Jesus Christ, our boys are coming!" Mama kneels on the ground in tears and raises her hands giving thanks to God.

The Soviet soldier looks at her with displeasure, waves to them, and moves on.

They stand there in the yard, confused. Danusia looks around with uncertainty. "Does that mean we're free now?"

"Not until we get Warsaw back," Zbyszek replies without hesitation.

"You are right, Son," Dad adds. "We must get Warsaw and our government back."

"But the Soviets can be in Warsaw tomorrow!" Danusia states the obvious.

"For this occasion we need a radio. And finally we can have one!" Dad announces and rushes out the door.

Zbyszek walks impatiently around the house. "Mama, I need to go back to Warsaw at once!"

"That means you would have to cross the frontline," Danusia observes.

"You see, I told you! It's all your fault! Now I will have to go on foot."

Dad returns home with a radio and urgently starts plugging it in. For a while, he gets only static over the airwaves, then a Soviet station, and finally the Soviet news. They all gather around the table. "Be quiet!" he roars at them, straining his ears for every bit of news. "The First Byelorussian Front has already reached Radzyń. It means the frontline is upon us," he spits the words in short intervals.

"It's less than an hour from Warsaw," Zbyszek exclaims.

The whistling and crackling grows and the Soviet station disappears. Dad nervously browses through the waves. Suddenly, they all hear a strong clear Polish voice.

"Warsaw Has Risen! Warsaw Has Risen!"

Zbyszek jumps up wildly.

"Be quiet!" they yell.

> At last the long-awaited day has come! The day for which we have been waiting five long years in anguish and pain but with dogged determination. Today, the Commander of the Home Army declared open war on the German invader. After five years of underground and resistance, the Polish soldiers professedly stand up to regain freedom for Poland, dignity for the Polish people, and administer justice for terror and crimes committed on the Polish soil. The time has come for the German invader to account for desecrating and destroying everything that's holy to us. An aura of liberty and freedom arises over Warsaw. Compatriots, to arms! Warsaw is calling upon you!

The speaker's voice fades away. The listeners remain speechless. Their hearts are utterly melted. Warsaw fights! Poland is rising! Liberty will be here within a matter of days!

Zbyszek almost cries in fury. His battalion is fighting, all his friends are fighting, and he seats idly here in Międzyrzec. He feels like a deserter in hiding. "I must go back, no matter what!"

"Don't worry, Son. The whole thing will be over soon, before you could even get there," Dad pats him confidently. From then on, they are glued to the radio around the clock.

The Warsaw Uprising, known as the Operation Tempest, was ordered by the Home Army (AK) Commander Bor-Komorowski with the approval of the Delegate of the Polish Government in London. The plan was to coordinate the takeover of the city with the Soviet final push across the Vistula River in order to assure liberation by the Polish forces and to establish an independent Polish administration.

On July 19, soon after the Soviets entered Eastern Poland, Moscow radio urged the Warsawians to rise. At the same time, the Germans started to evacuate civilian offices from Warsaw and called on Warsawians to report to work on fortifications around the city.[9] In an atmosphere of suppressed exuberance, the Warsawians were ready to rise against the hated oppressors on their own accord. On July 31, the Home Army spotted a Soviet patrol in the suburbs of Warsaw. At 5:30 PM that day, Bor-Komorowski gave the order to start Operation Tempest on August 1 at 17 PM. The long-awaited Hour "W" finally came.[10]

The response of Warsawians is unprecedented. In complete unity, the entire city stand up to fight, the old and the young, men and woman, communists and capitalists, all underground organizations, no matter what their affiliation or beliefs. On August 4, the underground press reports:

> The Home Army already controls most of Warsaw. The Polish Government in Great Britain has requested that the Home Army be considered as the regular Allied Army and be given full support of the Allied forces. The first Allied planes with arms and food for fighting Warsaw have already taken off from Brindisi in Italy.[11]

On August 5, 1944, General Rokossowski, commanding the fast-advancing First Byelorussian Front, receives a simple and unequivocal order from Stalin to stop the offensive on Warsaw and await further orders.[12] Suddenly, the Soviet offensive comes to an abrupt halt. The fleeing Germans immediately comprehend that sudden change of heart, stop their retreat, and send reinforcements to crash Warsaw.[13]

By halting the advances of the Soviet Army towards Warsaw, Stalin hoped for a quick defeat of the Warsaw Uprising.[14] Despite Churchill's urgent requests for permission for the Allied fighters to land on the Soviet side of the frontline, Stalin didn't approve the landing. In the first weeks of the uprising, the Allied planes, many of them with the Polish pilots, took off from Great Britain and Italy, carrying arms and food for fighting Warsaw. The round-trip non-stop fighter flights from England or Italy to Warsaw, 2800 kilometers without refueling, entailed unreasonable risk and extensive casualties. The entire Allied air support to Warsaw quickly became unsustainable due to heavy losses. After 199 sorties consisting of 97 Polish and 105 British flights, the air support was discontinued.[15]

By the end of the first week of the Uprising, the underground press reports:

> Warsaw is fighting! The Warsawians bravely hold their ground, desperately preserving their positions. However, the Soviet Army stationed at the bank of the Vistula River is not advancing while the Germans are sending reinforcements to Warsaw. The most brutal Nazi formations, SS Viking Panzer Division and SS Hermann Goring regiment with most murderous penal brigade thugs are believed to be moving towards Warsaw!

"What's going on?" Dad wonders. "Why are the Soviets stuck there?" He tunes in on his short-wave radio and catches a distant

Russian voice. Soon he flushes with anger. "This must be the end of the world!" He exclaims and heads to the door.

"What is it?" Frightened, Danusia stands in his way.

He looks at her reflexively and sits down again. "Unbelievable, just insane! The Soviets call the Home Army a handful of rebels... and...the Warsaw Uprising a gang of power-seeking criminals![16] Can you imagine this kind of iniquity! And they talk about some puppets in Lublin as the legitimate Polish government. No one has ever heard of those jerks!"

On August 11, the radio reports:

> After heavy fighting and extensive losses, the Warsawians have lost their positions in three districts: at Wola, Ochota, and Muranów. In the lost districts, the Germans conduct mass executions of the civilian population. It is reported that thousands of Warsawians are being executed every day.[17]

The listeners are seized by fear. What's happening? What's happening to their friends, to their neighbors, to their home? And how about the Polish Army that stands near Warsaw with the Soviet forces. Why don't they move to help Warsaw?

The next day the Warsaw radio station broadcasts a desperate plea for help. The Home Army Commander issued an order to all units of the Home Army in the country to provide reinforcements to Warsaw. The situation in the city is dramatic. The Allied air support has been terminated while the German air raids intensify. Every bit of help counts!

But the Soviet Army tightly controls the access to Warsaw from the east and makes sure that no units of the Home Army break through to Warsaw....

With every passing day, however, the drama of embattled Warsaw is gaining momentum on the international scene, putting more pressure on Stalin. On August 12, Churchill once again asks Stalin to provide support to the Warsaw Uprising. On August 18, a large number of American airplanes appear over the sky of Warsaw. All together 110 flying fortresses supported by 73 fighters make 1300 drops of arms and supplies for the Home Army.[18] By this time, however, the Home Army has been carved up into four different pockets of resistance and consequently intercepts only 380 drops.[19] On its return flight, the American mission suffers heavy losses and further flights are cancelled.

The next day, the Polish radio reports:

> Paris rose today! The French people take over their capital. The French Resistance closely cooperates with the American Command to coordinate their attacks inside the city with the final push of the American Army into Paris. Assailed from all fronts, the German garrison has begun to withdraw!

"Damn! I can't listen to this!" Dad shouts. "Is there a curse on us...?" He goes out to get some fresh air. Nearby, a group of neighbors gesticulates vividly.

"Something must have happened," he worries.

One of the women from the group walks towards him.

"What happened there?" he asks.

She gives him a wild look. "See there?" She bursts in fury. "See that smoke on the horizon! That's burning Warsaw!" she yells in a wild voice.

Dad stops, his eyes fixed on the pillar of smoke high in the sky. That's his home, his furniture, his books, his photo albums, his life....

"They will succeed, they just must hang onto their positions a little longer!" Zbyszek joins him from behind.

"Hoping for what? A miracle?"

"But Dad! The mint is very well fortified. Our group commander, Pełka, is excellent. He has the rank of Major in the Home Army."

"Yes, yes, Pełka is excellent, so what?" Dad stands in silence and watches the sky.

Throughout the entire war, Pełka, his real name Mieczysław Chyżyński, has been running a big underground operation, producing on a mass scale fake identification documents for the Home Army. This low-level quality control manager at the mint was a commander of the Home Army Group "PWB/17" in charge of defending the mint fortress in the Old Town.[20]

"Pełka's group was about to get *Arbeitskarte* for Józio, but they didn't make it on time...," Dad sighs. "You can't blame them, though. They saved so many lives."

In the following days, the main attack is aimed at the Old Town. The mint fortress represents the primary target in the Old Town. Heavy bombing continues around the clock. Relentless diving Stuka planes proceed with the systematic devastation of the city, street by street, house by house. The roar of approaching dive-bombers paralyzes the defenders of Warsaw. Some attempt to sing to control their fear, others pray, yet others are simply ready for their fate. To many, there is no going back: it's either win and regain their freedom and dignity, or die. To these men and women of Warsaw, life in oppression is not worth living anymore.

On August 26, the Poles listen to radio reports on the great victory parade in Paris. Fighting under American command, the French armored division was given the honor of spearheading the advance to Paris. General de Gaulle paraded down the Champs Elysées greeted by enthusiastic crowds of thousands of liberated Parisians. The Third French Republic had been restored![21]

While the victory parade takes place in Paris, the Poles learn that the Old Town has been lost in Warsaw. The mint was fighting to the last bullet but was ultimately overtaken by the SS forces, the gendarmerie, and a flame-thrower battalion supported by the Wehrmacht. The Home Army Group PWB/17 under the command of Major Pełka with less than 100 soldiers retreated from the mint towards the desperately defended Śródmieście district.[22]

A large group of civilians was left behind in the labyrinths of the mint's basement. Those left succumbed to such an unbearable level of mental anguish that they became unable to escape or even stand up. In addition, the withdrawing Army Group PWB/17 left behind about thirty heavily wounded friends. Doctor Petrynowska, known in the underground as "Rana," meaning "Wound," decided to remain in the building with her patients.

A herd of ferocious enemies swarmed the ruins of the mint from all directions. Talking in many different languages, the invaders had difficulties communicating with each other. The Nazi SS forces under the command of Colonel Schmidt consisted of about 1500 men representing all sorts of human refuse from many different countries and demonstrated blatant disregard to human life and any civilized norms.[23]

Plundering through the basement maze of the mint, the savage group burst into the medical shelter where Doctor Petrynowska was performing a surgery. She turned to them, saying: "Hier, Lazarett!"

"Move away!" one of them ordered.

"No, I can't move away right now! I am a medical doctor and can't leave my patients," she replied.

The SS-man clenched his teeth and opened fire with his machine-gun, killing Doctor Petrynowska and her patient instantly. Enraged, the conquerors proceeded to throw grenades on the beds of the wounded patients. Only a handful of nurses survived the slaughter. They were subsequently sent to dismantle the mint barricades and together with several more civilian men survived the initial fury of the attackers.

Most of the civilians found alive in the basement did not survive the onslaught, however. They all were loaded into *buda* trucks and sent to the Gestapo prison. None of them was ever seen again. All patients in two hospitals were killed on the spot. The entire civilian population was either killed or sent to concentration camps.[24] The Old Town was emptied in preparation for its final hour of absolute destruction.

A few days after the slaughter, a number of articles appeared in the German press, describing the glorious victory in the Old Town. *Das Reich* and *Signal* included the following article that was subsequently reprinted in the Polish media.

> For several days, the Reinefarth group attacked with heavy weaponry a large building complex in the Old Town. The front line extended for about 250 meters. Mine-throwers and heavy cannons tore open thick reinforced concrete walls, heavy bombing destroyed the courtyards, and Goliath tanks together with armor piercing artillery forced the defenders down from the higher elevations. But inside the molehill of cellars, in the maze of basements and corridors, the fight raged on while the monumental buildings were turned into a stack of rubble in a permanent cloud of smoke and dust. Eventually the forces of the Wehrmacht, SS, police, gendarmerie, and the flame-thrower battalion came together, the basement maze was ultimately overtaken and Colonel Schmidt received a report that the immense ruins at last have been captured.[25]

Dad listens to the news about the destruction of Warsaw flowing over the airwaves and feels numb. How strange.... The drama of Warsaw transcends any words and feelings. Warsawians are dying by the hundred of thousands; they will all die with Hitler breathing his last venomous breath and Stalin waiting in peace until the "wet work" is done for him. Even in their final, deadly grip, the two miscreants again join forces in destroying the Poles.

Troubled by the Polish situation, Roosevelt and Churchill write to Stalin again, expressing their concern over the international image of the Allied forces if the Warsaw patriots are hung out to be slaughtered. Under considerable pressure from his Allied friends, by mid-September Stalin decides to make some meaningless gesture towards fighting Warsaw. He is convinced that after six weeks of siege, the Uprising must be in its final days.

General Rokossowski who commanded the First Byelorussian Front stationed near Warsaw was of Polish origin. Together with General Berling commanding the First Polish Army formed by the Polish puppet communist government, Rokossowski was inclined to press for the offensive on Warsaw at the earliest possible opportunity. On September 8, he presented to his generals a plan to capture the district of Praga on the eastern bank of the Vistula River, just across from the fighting enclaves of the Home Army. At the meeting he asked General Berling to take the lead role in the offensive. By September 14, the combined Polish Soviet forces captured Praga and arrived within sight of tormented Warsaw.[26]

At that moment, Stalin, who had been under considerable pressure from the West to help the "Polish patriots," spoke with General Rokossowski. According to Rokossowski's subsequent recounts, Stalin, in a telephone discussion, expressed his desire to "provide help to the Uprising" and recommended using the Polish Army for the operation. Thus, on September 15, General Berling received an order to start preparations for crossing of the Vistula River and for descent operations.[27] At the same time, a courier from embattled Warsaw delivered an urgent request for help, indicating that the capitulation of Warsaw was a matter of days.

Under considerable pressure but totally unprepared, the Polish Army under the command of General Berling begins its descent on Warsaw the same night. By now, however, the German forces are fully prepared to repel the attack from the river side, lining up forty thousand well-armed men, 220 tanks, and about 416 cannons and mortars. Berling's Army also consists of about forty thousand men but they are poorly armed. The lack of landing equipment dramatically slows down the attack. Nevertheless, several Polish regiments reach the Czerniaków beachhead on the west side of the river. For five long days, the Polish Army struggles to preserve and strengthen its presence on the beachhead.[28] But their effort is doomed to fail from the outset because the Germans had plenty of time to put in place curtain fire for unwanted visitors. Many historians would later conclude that the only feasible way to conquer Warsaw in mid-September was through the encirclement of the city by the entire First Byelorussian Front.

In light of the heavy losses suffered by General Berling's forces, on September 20, General Rokossowski decides to send Soviet reinforcements to the Polish Army.[29] The 226th Infantry Regiment of the 8th Army arrives when the situation of the Polish forces is hopeless. On September 21, the Polish forces defending the Czerniaków beachhead send a desperate plea to General Berling: "Direct your fire on us!"[30] That night the Home Army left the Czerniaków beachhead through the city sewer and moved towards the last stronghold in the Mokotów district. Out of 42 barges and pontoons, only 8 barges with the soldiers of General Berling made it back to the east side of the Vistula River that night.[31] One may only wonder what was on Stalin's mind when he sent the Polish Army to Warsaw in mid-September.

Mokotów and Żoliborz, the last two districts of Warsaw, continued their solitary fighting until the General Command of the Home Army forced them to capitulate on September 30. The Warsaw Capitulation Act was signed on October 2, 1944, by Colonels Heller and Zyndram on behalf of the Home Army and by the Commander Von den Bach on behalf of the Germans.[32] Two days later, Stalin released General Berling from the command of the First Polish Army. Soon thereafter, General Rokossowski was transferred to command the Second Byelorussian Front. The First Byelorussian Front, together with the privilege of capturing Berlin, was handed to General Zukow.

"Warsaw has fallen!" the radio reports. Unbearable despair and fright courses through the hearts of the Polish people.

"What happened to all the people there?" Danusia asks in a hollow voice. "Old Mr. Gara, his daughters, the other friends, Wanda and Danka and Bruno and all the rest of them...?"

"According to the terms of the capitulation agreement, the Home Army soldiers become prisoners of war.[33] The civilian population is sent to a transition camp," the radio reports.

"Transition camp to what?" A mixture of irony and sarcasm resonates in Dad's voice.

"To the concentration camp of course!"

The smoke and dust over Warsaw doesn't settle, though. To the contrary, it will persist for several more months in front of the hopelessly horrified eyes of the Polish people.

While Warsaw's dramatic downfall is fresh in people's minds, the new bosses arrive in Polish towns and villages on the east side of the Vistula River. The new bosses speak Russian, the language that most of the Poles instinctively understand. The new bosses bring a new order as well. Some of the Poles are arrested instantly, many are sent to the Soviet Union, some are called for interrogations, yet others are given prominent positions in the newly formed local administration. Almost overnight, a new administration is created with totally arbitrary appointments. Young people are preferred. They are the hope of the new bosses. They can be molded and shaped according to their bosses' wishes.

Zbyszek is of great interest to them—a young, energetic and good-looking Warsawian who enjoys respect of the local people and yet can be easily guided. His family background is promising, too. His former affiliation with the Home Army raises some concerns though. He needs to be further rehabilitated. As a jumpstart to his future career, he is offered a position of director of the local farmers' cooperative.

Wow! Danusia is impressed. Her little brother would be the real director in the small town. But Dad is less impressed. "Let's wait and see. After all, who are they, the so-called Polish Government from Lublin? As far as I am concerned, our government is in London and these jerks are just Stalin's henchmen brought in suitcases by the Soviet Army, mere traitors."

"I shouldn't take this job then, should I, Dad?"

"It's your decision, Son. If you don't take it, they will find someone else. But beware. They first ask for your finger and before you know it, they grab your hand."

* * * *

On a quiet afternoon in 2001, Danusia, immersed in her armchair, holds a small photograph in her tiny trembling hand. Soon Konrad will be back from school, his parents will be back from work, and the house will be bursting with activity. But for the time being, Danusia enjoys the quiet moments of the day. She likes to spend these silent moments contemplating the best memories of her Zbyś, her beloved little brother. Zbyszek passed away in Warsaw just a year ago, at the age of 73. But she didn't go to his funeral and she didn't even visit his grave. She was too sick to travel to Poland. Her little brother was her hero, her mainstay through difficult times, and her great love. But she couldn't even say a prayer at his grave. Maybe one day she will go to Poland....

When she wakes up from her dreams, everybody is back and diner is ready. CNN reports on the American and British air attacks on the suburbs of Baghdad.

"Let's see the Polish news," Mae switches to TV Polonia.

"The Russian Army conducted two successful tests with strategic inter-continental ballistic missiles." They hear the voice of the TV Polonia political correspondent who interviews a left wing politician.[34] "So let's discuss this very troubling development."

"It is believed that Russia undertakes those steps in response to the American drive for military supremacy," the politician suggests. "In particular, the opposition of the Washington administration to the Comprehensive Nuclear Test Ban Treaty and their commitment to build the National Missile Defense System stimulates the arms race. What we observe on the international scene today should be of great concern to many. The arms control treaties are no longer viewed as a solution, and nuclear testing resumes all over the world. One of the Russian officials recently said that if the Americans deploy the National Missile Defense System and offer its benefit to Europe, the balance of power on the European Continent would be significantly changed."

"What do you read into this statement?" the journalist asks.

"The concern over the changing balance of power leads the Russians to increase their military presence and deploy nuclear weapons in the Kaliningrad region, right on the Polish borders."

"But this action violates the Russian commitment to assure that the Baltic Sea region remains free from nuclear weapons, doesn't it?" the journalist asks.

"Yes, but we must remember the Kaliningrad enclave represents a direct Russian border with the NATO block."

"The Russians officially denied any transfers of nuclear weapons to the Kaliningrad enclave," the journalist follows up, "but the findings of the American satellite surveillance contradict the Russian statement. Just a few days ago, the *New York Times* acknowledged that Russia deployed nuclear weapons in the Kaliningrad region. What steps, in your opinion, should Poland undertake in this situation?"

The politician moves nervously in his chair. "Obviously, this is a very urgent matter for Poland. We could present our concerns directly to Russia but as a member of the NATO Alliance we have to act through NATO channels as well. Our Defense Secretary recently submitted to the NATO Alliance the Polish request for international inspection of the Kaliningrad region. Unfortunately, the United States did not support our initiative. So far, the only result of our intervention has been an official statement issued by the NATO Secretary General that the Alliance 'took notice of the media reports with respect to the transfer of nuclear weapons to the Kaliningrad region.' Thus, our Ministry of Defense continues direct talks with Russia and tries hard to calm down the public hysteria."

"Talking about the public opinion," the journalist continues, "there have been some reports about a Russian–German deal with respect to Kaliningrad. We received many letters and phone call regarding this matter. It appears as if we are more afraid of the German–Russian rapprochement than of the nuclear weapons. Could you please comment on this matter?"

"It is appropriate to call it just a story or, rather, a rumor. If we believe that Kaliningrad plays a strategic role for Russia it would be rather unreasonable to believe that Russia would contemplate a sale of the Kaliningrad enclave to Germany. Those two philosophies contradict each other."

"As I understand it though, we are not talking about just a sale," the journalist argues. "We are talking about eliminating billions of dollars of Russian debt to Germany. It's kind of a forced sale, if you will."

"It is highly unlikely, but to put matters in perspective, Germany would have to obtain an approval for that kind of transaction from the

European Union. Until that happens everything remains in the realm of speculation."

"But many of our viewers, especially the older generation, already envision this event as a stepping-stone towards a future German request for the corridor through Polish territory, reminiscent of September 1939," the journalist pushes the issue.

The politician laughs. "Today there are very many air corridors across Poland and no one panics over them. I believe we tend to overreact...."

Danusia listens attentively and becomes visibly upset. "Overreact or not, we can't just sit and pray that somehow everything will be fine."

"Don't worry," her son calms her down. "This is another era. We have a global economy and multinational corporations today. No one in his right mind will fight for a piece of land here or there."

"You know, my dear, before the war, we heard all sorts of arguments from the so-called intellectuals convincing the public that nothing bad could happen to us. They were saying exactly the same thing—that this was the whole new era...."

"Maybe you are right, Mother," her son shakes his head upon reflection. "When it comes to Russian–German rapprochement, there has never been another era in their shared appetite for Poland."

"By the way," Konrad jumps in, "remember the book you borrowed for me about the Warsaw Uprising? Let me show you something." He rushes to his room and comes back with a thin, hardcover, well-illustrated book. "Look here!" He points to a black and white picture of a German soldier with his hands in the air, held at a gun point by the Home Army soldiers in the smoldering ruins of Warsaw. *Polish Bandits Capturing a German Soldier*, the photograph description reads.

"Let me see," Mae grabs the book and checks it over carefully. "This book is written by a German who took part in crushing the Warsaw Uprising!" she concludes with dismay. "And this was the only book about the Warsaw Uprising I could find in the main public library in Cleveland!" she exclaims in disbelief. "Yes, America is a free country," she thinks aloud. "The Germans have the right to brag about their abhorrent victories but it is our responsibility to write about this assault on humanity the way we experienced it."

"Except that it is very hard for us to think about this tragedy, let alone write about it," Danusia says quietly. "In the Warsaw Uprising, we lost 250,000 people, mostly civilians, our best youth and many children. It's more than the Hiroshima and Nagasaki losses combined, can you imagine that?"

"That's why the history is written by the victorious parties and not those who are defeated," her son observes. "And we always end up on the losing side, no matter how we play."

"But we should also remember," Konrad barges in with a remark, "that by engaging huge German forces, the Warsaw Uprising weakened the German resistance on the Western Front. In the middle of September, the Wehrmacht forces crushing the Warsaw Uprising were comparable in size to the German forces used by General Rommel in North Africa in the 1941–1943 campaign.[35] There is no doubt that the Warsaw Uprising provided a great relief to the Normandy campaign in the Western Front. That's where Giedzium with the Polish Armored Division under General Maczek fought the battles near Caen and Falaise, right?"

"Unfortunately, his efforts didn't pay off for Poland and the Normandy campaign was of no consequence to us," Danusia replies.

"We tend to feel guilty about all these defeats but that's wrong," Mae's eyes are blazing. "We shouldn't feel that way. When the Soviets stabbed us in the back in September of 1939, we didn't stand a chance, not because we were weak or because we neglected something but because the adversities were overwhelming. No other country in the world would withstand the coordinated Soviet–Nazi aggression. When the Germans leveled Warsaw to the ground in 1944 while the Soviets sunbathed on the other side of the river, we didn't stand a chance, not because we neglected something or made a mistake, but because we couldn't succeed against both miscreants aiding and abetting each other, and no one else in the world would have either."

"You are only partially correct," her husband says. "Many historians argue that the uprising was called too early and was inadequately prepared because our Government in London did not come to any agreement with Stalin in advance. If they were counting on Soviet support, they should have assured that support in advance, some would say. Without that kind of assurance, they took an unreasonable risk.

Stalin simply labeled them as power-hungry criminals and disregarded them all together."

Danusia laughs. "This assurance of Soviet cooperation wasn't as simple as one may think. Besides, the people were determined to fight. The uprising would have started spontaneously, no matter what.[36] But do you know what kind of conditions Stalin submitted to the Polish Government in London in exchange for the Soviet support?" Danusia sends him a provocative look.

"Some would say that looking at the results from today's perspective, the Polish Government should have accepted any conditions," Mae observes.

"Well," Danusia sighs, "just before the outbreak of the uprising, Stalin presented the Polish Government with four conditions under which he was willing to cooperate with them and give recognition to the Home Army. I don't remember all of them." Danusia strains her memory. "I know, however, that he requested the resignation of our President and the General Commander in London because he wanted to replace them with his own puppets."[37]

"As we know now, he did it anyway," her son adds.

"Next, he demanded that the Polish Government accept the so-called Curzon line, in other words the Ribbentrop–Molotov partition line. Putting it simply, it meant losing eleven million Polish citizens and one half of the Polish territory to the Soviet Union," Danusia replies.

"I understand how hard it would have been to accept this condition," Mae says. "But as we know today, that's precisely what happened no matter how strongly the Polish Government protested or objected to it."

"But how about the third condition? I wonder whether you or any reasonable decent person in the world would accept this one?" Danusia is ready to unveil her final blow. "Listen to this mastery of cynicism. Stalin had guts to demand from our Government the formal change of their position with respect to the Katyń genocide. In the fall of 1943, he called his own commission of experts, the so-called Burdenko Commission. It didn't take long for the prominent Soviet scientists to determine beyond any doubt that the Nazis committed the Katyń murders.[38] The date of the massacre was moved one year forward to 1941. Stalin demanded that our Government accept these farcical findings of the Burdenko Commission and adopt them as the official Polish position. Would you do that?" Danusia's eyes are getting round. They all put their heads down. "I guess I wouldn't," her son admits. "At any price," he adds with resignation.

"Have you heard the latest developments in the Katyń matter?" Mae asks. "Just recently, some British secret archives have been released to the public. Among them, some materials from the investigation of the Gibraltar airplane crash in which General Sikorski was killed. Apparently the documents refer to the NKVD as the perpetrator of the crime."

"That makes sense," her husband nods. "Stalin was obsessed with covering up the Katyń murders while Sikorski was relentless in digging up the truth."

"Do you know what else Stalin did?" Danusia challenges them again. "He requested that General Berling undertake special initiatives to convince the Polish people, in particular Polish soldiers, that the Nazis committed the Katyń crime. In January of 1944, the Polish puppet government appointed by Stalin issued a decree to commemorate the victims of the Katyń crime. Soon thereafter, the Polish Army held an official memorial ceremony in the Katyń Forest. All units of the Polish Army sent their representatives. The official ceremony began with the announcement of the Burdenko Commission report. The Soviets even allowed for a memorial mass to be concelebrated at the common graves site in Katyń.[39]

"After the war, I spoke with a man who took part in that ceremony. It was a very special moment for him because he himself was taken as a prisoner of war during the Soviet invasion. Moreover, he and the other soldiers from the Berling Army had many colleagues and close relatives buried in that Katyń forest. But you know what!" Danusia stops abruptly. "Back then, they all believed the Burdenko report! They really did! It took them many, many years to grasp the truth."[40]

"If they could believe it, maybe our Government could have bluffed and accepted Stalin's lie temporarily in order to save Warsaw and half a century of Polish independence," Mae wonders.

Danusia's eyes glitter. "I don't think their acceptance of Stalin's conditions would have saved anything. He would have taken over Poland anyway. But for sure the acceptance of this lie would have been a betrayal of those who died by Stalin's hand in that Katyń massacre, like my Julian."

"It could have saved Warsaw, though, because Hitler would not have been able to pour his insane rage for all his failures and defeats on that rebellious city. Our ancient, national treasure could have been saved.... But would it be worth it? I don't know...," Mae ponders.

"I don't understand one thing," Konrad who has been listening attentively, joins the discussion. "I keep hearing that Warsaw was leveled to the ground. There were many cities that were heavily damaged during the war through carpet bombardments and direct fighting, but they were never leveled to the ground. Airplanes and tanks can damage the buildings but they don't level the city to the ground."

"Well..., it was because there was never another city in the whole world that was destroyed just for the sake of being erased from the map...once and for all," Danusia says in a hollow voice. "The other cities like Stalingrad, Leningrad, or some German cities destroyed by the Allies towards the end of the war were destroyed in the battle, during the military actions, in an attempt to take them over, or in order to destroy the military industry. Warsaw was leveled to the ground after the uprising was already crushed. While recapturing the rebelling city, Hitler in his fury ordered that Warsaw be razed without a trace from the map and from human memory. No stone was to be left standing.[41] It was his order, literally. And the Germans executed his order, as always, with due diligence and great precision.

"After the Warsaw surrender, German Commander von dem Bach received an order to evacuate to Germany all raw materials, textiles, and furniture and subsequently level Warsaw to the ground. Countless trains were loaded with 'evacuated' goods and sent west.[42] Utilizing their last remnants of energy, the Germans began to demolish Warsaw street by street, house by house, and meter by meter, non-stop for over three months. They burned, blew up, and destroyed everything, including all houses, museums, archives, official buildings, and churches, starting with the Old Town, the Cathedral, the King's Palace, King Zygmunt Column, and continuing with the historic buildings, one by one. Only the Palace on the Water in the Łazienki Park was spared. It was not on the demolition order because it was in the park....

"By December 1944, Warsaw was turned into a desert of rubble. Hitler's press proudly announced that Warsaw was forever erased from the map."[43] Danusia stops. Her mind ventures back to the wreckage of Warsaw. The image of the dead town is dreadfully vivid in her memory. The Warsaw catastrophe was so great that some people really doubted whether the city could ever be rebuilt. Throughout history, countless cities have been destroyed by wars and natural disasters. But the destruction of Warsaw was different. It was driven by sick hatred and mad desire to annihilate the symbol of the spirit of the Polish nation, to erase this rebellious symbol from human memory once and for all.

"Right after the Germans were done with the top-quality, high precision, total demolition of Warsaw, the Soviets were ready to ride in," Danusia continues with bitter irony in her voice. "Konrad, do you remember when the Soviets entered Warsaw? In January of 1945, right? From October through January, the Germans had been working diligently, erasing Warsaw from the map. By January, they completed their vicious task and were ready to move out anyway. On January 17, 1945, the Soviets entered the deserted rubble of the dead city.

"Yes," Mae pats Konrad on the shoulder, "that's a true story, it's not a thriller. You should remember that!"

40. Major Mieczysław Chyżyński (Pełka)

41. Roman Marchel, PBW/17.
First Week of Warsaw Uprising

42. Home Army captures German prisoners after seizing the PAST buildin

43. State Mint Complex (PWPW)
Apartment building marked with "A"

44. PWPW apartment building before the war

45. German tank at the ruins of the PWPW apartment building, September 1944

15

The Soviet Army takes over Międzyrzec. Emaciated Soviet soldiers flood the area. Local units of the Home Army retreat to the surrounding forests. A new type of fear and apprehension grips the small town.

Young Zbyszek doesn't worry about anything. He is already nineteen and deeply in love with a beautiful blonde from the neighboring town. Walking down the street, he is totally consumed by the thought of seeing his girlfriend later that day. Suddenly a Soviet soldier blocks his way. "Do you have a watch?"

"Yeah," Zbyszek replies, rather bewildered.

"Give it to me because I need a watch," the Soviet says.

Zbyszek takes a step back. It's not a question whether he wants to give away the watch or not. He can't give it away because the watch is not his. It's a very special watch. It's Józio's watch, an object of great sentimental value to all of them. Zbyszek scrutinizes the Soviet carefully. Not much older than he, the Soviet doesn't look violent or aggressive but rather very determined to have a watch.

"Well, I can't give you this watch because it's not mine," Zbyszek replies calmly. "But why don't you come with me? Maybe I will find another watch for you."

Zbyszek knows that Dad is an expert in dealing with the Soviets. With his fluent Russian, seaman-like manners, and expertise in drinking vodka, he spends a lot of time with the Soviets lately. So, let him deal with this one, too. As they walk towards the house, Zbyszek tries to sound friendly, making sure that his voice does not betray his nervousness. But what if Dad isn't home? As they enter the house, he hears Dad's voice from a distance and relaxes.

"Dad, let me introduce my friend. This is Grisha," he points to the Soviet. "I thought you could help Grisha." He sends Dad a signal, discreetly rolling his eyes.

"Please sit down, Comrade!" Dad invites Grisha and looks around for a bottle of vodka.

The two men start talking and drinking. But as time passes, Grisha becomes more agitated. He keeps repeating over and over again that he needs a watch. Danusia, working next door, listens to the growing tension in his voice with apprehension. "I need a watch! Do you understand? I need a watch!" Grisha starts shouting.

"That's it! I have to do something about this." She hurries into the room. "You want a watch, right?"

Caught by surprise, the Soviet murmurs something.

"Okay then, here you are!" In a decisive gesture, she unfastens her small plastic watch and throws it on the table. "Take it!"

Grisha is thrilled. He takes the watch and looks it over with delight. "Thank you, Miss! Thank you!" He almost cries with joy and wants to kiss Danusia.

"You're welcome!" She stops him with her hands. "No problem."

Dad grabs Grisha's hand. "Sit down, Comrade, sit down."

"No, no! I have to return the favor. I will get you a bike." He looks at Danusia with great gratitude.

"Oh, I don't need any bike. I have one." In fact, Danusia doesn't have any such thing. But how could the Soviet get her a bike? Probably he would take it from Danusia's neighbors. "No, no! I really don't want a bike. I don't want anything. Just keep the watch and don't worry," she insists.

"I have to get you a bike," Grisha keeps repeating and heads to the door.

Uff, he is finally gone. They relax.

"All the Soviets are after all kinds of watches these days. I wonder why?" Dad shakes his head.

"I'm glad he was satisfied with this small watch," Danusia sounds triumphant. "Recently, I heard about a similar incident. The Soviets got a small Swiss watch but they weren't pleased with it. It was too small. They wanted a big watch. So eventually they settled on a big clock and were much happier with it. Hmm, how about our clock.... It's in Warsaw...or rather *was* in Warsaw...."

Zbyszek shows up in the door. "Oh, I see you got rid of Grisha."

"Yes, but at a price." Dad is upset. "Danusia had to sacrifice her watch."

"Well, but this way we saved Józio's watch," Zbyszek replies. "I had to bring him home to distract his attention from Józio's watch. He was determined to get Józio's watch."

"Then, I guess, it was worth it," Danusia sighs.

Two hours later, someone knocks at the door.

"Oh, no!" Danusia spies Grisha through the glass door.

"Miss," Grisha says proudly, "here is the bicycle for you!" He points to a big bicycle parked in front of the house.

Danusia can't believe her eyes. He really brought her a bike. She goes out to take a better look at the booty. "It's a Soviet bicycle," she concludes with astonishment, checking some Cyrillic letters on the green frame. "At least it's not taken from the next door neighbor," she sighs with relief. "And it's very solid too." She smiles and waves to Grisha who is hurrying away.

Zbyszek and Dad come out to see the bicycle. Little Ela follows wobbling on her tiny feet. Mama steadies her gently with her hands.

"Can you imagine? This is a pretty good bike!" Dad exclaims. "You made quite a good deal, Danusia. You can even ride this bike together with Ela."

"I have to try it first. It looks a little too heavy for me." Danusia gets on and takes a short ride, hopping from one side to another. Dad adjusts the seat easily.

"Great!" Danusia marvels. "It's perfect. Now I can ride the bike to the post office to send a letter to Koło."

With the advancement of the Soviet troops, there are two barriers between Międzyrzec and Koło: one is the Soviet-German frontline and the other is Hitler's General Government border. For all practical purposes, the communication between Danusia and Józio's family in Koło is completely cut off. Everybody knows it but Danusia doesn't accept this reality and with naive determination keeps sending letters to Koło, one after another, requesting in vain the return of her Jędruś.

She hasn't seen her little son for nearly twenty months. Jędruś is three-and-a-half years old by now. For certain he is a charming boy, running, talking, and playing cheerfully but Danusia is not privy to the joy of watching him grow up. Her anguish intensifies with each passing day.

"You made a grave mistake by giving your child away," an old woman tells her. "By now your son doesn't even remember his mother.

He is already attached to that other woman. To him she became his real mother. You've already lost your child."

Danusia's painful fury over her lost child grows stronger and stronger. Bitter resentment and helpless despair tear her heart and soul. Planning a trip to Koło becomes her daily obsession. The charming dark eyes and soft laughter of her little daughter crawling around doesn't bring much relief from the overwhelming sense of guilt and frenzied longing for her son.

In the meantime, Ela develops nicely. She walks and talks already. With her big brown eyes, soft curly dark hair, and a charming smile, she is a delight of the entire neighborhood. A curious and energetic baby, she is everywhere. She has to be watched non-stop. Any time she becomes quiet, it's a sure sign of trouble.

One day Ela disappears for a while. Eventually Dad finds her busy dismantling his radio under the table. "Elunia!" He wrings his hands. She turns her sparkling eyes on him with innocent confidence. He takes her in his arms and gives her a big kiss. "My darling, you just broke my client's radio. I am not sure whether I can fix it now." He gently ruffles her hair.

Dad is totally defenseless against Ela's charms and completely crazy about his little granddaughter. He often takes her for walks and likes to play with her in the park. He frequently works next to her bed when she takes a nap during the day. While Mama and Danusia take care of the daily chores, Dad is Ela's faithful companion.

Another Christmas is fast approaching. It is already the sixth Christmas of the war and there is less and less hope now for better days ahead. After all the years of Nazi carnage, one invader has merely replaced the other. Warsaw is destroyed; the Home Army is once again in hiding; the Polish press is more suppressed than ever. The *Bulletin* is rarely published these days. Radio broadcasts from the Polish Government in London is limited and more pessimistic than ever.

An operation of the Allied forces in Belgium and Holland code-named "Market Garden" failed miserably in the fall of 1944. Together with it, hopes of liberating Poland with the Polish Armed forces under the command of the Polish Government in London have also vanished. The fate of Poland has been handed to Stalin on a silver platter.

The shrewd tyrant didn't waste any time. Back in July of 1944, he sent a ready-made pro-Communist administration to Poland. The so-called Polish Committee of National Liberation was installed in Lublin in direct opposition to the legitimate Polish Government in London, and another bloody selection process has been spreading through the devastated country: anyone suspected of opposing the Communist Government in Lublin was promptly eliminated.[1]

In the beginning of 1945, thousands of Soviet tanks roll into Eastern Poland and millions of Soviet soldiers flood the country in preparation for the final push toward Berlin. The roads are crammed with a deluge of soldiers, with columns of military vehicles, and the army support units, all advancing west. Crowds of Soviet officers come to Międzyrzec in search for a better place to stay before the final western offensive.

The Soviet Special Forces follow the Soviet Army to Poland just as before. And, as in 1939, the NKVD began purging the Polish population of its few remaining active elements. The Home Army members are gradually arrested. The lower-ranking individuals are evaluated for fitness to join the communist armed forces. The higher-ranking Home Army officers are sent to Moscow for propaganda trials.[2] Poles are again incarcerated, shipped to the Soviet Union, or simply eliminated. In every town and village, local leaders, elders, and factory managers are subjected to ideological scrutiny and either replaced outright or scheduled for future replacement. All farms and businesses are confiscated and nationalized. Peasants and workers are lured to the new order by being offered lucrative positions and bright opportunities.

One day Zbyszek does not come home as expected. Mama starts worrying when one of the neighbors hurries in, yelling: "Zbyszek! Zbyszek is arrested! They've arrested him!"

"Who are they?" Danusia asks in stomach-sinking terror.

"Dawidowicz, of course!" the neighbor replies. "He took the boy to the heavy security prison," the breathless man adds.

Dawidowicz is the bearer of the new order to Międzyrzec. As the Polish right hand of the NKVD, he holds himself as a representative of the People's Government in Lublin and runs the infamous selection process in Międzyrzec. His arbitrary victims disappear without a trace. He hasn't been on the job long but already enjoys the worst possible reputation. People hate him for his cruel and collaborative behavior.

Deeply shaken, Danusia rushes to the prison and the guard takes her to the visitors' cell. Soon Zbyszek's confused face appears in a small window behind heavy bars.

"Zbyś, my love! Why did they arrest you?"

He shrugs with resignation. "I don't know. I honestly don't know!" They stare at each other in silence.

"Here you are, Danuś. Take this watch. It's your memory of Józio. You better keep it." He unfastens the watch and hands it over to her.

"No! Keep it. I don't want it!" she cries.

"You must take it." he insists.

Visiting time is over. The window shuts down abruptly and Zbyszek's face disappears.

That night Danusia and Mama don't get any sleep. Dawidowicz's victims are quickly disposed of. They are either killed in the basement or sent east, to the "white grizzlies," as they say around town.

Early the next morning, Danusia waits for Dawidowicz in front of his office. He finally shows up but is not eager to talk with her. He is busy today and will be busy tomorrow as well. She may come back after tomorrow, if she so desires.... And by the way, he arrested Zbyszek pursuant to an NKVD order.

On the way home, Danusia feverishly strains her mind. She must do something quickly. After tomorrow there will be no trace of Zbyszek. Suddenly Mama shows up in front of her. Mama! That's right! She must help!

"I saw him, Mama. He is fine for now, but we must do something immediately. Remember this Soviet woman who came over to the salon just a couple days ago to have her hair done? She was a medical doctor and her husband was some sort of a high-ranking Soviet officer. We must find them! Do you know where they're staying?"

Mama is shaking. She closes her eyes and knits her brows with great effort. "If I am not mistaken, she said she was staying at the Palace. Yes, that's what she said."

"Let's go then." Danusia and Mama rush to the Palace at the outskirts of the town.

"We need to see the Soviet lady doctor that's staying here," Danusia confidently says to the guard.

"What do you want?" he asks suspiciously.

"We are from the hair salon. We're here to do her hair," Danusia explains.

"Okay then, go to the second floor."

The Soviet woman opens the door and greets them amiably. She already knows a lot about Danusia and her tragic story, she knows about Auschwitz, about Józio's death, and about the two children. She remembers little Ela's charming sparkling eyes.

"Please help us, please help!" Danusia bursts into tears and sobbing, tries to explain the problem.

"Did he say *NKVD*?" the Soviet doctor asks in disbelief.

Danusia nods.

"Please calm down, we'll see what can be done. My husband is the NKVD chief for this area. He'll find out what is going on." Danusia and Mama almost faint upon learning that this tall blond man who came to their salon the other day is the chief of the feared NKVD police.

"You wait here and I'll find out what is going on with your Zbyszek," the woman says, leaving the room. In fifteen minutes, she comes back with her husband. The tall handsome Soviet glances at the two terrified women amicably. "Let's go," he says to them. Danusia and Mama timidly get up and hastily follow him.

"I checked our records and we didn't give any order to arrest your son," the Soviet says, walking down the street. Seeing the tall Soviet approaching, the prison guard hastily opens the gate. They proceed straight to Dawidowicz's office. In front of his door, the Soviet turns to them: "Please wait here." He then goes in without knocking and energetically shuts the door. Several seemingly endless minutes pass by before the door opens again and the two men emerge.

"He will take care of you," the Soviet says.

Dawidowicz looks at Danusia with a strained smile and stutters with difficulty, "Your brother will be released. You may wait for him here."

Danusia squeezes Mama's hand and looks with gratitude at the Soviet.

Later that day, they walk home with Zbyszek marching erect between Mama and Danusia. The whole neighborhood is puzzled. Dawidowicz has already announced that Zbyszek would be sent to the white grizzlies.

At home, Dad is in the process of finishing his fourth pack of cigarettes when they all walk through the door in triumph. "Zbyszek!" His cigarette falls, burning a hole in the green tablecloth. "It must be a miracle!" He can't believe his eyes.

"But why did they arrest you in the first place?" Mama still worries.

Zbyszek shrugs helplessly.

"You should know why, my son," Dad admonishes him. "At the party this weekend you yapped about killing all the communist traitors. You must control yourself, Son! Eyes and ears are everywhere these days"

"But Dad! I was just joking!" Zbyszek replies in shock.

"Now you know that they don't have a sense of humor."

In the middle of January, the final Soviet counter-offensive begins. On January 17, 1945, the First Byelorussian Front and the Soviet-controlled First Polish Army under the command of newly appointed General Popławski easily take over the ruins of Warsaw. The horrifying news about the total destruction of Warsaw spreads immediately throughout the Soviet-occupied part of Poland.

"There is no Warsaw anymore," people whisper in horror.

"And where are the Warsawians?" everybody asks. "What happened to them?"

"Those who survived have been sent to the concentration camps," some reply.

"How many died?" people wonder.

"Hundreds of thousands," others whisper back.

This is not the first destruction of Warsaw in this war. During the defense of Warsaw in September of 1939, about fifteen percent of the city lay in ruins and about ten thousand Warsawians lost their lives. As a result of the Warsaw Ghetto Uprising in 1943, about seven thousand people were killed and another fifteen percent of the town lay in ruins. But the latest tragedy transcends human comprehension. More than two hundred thousand are dead and all the survivors are in the concentration camps.[3] There is no Warsaw to speak of and there are no Warsawians left….

"We saved Zbyszek's life by calling him to come here that day, just before the outbreak of the uprising," Mama keeps repeating with fanatical passion.

"But what happened to our friends at the mint?" Dad asks in vain. They are devastated beyond words. Dad goes to the local bar to get more information and some relief. Late at night, he walks down the street with a group of Soviet soldiers. Loud drunken voices awaken the quiet neighborhood. Mama runs out and brings Dad inside.

"No more pubs!" she orders categorically.

As the front line moves west, a strange letter arrives. In the turmoil of the counter-offensive, letters are almost unheard of. "It's not from Koło!" Danusia concludes with angry disappointment. "It can't be from Koło," Dad observes. "The front line hasn't reached Koło yet."

They carefully inspect the envelope. "Red Cross," Zbyszek reads the nearly illegible letters in the corner and hastily tears it open. "What is it? Another envelope?" Mama whispers as the rest of them hold their breath. A sender is not indicated on this one. Only their names are written in big letters on the front. Zbyszek takes a sharp knife, carefully cuts it open at the top, pulls out a sheet of notebook paper, glances at both sides, and announces: "It's from Wila, from Dryświaty!"

"At last!" Dad gasps with excitement.

"Our Loved Ones!" he begins reading as they all surround him tightly.

> We worry about you very much. Warsaw suffered such a terrible destruction. Please let us know where you are and how everybody is doing. We have just come home from the east after four long years of the labor camp. Our parents are no longer alive. There are big changes around here. We can't return to our home. The Soviets took over the administration of the villages. They are saying that the entire Dryświaty region and Vilnius and even Nowogródek and Grodno belong to the Soviet Union now. If there is to be any Poland at all, they say, it will be around Warsaw and west of Warsaw. Many of those who returned from Siberia are anxious to move west to make sure they don't end up on the Soviet side of the border. We also want to move to Poland, wherever that Poland may be today.
>
> I very much hope that this letter will find you in good health. Please write back as soon as possible. We all are anxiously awaiting any news from you!
>
> With love,
> Wila

* * * *

It's a Friday evening in the first spring of the third millennium. Danusia shuffles along hastily in her warm slippers. She had a busy day today. Early in the day, a Polish priest came down from Cleveland with the holy sacraments in preparation for Easter. It is a priceless experience to receive confession and Holy Communion in Polish. The Polish priest can't visit her more often than twice a year. Danusia is still excited about his visit but now she rushes to get to bed. Tomorrow she will have another busy day. She must get up very early, at 6 AM, because her private hair stylist comes at 7 AM.

Rossita comes every Saturday before her regular workday to style Danusia's hair. Rossita has to get up before dawn and drive in the drizzly Ohio morning in order to visit Danusia. She goes through the pain of this early morning exercise not for the financial benefit of it but because of some unreasonable desire to be with Danusia and her family. A rational observer would never understand this odd relationship.

Rossita is an attractive blonde in her mid-thirties. She is of average height, slender, and refined. With her delicate-featured face and a high-pitched voice, she come across as much younger, almost childish. She has recently immigrated to the United States from what was once the Soviet Union but with the demise of the Soviet empire became Byelorussia. Because of her Jewish husband, she was able to immigrate to the United States.

Rossita is Polish though. Her family comes from the Polish territories incorporated into the Soviet Union as a result of World War II. Rossita was raised by her grandmother in a small village near Grodno. Rossita's mother, after divorcing her father, moved away. Her father was subsequently killed while on duty in the Soviet Marine Corps. Departing for the United States, Rossita left her beloved grandmother alone in the village near Grodno. The sense of guilt for leaving behind her dearest Grandma is Rossita's daily obsession. The early Saturday morning time with Danusia is Rossita's attempt to redeem that unsettling guilt.

"I like to style your hair because I can speak Polish with you," she explains. "I spoke Polish with my Grandma."

"And you are the only one who can curl my hair so well," Danusia replies. "For all these years in the United States, I couldn't find anybody who could style my hair the way I want it. They don't do the curling the way I need to have it done," Danusia sighs. "I am very happy that I found you...."

"I understand. I used to curl my Grandma's hair that way," Rossita sounds nostalgic. "My Grandma is such a lovely person.... You know, you often sound like her...." They both laugh cheerily.

"My Grandma is an incredible woman. Her life was so tragic and yet she never lost that sparkling optimism and faith in people. I often think that if I were her I wouldn't be able to survive all what she had been through."

"Was she in Siberia?" Danusia asks flatly.

"Yes, she was.... Like all of them...," Rossita replies quietly. They both fall silent.

"And her husband was killed in Katyń," Rossita adds in a blunt voice.

"I am sorry to hear that, Rossita," Danusia mutters gently. "I know how much you suffered out there. I know it very well.... My boyfriend was murdered in Katyń, some of my close relatives were killed by the Soviets, and the others were deported to Siberia."

The intense odor of hairspray pricks their throat and Danusia starts coughing. "Do you know that the official memorial for the families of the Katyń victims was finally held at Katyń this year...after all these years," she chokes out. Rossita hands her a glass of water.

"Yes, I know, but my Grandma couldn't go, or rather, wasn't able to go."

"When was she deported to Siberia? Was it early on in 1940, or later, towards the spring?"

"If I am not mistaken, she was deported in the second phase of the whole operation, that would be March or April of 1940."

"She was lucky then," Danusia says with a hint of irony in her voice. "My family in Dryświaty was deported early on, in February. The NKVD squads with the help of local collaborators broke into their homes in the middle of a deadly cold winter night and ordered them to leave. My uncle, who was a prominent landowner in the area, didn't want to leave, so he was shot on the spot. Then his traumatized wife and two children were dragged to some kind of a common room where all the other terrified Poles were forced into from all directions. From there, they were sent to the train station and loaded into those infamous rusted cattle wagons, about sixty people in each."[4]

"That's right. This is exactly what my Grandma told me about the trip!" Rossita tries to hide her emotions. "My Grandma often talked about that journey, the unspeakable hunger, thirst, and cold. But she also told me about the songs that resounded throughout the train at least at the beginning of the trip. *We'll not abandon the land we hail* is the song that she remembers the most...." Rossita tries to recall the melody.

"My cousins from Dryświaty, Wila, Franek, and their mother, were loaded into one of these cattle wagons in minus-forty degree weather. Only half of the people survived that trip. Younger children were dying en mass. At occasional stops, the Soviets collected the bodies of the dead, mostly children and elderly, and threw them into the ditches along the rail tracks. The parents made desperate but mostly futile attempts to at least bury their children. My cousins, thank God, were older back then, like fifteen and nineteen, and they managed to survive the trip. But their mother died on the train towards the end of the journey ...and...."

"And what happened to her?"

"Well...the Soviets simply threw her body from the moving train."

"So, your cousins don't even have their mother's grave...."

"Right...."

Rossita turns on the blow dryer and the growling noise passes through the sleeping house.

"My cousins returned from Siberia to Dryświaty in 1944," Danusia goes on. "By that time, their house and the entire estate was confiscated and turned into a collective farm. After the war we arranged for their repatriation to Poland. But why didn't your grandmother move to Poland during the repatriation period?"

"At that time we didn't have any family left in Poland," Rossita replies. "My Grandma's family in the Zamość region disappeared from the face of the earth. Today we know that they were all killed. No one survived. Besides, Grandma was so depressed that she wasn't capable of going through another fight to get Soviet permission to move to Poland."

"You're right. I remember we were fighting for all of our cousins from Dryświaty. First, we applied for Wila and Franek," Danusia tries to recall the process. "And for Wila's son," she adds, straining her memory. "I didn't know about that...but when Wila finally came to

Poland she told me the story. She was brutally raped in the labor camp in Siberia by the camp guard...and forced to have that unwanted child.... Poor Wila.... She was my age...," Danusia blinks her eyes in pain. "You know, I often wonder whether she was able to love that child."

"It's beyond my imagination." Rossita turns off the blow dryer. The silence stets in.

"I understand that only now the details of the Soviet persecutions of the Polish population are coming to light," she finally says.

"Right," Danusia smiles sadly. "Under the communist regime, any mention of the Polish problem in the east meant certain imprisonment. The subject was effectively dead for half a century."

"Recently I've read that those Siberian death trains transported close to two million Polish civilians during those memorable days of 1940. The Soviets set up about two thousand forced labor camps for the Poles in the Russia Far East. I heard that some people were deported even to Kazakhstan," Rossita says.

"Some of my cousins, like Uncle Vince and Bolek were lucky, though. I always thought they were spared because they didn't own any land. They merely leased the land and didn't have many possessions."

"I don't think the ownership was the selection criterion," Rossita insists. "In our region, all the government workers were deported, all the forestry workers were deported, and all the teachers and priests were deported, too. Apparently in 1940, Stalin had his sweet revenge on the Poles, liquidating us on all fronts."

"He certainly did." Danusia looks in the mirror. Her thin brown hair is perfectly curled and stylishly pouffed over her forehead. Her hair is a source of great pride for Danusia. At 78, she has not a single gray hair; it's naturally brown!

"Thank you Rossita, my dear. It's perfect. I always look forward to our Saturday early morning togetherness."

Rossita kisses her cheek. "Bye, Danusia, see you next week."

* * * *

With the inflow of the Soviets to Międzyrzec, Jasia's business is booming but she fears for her family's safety. The town has been flooded with soldiers.

"You must watch Ela today," she says to Alek one day. "I have to go to the other salon and I am taking Danusia with me." Jasia has recently opened another salon on the opposite side of town and works round the clock to keep up with the demand.

At around noon, Dad shows up at the other salon. "Danusia, you have to go home to watch Ela. A Soviet that I met the other day came over. I have to go with him now."

"You better watch those Soviets. You never know what they're after these days." Mama scrutinizes Dad carefully. He looks completely sober and talks in a business-like manner. Probably he has to take care of some business, she concludes and starts taking off her apron.

"No, no!" Dad protests. "Danusia is the mother. She should go. You can stay here and let Danusia watch after her daughter."

"That's okay. I'll go," Mama says. "She'll go next time."

At home, a Soviet officer sits at the table. His military insignia indicate that he is a Captain in the Soviet Air Force. Next to him, little Ela plays with a tiny pink elephant. "Hello," Mama says but the stranger doesn't reply. Without looking at her, he gets up and turns to Dad. "Let's go!"

Mama shrugs at his rudeness and picks up Ela. "I have to give you something to eat, my little tot."

Dad puts on his sheepskin coat and leaves, following the Soviet in silence. "Let's go in here," the Soviet points to a nearby house on the opposite side of the street. They walk through the door, through a dilapidated hallway, up the stairs, and into a dark room on the first floor. A shabby desk and two chairs stand in the center of the otherwise empty room. The Soviet picks up some firewood from the floor, drops it into a small stove in the corner, and pulls out a bottle of vodka with two glasses from nowhere.

"Okay, Alek," he starts slyly, "as I was saying, we need good people." He considers Alek, pouring vodka into his glass. "People like you, Comrade! We will be building a new country here, a new society...a *better* society for the working poor. You could make a difference in building a better future for your people, Alek!"

Dad observes the Soviet attentively. "But specifically, what kind of work do you have in mind?" he asks, weighing his words carefully.

The Soviet raises the glass and quickly pulls back his hand. "We are in the process of putting together a new organization here. At this stage of the building of the new society, we need the best people for the security forces. You have the unique opportunity to build a great career with us." The Soviet's eyes sparkle.

"Security forces...", Dad repeats blankly. "Like Dawidowicz, you mean?"

"You see, that's our problem. Dawidowicz is not up to the job. We don't want people like Dawidowicz who tend to use their positions to square old accounts or for private gain. We want quality people like you, Alek. People who believe in the idea of the international brotherhood of the proletariat, who are committed to building a better society for their people, who have communist ethics, and will help us purify society of the reactionary elements that may prevent us from achieving this historic mission."

"To purify society," Alek repeats in vain. "It means spying on my own people and persecuting them...."

"You shouldn't be looking at it that way!" the Soviet is visibly displeased with Alek's comment. "You are a part of the greater cause! You will be building the Communist Society. This great cause requires short-term sacrifices. We have to make sacrifices in the name of Communism."

"It means more bloodshed for this already crucified nation...." Alek takes the glass of vodka and pours it straight down his throat.

"For the true Communist, the notion of a nation doesn't exist. It's an outdated and empty concept. Only the working people matter. Only the classes matter, and we fight for a better life for millions and billions of people, no matter what their nationality is. Soon, nations will become obsolete. The international fraternity of working people cooperating in peace and harmony throughout the world will replace nations."

"No nation. Right!" Alek growls sarcastically. "That's why you aided and abated the Germans in annihilating the Warsawians!"

"Your comments sadden me, my friend. I was hoping to avoid this sensitive subject but since you raised it, apparently you must be reminded about the collaborative attitude of your bourgeois government in London towards the Germans. They were the ones who shielded the Nazis and tried to smear the Soviet Union, accusing us of this abominable Katyń massacre. Poland must pay the price for collaborating with Germany in damaging the reputation of the greatest country humankind has ever seen!" the Soviet states with an ominous glint in his eyes.

"Collaboration with Germany???" Alek exclaims, getting up, his cheeks flushing hotly. "You all are either idiots or devils!" he starts yelling. "You and your Communist leaders are nothing more than a bunch of mad imperialists hungry for world domination at any cost!" Alek laughs with dramatic irony, pacing and gesticulating in fury. "No nations? Sure! As long as YOUR NATION makes territorial gains at Poland's cost. No nations! Sure! As long as YOUR NATION runs the world, right? You're the same bunch of miscreants as the Nazis...!" He glances at the Soviet and the last word dies down on his lips. With a contemptuous look on his face, the Soviet stands still, pointing a small handgun at his chest. "Sorry, Comrade, but you are useless to the Cause," the Soviet pronounces ceremoniously and pulls the trigger.

* * * *

Late in the evening, someone knocks on the window. "*Pani* Jasia, *Pani* Jasia! Your husband has been shot! Go to that building, upstairs!"

Mama stands like a pillar of salt. Her hands are shaking, her mind is gone; she is paralyzed from head to toe. But Danusia dashes out, talks briefly with the man, and runs to the building. By the time she reaches the small dark room, Dad lies on the floor with his chest neatly bandaged all around. He is conscious. She looks at him, then at the half-emptied bottle of vodka, and screams in fury.

"Oh, Dad! What did you do!" she bursts out furiously. "You ran into your destiny!"

"Right," he says quietly. "The Germans incarcerated me but my Soviet shot me...."

"To which hospital do you want to take your father?" a Soviet nurse asks. "Polish or Russian?"

Danusia looks at her in shock. "To the Polish...of course...!" she says, confused.

Dad survives the night. In the morning, a senior doctor comes, checks him out, and orders immediate surgery. One of his lungs and stomach are badly damaged. Danusia and Mama stay at the hospital. Only Zbyszek is not around. After the NKVD incident, he moved to another town, closer to his girlfriend.

Dad is taken to the operating room. Two Russian doctors assist the Polish doctor in the operation. After three long hours, the operation is over and the two Russians leave the operating room.

"How was it? How is Dad doing?" Danusia jumps at them.

"Your doctor performed a state of art operation," the older Russian replies.

"Will he survive?"

The doctors exchange awkward looks. "Will he survive…? Hmm, only God can answer that question."

In the evening, Dad is transported to his room. He is conscious but in great pain.

"Do you want to see the priest?" the nurse asks.

"No, my Dad doesn't want to see any priests!" Danusia replies with anger.

Dad watches them from under his half-opened lids, then slowly moves his hand, and calls the nurse. "Yes, I want to see the priest," he whispers.

Danusia bursts into tears. The Polish doctor comes to the room to check on Dad. She is an experienced and a very strict lady. She orders that a bag of ice be placed on Dad's fresh stitches and asks Danusia and Mama to leave the room. "He needs good rest," she explains.

"But he also needs good care," Danusia argues with her. "And we want to watch him throughout the night."

"Don't worry about that. Our nurses are excellent. They will take good care of him," the doctor replies firmly.

Willy-nilly, they kiss Dad, and slowly leave the room. "Let him sleep," Mama says with resignation.

In the hallway, they meet a breathless Zbyszek. He has just arrived. "Run and ask them to let you in," Danusia instructs him quickly. But the hall has been already locked for the night and no one can get in.

Early in the morning, they all are back at the hospital. Zbyszek dashes in first, very anxious to see Dad. The hall is open. He rushes to the door that Danusia pointed out to him and stops, bewildered. Danusia and Mama soon join him. Dad is not in the room. His bed is empty. A patient in the other bed looks at them rather upset and turns away. A nurse shows up from behind and asks them to step back.

"Where is…?" Zbyszek shouts wildly.

"I am sorry," the nurse drops her eyes and lowers her voice, "he passed away in the night."

"NO!!!" Zbyszek howls.

"NO!!!" Mama cries.

Danusia slides against the wall and collapses.

"Where is he?" Zbyszek can't stop yelling.

"In the charnel house, across the street," the nurse explains.

"Here, drink some water," another nurse hands them cups of cold water.

Grieving and clinging to each other, they walk together to a small charnel house. There in the open casket in the center of the gloomy room, Dad lies in silence. His raven-black hair spread on the white sheet is strikingly alive. But his yellowish, rigid face displays painful calm, his lips are tightly closed, and his stomach is bulged out like a balloon.

Mama prays, cries and sobs desperately. Danusia sits like a mummy, still numb from pain and disbelief.

"Father, I promise you, I will kill this Kola, this Soviet who killed you!" Zbyszek says in a half-whisper, sobbing heavily.

In the end, they go home deeply absorbed in their infinite grief. Before long, an urgent pounding on the door interrupts their mourning.

"Open the door!" they hear loud Soviet voices.

Mama walks to the door and opens it slightly.

"We need your man," a Soviet soldier tells her.

"You just killed my man!" she replies with furious intensity.

"But we need this young man," the soldier says.

"What? You don't have enough! You still need more victims, you bloodsuckers! Never! Over my dead body!" she screams.

The Soviet pushes through the door. She throws herself on him. "Never! Never!" she screams hysterically, hitting the Soviet indiscriminately with her fists. Danusia rushes to the door and tries to drag her away. Zbyszek shows up. "Mama, calm down please," he yells.

"Young man, you must go with me. This is an NKVD order," the Soviet announces, straightening his uniform after Mama's attack.

Mama grabs Zbyszek's hand. "No. I won't let you go! NO!!!" she cries wildly.

46. Józek and Alek common grave, Międzyrzec, 1973

47. Polish flag over Monte Cassino, Italy

48. Poland after World War II

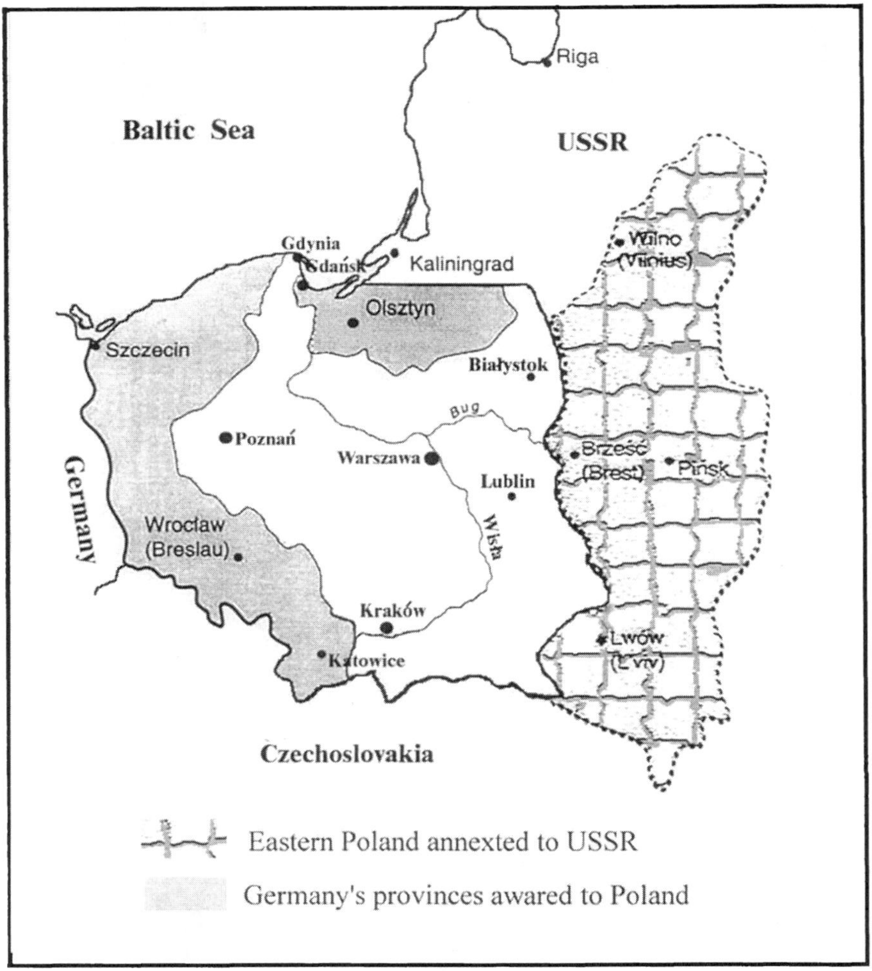

"Mama, I will go with Zbyszek," Danusia declares. "I will protect him, trust me, I will."

"No, no! For God's sake, don't go! They will kill you, too. Don't go, please."

Danusia and Zbyszek put their coats on and go out with the Soviet, leaving Mama at home in bottomless despair.

At the NKVD building, the guard orders Danusia to wait in the reception room and takes Zbyszek away. She panics. There have been instances where a woman came here with her husband or brother, she was then asked to wait and when, after hours of waiting, she asked about her loved one again, the response was: "Who? There's nobody here with that name. You must be hallucinating." Those husbands and brothers have not been seen since such hallucinations.

Danusia intensely reviews her options. She must do something quickly. But what? Her tall blond Soviet left the area and is no longer available. Dawidowicz is her worst enemy anyway. What to do, what to do? She feverishly searches for a solution. But she is lucky this time. She won't be accused of hallucinating. Instead, after a half-hour wait, she gets her Zbyszek back.

"Let's get out of here!" he says in an undertone. They walk out into the dark cold January night without any guard.

"Are you free?" she asks fearfully.

"For now at least," he replies. "Oh, my God! Mama! She must be agonizing there! Let's go!" Zbyszek grabs her hand and starts running.

At home, Mama is already hallucinating. "Zbyś, my love! Is it you or is this just the dream?" she touches his hair lovingly but with a deranged smile. "Is it really you?"

"Mama, calm down! It's me, it's the real me!" He embraces her tightly. "I'm back. See, I'm alive and I'm even hungry," he tries to smile through his tears.

Semi-conscious, Mama desperately clings to Zbyszek. Danusia checks on sleeping Ela, makes a warm meal, adds firewood to the stove, and asks them to the table.

"Now tell us what this whole thing was about," she asks Zbyszek.

He nervously looks around the room and signals that it's dangerous to talk about it. Danusia bows over the table and whispers. "Just tell us a little bit."

"Remember, when I said that...I would kill that Soviet?" He mouths, hardly producing a sound.

"Yes, but that was at the charnel house and there was nobody but us in that room," she whispers back, her eyes growing round.

"Well, apparently someone overheard me there. That's why they called me...to tell me that if I touched that Soviet," he hesitates for a moment, looking rather disheartened, then finishes in a faint voice. "Then...they will execute the entire family, all of us."

Silence sets in. They all busy themselves with scrambled eggs, chewing slowly and swallowing hard.

Dad's funeral is modest and quiet, with just a few people attending. Dad is laid to rest next to Józio. Two simple wooded crosses stand next to each other. On the first cross, the inscription reads: "A Nazi bullet cut short your young life." On the second cross, the inscription reads: "A Soviet bullet so unexpectedly carried you away." A small crowd surrounds the grave staring in silence at the sepulcher. Some try to pray, some wipe away tears. Branches of evergreens and a few flowers cover the fresh but already frozen soil. "Beware!" someone whispers. "THEY may not like the inscription."

Indeed, when they return the next day, Dad's cross is gone all together. Zbyszek picks up some branches and puts together another cross. They stand there praying in silence and holding back tears. The cold stings their cheeks and numbs their lips. Little Ela wiggles with impatience in her carriage.

"We have to think about planting some flowers for Dad."

"Yes, I must plant daffodils and tulips," Danusia pledges. "The same as I planted for Józio."

"We have to build a new twin grave, from stone this time...," Zbyszek clenches his fists. "We will build a strong twin grave with the inscription engraved in stone."

"Let's go," Mama whispers.

On the way home Zbyszek holds Mama and Danusia close and whispers: "The Soviets have arrested Dad's murderer, this Captain Kola. They said that he would stand trial for murder."

"Really?" Danusia sighs with disbelief.

"Yes, except that they said they would bring their own judges from Russia."

"Aha, that's the trick," Mama sounds sarcastic. "What kind of trial will that be?"

"I don't even want to know," Zbyszek replies. "I can't stand it anymore." He ponders for a while then continues. "Mama, I have to go to Warsaw now. I must check what's going on there."

"Where do you want to go? There is only rubble there," Mama says in a dejected voice.

"I think I will find some place to stay on the east side of the river, somewhere in Praga. Maybe one of Dad's friends will give me a room to stay in. From there, I can go and see what's going on with our home."

"That's a good idea." Danusia supports him. "Why don't you go and find some place to stay. I must go to Koło as soon as the front line passes it. Once I hear that the Soviets are in Poznań, I must go immediately."

"Danusia, you can't go right away. It's too dangerous. You must wait a little. And besides, you shouldn't go in this freezing cold." Zbyszek tries to slow her down, too. "You can't travel with Jędruś in forty degree weather."

One sunny but frosty morning, Zbyszek takes off for Warsaw. With fear and concern, Mama blesses him for the trip. "Be careful, Zbyś. Please be very careful and write to us often."

Ten days later, a letter comes from Zbyś. He made it safely to Praga, and now is staying with Dad's friends at Jagiellońska Street. Mama is relieved. They will take good care of him.

Towards the end of February, the long-awaited news comes. The frontline has reached Poznań. Danusia is ecstatic. "I am going!" she declares with determination.

"You can't go through Warsaw," she learns at the train station. "The Warsaw line is closed. And there are no trains to Poznań yet. You can only hope to catch some charter trains that occasionally run to the frontline."

With a grim face, Mama gives her all the money and blesses her in tears. Danusia hugs and kisses little Ela. "Be good, my little tot. Mommy will be back soon. You will have your big brother back, darling." She looks at her devastated Mama. "I'll be fine! Don't worry,

Mama." She takes just a small handbag and takes off for the train station.

The journey is bizarre from the start. "Take the train to Łuków, and from there, go to Piława and Skierniewice," she is instructed. The station and all the trains are jammed with excited people trying to return home. Squeezed in like a sardine, Danusia reaches Skierniewice one day later. At last she is on the west bank of the Vistula River. Swaying from exhaustion, she gets off the train with tottering steps and reaches the pub at the train station. "Please give me something to eat," she whispers.

"And how are you going to pay?" the bartender asks.

"I have money," she takes out some bills.

"Are you joking? You want to pay me with this junk paper? Don't you know it's useless?"

Danusia's round eyes fill with tears. "Please give me something to eat. I haven't had anything for more than a day," she begs.

The bartender looks at her with disgust. "Another one," he mutters. "It's as if I'm running a soup kitchen for the homeless here...," he grumbles even more. "I can only give you a piece of bread and hot tea."

Danusia slowly chews the dried bread. Dark, tasteless tea warms her from the inside. Her next destination is Łowicz. The train to Łowicz may come in the evening, but it's not certain. She falls asleep on a stinky bench next to other weary traveling wrecks. The sudden commotion in the waiting room wakes her up just in time for the Łowicz train. She rushes out and the crowd carries her to the train. The ride to Łowicz is short. She arrives there in the middle of the night and ends up in yet another waiting room. Now she needs a train to Poznań. But there are no trains to Poznań yet.

"You just wait and hope for some charter train," she is informed.

"How long do I have to wait?" she asks in despair.

"We usually have something once a day," a woman at the information window smiles agreeably.

The next day in the afternoon, a cattle train pulls into the station. "The Poznań train!" The crowd spreads the exciting news. The wagons at the front of the train are locked but the wagons at the back are wide open and empty. The crowd flows toward the rear, everybody gets in and there is still some room inside.

As the train starts moving, Danusia, exhausted, sinks with relief onto the floor. This is the final stage of her endless journey. Soon she will have her Jędruś back, her little darling. She looks around cheerfully and notices many exhausted but expectant faces next to her.

"I was driven out of my home and deported in the wagon like this one over three years ago," a man with a peasant accent says.

"I was, too," someone else adds. "Except that the doors of those wagons were tightly locked back then."

All the travelers turn their eyes to the wide open doors of their cattle wagon. A serene view of the countryside awaking from its winter sleep and a frigid draft of fresh air brings intense pleasure.

"It's so wonderful to be able to return home at last," a woman sighs.

"Even if there may be no home left," someone else adds.

"But at least it's our place on this Earth...."

People pull out sandwiches, crackers, carrots and fruit. A woman sitting on the opposite side of the wagon offers Danusia an apple. A middle-aged man sitting next to her shares his cheese sandwich with her. The train passes through small villages and towns. Some villages are untouched, some are badly burned, many towns are in ruins, some roads are damaged but most are operational. The train doesn't stop anywhere, only slows down while passing through the stations. The passengers one by one jump out of the moving train at these semi-stops.

"It won't stop in Koło either," her neighbor says. "You will have to jump. But you must jump either before the station or after the station. The ground is softer...."

Danusia looks at the man fearfully.

"You have to take off your shoes and throw them out first, together with the suitcase," he instructs her. "Don't worry. I'm getting off in Koło, too. I'll help you." He walks to the door and takes a peek towards the front of the train. "We're almost there. I prefer to jump before the station. There is a nice rail-bed there."

Danusia is speechless. She has finally made it to Koło. Trembling with emotion, she gets up. This is Koło then! She looks at the yellowish, thawing fields. Now she only has to jump. The train begins to slow down. She takes off her shoes and holds them tightly.

"I'll go first but you must go right after me," the man instructs her again. "And remember, your shoes and the bag go first."

The train slows even more. The cold breeze loses its strength.

"Let's go! Now!" The man jumps, falls down but quickly gets up, and runs with the train. "You must jump now!" he yells.

"Please catch me!" Danusia yells back and throws out everything to empty her hands.

"Now!" he gives her an order and she jumps right at him. They both roll down the hill. Such a strange experience.... Danusia is in shock.

"Are you okay?" the man asks her while trying to get up.

"I think so," Danusia replies, trying to move her legs.

"You are quite a brave woman," he observes, looking at her with admiration.

"I am doing this for my son," she declares with determination.

He picks up her bag. "Here.... Do you know where to go?"

"No, I've never been here."

He escorts her to the main road and points to the church tower. "Go towards that tower. It's not that far, about half-an-hour walk. Near that church ask the people again. And good luck! I'm going that way." He smiles and waves to her.

"Thank you!" she replies and turns towards the church tower.

Her heart is pounding as she approaches the church. "You have to go further," people advise her. "Another ten minute walk. It's a small house on the corner, there," someone else says. "You'll see. Some children are playing in the yard."

"Some children...," she repeats nervously and quickens her pace. Soon she passes along the fence of a small house. Leaves are neatly raked in the yard and rows of flowerbeds are ready to blossom. Acrid smoke from burning leaves reaches her—spring cleaning is under the way. Suddenly she hears voices. One more turn and she stands in front of the gate. Inside, several toddlers are running around screaming and shouting. They are playing a war game.

"Jędruś, which one is Jędruś? Am I going to recognize him?" In despair, she sifts thoroughly through the little faces. But the choice is easy. There is only one blond kid, only one pair of big blue eyes, only one Jędruś, her Jędruś. She walks through the gate and extends her arms towards him.

"Jędruś, my love. Your Mama came."

Marysia appears in the doorway; tears pour down her face.

The boy stops, looks at Danusia severely, and points his stick at her. "Move away, Miss! I will kill you if you don't move."

Danusia freezes. Unspeakable pain tears her heart and her face flushes hotly. She bites her lips, pulls her hands back, and gets up without even touching the blond, dear hair. Her pain suddenly turns into rage. She looks at Marysia with hatred. "It's her fault. It's all her fault." Danusia's fury grows with every second. "She took away my Jędruś, she didn't even tell him about my existence. She made him forget his mother, *she* wanted to be the mother to him...." Danusia's eyes grow fierce.

"I am taking Jędruś back, now! I am leaving with him immediately," she says with cold determination.

Marysia starts sobbing loudly. "You can't take him immediately," a man's voice reaches her from inside the house and Kazik shows up at the door.

"Don't cry, Auntie! I'll protect you!" Little Jędruś runs to Marysia's rescue.

Danusia glares at Kazik like a tiger. She's ready for the fight. Her deepest and strongest feelings of motherhood have been badly hurt. Her whole sense of identity and self-worth has been damaged. She is the mother, the biological mother, the real mother, and nobody will ever stop her from claiming her child. Her maternal instincts boil; jealousy and rage overwhelm her.

"Please come in, Danusia," Kazik invites her inside.

"No! I am leaving right away! I won't wait even a minute longer, I have been already waiting much too long!" she shouts, trying to reach for Jędruś, but the boy runs away, crying in fear.

"Please come in, just do it for Jędruś," Kazik insists.

She pulls back angrily, realizing she has no choice but to go inside. Marysia follows, sobbing heavily.

"Please sit down, you must be tired. I'll give you something to eat," Kazik tries to calm her down.

"Don't bother. I don't want to eat anything."

"Then I'll give you something to drink."

They fall silent. Danusia paces back and forth. Kazik hands her a glass of milk.

"Sit down, please, and don't be so upset. Everything will be fine. But tell us, how have you been? We have been worrying about you all out there. The Russians are very dangerous."

Danusia sits down. Her rage slowly subsides and terrible exhaustion takes over. They don't know anything about Dad, she realizes. Another pain and loss tear at her heart.

"My Dad is dead," she says quietly.

"Oh, my God!" Marysia utters a cry. "What happened?"

"The Soviets shot him," she replies.

They all sit quietly, staring at nothing.

"Can I take your coat?" Kazik reaches out to her.

"Yes," she acquiesces.

Marysia moves closer to her. "Please stay with us for a couple more days. It will be better that way…"

Danusia reluctantly agrees. The next few days, she spends mostly with Jędruś. He has to get used to his mother before she takes him home. They all need some transition time. But these are very hard and painful days for Danusia. Time and again, Jędruś rejects Danusia and runs to Marysia for comfort.

"The old women were right. I should have never given Jędruś away." Those two years and two months in the life of the four-year-old, she's lost them forever. Danusia deeply feels the terrible loss and can't wait to reclaim Jędruś.

"The trains are not yet operational." Kazik tries to delay her departure. But she goes to the train station, talks with some people in town, and quickly solves the problem.

"There are some Soviet military trucks that are going towards Warsaw from here. I already talked to them and they have agreed to give me a ride. We are leaving tomorrow morning," she declares.

Marysia bursts into tears but Danusia is merciless. "We're leaving no matter what," she repeats.

The next morning, little Jędruś holding Marysia and Danusia's hands, walks to the Soviet military dispatch center. With a heavy valise in his hand, Kazik nervously gives Danusia last-minute advice on how to look after Jędruś. The dispatch center is chaotic and crowded. All the trucks are full.

"You have to wait," a Soviet traffic coordinator informs Danusia.

But she doesn't want to wait. The tension grows. Jędruś becomes upset and Kazik presses her to return home.

"It's too dangerous. You shouldn't travel that way. It's too dangerous for you and for Jędruś...."

She can't take it anymore. Without saying a word, she grabs Jędruś and rushes to an incoming truck.

"Please take me towards Warsaw! I must go immediately!"

The driver is taken by surprise. He already has a companion in his truck cab. Danusia's eyes grow desperate. "Please!" she begs him.

"*Nu davay*," the driver reluctantly agrees.

With Jędruś in her arms, she climbs up, ignoring the dispatcher and leaving behind a terrified Marysia and an astonished Kazik.

"There is no Warsaw anymore, you know that...," the Soviet quizzes her. "So, where do you really want to go?" He tries to make some sense out of Danusia's desperate plea.

"I have to get to Praga. That's across the river from Warsaw," she replies. "There's a temporary pontoon bridge on the Vistula River now."

"We will see." The driver scratches his head. The truck slowly starts moving. Danusia doesn't look back. She doesn't want to see Marysia's tears and doesn't want to listen to Kazik's endless concerns. Kazik throws the suitcase in the back of the departing truck. Jędruś at first is fascinated with the military vehicle but soon realizes that Marysia is not with him and starts whimpering and crying. Danusia tries to calm him down but the crowded stinky cab is very noisy and uncomfortable. They bounce up and down on the hard-edged bench on the bumpy road. Once they leave Koło, the Soviets start singing beautiful, nostalgic songs. How strange.... To her surprise, Danusia recognizes some of the songs. Her father used to sing them too. Holding Jędruś tightly in her arms, she joins in the singing. Jędruś calms down and falls asleep.

Danusia relaxes. After years of yearning for her little boy, after weeks of fiercely competing for his each and every look, smile, and gesture, she has reclaimed him at last. She feels his rhythmic breathing and the pleasant warmth of his small body. In a few hours, she will be in Praga where Zbyszek and maybe even Mama with Ela await her. Her eyelids become heavy and she is on the verge of falling asleep. At last they will all be safe and reunited. Her mind is blurry and she flows in her dream. The bright light shines though the curtains of the State Mint apartment. Dad gently asks her to get up, Mama prepares breakfast, Zbyszek does his morning pushups, and Józio takes out a while shirt from the wardrobe, while Ela and Jędruś happily play on the carpet. Dressed in a long silk robe, Danusia moves around. The house is warm, cozy, and clean. Soft colorful toys are scattered on the carpet....

The truck roars heavily, slows down, stops, jerks, stops abruptly, and starts moving again. Danusia slowly wakes up from her dream and suddenly finds herself in the gray dreary void. "What's that?" Her eyes open wide. A boundless desert of gray desolate rubble surrounds her. Solitary stumps and notched fragments of walls along the way look like repulsive avant-garde sculptures. A chill gust of smoke and rot envelops her. An abstract five-foot high configuration of strange serpents aggressively shines in the reddish afternoon rays in front of them. As the truck moves closer, the shiny serpent looks more like a mountain of gigantic spaghetti. Danusia strains her eyes. As the truck continues moving forward, the mountain of spaghetti turns into a colossal entanglement of tram rails.

"Unbelievable! There's nothing left here," the driver exclaims.

Danusia is unable to emit a sound. Is this Warsaw? Where is her home, her school, her friends, this place of her great pride and happiness? Where is it now? It can't be it! Boundless rubble, bomb craters, barbed wires, dead tanks, barricades, crosses, rats, death, stench, and this horrible ringing silence.... She closes her eyes. Cold sweat drenches her body. She only needs to get to Praga. She folds Jędruś to her breast. The boy looks around curiously. The serene desert of ruins attracts his attention.

The bridge must be very close, just nearby. But Danusia can't recognize the streets. There is no single familiar building left or a single street sign standing. It is even impossible to figure out how the streets go. The truck moves sluggishly in a column of all sorts of strange vehicles and carriages along the passageway cut through the rubble. The entire procession heads towards the pontoon bridge.

In somber silence they reach the bridge. Danusia desperately wants to look back but deep inside is afraid to turn her head. In front of them, a real city pulsates with life. Wide streets are mostly cleared of rubble, crowded houses are being renovated in a rush, small shops are flourishing, and unruly markets are booming. Herds of travelers with odd bundles and packages are rushing in all directions, mingling with many formally dressed, middle-aged people looking more or less like government officials. Praga takes over the function of the capital city.

The Soviet stops on a small street in front of a shabby apartment building. Danusia jumps out to check the address. But Zbyszek is already rushing to the truck. Mama with Ela in her arms greets them from the door. Jędruś is shocked and intimidated but he does recognize his grandmother and reluctantly accepts her kisses. He doesn't like little Ela though. After all, he doesn't know his little sister at all.

The Półkośniak family welcomes Danusia, Jędruś and the Soviets to their small two-bedroom apartment without any hesitation. They are doing their best to manage in these extraordinary circumstances. The Soviets are treated to a good meal and a bottle of vodka. They stay overnight and are back on the road in the morning.

"Zbyszek, we have to go to see our house," Danusia says after the Soviets are gone.

Zbyszek looks at her in disbelief. "Our house is gone, don't you know that…?"

"But I must go there. Please take me there!" she insists.

"What is it that you want to see?" Zbyszek asks cynically.

She turns to him abruptly but controls her anger. "Would you go with me, please?"

He takes a step back and lowers his voice, "Okay, I guess I will."

"No way! You are not going anywhere!" Mama explodes. "There are landmines everywhere!"

"The Germans planted these landmines to prevent us from coming back," Mr. Półkośniak says quietly. "Just to make sure we never return to Warsaw…," he adds.

"Yes, but our sappers have been working around the clock to identify the minefields for several weeks already," Zbyszek replies. "The mines are clearly marked everywhere. They're probably marked near our house, too."

Soon Danusia crosses the pontoon bridge again, only this time in the opposite direction. The horizon in front of her is mysterious: a silent stony desert with dramatic solitary stumps. Only on the banks of the Vistula River does she notice some commotion and small fumes here or there.

"What's that?" she points towards the other shore.

"People are digging shelters," Zbyszek replies. "They can't return to their homes, so they dig temporary shelters on the banks of the river until their houses are rebuilt."

"How can they live in the holes like that?" Danusia is puzzled.

"Remember how Dad dug a shelter for us in Międzyrzec? His shelter was pretty good. We could have survived there for some time, if needed. A shelter like that keeps the heat rather well. Some people even put small stoves in there. You see those pipes sticking out of the ground? Those are stove chimneys. You see some smoke coming out of them?" Zbyszek stretches his hand.

"That's incredible...." Danusia looks around with subdued disbelief. Soon they cross the bridge and enter the abyss of ruins, passing through rubble, scrap iron, wires, helmets, weapons, personal belongings, and crosses. Zbyszek walks in front.

"Follow my footsteps," he orders.

"Do you know where to go?" Danusia wonders.

"Don't worry, I never get lost on the way home," he replies, laughing.

After a long exhausting walk, Zbyszek slows down. "See there!" He points to the wreckage in front of them.

Danusia takes a couple more steps. "Our fence?"

"Yes," he nods. "The same good old fence—undamaged...."

"And how about the gate?" Danusia asks in vain.

"There is no gate.... And old Gara is gone too...," Zbyszek says in a dejected voice. They approach the fence, maneuvering carefully between the mines marked in red circles on the ground.

"What happened to the Gara family?" Danusia asks in a frightened voice.

"Old Gara was killed at the beginning of the Uprising. People say that he sought death.... After losing Zenek, he lost his purpose in life...and didn't bow to the bullets."

"And what happened to the girls?"

Zbyszek takes a deep breath. "They fought in the Uprising too, acting as nurses, messengers and even soldiers and…."

"And what?" Danusia can't stand his hesitation.

"I heard that Marysia survived but was sent to the concentration camp, together with Wanda Tołłoczko and Danusia Staniszewska."

Grasping cold metal poles with both hands, Danusia pushes her face against the fence and swallows her tears. Her head is buzzing. Death and destruction everywhere. Her town, her home, her life—all lay in ruins. How much more one can endure?

"But many concentration camps have been already liberated," Zbyszek adds. "Auschwitz and Treblinka are already liberated…! There is a chance that they've survived."

Suddenly, loud pounding comes from the ruins of the house. Danusia shrinks. Zbyszek looks around, signals her to be quiet, and starts moving towards the noise. Danusia follows. They move along the fence towards their apartment. The noise grows louder. Soon they find themselves in front of a big gloomy hole in the thick cracked wall. It's their living room window! Rhythmic banging and clouds of fetid dust belch from the murky pit. Zbyszek shields Danusia with his body. She strains her eyes from behind his back. A lanky silhouette inside works energetically with a hatchet.

"It's a Soviet soldier," Zbyszek whispers.

"But what is he doing…?

"Let me see…. Oh gee! He is chopping up our wardrobe!" Zbyszek makes a stunning observation.

"Looks like he needs some firewood to keep warm," Danusia says with resignation.

"But he is chopping up our fancy wardrobe! Remember how Mama loved this wardrobe?"

"Let's go, Zbyś," Danusia pulls his sleeve. "Let's go, darling. After all, what difference does it make?"

Upon reflection, Zbyszek nods and obediently turns back. "Right, what difference does it make now?" he repeats hopelessly.

In tense silence, they maneuver through the minefield. "The mint played a key role in the Uprising," Zbyszek breaks the silence. "Major Pełka was in charge of the defense of the mint complex. Do you know who he was?" They stop and look at each other. "You would never believe it!" Zbyszek says severely. "It was Mieczysław Chyżyński, this quiet man who worked at the mint as a quality control inspector during the occupation. He was a Major in the Polish Army before the war."

"I remember now," Danusia's eyes grow round. "Dad had always so much respect for that man."

"That's right. And you know what else? He was the one who was running the Underground Printing Operations for the Home Army throughout all those years of the war!"

"That's incredible. I couldn't quite understand back then why Chyżyński was so respected by everybody. Now I understand! And now I understand why Dad frequently talked to him when Józio came back from Auschwitz." Danusia looks at Zbyszek. "Do you know what happened to him?"

"I know for sure that he did survive the Uprising. As a prisoner of war, he was probably shipped to some sort of a German camp."

"How do you know all this?"

"From Bruno. I met him in Praga. He escaped the Germans via underground sewer pipes."

"Sewer pipes! How disgusting."

Zbyszek laughs. "I had the same reaction. But after listening to Bruno, I totally changed my perspective. He told me that the sewer channels played a key role during the entire Uprising. It was the primary way to move around. And what's most incredible—they didn't mind it at all. In fact it was a very happy time for them. They were fighting for independence, they were free and they had hope.[5] And those are the most precious things in life!" Zbyszek swallows hard. "And I wasn't there with them...," his voice breaks down.

"Stupid you! Do you think you would have made a difference and saved Warsaw?" Danusia raises her voice. "Look! Look around! Do you see all these crosses?" She waves her hands in despair. "You would be just one of them, nothing else, just that!"

"Many of our friends chose to die in freedom instead of lingering in oppression," Zbyszek replies dramatically. "It was their conscious decision. And I admire them for that!" he shouts. "Do you remember the Andrusiak brothers?"

"I remember the name," Danusia replies shyly. "Do you mean the twins?"

"Right. I attended *Komplety* with them. They felt very strongly that it's better to die fighting than to suffer in oppression. And they both lost their lives in the Uprising. They are buried not that far from here. Let me show you!" Zbyszek grabs Danusia's hand energetically. "They already have a permanent place.... Their mother moved their bodies from the street debris to the cemetery."

With effort they push their way through the rubble but Zbyszek knows his way well. "A cemetery," Danusia thinks. "The whole city is one big cemetery. What difference does it make whether one is buried in the cemetery or not...? Can one really distinguish a cemetery around here? And their mother." This thought gives her a jolt. The image of Mrs. Andrusiak suddenly hits her hard. That gentle smiling woman, so selflessly devoted to her beloved sons...the MOTHER!

They enter the cemetery. It's not much different here. The sea of rubble spreads everywhere except that here there are many more crosses standing erect in long straight rows. Zbyszek moves slowly along those rows and stops at a grave a little wider than the rest. Next to the cross, a big stone strangely hangs in the air. Danusia quietly joins him. The flying stone captivates her.

"Mrs. Andrusiak carved that stone into the shape of a tear and mounted it like that here," Zbyszek says in anticipation of her question. They kneel down and pray in silence.

"You will find many familiar names on these crosses," Zbyszek says, getting up. "Most of those buried here are our age," he adds. "Oh, I must show you something." They walk among the graves, some with inscriptions, some without any names, and stop at another strange grave. A big metal plate hangs high on the cross.

"Krzysztof Kamil Baczyński," Danusia reads the name out loud. "I know the name but I am not sure...," she looks at Zbyszek inquiringly.

"Remember that poem in the *Bulletin*? The one about the trains emptied by sadness?"

They stare in silence at the black plate with script letters painted in white.

And you left, my fair son, with a dark weapon into the night,
And you felt, in the minutes' sound, how the evil bristled.
Against falling, your hand blessed the earth.
Was it a bullet, dearest son, or the heart burst?

"Shooting with jewels!" Danusia says in an empty voice. "I understand it now. He was our next Mickiewicz."

"He was only twenty-three years old." Zbyszek gently takes her hand. "His wife, Basia, was also killed in the uprising. They are buried here together. "

"They were...my age.," Danusia whispers and unspeakable sorrow wells up in her.

"Remember this?" Zbyszek half whispers, staring at the grave.

You are like the humongous old tree,
My nation, like the audacious oak (...)
Carpenters plow your body
And dig your roots with a graver (...)
Your leafs are chopped and smashed (...)
Your fiery eyes are gouged out (...)
Your body is ground into dust (...)
You stand there, ragged in solitude (...)
Tearing the grapples of your claws
Into the wounds of your land
And dream the reverie of disdain (...)

Danusia looks down. Something intensely green catches her teary eyes. A tiny flower in the center of the grave is about to unfold its wings. She kneels down and bows over the stiff cold soil. "Red tulip!" she whispers with excitement. Nourishing drops of crystal dew are covering its fleshy green leaves and reddish petals. The red tulip is about to bloom. Its intense freshness mesmerizes her. Baczyński's poem comes to her mind.

But the eternal clock is ticking (...)
Listen to that heart. That heart beats!

49. Ruins of King Palace and King Zygmunt Column, Old Town after the Warsaw Uprising

50. Danusia and Karol, 1951 Wedding

Epilogue

A staunch anti-Nazi ally, Poland suffered so much and ultimately gained so little.[1] Although a member of the winning coalition, postwar Poland fell under Stalin's tyranny and for another half a century struggled for its independence and freedom.

After the war, Danusia completed her education and became an elementary school teacher. In 1951, she married Karol Binienda, a graduate of the University of Warsaw School of Law. Karol was the best husband she could ever dream of. He loved her dearly and was like a real father to her children. Danusia had two more children with Karol. In the 1970's, the couple left Poland and came to the United States in search of a better future. The Solidarity Movement upheaval of the early 1980's and the imposition of the Martial Law on December 13, 1981, forced Danuta's children to leave Poland and follow their parents into freedom.

In 1987, a British journalist, Neal Ascherson, wrote: "Poland remains a smoking volcano whose eruption could shatter all calculations."[2] Indeed, the unrelenting struggle of the Polish people for independence, strengthened by the moral support of Pope John Paul II and the organizational framework of the Solidarity Movement, ultimately led to victory. In September 1989, the first non-communist government led by Tadeusz Mazowiecki took over power in Poland and set the stage for the tearing down of the Berlin Wall.

In July 1997 Poland, along with the Czech Republic and Hungary, was invited to join the North Atlantic Treaty Organization. The United States Senate ratified Poland's admission to NATO on April 30, 1998, by a vote of 80 to 19.[3] Ms. Barbara Mikulski, a United States Senator of Polish descent, addressed the United States Senate on this historic occasion:

> My great-grandmother had three pictures on her mantelpiece: One of Pope Pius XII, because we were Catholic and are Catholic and that was her Pope, my uncle Joe who was on the Baltimore City Police Department and we were so proud of what he had achieved; and the

> other picture, of Franklin Delano Roosevelt because of what he had done for working people.
>
> But after Yalta and Potsdam, my great-grandmother turned the Roosevelt picture face down on her mantel and she let it stay there until the day she died because of what happened at Yalta and Potsdam. That is why many of us cannot forget the history of that region, the placing of a nation and the other nations, the captive nations, involuntarily under the servitude and boot heel of then the evil empire.
>
> But my support for NATO enlargement is not based on nostalgia, nor is it based on the past; it is based on the future. [...] I support NATO enlargement because I believe that it will make America and Europe more stable and more secure.[4]

A declaration in support of the NATO enlargement signed by sixty United States Generals proclaimed:

> The lessons of history are clear. Two World Wars and one Cold one have established beyond question that American security and European security are inseparable. In the aftermath of World War I, America turned its back on Europe, only to have America's sons and daughters pay the price a generation later. We cannot afford to make that mistake again.[5]

Notes

Chapter 1

1. Jan Karski, *Wielkie Mocarstwa Wobec Polski* (Warszawa: Państwowy Instytut Wydawniczy, 1992), pp. 371-372.

2. Allen Paul, *Katyn; The Untold Story of Stalin's Polish Massacre* (Charles Scribner's Sons, 1991), p. 282.

3. J. K. Zawodny, *Death in the Forest; The Story of the Katyń Forest Massacre* (University of Notre Dame Press, 1962), p. 41.

4. *The Goebbels Diaries, 1942-1943.* Louis P. Lochner, 1st edition (Garden City, NY: Doubleday Co., 1948), p. 347.

5. See Piotr Wandycz, *The United States and Poland* (Harvard University Press, 1980), p. 269.

6. Crister S. and Stephen A. Garrett, "Death and Politics: The Katyn Forest Massacre and American Foreign Policy," *East European Quarterly* XX, No. 4, (January 1987) p. 435.

7. Zawodny, *Death in the Forest*, p. 64.

8. General Oberhauser's Testimony, International Military Tribunal, Nuremberg, Vol. XVII, p. 286, 1945–1946.

9. Tadeusz Piotrowski, *Poland's Holocaust* (McFarland & Company, 1998), p. 269.

10. Adam Moszyński, *Lista Katyńska* (London: Gryf, 1977), p. 171.

11. Rafał Korbal, *Słynne Bitwy w Historii Polski* (Poznań: Podsiedlik, Raniowski i Spółka, 1997), p. 40.

12. *Ibid.*, p. 41.

13. Józef Buszko, *Historia Polski 1864-1948* (Warszawa: Państwowe Wydawnictwo Naukowe, 1983), p. 243.

14. *Ibid.*, p. 249.

15. Norman Davies, *Europe, A History* (Oxford University Press, 1996), p. 943.

16. *Ibid.*, p. 942.

17. Buszko, p. 248.

18. Gymnasium is an equivalent of Middle School.

19. Janusz Tazbir, ed., *Zarys Historii Polski* (Państwowy Instytut Wydawniczy, 1980), pp. 637-638.

20. Davies, *Europe, A History*, p. 978.

21. Tazbir, p.622.

22. A. Garlicki, *Józef Piłsudski 1867-1935* (Warszawa: Czytelnik, 1988), pp. 687-684.

23. Buszko, pp. 305-307.

24. *Ibid.*, pp. 330-332.

25. Davies, *Europe, A History*, p. 990.

26. *Ibid.*, p. 991.

27. Władysław Pobóg-Malinowski, *Najnowsza Historia Polityczna Polski 1864-1945* (London: Gryf Printers, 1956), p. 659.

28. Upon seizing power, the Nazis began to incite its German minorities in the neighboring countries to demand more independence. Fearing German domination,

Poland immediately submitted to the Western Powers the Polish request to treat the sizable Polish minority in Zaolzie "al pari" with the German minority. Their request was accepted. As the Germans kept raising their demands for Sudety, the Poles responded by keeping up with their demands to Zaolzie. See Wacław Jędrzejewicz, *Rola Józefa Piłsudskiego w Odbudowie i Umacnianiu Państwa Polskiego* (Józef Piłsudski Institute of America, 1984), p. 70.

29. Józef Wójcicki, *Wolne Miasto Gdańsk 1920-1939* (Warszawa: MON, 1976), p. 312.

30. Peter Young, ed., *Illustrated World War II Encyclopedia*, Volume I (H. S. Stuttman Inc. Publisher), pp. 11-13.

31. Buszko, p. 333.

32. Davies, *Europe, A History*, pp. 992-995.

33. Buszko, p. 333.

34. Karski, *Wielkie Mocarstwa Wobec Polski*, p. 234.

Chapter 2

1. Buszko, p. 262.

2. Davies, *Europe, A History*, p. 995.

3. *Ibid.*, pp. 995-998.

Chapter 3

1. See also: *Historia, Encyklopedia Szkolna* (Warszawa: Wydawnictwa Szkolne i Pedagogiczne, 1993), p.706.

2. Rafał Korbal, *Polacy na Frontach II Wojny Światowej* (Podsiedlik, Raniowski i Spółka, 1999), p. 4.

3. Wójcicki, p. 285.

4. Norman Davies, *Heart of Europe, A Short History of Poland*, (Oxford: Clarendon Press, 1984), p. 126.

5. Buszko, pp. 332-333.

6. For an in-depth analysis of Soviet negotiations with the British, French and Germans, see Jan Karski, *The Great Powers and Poland 1919-1945* (University Press of America, 1985).

7. Michael Wright, *The World at Arms, The Reader's Digest Illustrated History of World War II* (London: Readers Digest Association Inc., 1989), p. 25.

8. Davies, *Europe, A History*, p. 997.

9. For a detailed analysis of the August 25, 1939 Agreement of Mutual Assistance Between the United Kingdom and Poland see Anita Prażmowska, *Britain, Poland and the Eastern Front, 1939* (Cambridge University Press, 1987), pp. 161-166.

10. Buszko, pp. 362-365.

11. Korbal, *Polacy na Frontach II Wojny Światowej*, p.6-7.

12. Karski, *The Great Powers and Poland*, p. 316.

13. Davies, *Europe, A History*, pp. 1032-1033.

14. Paul, *Katyń*, p 19. See also Davies, *Europe, A History*, p. 996.

15. Piotrowski, *Poland's Holocaust*, pp. 21-33.

16. Paul, *Katyń*, p.30.

17. Prażmowska, *Britain, Poland and the Eastern Front, 1939*, p.190.

Chapter 4

1. *Historia, Encyclopedia Szkolna*, p. 707.
2. District of Warsaw.
3. Young, p. 20.
4. *Ibid.*, p.20.
5. Korbal, *Polacy na Frontach Drugiej Wojny Światowej*, p. 5.
6. *Ibid.*, pp. 8-9.
7. For the behind-the-scenes politics of the British and French declaration of war, see Karski, *The Great Powers and Poland 1919-1945*.
8. Buszko, p. 365.
9. *Ibid.*, p. 365-366.
10. *Ibid.*, p.366.
11. For Polish negotiations on the purchase of arms, see Prażmowska, *Britain, Poland and the Eastern Front, 1939*, p.124.
12. Korbal, *Polacy na Frontach II Wojny Światowej*, p. 10.
13. For the Soviet political maneuverings, see Karski, *The Great Powers and Poland 1919-1945*.
14. Korbal, *Polacy na Frontach II Wojny Światowej*, p. 11.
15. Young, p. 39.

Chapter 5

1. Young, p.40.
2. Paul, p. 63.
3. *Ibid.*, p. 64.
4. *Ibid.*, p. 63.
5. Davies, *Europe, A History*, p. 1002.
6. Piotrowski, p. 23.
7. *Historia, Encyclopedia Szkolna,* p. 709.
8. Tazbir, p. 675.
9. Piotrowski, p. 6.
10. Karski, *The Great Powers and Poland, 1919-1945*, p. 329.
11. *Ibid.*, p. 330.
12. *Ibid.*, p. 329.
13. Paul, pp. 65-67.
14. *Ibid.*, p. 67.
15. Davies, *Heart of Europe, A Short History of Poland*, p.73.
16. *Historia, Encyklopedia Szkolna,* p. 546.
17. Piotrowski, p. 25.
18. *Ibid.*, p. 23.
19. By 1942, ZWZ had over 200,000 members and on February 14, 1942 was transformed into the Home Army. For history of the Home Army and other resistance organizations see *Historia, Encyklopedia Szkolna*, pp. 530-533.
20. By February 1940, the German army had conducted 100 executions on the Polish soil. For examples and details of such mass executions, see Piotrowski, pp. 25-26.

Chapter 6

1. Paul, *Katyń*, p.70.
2. *Ibid.*, p. 72.
3. *Ibid.*, p. 74. For the description of the camp life see also Stanisław Świaniewicz, *W cieniu Katynia* (Czytelnik, 1990); J. Snopkiewicz, A. Zakrzewski, and J. Jaruzelski, *Dokumenty Katynia* (Interpress, 1992); Zawodny, *Death in the Forest*; Kazimierz Węgrzecki, *Czarne Plamy Historii* (London: Veritas Foundation, 1990).
4. Zawodny, *Death in the Forest*, p. 3.
5. Young, p. 65.
6. For the examples of interrogations, see Paul, *Katyń*, p.77.
7. *Ibid.*, p.77.
8. Świaniewicz, p. 100.
9. Zawodny, *Death in the Forest*, pp. 104-106.
10. Paul, *Katyń*, pp. 106-107.
11. *Ibid.*, p. 107.
12. *Ibid.*, p. 108; See also Vladimir Abarinov, *The Murderers of Katyń* (New York: Hippocrene Books Inc., 1993), p. 66.
13. For the analysis of the final moments of the Katyń victims compare Paul, pp. 110-111; Zawodny, *Death in the Forest*, pp. 110-112; and Abarinov, pp. 69-71.
14. Zawodny, *Death in the Forest*, pp. 19-20.
15. Paul, p. 114.
16. *Ibid.*, p. 114.
17. General Sikorski signed the Polish Soviet Agreement on July 30, 1941, under great pressure from the British Government and despite the opposition of his own cabinet. The Agreement did not address the Polish-Soviet borders.
18. Paul, pp. 157-160.
19. Paul, pp. 114-115.
20. Abarinov, pp. 91-93.
21. Paul, p. 114. See also Natalia Lebedeva, *Katyń* (Warszawa: Dom Wydawniczy Bellona, 1998).
22. The Beria document contains reference to special proceedings to be applied to the Poles that were considered to be hardened and uncompromising enemies of the Soviet authority. Examination of the Polish detainees should be carried out without summoning them and without bringing charges. The cases should be examined and the verdicts pronounced by a three person special tribunal consisting of Comrades Merkulov, Kabulov and Bashtakov. For the full text of the Beria document, see Piotrowski, pp. 15, 269-270.
23. *Ibid.*, p. 297.
24. Zawodny, *Death in the Forest*, p.64.
25. *Ibid.*, p. 64.
26. For an excellent discussion of the Katyń case at the Nuremberg trial, see Zawodny, *Death in the Forest*.
27. For a detailed analysis of the policy of Great Britain and the United States towards the Katyń matter, see Zawodny, *Death in the Forest*.

Chapter 7

1. Korbal, *Polacy na Frontach Drugiej Wojny Światowej*, p. 19.

2. *Ibid.*, p. 19.
3. *Ibid.*, p. 18.
4. For more information on the Polish Resistance see Davies, *Heart of Europe, A Short History of Poland*, pp. 72-73.
5. Korbal, *Słynne Bitwy w Historii Polski*, p. 48.
6. Korbal, *Polacy na Frontach Drugiej Wojny Światowej*, p. 20.
7. Tazbir, p. 681.
8. During the German occupation of Poland, the merciless and systematic campaign of biological destruction of the Poles took place. By 1940 over 52,000 persons had died in Nazi-occupied Poland, many by execution. For a detailed account of the Nazi terror in occupied Poland, see Piotrowski, pp. 21-33.

Chapter 8

1. About Delegatura Rządu RP na Kraj, see *Historia, Encyklopedia Szkolna*, p. 534.

Chapter 9

1. Korbal, *Polacy na Frontach Drugiej Wojny Światowej*, p. 23.
2. For an in-depth analysis of the formation of the Polish Air Force in Great Britain, see Anita Prażmowska, *Britain and Poland 1939–1943: The Betrayed Ally* (Cambridge University Press, 1995), pp. 73-75.
3. *Historia, Encyklopedia Szkolna*, pp. 259-260.
4. For the analysis of the Grunwald Battle, see Leszek Podhorodecki, *Sławne Bitwy Polaków* (Wydawnictwo Mada, 1997).
5. Davies, *Heart of Europe, A Short History of Poland*, pp. 294-296.
6. *Ibid.*, pp. 296-299.

Chapter 10

1. For stories describing the arrival in Auschwitz in 1940 see Zygmunt Zonik, *Alert Trwał 5 Lat* (Młodzieżowa Agencja Wydawnicza, 1989).
2. Danuta Czech, *Auschwitz Chronicle* (New York: Henry Holt and Company, 1997), p. 26.
3. *Ibid.*, p. 10.
4. *Ibid.*, p. 9.
5. *Ibid.*, p. 17.
6. *Ibid.*, p. 27.
7. *Numery Mówią–Wspomnienia Więźniów KL Auschwitz* (Katowice: Wydawnictwo Śląsk, 1984), p. 50.
8. *Ibid.*, p. 51.
9. *Ibid.*, p. 56.
10. Czech, p. 19.
11. *Numery Mówią–Wspomnienia Więźniów KL Auschwitz*, p. 65.
12. Czech, p. 32.
13. *Ibid.*, p. 35.
14. *Numery Mówią–Wspomnienia Więźniów KL Auschwitz*, p. 69.
15. *Ibid.*, p. 73.

16. *Ibid.*, p. 69.
17. *Ibid.*, pp. 70-71.
18. *Ibid.*, p. 72.
19. *Ibid.*, p. 55.
20. Czech, p. 59.
21. *Ibid.*, p. 76.
22. *Ibid.*, p. 76.
23. *Ibid.*, p. 80.
24. In August of 1941, Hitler issued a secret order to weed out Russian political officers from the prisoners of war camps and to transfer them to the nearest concentration camps for liquidation. A small group of Russian prisoners of war is selected for the first experimental killing with Zyklon B in the gas chamber. See Czech, pp. 84-85.
25. *Ibid.*, p. 100.

Chapter 11

1. Czech, p.130.
2. *Ibid.*, p. 121.
3. In 1943 the Polish Underground Press published a Polish version of Arkady Fiedler's book entitled *Dywizjon 303* written in Great Britain in 1942. The English version of this book was also published in 1943 in Great Britain and in the United States.
4. Davies, *Europe, A History*, p. 1008.
5. Korbal, *Słynne Bitwy w Historii Polski*, p. 51.
6. Robert Gretzyngier and Wojtek Matusiak, *Polish Aces of World War II* (Osprey Publishing, 1998), p. 25.
7. *Ibid.*, p. 85. Many Western sources refer to Joseph Frantisek, a Czech flying with Squadron 303 who recorded 17 confirmed kills and one probable, as the top ace of Squadron 303.
8. *Ibid.*, pp. 85-87.
9. *Ibid.*, p. 85.
10. Korbal, *Polacy na Frontach II Wojny Światowej*, p. 23.
11. *Ibid.*
12. *Ibid.*
13. Davies, *Europe, A History*, p. 1008.
14. *Ibid.*
15. Czech, p. 136.
16. Korbal, *Słynne Bitwy w Historii Polski,* p. 55.
17. *Historia, Encyklopedia Szkolna*, p. 339.
18. *Ibid.*, p. 340.
19. *Ibid.*, p. 340.
20. *Ibid.*, p. 342.
21. *Ibid.*, p. 339.

Chapter 12

1. For a description of various types of identification documents introduced by the Nazis for the Polish population, see Korbal, *Polacy na Frontach Drugiej Wojny Światowej*, p. 49.

2. *Ibid.*, p. 48. Through constant ID inspections, the Nazis tried to control the situation in Poland. Every German was authorized to stop and check the ID of any Pole or Jew. The Polish Underground ran the production of fake identification documents on a large scale.

3. Tazbir, p. 682.

Chapter 13

1. Forbidding manicures is yet another example of many rules introduced by the Nazis to humiliate the Poles.

2. Tazbir, p. 686.

3. *Historia, Encyklopedia Szkolna*, p. 358.

4. *Ibid.*, p. 359.

5. J. T. Gross, *Neighbors: The Destruction of the Jewish Community in Jedwabne, Poland* (Princeton University Press, 2001).

6. Testimony of Father Edward Orłowski by Eugeniusz Marciniak, *Jedwabne w Oczach Świadków* (Wydawnictwo Duszpasterstwa Rolników, 1999).

7. Istvan Deak, Jan T. Gross, and Tony Judt, *The Politics of Retribution in Europe; World War II and its Aftermath* (Princeton University Press, 2000), p. 94. See also J. T. Gross, *Revolution From Abroad* (Princeton University Press, 1988).

8. J. R. Nowak, "A Żydzi Całowali Sowieckie Czołgi," *Głos*, February 24, 2000.

9. Testimony of Father Edward Orłowski, *op. cit.*, p. 8.

10. The Jewish collaboration with the Soviets was not a primary focus of research for the Polish historians mostly preoccupied with the Soviet atrocities. Nevertheless, many eyewitness accounts refer to Jewish neighbors as Soviet informants and collaborators—see, for example, Stanisław Jaczyński, *Zagłada Oficerów Wojska Polskiego na Wschodzie Wrzesień 1939–Maj 1940* (Warszawa: Dom Wydawniczy Bellona, 2000), p. 535; see also Mark Paul, *Neighbours on the Eve of the Holocaust* (Toronto: Pefina Press, 2001).

11. Testimony of Father Edward Orłowski, *op. cit.*

12. See Mark Paul, *Neighbours on the Eve of the Holocaust.*

13. *Śledztwo Instytutu Pamięci Narodowej w Sprawie Zbrodni w Brzostowicy.* Dziennik Internetowy PAP 04/10/2001.

14. Testimony of Father Edward Orłowski, *op. cit.*, p. 7.

15. *Ibid.*, p. 5.

16. See Piotrowski, *Poland's Holocaust.*

17. Davies, *Europe, A History*, p. 1328.

18. *Historia, Encyklopedia Szkolna*, p. 420.

19. *Ibid.*, pp. 414-415.

20. Prażmowska, *Britain and Poland 1939–1943: The Betrayed Ally*, p. 191. See also Bolesław Wierzbiański, *Techeran Jałta Poczdam; Reportaż w Przeszłość* (Bicentennial Publishing Corp. Inc., 1985), pp. 21-22.

Chapter 14

1. *Historia, Encyklopedia Szkolna*, pp. 530-538.

2. *Ibid.*, p. 359.

3. The real names of the female agents are Hanna Szarzyńska, Maria Stypułkowska and Elżbieta Dziembowska. See Korbal, *Polacy na Frontach II Wojny Światowej*, p. 43.

4. Wright, p. 334.

5. *Ibid.*, p. 336.

6. *Ibid.*, pp. 338-339.

7. *Ibid.*, pp. 284-287.

8. *Ibid.*, pp. 285-287. See also Tadeusz Panecki, *2 Korpus Polski w Bitwie o Monte Casino* (Warszawa: Wydawnictwo Bellona, 1994).

9. Davies, *Heart of Europe, A Short History of Poland*, p. 77.

10. *Historia, Encyclopedia Szkolna*, p. 454.

11. *Ibid.*, p. 456.

12. Stanisław Jaczyński, *Zygmunt Berling; Między Sławą a Potępieniem* (Książka i Wiedza, 1993), p. 284.

13. Tadeusz Sawicki, *Front Wschodni a Powstanie Warszawskie* (Warszawa: Państwowe Wydawnictowo Naukowe, 1989), pp. 53-55.

14. Earlier in the year, the Home Army Command ordered Operation Burza in Eastern Poland. The goal of the Operation Burza was to sabotage the retreating German forces and take over the administration of the liberated Polish territories. Starting in 1943, the Home Army assisted the advancing Soviet Army in liberating Halubin, Kovel and Włodzimierz, later on in liberating Vilnius, Lwów, and Lublin, and subsequently Bialystok, Kielce, Kraków and Łódź regions. All together, over 100 thousand armed men under the command of the Home Army supported the Soviet troops in liberating Eastern Poland, taking upon themselves the role of hosts.

But Stalin was not pleased with this assistance. In his view already acquiesced to by the Big Two at Teheran, Poland's eastern provinces were officially part of the Soviet Union. Having severed diplomatic relations with the Polish Government in Great Britain, Stalin viewed the Home Army as the reactionary enemy force. Consequently the Home Army found itself in a dramatic situation. For example, Colonel Krzyżanowski commanding the Home Army forces of about five thousand men liberated Vilnius and Novogrod. One week after the liberation of Vilnius, Krzyżanowski was arrested by the NKVD and deported to Siberia. Many of his soldiers shared his fate.

15. *Historia, Encyklopedia Szkolna*. p. 456. For the memoirs of the Polish pilot from RAF Squadron 301, see J. K. Zawodny, *Uczestnicy i Świadkowie Powstania Warszawskiego* (Warszawa: Wydawnictwa Naukowe PWN, 1994), pp. 353-359.

16. For the analysis of the Warsaw Uprising, see also Adam Zamoyski, *The Polish Way* (Franklin Watts, 1988), pp. 365-369.

17. *Historia, Encyklopedia Szkolna*, p. 456.

18. *Ibid.*

19. *Ibid.*

20. Juliusz Kulesza, *Z Tasiemką na Czołgi* (Czytelnik, 1984), p. 228.

21. Davies, *Europe, A History*, p. 1041.

22. Kulesza, *Z Tasiemką na Czołgi.*

23. *Ibid.*, p. 231.

24. *Ibid.*, p. 232.

25. *Ibid.*, 234.

26. Jaczyński, *Zygmunt Berling*, p. 282.

27. *Ibid.*, p. 286.

28. *Ibid.*, pp. 292-299.

29. *Ibid.*, p. 297.

30. *Ibid.*, p 298.

31. *Ibid.*, p. 300.

32. *Historia, Encyklopedia Szkolna*, p. 458.

33. The Home Army soldiers were considered as Allied forces and were afforded the prisoner-of-war status. The civilian population was sent to the concentration and labor camps.

34. The first missile Topol-M went off from Plesieck in the European part of Russia and after traveling 8000 kilometers landed at Kamchatka. The other missile went off from the submarine at the Barents Sea and landed also at Kamchatka.

35. Sawicki, *Front Wschodni*, p. 164-167.

36. Zawodny, *Uczestnicy i Świadkowie Powstania Warszawskiego.*

37. A. Paul, *Katyń*, p. 286.

38. Zawodny, *Death in the Forest*, pp. 157 –161.

39. Jaczyński, *Zygmunt Berling*, pp. 219-221.

40. *Ibid.*, p. 223.

41. Davies, *Europe, A History*, p. 1041.

42. *Klisze Pamięci; Z Fotokroniki Powstania Warszawskiego* (Warszawa: Agencja Omnipress, 1984), p.95.

43. Buszko, p. 397.

Chapter 15

1. Davies, *Heart of Europe*, p. 76.

2. See for example, Process Moskiewski, *Historia, Encyklopedia Szkolna*, p. 469.

3. *Historia, Encyklopedia Szkolna*, p. 458.

4. See also Piotrowski, *Poland's Holocaust*, pp. 7-20; A. Paul, *Katyń*, p. 64; Davies, *Heart of Europe*, p. 67.

5. Juliusz Kulesza, *Reduta PWPW* (Warszawa: Instytut Wydawniczy Pax, 1989); Piotr Stachiewicz, *Starówka 1944* (Warszawa: MON, 19830; Andrzej Czarski, *Najmłodsi Żołnierze Walczącej Warszawy* (Warszawa: Instytut Wydawniczy Pax, 1971); Romuald Śreniawa-Szypiorowski, *Powstanie Warszawskie* (Warszawa: Wydawnictwo Naukowe PWN, 1994); *Świadectwa Powstania Warszawskiego 1944,* Kuria Metropolitalna Warszawska 1988.

Epilogue

1. Neal Ascherson, *The Struggle for Poland,* Random House, New York, 1987.

2. *Ibid.*

3. *Protocols of the North Atlantic Treaty of 1949 on the Accession of Poland, Hungary, and the Czech Republic,* 105th Congress, 2nd sess., Treaty Document 105-36, *Congressional Record,* 144, no. 51, daily ed. (30 April 1998): S3907.

4. *Protocols to the North Atlantic Treaty of 1949 on Accession of Poland, Hungary, and the Czech Republic*, Cong. Rec. 105th Cong., 2nd sess., *Congressional Record* (March 18, 1998) 144: 2196-2197.

5. *Protocols to the North Atlantic Treaty of 1949 on Accession of Poland, Hungary, and the Czech Republic*, Cong. Rec. 105th Congress, 2nd sess., *Congressional Record* (March 18, 1998) 144: 1999-2200 (Declaration of Support for NATO Enlargement).

List of Illustrations and Maps

Bibliography

Abarinov, Vladimir. *The Murderers of Katyń*. New York: Hippocrene Books, Inc., 1993.

Akavia, Miriam. *An End to Childhood*. Vallentine Mitchell, 1995.

Ascherson, Neil. *The Struggle for Poland*. New York: Random House, 1987.

Baczyński, Krzysztof Kamil. *Śpiew z Pożogi*. Warszawa: Spółdzielnia Wydawnicza "Wiedza," 1947.

____. *Poezje*. Piotr Matywiecki (opracowanie). Państwowy Instytut Wydawniczy, 1996.

____. *Wiersze*. Elżbieta Kozłowska-Świątkowska (opracowanie). Krajowa Agencja Wydawnicza, 1984.

____. *Utwory Wybrane*. Kazimierz Wyka (opracowanie). Kraków: Wydawnictwo Literackie, 1964.

Bartelski, Lesław M. *Powstanie Warszawskie*. Warszawa: Iskry, 1981.

Buszko, Józef. *Historia Polski 1864-1948*. Warszawa: Państwowe Wydawnictwo Naukowe, 1983.

Cannistraro, Philip, Edward D. Wynot, Jr., and Theodore P. Kovaleff, eds. *Poland and the Coming of the Second World War; The Diplomatic Papers of A. J. Drexel Biddle, Jr., United States Ambassador to Poland 1937-1939*. Columbus: Ohio State University Press, 1976.

Carley, Michael J. *1939: The Alliance That Never Was and the Coming of World War II*. Ivan R. Dee Publisher, 1999.

Cholewczyński, George F. *Poles Apart; The Polish Airborne at the Battle of Arnhem*. New York: Sarpedon, 1993.

Ciechowski, Jan M. *Powstanie Warszawskie – Zarys Podłoża Politycznego i Dyplomatycznego*. Warszawa: Państwowy Instytut Wydawniczy, 1984.

Czarski, Andrzej. *Najmłodsi Żołnierze Walczącej Warszawy*. Warszawa: Instytut Wydawniczy Pax, 1971.

Czech, Danuta. *Kalendarz Wydarzeń w KL Auschwitz*. Wydawnictwo Państwowego Muzeum w Oświęcimiu Brzezince, 1992.

____. *Auschwitz Chronicle, 1939-1945*. New York: H. Holt, 1997.

Dallek, Robert. *Franklin D. Roosevelt and American Foreign Policy, 1932-1945*. New York: Oxford University Press, 1979.

Dallek, Robert, ed. *The Roosevelt Diplomacy and World War II.* Holt, Rinehart and Winston, 1970.

Davies, Norman. *Europe, A History*. Oxford University Press, 1996.

____. *God's Playground: A History of Poland.* Vol. 2: *1795 to Present*. New York: Columbia University Press, 1982.

____. *Heart of Europe, A Short History of Poland.* Clarendon Press, Oxford, 1984.

Deak, Istvan, Jan Gross and Tony Judt. *The Politics of Retribution in Europe; World War II and its Aftermath.* Princeton University Press, 2000.

Dunin-Wąsowicz, Krzysztof. *Warszawa w Latach 1939-1945*. Warszawa: Państwowe Wydawnictwo Naukowe, 1984.

Fiedler, Arkady. *Dywizjon 303.* Wydawnictwo Poznańskie, 1971.

Garlicki, Andrzej. *Józef Piłsudski 1867-1935.* Warszawa: Czytelnik, 1988.

Garrett, Crister S. and Stephen A. *Death and Politics: The Katyń Forest Massacre and American Foreign Policy.* East European Quarterly, XX, No. 4 (January 1987), p. 429.

Goebbels, Joseph. *The Goebbels Diaries.* ed. and trans. Louis P. Lochner, Garden City, New York: Doubleday Co., 1948, p. 347.

Gretzyngier, Robert and Wojtek Matusiak. *Polish Aces of World War II.* London: Osprey Aircraft of the Aces, Osprey Publishing, 1998.

Gross, Jan. *Neighbor: The Destruction of the Jewish Community in Jedwabne, Poland.* Princeton University Press, 2000.

____. *Revolution from Abroad.* Princeton University Press, 1988.

Historia, Encyklopedia Szkolna. Warszawa: Wydawnictwa Szkolne i Pedagogiczne, 1993.

Hort, Weronika (Hanka Ordonówna). *Tułacze Dzieci.* Originally published by Bejrut: Instytut Literacki, 1948; reprinted Warszawa: Państwowy Instytut Wydawniczy, 1990.

International Military Tribunal, Nuremberg, Vol. XVII, 1945-1946.

Jaczyński, Stanisław. *Zygmunt Berling; Między Sławą a Potępieniem*. Warszawa: Książka i Wiedza, 1993.

____. *Zagłada Oficerów Wojska Polskiego na Wschodzie, Wrzesień 1939 Maj 1940.* Warszawa: Wydawnictwo Bellona, 2000.

Jankowski, Stanisław M. and Edward Miszczak. *Powrót do Katynia.* Krajowa Agencja Wydawnicza 1990.

Jasiewicz, Krzysztof. *Ziemianie Wobec Własnej Zagłady*. Przegląd Wschodni, Volume V, pp. 95-118 (1998).

Jędrzejewicz, Wacław. *Rola Józefa Piłsudskiego w Odbudowie i Umacnianiu Państwa Polskiego*. Józef Piłsudski Institute of America, 1984.

Karski, Jan. *The Great Powers and Poland 1919-1945*. Lanham, NJ: University Press of America, 1985.

____. *Wielkie Mocarstwa Wobec Polski 1919-1945*. Warszawa: Państwowy Instytut Wydawniczy, 1992.

Klisze Pamięci; Z Fotokroniki Powstania Warszawskiego. Warszawa: Agencja Onipress, 1984.

Kmita-Piorunowa, Aniela and Kazimierz Wyka (eds.). *Krzysztof Kamil Baczyński Utwory Zebrane II*, Kraków: Wydawnictwo Literackie, 1994.

Korbal, Rafał. *Polacy na Frontach II Wojny Światowej*. Poznań: Podsiedlik, Raniowski i Spółka, 1999.

____. *Słynne Bitwy w Historii Polski*. Poznań: Podsiedlik, Raniowski i Spółka, 1997.

Kordek, Ryszard Henryk. *Blizny Krwawią*. Kraków/Wrocław: Wydawnictwo Literackie, 1986.

Kubiak, Michał. *Tacy Byliśmy*. Warszawa: Wydawnictwo Ministerstwa Obrony Narodowej, 1981.

Kulesza, Juliusz. *Z Tasiemką na Czołgi – Wspomnienia Walk na Starym Mieście w Sierpniu 1944 Roku*, Warszawa: Czytelnik, 1984.

____. *Reduta PWPW; Polska Wytwórnia Papierów Wartościowych w Konspiracji i w Powstaniu Warszawskim*. Warszawa: Instytut Wydawniczy Pax, 1989.

Lane, Arthur Bliss. *I saw Poland Betrayed*. The Bobbs-Merrill Company, 1948.

Lebedeva, Nataliya S. *Katyń – Zbrodnia Przeciwko Ludzkości*. Warszawa: Dom Wydawniczy Bellona, 1998.

Levi, Primo. *Survival in Auschwitz – The Nazi Assault on Humanity*. Translated by Stuart Woolf, Touchstone Books, Simon & Schuster, 1996.

Liblau, Charles. *Kapo z Auschwitz*, Wydawnictwo Państwowego Muzeum w Oświęcimiu-Brzezince, 1996.

Lipińska, Grażyna. *Jeśli Zapomnę o Nich*. Editions Spotkania, 1988.

Lukas, Richard C. *Bitter Legacy; Polish-American Relations in the Wake of World War II*. The University Press of Kentucky, 1982.

____. *Forgotten Holocaust. The Poles under German Occupation 1939-1944*. New York: Hippocrene Books, Inc., 1997.

Łojek, Jerzy (Leopold Jerzewski). *Agresja 17 Września 1939 Roku*. Warszawa: Instytut Wydawniczy PAX, 1990.

Majewski, Adam. *Zaczęło się w Tobruku*. Wydawnictwo Lubelskie 1973.

Marciniak, Eugeniusz. *Jedwabne w Oczach Świadków*. Wydawnictwo Duszpasterstwa Rolników, 1999.

Materski, Wojciech (opracowanie). *Katyń – Dokumenty Zbrodni*. TRIO, 1995.

Mikołajczyk, Stanisław. *The Rape of Poland: Pattern of Soviet Aggression*. Originally published in 1948; reprinted Westport, CT: Greenwood Press, 1972.

Morton Blum, John, ed. *The Price of Vision; The Diary of Henry A. Wallace 1942-1946*. Boston: Houghton Mifflin Company, 1973.

Moszczyński, Adam (opracowanie). *Rozstrzelani w Katyniu. Alfabetyczny Spis 4410 Jeńców z Kozielska*. London, 1972.

Muller, Fillip. *Eyewitness Auschwitz*. Chicago: Ivan R. Dee, 1999.

Niekrasz, Lech. *Operacja Jedwabne – Mity i Fakty*. Wrocław: Nortom, 2001.

Nowak J. R. "A Żydzi Całowali Sowieckie Czołgi." *Głos*, 24 luty 2000.

Nowak-Jeziorański, Jan. *Kurier z Warszawy*. London: Odnowa, 1978.

O'Connor, Raymond G. *Diplomacy for Victory; FDR and Unconditional Surrender*. New York: W. W. Norton & Company, Inc., 1971.

Panecki, Tadeusz. *2 Korpus Polski w Bitwie o Monte Cassino; Z Perspektywy Półwiecza*. Warszawa: Wydawnictwo Bellona, 1994.

Paul, Allen. *Katyń – The Untold Story of Stalin's Polish Massacre*. Maxwell Macmillan International, 1991.

Paul, Mark. *Neighbours on the Eve of the Holocaust*. Toronto: Pefina Press, 2001.

____. *A Tangled Web; Polish-Jewish Relations in Wartime Northeastern Poland*. Toronto: Pefina Press, 2002.

Perlmutter, Amos. *FDR & Stalin – A Not So Grand Alliance, 1943-1945*. University of Missouri Press, 1993.

Piotrowski, Tadeusz M. *Poland's Holocaust. Ethnic Strife, Collaboration with Occupying Forces and Genocide in the Second Republic 1918-1947*. McFarland & Company, Inc., 1998.

Pobóg-Malinowski, Władysław. *Najnowsza Historia Polityczna Polski 1864-1945*. Tom Drugi. London: Gryf Printers (H.C.), Ltd. 1956.

Prażmowska, Anita. *Britain, Poland and the Eastern Front, 1939*. Cambridge University Press 1987.

Prażmowska, Anita. *Britain and Poland, 1939-1943, The Betrayed Allied.* Cambridge University Press, 1987.

Protocols on the North Atlantic Treaty of 1949 on the Accession of Poland, Hungary, and the Czech Republic, 105th Congress, 2nd sess., Treaty Document 105-36, *Congressional Record,* 144, no. 51, daily ed. (30 April 1998): S3907.

Sawicki, Tadeusz. *Front Wschodni a Powstanie Warszawskie.* Warszawa: Państwowe Wydawnictwo Naukowe, 1989.

Snopkiewicz, J., A. Zakrzewski, and J. Jaruzelski. *Dokumenty Katynia.* Warszawa: Interpress, 1992.

Stabra, Stanisław. *Chwila bez Imienia – O Poezji Krzysztofa Kamila Baczyńskiego.* Verba, 1992.

Stachiewicz, Piotr. *Starówka 1944.* Warszawa: Ministerstwo Obrony Narodowej, 1983.

Stochowa, Zofia (opracowanie). *Numery Mówią – Wspomnienia,* Katowice: Wydawnictwo Śląsk, 1984.

Szczęśniak, Andrzej Leszek (opracowanie). *Katyń: Lista Ofiar i Zaginionych Jeńców.* Warszawa: Wydawnictwo Alfa, 1989.

Śledztwo Instytutu Pamięci Narodowej w Sprawie Zbrodni w Brzostowicy. Dziennik Internetowy PAP 04/10/2001.

Śreniawa-Szypiorowski, Romuald (opracowanie). *Powstanie Warszawskie.* Warszawa: Państwowe Wydawnictwo Naukowe PWN, 1994.

Świadectwa Powstania Warszawskiego. Kuria Metropolitalna Warszawska, Wydział Duszpasterstwa, 1988.

Świaniewicz, Stanisław. *W cieniu Katynia.* Paryż: Instytut Literacki, 1976.

Świebocki, Henryk, ed. *London has been informed.* Oświęcim: The Auschwitz-Birkenau State Museum, 1997.

Tazbir, Janusz (opracowanie). *Zarys Historii Polski.* Państwowy Instytut Wydawniczy, 1980.

Tucholski, Jędrzej. *Cichociemni.* Warszawa: Instytut Wydawniczy Pax, 1985.

United States Senate. Senator Milkulski of Maryland speaking on the NATO enlargement.105th Congress, 2nd., sess., *Congressional Record* (18 March 1998), vol. 144, no. 30.

Wandycz, Piotr S. *The United States and Poland.* Harvard University Press, 1980.

Węgrzecki, Kazimierz. *Czarne Plamy Historii.* London: Veritas Foundation, 1990.

Wierzbiański, Bolesław. *Teheran Jałta Poczdam – Reportaż w Przeszłość.* New York: Bicentennial Publishing Corp., Inc. 1985.

Wojcicki, Józef. *Wolne Miasto Gdańsk 1920-1939.* Warszawa: Ministerstwo Obrony Narodowej, 1976.

Wright, Michael. *The World at Arms, The Reader's Digest Illustrated History of World War II.* London: Reader's Digest Association Inc., 1989.

Young, Peter, ed. *Illustrated World War II Encyclopedia,* Volume I, H.S. Stuttman Inc.

Za Naszą I Waszą Wolność. New York, Polish Information Center, 1941.

Zagajewski, Adam, *Two Cities; On Exile, History, and Imagination.* New York: Farrar, Straus & Giroux, 1995.

Zagórski, Wacław. *Wicher Wolności – Dziennik Powstańca.* London: Polska Fundacja Kulturalna, 1984.

Zamoyski, Adam. *The Polish Way. A Thousand-Year History of the Poles and Their Culture.* Franklin Watts, 1988.

____. *The Forgotten Few – The Polish Air Force in the Second World War.* New York: Hippocrene Books, Inc., 1996.

Zawodny, Janusz K. *Death in the Forest. The Story of the Katyń Forest Massacre.* University of Notre Dame Press, 1962.

Zawodny, Janusz Kazimierz. *Uczestnicy i Świadkowie Powstania Warszawskiego; Wywiady.* Warszawa: Wydawnictwo Naukowe PWN, 1994.

Zonik, Zygmunt. *Alert Trwał 5 Lat.* Warszawa: Młodzieżowa Agencja Wydawnicza, 1989.